D1827577

Data Structures
Using Pascal

Data Structures
Using Pascal

- **Samuel E. Rhoads**
  Honolulu Community College

- **Michael V. Gearen**
  Punahou School

 **Wm. C. Brown Publishers**

Book Team

Editor *Earl McPeek*
Developmental Editor *Linda M. Meehan*
Production Editor *Jane E. Matthews*
Designer *Eric Engelby*
Art Editor *Janice M. Roerig*

 Wm. C. Brown Publishers

President *G. Franklin Lewis*
Vice President, Publisher *George Wm. Bergquist*
Vice President, Operations and Production *Beverly Kolz*
National Sales Manager *Virginia S. Moffat*
Group Sales Manager *Vincent R. Di Blasi*
Vice President, Editor in Chief *Edward G. Jaffe*
Executive Editor *Earl McPeek*
Marketing Manager *Elizabeth Robbins*
Advertising Manager *Amy Schmitz*
Managing Editor, Production *Colleen A. Yonda*
Manager of Visuals and Design *Faye M. Schilling*
Production Editorial Manager *Julie A. Kennedy*
Production Editorial Manager *Ann Fuerste*
Publishing Services Manager *Karen J. Slaght*

WCB Group

President and Chief Executive Officer *Mark C. Falb*
Chairman of the Board *Wm. C. Brown*

Cover Image: The Nest of Dragons, © Samuel E. Rhoads.
A dragon curve is a recursively generated series of line segments that
form a path from one point to another. The "Nest of Dragons" consists
of four dragon curves, each starting at the same point but ending at four
points on a spiral. The program that produced the image was written in
Pascal, and is available from the authors upon request.

Copyright © 1992 by Wm. C. Brown Publishers. All rights reserved

Library of Congress Catalog Card Number: 91–73409

ISBN 0–697–11173–3

No part of this publication may be reproduced, stored in a retrieval
system, or transmitted, in any form or by any means, electronic,
mechanical, photocopying, recording, or otherwise, without the
prior written permission of the publisher.

Printed in the United States of America by Wm. C. Brown Publishers,
2460 Kerper Boulevard, Dubuque, IA 52001

10 9 8 7 6 5 4 3 2 1

For:

David, Beth Ann, Brigid, Claire and Chrissy

Contents

Preface

Computer programming is problem solving with a computer. A computer programmer does much more than write code in some language. A computer programmer must be able to make sure the problem being solved is well-defined, must be able to solve the problem, must know how to use appropriate data structures for the solution, must be able to turn the solution into an algorithm, and must be able to code the algorithm in a suitable language. The resulting program must be tested and debugged. The entire process must be documented.

This book is a textbook in computer problem solving and it covers all of the points above. However, the emphasis of the text is on three of the above steps. We concentrate on writing algorithms and designing data structures for the solution, and we introduce the Pascal necessary to implement the programs.

The text introduces an algorithmic language in the first chapter and uses it throughout the rest of the book. It is very important that a computer programmer is able to express a solution to a problem as a series of small steps, i.e., as an algorithm. By using an algorithmic language distinct from the language in which the code is written, the programmer is able to concentrate on the solution to the problem rather than on the syntax of the coding language. We develop algorithms for every solution, and we do not develop the algorithms in Pascal. We strongly recommend that all programmers do the same. There is always the temptation to start coding too soon, and that temptation must be resisted. It's all too true that "the sooner you start coding your program, the longer it's going to take." It's also likely that the resulting program will not be as well written as it should be.

Computer programmers must understand data structures, and must be able to choose appropriate data structures for the solutions to the problems they solve. This text uses an "abstract data type" approach to the development of data structures. Rather than introduce, for example, a stack as an array, or as a linked list, we introduce it as an abstract data type that has a fixed set of fundamental operations which can be performed on it. The *implementation* of a stack might be an array or a linked list, but the stack is abstract. The programs developed in the book treat all data structures in this manner.

The typical reader might not have a strong background in recursion. We discuss recursion by assuming at the start that the reader has some experience with it, but perhaps not a great deal. By the time you complete the chapters on binary trees, you will have gained a great deal of experience with recursion.

We use Standard Pascal as the language in which to write the code, and we assume the user of the text has had a previous course in Pascal before using this book. In particular, we assume the reader has a fairly complete understanding of Pascal. The only major portion of Pascal that you might not have any experience with is the use of pointers. We cover pointers in considerable detail; starting in chapter 4 and throughout the remainder of the text.

We've included an appendix which contains "rail-road track" syntax diagrams for Pascal. If you have a question regarding Pascal's syntax, you can consult the appendix and, perhaps, get your question answered. An examination of our Pascal code will reveal our style. We do not include superfluous semicolons as some people do, and we indent the ⟨if statement⟩ and ⟨repeat statement⟩ in what we consider a logical manner. Other authors and programmers indent differently. We would argue, however, that whatever style you adopt, you should be consistent. A sloppily indented program is very hard to understand and debug.

The Level of the Course

The text is designed for use at the college level in a typical data structures course, and covers the Association of Computing Machinery (ACM) recommended curriculum for CS2. It is also designed for use in the Advanced Placement Computer Science course at the high-school level and covers the material recommended for the second semester Advanced Placement Course, (i.e., Computer Science AB).

Stop and Think

At various places in the book you will see a little computer character holding a stop sign.

This indicates a place for you to pause in your reading and either think extra carefully about what is being said at that point or take a few moments and do some sort of calculation before reading on. Please stop and do whatever the text suggests before reading further whenever you see this character. It will help in your understanding of the material.

Exercises

We include many carefully selected exercises. Many of the exercises amount to finishing parts of a problem solution discussed in the text, and many are independent problems. We would not expect the average reader to attempt all of the exercises. The instructor should pick and choose exercises appropriate for the class being taught.

Covering the Entire Book

While this book is designed for a one semester course, it might turn out that there is insufficient time to cover all the material in one semester. If that is the case, many of the topics in chapters 8–12 can be covered independently of the others, so, with a bit of planning, the instructor can pick and choose among them. In particular, chapter 12 is considered optional. It's not likely that the average class will cover the material on random number generation, but the material is there for a faster than average class, or possibly as extra credit material for faster students.

Acknowledgments

We would like to acknowledge those who have assisted in the preparation of the book.

First, our students and colleagues. We owe our thanks to the many students over the years who have helped us formulate our thoughts on how computer programming should be taught. These students have suffered through various drafts of this book and have added considerably to its final form. As the book neared completion, we were helped by a number of students and colleagues who offered specific suggestions or found errors in the text. In particular, we'd like to thank Tim Wilson and Dennis Chen. Tim has read several drafts of the manuscript, taught the course using the text in early forms and offered many useful suggestions. Dennis used the book in a class at Honolulu Community College and found several serious errors that we might not have found otherwise. Of course any remaining errors are our responsibility, and we will appreciate being notified of them. The current bounty for the first report by one of our students of a "serious" error (i.e., other than a typographical error) is $2.00.

Second, we would like to recognize the support of the schools where we teach. Honolulu Community College and Punahou School have both allowed us the use of their facilities while the text has been in preparation and have been understanding about the number of hours we have spent on its preparation.

Third, we would like to thank the reviewers who have offered their thoughts and suggestions: Ijaz A. Awan, Savannah State College; Chaitanya Baru, University of Michigan; Edward L. Bosworth, Athens State College; Helen Casey, Sam Houston State University; Frank A. Chimenti, Liberty University; Edward Crosson, Siena College; Daniel J. Falabella, Albright College; Evan Noynaert, Missouri Western State College; and Evelyn Rozanski, Rochester Institute of Technology. Their careful reading of the text and many suggestions have aided us a great deal in preparing the manuscript. It is a much better textbook as a result of their help.

Special thanks go to our editors, Linda Meehan and Jane Matthews, and the rest of the people at Wm. C. Brown Publishers. Their enthusiastic belief in computer science textbooks emphasizing the whole process of programming, rather than coding in a particular language, has made this book possible.

The manuscript for this book has been prepared with TEX and LaTeX. We want to thank Donald E. Knuth and Leslie Lamport for producing these wonderful aids. One of the unanticipated joys of writing the book has been learning TEX and LaTeX, and in reading *The TEXbook*.

Finally, to Pui Hin and Barbara: once again, thanks for putting up with us during the months when we surely spent more time thinking about this than you would have liked.

Chapter 1

Programming: Algorithms and Pascal

My favorite way to describe computer science
is to say that it is the study of algorithms.
An algorithm is a precisely defined sequence
of rules telling how to produce specified
output information from given input information
in a finite number of steps.
— Donald E. Knuth

Programs, after all, are concrete formulations
of abstract *algorithms* based on particular
representations and structures of *data*.
— Niklaus Wirth

1.1   Overview of the Chapter

The primary purpose of this chapter is to introduce the reader to our algorithmic language. A fundamental premise we make concerning the discipline is that computer programming is not the same as coding. Programming is much more than just learning how to use a particular programming language, like Pascal. Programming is problem solving, and "problem solving" implies the need to solve a given problem in addition to coding the solution in some language. We introduce what we call the "Five + Steps" of programming, and we discuss our algorithmic language. Our language is designed to allow us to express a solution to a problem in a language independent, step-by-step manner without having to worry about the details of a particular language, such as syntax requirements and/or types.

Virtually all "real" computer programs are written in a top-down fashion using modules. We introduce our way of listing the parameters sent to a subprogram, our way of indicating whether they are passed by value or by reference,

our way of stating pre- and postconditions, and our way of calling procedures
and functions. While these ways are similar to the way that the same things are
done in Pascal, they are not as restrictive as the syntax rules of Pascal require,
leaving us with the freedom to say what we want to happen at a slightly higher
level than required in Pascal. The careful development of an algorithm prior to
sitting down and writing a program almost always makes the job easier. The
essentials of the solution are easier to concentrate on, and one is not distracted
by the syntax and semantic details of the language.

We expect the reader to be familiar with the basic elements of Pascal, such
as the *assignment statement*, the *if statement*, the basic input and output statements (*read* and *write*), and the three looping statements: the *while statement*,
the *repeat statement* and the *for statement*. We also expect the reader to be familiar with arrays in Pascal. We expect the reader to have had some experience
with records, but perhaps less than with those things mentioned above.

We do not expect the reader to be familiar with pointers in Pascal, and we
discuss pointers in considerable detail throughout the text.

Recursion is also covered in considerable detail throughout the text, although we expect the reader to have had some experience with recursive functions and procedures.

1.2   The Five + Steps

In the companion volume to this text, we introduce what we call the FIVE +
STEPS. Here they are again:

1. Define the problem.
2. Find a solution to the problem.
3. Design and write an algorithm for the solution.
4. Code the algorithm in some computer language.
5. Test and debug the program.

    + Document continuously.

Many people think that computer programming is essentially the same thing
as writing a program in some language, like Pascal. We don't agree. Programming amounts to much more than coding. You will notice that the fourth step
in the FIVE + STEPS is the coding step. Computer programmers are expected
to do a lot more than write code. In the real world, they have to solve problems, and they have to be able to express their solution in a step-by-step manner
before it can be implemented in code.

Often, real world problems are not well stated, and as a result, a programmer
has to be able to tell when the definition is not complete as well as help the
person stating the problem get the definition clear. There are many horror
stories about hours and hours of time spent solving problems that weren't the
right problem in the first place.

Solving complex problems is best done using a *top-down* approach. Such problems are broken down into smaller, simpler problems, and those are perhaps further refined, until the remaining problems are simple enough to be solved directly.

Once the problem is solved, beginners often rush into the coding step without carefully expressing the solution in a step-by-step manner as an *algorithm*. A good algorithm should be detailed enough that someone unfamiliar with the problem could understand the steps and follow them using pencil and paper.

We pay attention to these matters in this text; we are careful to make sure the problem definition is clear before setting out to solve it. We make sure a solution is well understood before attempting to express the solution algorithmically. We spend a lot of time on the algorithms we develop. Only after the algorithm has been well thought out should a programmer start implementing it, and that's the way we do it in this book. When we write an algorithm, we are careful about expressing what we want the computer to do, but we are not nearly as formal about the expression of the steps as we have to be when writing code. The following sections discuss the algorithmic language we use.

1.3   Algorithms

Algorithmic Language

As we introduce the algorithmic language we'll use in the book, we'll also review some of the basic concepts encountered in programming.

Assignment

One of the most common things done in a computer program is to put something in a variable. This is called *assignment*. To do this we need to know the name of the variable and the value that we want to put there. In our algorithms, we'll use the word *store* to indicate assignment, and we'll express the assignment from left to right. That is, when we want to store the value of some expression in a variable, we'll write:

>   *store* ⟨*expression*⟩ *in* ⟨*variablename*⟩

However, we won't treat the algorithmic language as formally as we have to treat Pascal; e.g., on occasion we'll write such things as:

>   *add 1 to Top*

Rather than something like:

>   *store Top + 1 in Top*

In general, we'll treat an algorithm as something that can be read by a human and will use human language when it seems easier to understand. At the same time, we'll be careful to write algorithms on a low enough level that it will be easy to turn the steps in the algorithm into code.

Selection

Nearly all programs use *selection*. Selection is the ability to have the computer make some sort of test, and decide, on the basis of the outcome of the test, whether to execute one series of steps or another. We'll use the common *if...then...else* construction, and will use indentation to tell which steps are in the *then* part and which steps are in the (optional) *else* part. For example, you will see such constructions as:

if ⟨*condition*⟩
   then
      ⟨*step*⟩
      ⟨*step*⟩
      ⋮
      ⟨*step*⟩
  else
      ⟨*step*⟩
      ⟨*step*⟩
      ⋮
      ⟨*step*⟩

There will also be times when we want to have a program do *multi-way selection*. That is, rather than have a true/false test and only two possible paths to follow, there are times when we want the program to decide which of several paths to follow. In such a case we will use a *when* construction like the following:

when ⟨*expression*⟩ *is*
   ⟨*constant list*⟩; ⟨*step*⟩(s)
   ⟨*constant list*⟩; ⟨*step*⟩(s)
   ⋮
   ⟨*constant list*⟩; ⟨*step*⟩(s)

The meaning should be obvious: evaluate the expression, find a constant in one of the constant lists that matches the value of the expression, and execute the step or steps following that constant. This *when* structure is very similar to the Pascal *case statement*, but we will not be as formal in our algorithms as the *case statement* requires in Pascal.

Looping

A third familiar construction involves *looping*, also known as *repetition* or *iteration*. We'll use three kinds of loops, a *loop while*, a *loop until* and a *loop for*. A *loop for* will be used in those situations where the number of times the loop is going to be executed is known in advance, or where the loop has definite starting and ending points. Otherwise, a *loop until* will be used for those loops where the body of the loop will always be executed at least once, and a *loop while* for those cases where the body of the loop might sometimes be skipped. We'll assume the ⟨*condition*⟩ that's being tested is tested at the end of a *loop until* and at the beginning of a *loop while*. Furthermore, we'll assume that a *loop while* continues as long as the test is true, and a *loop until* continues as long as the test is false. All of these assumptions are consistent with the ways these loops are implemented in Pascal. As with the *if...then...else*, we'll use indentation to indicate the body of the loop. For example, a *loop until* will be written in this manner:

```
loop
    ⟨step⟩
    ⟨step⟩
      ⋮
    ⟨step⟩
    until ⟨condition⟩
```

A *loop while* will be written like this:

```
loop while ⟨condition⟩
    ⟨step⟩
    ⟨step⟩
      ⋮
    ⟨step⟩
```

And a *loop for* written as either:

```
loop for ⟨index⟩ going from ⟨expression⟩ to ⟨expression⟩
    ⟨step⟩
    ⟨step⟩
      ⋮
    ⟨step⟩
```

or—in those cases where the loop should go from larger values to smaller:

loop for ⟨index⟩ going from ⟨expression⟩ down to ⟨expression⟩
   ⟨step⟩
   ⟨step⟩
   :
   ⟨step⟩

Input and Output

We'll often want to have our programs do output and input. We'll use *display* for output and *accept* for input. That is, when we want to see the value(s) of some expression(s) on the terminal screen, we'll write:

display ⟨expression list⟩

and when we want the computer to wait for the user to enter a value at the keyboard, and store the value entered in a variable, we'll write:

accept ⟨variablename⟩

There will be times that we want something written to and/or read from a file. In these cases we'll simply use the words *write* and *read* and include the name of the file. If a file is to be read from, we'll normally include a step something like:

prepare ⟨filename⟩ to be read from

at the point where the file should be opened for input, and a similar step at the point where a file should be opened for output.

Procedures and Functions

Naturally, we'll make use of top-down problem solving methods in the book, and we'll make regular use of procedures and functions in our algorithms. Procedures will be modules that perform some sort of task, and functions will be modules that calculate and return a single value. Modules that need to have data sent to them, or that modify and return some data, will have those data clearly indicated. These data items are known as "parameters."

Depending on the needs of the calling module or the purpose of the module being called, there are two methods of passing parameters. Sometimes we send the parameters themselves, and other times we send copies of the parameters, leaving the actual parameters unchanged.

When the value of a parameter is changed in a module *and* when that parameter's changed value is to be returned to the calling routine, the parameter is said to be "passed by reference." In all other cases, the parameter is said to be "passed by value." We'll always be careful to indicate how every parameter is passed to one of our modules; i.e., by value or by reference.

Rather than try to make a list of rules for writing procedures, let's look at a couple of samples of how we do it.

Example of a procedure

Suppose, first, that we need a procedure that exchanges the values of two variables. Choosing the name *Swap* for the procedure, we would write the algorithm as follows:

```
START OF Swap(First, Second)
Passed by reference: First, Second

store First in Temp
store Second in First
store Temp in Second

END OF Swap
```

The formal parameters are *First* and *Second*, and *Temp* is a local variable. The two parameters are passed by reference, because their values are being swapped in the routine and passed back to the calling module that way. Notice that we do not worry about what type the three variables are. While there are times when type information is needed in an algorithm, when it's not needed, we'll not clutter the algorithm with it.

Example of a function

On the other hand, suppose we need a function that calculates the greatest common divisor of two integers. This is how we would write the algorithm for it:

START OF GCD(First, Second)
Precondition: First and Second are positive integers

store the remainder of First ÷ Second in Remainder
loop while Remainder > 0
    store Second in First
    store Remainder in Second
    store the remainder of First ÷ Second in Remainder
return the value stored in Second

END OF GCD

This routine utilizes the well-known Euclidean algorithm. If you're not familiar with the Euclidean algorithm, trace this routine with a few pairs of integers to get comfortable with it.

Notice that we do not indicate how the parameters are passed to GCD. Since parameters are almost always passed by value to a function—in order to avoid *side effects*—we'll not indicate how the parameters are passed to a function when they are passed by value. If it ever happens that we do pass a parameter by reference to a function, we'll make that fact clear at the beginning of the algorithm.

Notice that we use the word *return* to indicate what value a function returns. Since procedures don't "return" values, we'll never see the word *return* used in a procedure; that will give the reader another reminder as to whether the routine is a procedure or a function.

Preconditions and Error Checking

Notice also that we carefully state any preconditions that the routine assumes. Different people have differing philosophies concerning error checking, and where it should be done. Our philosophy is simple: the *calling* routine should do any necessary error checking. It's the responsibility of the programmer to make sure the necessary checks are done before any routine having preconditions is called. If all error-checking is done at a high-level, then the lower-level routines won't have to take time to do it; as a result, the program will be more efficient. This programming style puts more responsibility on the programmer and requires more discipline, but that's as it should be.

Indentation

We should emphasize our conventions regarding writing algorithms, in particular, the way that we indent. Indentation makes it clear just which steps are done at which time. Those steps that are done only when a condition is *true*, as in an *if...then*, should be indented. Those steps that are in a loop should be indented. Another skeleton of an algorithm might help.

START OF ALGORITHM

⟨*step*⟩
⟨*step*⟩
loop while ⟨*condition*⟩
    ⟨*step*⟩
    ⟨*step*⟩
    if ⟨*condition*⟩
        then
            ⟨*step*⟩
            ⋮
            ⟨*step*⟩
        else
            loop
                ⟨*step*⟩
                ⋮
                ⟨*step*⟩
                until ⟨*condition*⟩
    ⟨*step*⟩
    ⟨*step*⟩
⟨*step*⟩

END OF ALGORITHM

The above algorithm consists of four main steps. The first two and the last are unspecified. The third step is a *loop while*. The body of this loop consists of five steps, the third of which is an *if...then...else*. In the *then part*, there is an unspecified number of steps. In the *else part*, there is one step, a *loop until*.

Recursion

We use recursion freely in our algorithms. When a procedure or function needs to call itself, we simply have it call itself. In the later chapters of the book, we'll see many examples of recursive routines, both in Pascal and in our algorithmic language. We hope these examples take away much of the mystery of recursion, and that you come away from them feeling very comfortable with the power of recursion.

For example, here is a recursive algorithm for the mathematical function factorial:

START OF Factorial(N)
Precondition: N is a non-negative integer

if N = 0 or 1
    then
        return 1
    else
        return N × Factorial(N − 1)

END OF Factorial

1.4   Summary and Review

This primary purpose of this chapter is to introduce the reader to the FIVE + STEPS of programming and to the algorithmic language we use. The discussion covered a number of "fundamental concepts" or "primitives" of computer programming.

- We discussed the concept of assignment and the use of variables. We indicated that we will use the word "*store*" to indicate assignment, and that assignment in our algorithms is "left to right"; i.e., *store Num2 in Num1* means to change the current value of *Num1* to the current value of *Num2*. In Pascal, this is expressed as **Num1 := Num2**.

- We discussed the notion of selection, the ability to have the program make some sort of test, and, depending on the result of the test, execute one series of steps or another. We also mentioned multi-way selection.

- We discussed the concept of looping: that ability to have the program execute a series of steps over and over. We described three kinds of loops, the *loop until*, the *loop while* and the *loop for*.

- We discussed input and output, and illustrated how we will indicate input and output in our algorithms.

- We discussed "top-down programming" (also known as "modular programming"), and we discussed parameter passing. It is important to understand the difference between passing parameters by value versus passing them by reference. It is also important to understand the difference between subroutines that are procedures versus those that are functions. A procedure is a routine that performs a task of some sort, and a function is a routine that returns (or "has") a value.

- We discussed "recursion." Many of the routines in this book will be written recursively. We expect the reader of this book to have had some experience with recursion, although not necessarily a great deal.

Chapter 2

Order of Magnitude

> Computers are not smarter than people,
> but they are smarter than programmers.
> — James Heasley

2.1 Overview of the Chapter

In this chapter we discuss the efficiency of algorithms. The goal is to develop techniques that measure the efficiency of an algorithm. As examples of the way the techniques are used, we analyze several searching and sorting algorithms. We discuss the notion of "order of magnitude" of an algorithm and introduce the "Big-O" notation. We also define the notion of "stability" for sorting algorithms.

2.2 Introduction

We want to be able to answer the question "How efficient is this algorithm?" for any given algorithm. Before we can answer that question, we have to come to some agreement as to what we mean by efficiency. Perhaps the first definition that comes to mind is related to speed. One algorithm would surely be considered more efficient than another if the first one got a particular job done faster than the second one did. There are problems with this definition, but it comes pretty close to what we want.

We have to be careful not to let other factors affect our conclusions. For example, if the first algorithm was implemented in a more efficient manner than the second, we would not want that to be the determining factor. Similarly, if the first algorithm was run on a faster computer, we would not want that to lead us into deciding that the algorithm is better. Also, we will want a more absolute measure of efficiency. We might not always have two algorithms to compare to one another; we will want to be able to look at a given algorithm and make some statements about its efficiency without having to compare it to another algorithm.

2.3   Searching Algorithms

To introduce the methodology we'll use to measure the efficiency of algorithms, we'll use two searching algorithms: a linear search algorithm and a binary search algorithm.

Linear Search

Let's start with an easy example: a *linear search*. A linear search searches through an array by examining the elements of the array one at a time, comparing each to a "*Key*" and continuing until either an element equal to the key is encountered or the end of the array is reached. We use this method when the list we're searching is in no particular order, or when the number of items in the list is very small. Here's an algorithm for a linear search:

```
START OF Linear Search(A, N, Key, Found, Place)
Passed by value: A (an array of N elements), N, Key
Passed by reference: Found, Place
Postconditions: If the Key is in the array, Found is set to true and
                Place set to the location. Otherwise, Found is false.


store false in Found
store 1 in Place
loop while not Found and Place ≤ N
    if A_Place = Key
        then
            store true in Found
        else
            add 1 to Place


END OF Linear Search
```

As the postcondition states, if the key is in the array, *Found* is set to true and *Place* is set to the index of the element containing the key. Otherwise, *Found* is set to false.

How efficient is a linear search? To answer this question, suppose we have a list of N elements in an array. To simplify our work a little, suppose that we know that a particular value, the key, is in the list and we plan to do a linear search to find out which location it's in. How long, on the average, will it take us to find the location of the key? If we're very lucky, we might find it on the first look; that is, the key might be in the first position in the array. On the other hand, if we are not lucky, we might not find it until the last look; we might have to look at all N elements until we find it.

Assuming that the elements are in no particular order, the average number of comparisons between the key and elements of the array required to locate the position of the key would be $N/2$. If the array had 100 elements in it, we would have to compare the key with 50 elements, on the average, before we found where it was.

Now, suppose we increase the number of elements in the array. Let's double the number to 200. What then would be the average number of comparisons? It would take, on the average, 100 comparisons, just twice what it took before. As the number of elements in the array increases, the time it takes us to locate a particular element increases at the same rate. Let C stand for the number of comparisons and N stand for the number of elements in the array. The relationship between C and N can be expressed as

$$C = N/2.$$

Since this equation describes a straight line when graphed, we call the relationship between the number of comparisons and the number of elements in the array a *linear* relationship. As a matter of fact, that's why we call it a linear search.

Binary Search

Now let's turn to a *binary search* technique. Suppose now that the list is in ascending order, and, as before, suppose we need to know whether or not the key is in the array. If it is, we need to know where it is. This time, let's not assume the key is in the array; rather, let's assume we don't know whether or not the key is in the array. A binary search depends on the fact that the list is in either ascending or descending order. It doesn't matter which—we can handle either situation—but we need to know which way it's arranged, so we'll assume it's in ascending order.

We first examine the element in the middle of the array by comparing it to the key. If this element equals the key, we take note of where we are in the array and exit. If it's smaller than the key, we discard the first half and continue searching in the second half. If it's larger, we discard the second half and continue searching in the first half. Each time we examine the element in the middle of those remaining. This continues until either we find the key or until no elements remain. An algorithm for a binary search is on the next page.

```
START OF Binary Search(A, N, Key, Found, Place)
Passed by value: A (an array of N elements), N, Key
Passed by reference: Found, Place
Precondition: The array A is arranged in ascending order.
Postconditions: If the Key is in the array, Found is set to true and
                        Place set to the location. Otherwise, Found is false.


store 0 in Left
store N+1 in Right
store false in Found
loop while Left+1 < Right and not Found
    store the index halfway between Left & Right in Place
    if A_Place = Key
        then
            store true in Found
        else
            if A_Place < Key
                then
                    store Place in Left
                else
                    store Place in Right


END OF Binary Search
```

Just as with the linear search, if the key is in the array, *Found* is set to true and *Place* equals the index of the element containing the key. Otherwise, *Found* is set to false.

Supposing that the key is present, how many "looks" in the array will it take us? If we are very lucky, we will find it on the first look. If we don't find it then, we have only half the array to continue searching. If we don't find it on the second look, we will have only 1/4 the array to continue to search. After the third look, if we haven't found it, we will only have 1/8 of the array to search.

How many "looks" will be required in the worst case? That is, what's the maximum number of times we will have to look at an element in the array?

Let's try a specific example before we go any further. Suppose the array has 100 numbers to start with. If we don't find the key on the first look, there will be at most 50 numbers left. If we don't find it on the second look, there will be at most 25 numbers left; third look, 12 numbers; fourth look, six numbers; and fifth look, three numbers. If we don't find it on the sixth look, we will know for certain on the seventh look whether the number is in the array or not. Thus, we are sure that, even in the worst case, we will either find the key in seven looks or know that it's not in the array.

Before you go on, be sure to compare this to a linear search which would require an average of 50 looks and a maximum of 100.

That was a lot of work we won't want to go through every time. Fortunately, there is an easier way. Consider the table in figure 2.1.

Looks	Number Remaining
0	N
1	$N/2$
2	$N/4$
3	$N/8$
4	$N/16$
$\vdots$	$\vdots$

Figure 2.1 Number of Looks versus Number Remaining

We want to know the number of looks that will insure the number remaining in the portion of the array left to be searched is zero. The number remaining will be zero when the denominator in the second column is larger than N. The denominator is 2 raised to the *number of looks* power. If we let x stand for the number of looks, when will 2^x be larger than N?

The answer to this can be expressed using the logarithm function. Recall from your algebra class that $\log_2 N$ is the power that we have to raise 2 to in order to get N. That is, if $\log_2 N = x$ then $2^x = N$.

It's also the case that if $2^x > N$ then $x > \log_2 N$. We want the first integer, x, such that $2^x > N$. That's equivalent to saying the first integer, x, such that $x > \log_2 N$. (We want an integer because the number of looks cannot be a fraction.) Since we want the first integer that is strictly greater than $\log_2 N$, it's easier to find the first integer that is greater than or equal to $\log_2(N + 1)$. The '+1' will only become important when N is a power of 2. Trace the bubble sort on an array with, for example, 128 elements and see how many looks it takes in the worst case.

There is a function, called the "ceiling" function, that returns the next greatest integer when sent a real number. Different math books use different symbols for this function; we'll use:

$$\text{Maximum Looks} = \lceil \log_2(N + 1) \rceil$$

where $\lceil X \rceil$ means the first integer greater than or equal to X. Don't worry about the notation; we're not going to dwell on it.

Let's check this with our earlier example. If $N = 100$, what is $\lceil \log_2(N+1) \rceil$? $\log_2 101 \approx 6.65821$ and the next integer greater than that is 7, which agrees with what we said earlier.

So what have we accomplished? Let's look at another example. Suppose N equals 200. How many looks will it take in the worst case? $\lceil \log_2 201 \rceil$ equals 8. We doubled the number of elements, but the maximum number of looks required only went up by one! If N is 400, it would take 9 looks. Indeed, if N were 1 million, it would only take 20 looks in the worst case! Well, of course; that's how the binary search works. That's not such a surprise, but we have developed a very useful formula. Let's repeat it for the record:

> In a binary search routine, where the number of elements in the array is N, the maximum number of comparisons, C, between the key and elements of the array needed to determine whether or not the key is in the array is given by:
>
> $$C = \lceil \log_2(N + 1) \rceil.$$

2.4   Order of Magnitude

We got onto this tack by trying to answer the question, "How efficient are the searching routines?" We are close to being able to formulate an answer.

Let's again consider the number of comparisons each algorithm requires. The linear search requires an average of $N/2$ comparisons. As we saw, if the number of elements in the array doubles, the number of comparisons also doubles. The binary search requires a maximum of $\lceil \log_2(N + 1) \rceil$ comparisons. If the number of elements in the array doubles, the maximum number of comparisons goes up by only one.

Suppose the number of elements in the array triples. How many more comparisons will be needed? The answer is easy for the linear search; the average number of comparisons will also triple. How about for the binary search? The maximum number of comparisons required for N elements is $\lceil \log_2(N+1) \rceil$ and the maximum number required for $3N$ elements is $\lceil \log_2(3N + 1) \rceil$. How do these numbers compare? For a particular value of N, the calculation is easy, but the formula:

$$\frac{\lceil \log_2(3N + 1) \rceil}{\lceil \log_2(N + 1) \rceil}$$

does not reduce in any straightforward way.

Rather than try to find specific numerical quantities, we use the relationship between the number N and the number of comparisons to express the efficiency of the algorithm. When the number of comparisons required is related to the number of elements, N, by some formula, say $g(N)$, we say that the number of comparisons is of *order of magnitude* $g(N)$. For our two examples, the linear search is of order of magnitude $N/2$, and the binary search is of order of magnitude $\lceil \log_2(N + 1) \rceil$.

The Big–O Notation

There is a common notation for this, called the *Big-O* notation. If the order of magnitude between the number of elements N and the number of comparisons is $g(N)$, one writes $O(g(N))$ instead of the words "order of magnitude $g(N)$."

Let's look at that a bit more carefully. If the formula $g(N)$ has several terms, we will only consider the term which increases fastest as N increases. For example, if $g(N)$ happened to be $N^2 + N$, we would say that the relationship is "of order of magnitude N^2," or $O(N^2)$. For larger values of N, the low order terms have virtually no effect on the time it takes compared to the highest order term.

Next, if there is a constant before the largest term, we will drop the constant. That is, if $g(N)$ happened to be $5N^2 + 4N$, we will still say that the relationship is $O(N^2)$. The reason for this is we are characterizing how the number of comparisons depends on different values of N, not the actual performance for a particular N, and the constant will always cancel out when we compare different values of N.

An example might help. Suppose that the number of comparisons is $5N^2$. If N is doubled, the number of comparisons is $5(2N)^2$, which is 4 times what it was before; the 5 cancels out. The same is true no matter what the constant is; the number of comparisons increases by a factor of four when N is doubled. We're going to use these techniques on some sorting algorithms next, but before we do, we need to clear up some more details.

First, you will have noticed that we referred to "the average number of comparisons" while discussing the linear search and "the maximum number of comparisons" while discussing the binary search. It really doesn't matter. Since the average number of comparisons was $\frac{1}{2}N$, and since we're going to drop the $\frac{1}{2}$ anyway, we still get $O(N)$ for the linear search.

We must not be careless if we attempt to discuss the average number of looks with the binary search. Even though the minimum number of possible looks is 1 and the maximum is $\lceil \log_2(N + 1) \rceil$, the average number is *not* the sum of these two numbers divided by 2. By 'average number' we mean something like the average number of looks we will have to make if we search the array many times, each time searching for a different number. It makes a difference whether the search is successful or not. If the search in not successful, the number of looks equals the maximum number of looks. If we always search for a value that is in the array, we will find it, on average, just before or on the last look. Thus the 'average number' of looks will be close to the maximum number of looks. This turns out to be more complicated than we want to get into in this text, so we'll just stay with the maximum. Also, notice that we drop the '$\lceil$' and the '$\rceil$' as well as the 1. As N gets large, the difference between the real value $\log_2 N$ and the integer $\lceil \log_2(N + 1) \rceil$ is very small and can be safely ignored.

Finally, since the base of the logarithm can be changed by simply multiplying by a constant—that is:

$$\log_2 N = \frac{\log_b N}{\log_b 2} = \frac{1}{\log_b 2} \log_b N$$

for any base $b > 1$—and we're going to drop the constant in front anyway, it isn't important that we use base 2.

In summary, the linear search is $O(N)$ and the binary search is $O(\log N)$.

2.5   Sorting Algorithms

We turn now to sorting. When we considered searching algorithms we were concerned with the number of comparisons that had to be made. Now we'll also have to take into account the steps involved in moving elements of the list around to achieve the desired order.

We'll consider several different well-known sorting algorithms and determine their orders of magnitude. As we said in the introduction to this chapter, the most basic thing we want to measure is speed. After eliminating factors such as which language is used to implement the algorithm and which computer the program is run on, we want to know how fast an algorithm is. We'll be discussing some famous sorting algorithms: the bubble sort, two versions of the insertion sort and the heap sort. There are many different sorting algorithms known, and we won't discuss more than these four in this chapter. We'll leave the analysis of some of the others for the exercises and will discuss others in later chapters.

Figure 2.2 contains a table of values for reference and comparison. We include times for the four algorithms we will discuss and some others as well. Each sorting algorithm has been written in Pascal as efficiently as possible. The numbers in the array were chosen at random—it turns out, as we will see, that some algorithms work very differently on numbers that are already in order, or nearly in order.

It may be easier to get a feeling for the differences in these times if we graph the numbers. Figure 2.3 shows the numbers from figure 2.2 plotted as the number of elements versus the time each algorithm took.

A few comments before we get into the analyses. Notice that the bubble sort is much slower than the rest. It takes over four minutes to sort 2000 real values, while the heap sort takes only about five seconds for the same array. Notice that the binary insertion sort is quite a bit better than the linear insertion sort, and that the selection sort and the linear insertion sort are almost identical. Finally, notice that each of the times required for the first four sorts *quadruples* as the number of elements in the array doubles. This should give you a clue as to what the order of magnitude is for each of these four algorithms.

Time, in seconds, required to sort an array.

Sorting Algorithm	Number of Elements				
	125	250	500	1000	2000
Bubble Sort	0.94	3.76	15.62	62.03	248.30
Selection Sort	0.50	2.01	7.97	31.72	126.69
Linear Insertion Sort	0.50	1.97	8.38	32.79	129.68
Binary Insertion Sort	0.22	0.74	2.91	10.91	42.02
Shell Sort	0.17	0.44	1.09	2.76	6.21
Heap Sort	0.19	0.47	1.06	2.42	5.35
Quicksort	0.11	0.22	0.51	1.13	2.57

Figure 2.2 Numbers Originally in Random Order

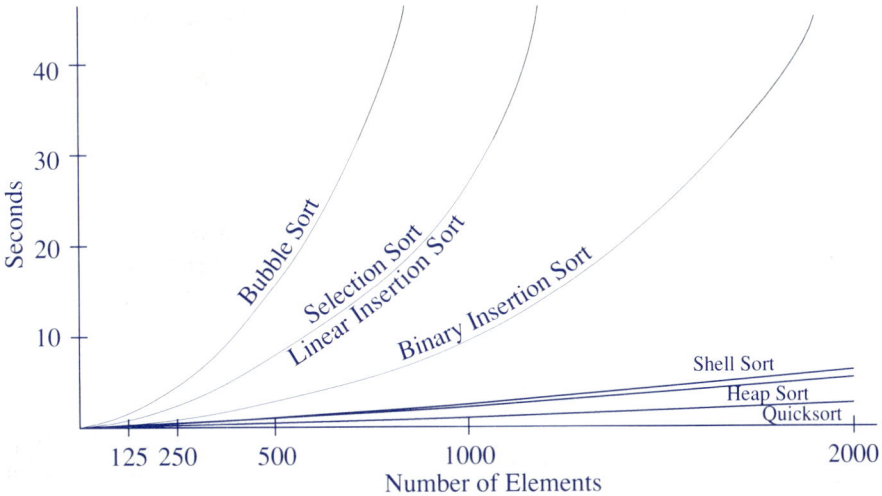

Figure 2.3 A Graph of the Data in Figure 2.2

The Bubble Sort

We want to determine the order of magnitude of the bubble sort. There are many versions of the bubble sort algorithm, but they are all characterized by the fact that the sorting is accomplished by exchanging ("swapping") the contents of adjacent locations in the array. An algorithm for one version of the bubble sort is on the next page.

```
START OF The Bubble Sort(A, N)
Passed by value: N
Passed by reference: A (an array of N elements)

store N−1 in j
loop
    store 1 in LastSwap
    loop for i going from 1 to j
        if Aᵢ > Aᵢ₊₁
            then
                call Swap(Aᵢ, Aᵢ₊₁)
                store i in LastSwap
    store LastSwap−1 in j
    until LastSwap = 1

END OF Bubble Sort
```

Our goal is to find a formula relating the number of elements in the array, N, to something that measures the time the algorithm takes. When we were discussing searching earlier, we always counted the number of comparisons that were made between the key and elements of the array. Since we don't have a key, let's count the number of times one element of the array is compared to another. It would also be possible to count the number of times an element of the array is moved, but let's stay with comparisons for now.

Consider the *if...then* in the middle of the algorithm. The test in this *if...then* will be done every time the inner loop is executed. If we can estimate the number of times it is executed, we'll have a good idea of how much time the algorithm takes.

Let's do a "worst case" estimation. Suppose that the array is in descending order. Every time the test is done, the two elements will be out of order. Then *LastSwap* will get set to the last value of i before the inner loop is exited. Thus j will always be decremented by 1 each time, and the outer loop will get executed $N-1$ times. The inner loop will be executed $N-1$ times the first time through the outer loop, $N-2$ times the second time, $N-3$ times the third time, etc. Thus, the comparison in the *if...then* will be done

$$S = (N-1) + (N-2) + (N-3) + \cdots + 2 + 1$$

times.

There are formulas for this sum, but rather than look it up, we can quickly develop it. Let S stand for the sum, and write the entire series down twice, but the second time write it down in the opposite order:

$$
\begin{aligned}
S &= (N-1) &+& (N-2) &+& (N-3) &+ \cdots +& 2 &+& 1 \\
S &= 1 &+& 2 &+& 3 &+ \cdots +& (N-2) &+& (N-1)
\end{aligned}
$$

Now add the two series vertically; i.e., by adding the first term of the first series to the first term of the second series, etc. The sum of the two first terms is N. The sum of the two second terms is N. In fact, the sum of *every* pair of terms is N. We have $N-1$ numbers each of which is N. That equals $N(N-1)$. But, since we added the whole thing twice, this equals $2S$. We have to divide by 2 to get the correct answer. So, the sum, S, is:

$$S = \frac{N(N-1)}{2}.$$

Rearranging slightly, we find that the maximum number of comparisons required by the bubble sort is:

$$S = \tfrac{1}{2}N^2 - \tfrac{1}{2}N.$$

According to the rules we agreed on earlier, we can state that the bubble sort is $O(N^2)$.

Remember, this means the time required to sort the array increases as N^2. Or, if N is doubled, the time will be increased by a factor of four. If N is increased by a factor of 4, the time will be increased by a factor of 4^2, or 16. These calculations are borne out by the numbers in figure 2.2.

Sorting an Already Sorted Array

It's interesting to note that we did a worst case estimation of the bubble sort while the times in figure 2.2 were for random data. The times show that the bubble sort is $O(N^2)$ even when the numbers are chosen at random. Had we chosen the numbers differently, e.g., had they been in order to start with, the results would have been quite different. Figure 2.4 illustrates what we are talking about. The same program as before was run, but this time, instead of choosing the numbers at random, they were put in the array in ascending order.

The two tables make it clear that the algorithms perform differently when sorting random numbers than they do when sorting numbers that are already in order. Some algorithms perform much better, some perform much worse, and others don't show much change. We'll be referring to these tables again when we analyze the other algorithms.

Time, in seconds, required to sort an array.

Sorting Algorithm	Number of Elements				
	125	250	500	1000	2000
Bubble Sort	0.00	0.03	0.03	0.08	0.14
Selection Sort	0.50	2.11	8.35	33.28	132.96
Linear Insertion Sort	0.03	0.06	0.11	0.19	0.34
Binary Insertion Sort	0.05	0.11	0.27	0.66	1.51
Shell Sort	0.08	0.19	0.41	0.93	2.06
Heap Sort	0.22	0.50	1.10	2.59	5.60
Quick Sort	0.72	2.75	10.65	42.12	167.84

Figure 2.4 Numbers Originally in Ascending Order

The Insertion Sort

Let's next analyze the insertion sort. The insertion sort is something akin to sorting a hand of cards in a bridge game. You pick up the cards one at a time and place each card in order with the ones already in your hand. We'll develop two versions of the insertion sort. Here's our first version:

```
START OF Linear Insertion Sort(A, N)
Passed by value: N
Passed by reference: A (an array of N elements)

loop for j going from 2 to N
    store A_j in Temp
    store j−1 in i
    store false in Found
    loop while not Found and i > 0
        if A_i > Temp
            then
                subtract 1 from i
            else
                store true in Found
    store i+1 in Place
    loop for i going from j−1 down to Place
        store A_i in A_{i+1}
    store Temp in A_{Place}

END OF Linear Insertion Sort
```

Starting with the second element in the array, we put each element in a temporary variable, search through the array to the left for the place where the element belongs, slide those that are larger than the temporary value to the right one slot, and insert the temporary value into A_{Place}, continuing until we come to the end of the array. Trace the algorithm on a small array until you understand it.

We call this the "linear insertion sort" because we do a linear search for the place to insert *Temp* each time.

As before, let's concentrate on comparisons. We'll want to estimate how the number of comparisons increases with the value of N. Let's start with a "worst case" analysis again. Suppose that the array is originally in decreasing order. Every time we insert an element, we will have to slide down every element from the first through the current $(j-1)^{\text{st}}$ and then put the element being inserted at the top of the array. That is, when we are inserting A_2, we will compare *Temp* with A_1 and decide to insert *Temp* above A_1, sliding A_1 down first. When we come to A_3, we will compare *Temp* with A_2 and then with A_1, deciding to slide both of these elements down and inserting *Temp* in position 1. Finally, when we are ready to insert A_N, we will compare *Temp* with all of the elements from A_{N-1} though A_1. The total number of comparisons is the sum of:

$$1, 2, 3, \ldots, N-1.$$

But that's the same total we got earlier:

$$\frac{N(N-1)}{2}.$$

As before, this simplifies to:

$$\tfrac{1}{2}N^2 - \tfrac{1}{2}N.$$

And we conclude that the *worst case* performance of the insertion sort is $O(N^2)$.

That was a worst case analysis. How about an "average case" analysis? Can we handle that? Sure. Let's suppose that the array is originally in random order. Sometimes we will have to insert the next element near the top, sometimes near the bottom and sometimes in the middle. On average, the number of comparisons required to find the place to insert *Temp* will be about half the value we got before. That is, the total number of comparisons will be, on the average, the sum of the values:

$$1, 1, 3/2, \ldots, (N-1)/2.$$

(The first number is 1, not 1/2 since we always have to make at least one comparison.)

This is the same as the previous series except there's an extra $1/2$ in front, and each term has $1/2$ in front of it. We can factor the $1/2$ out and the total becomes:

$$1/2 + \tfrac{1}{2}(\tfrac{1}{2}N^2 - \tfrac{1}{2}N).$$

Since the low order terms and the constant in front are dropped, as discussed earlier, the *average case* performance of the insertion sort is the same as it is for the worst case: $O(N^2)$.

The Insertion Sort with a Binary Search

Now let's turn to a second version of the insertion sort. This version replaces the linear search with a binary search. This sorting algorithm is very similar to the algorithm for the insertion sort with a linear search. The only difference is in the search part.

Here's the algorithm:

```
START OF Binary Insertion Sort(A, N)
Passed by value: N
Passed by reference: A (an array of N elements)

loop for i going from 2 to N
    store A_i in Temp
    store 0 in Left
    store i in Right
    loop while Left + 1 < Right
        store (Left + Right) / 2 in Middle
        if A_Middle ≤ Temp
            then
                store Middle in Left
            else
                store Middle in Right
    loop for j going from i-1 down to Right
        store A_j in A_{j+1}
    store Temp in A_Right

END OF Binary Insertion Sort
```

Before we get into the analysis of this algorithm, you should make sure you understand it. Trace the search part on an array with 15 numbers or so. Do you see why *Right* starts off at i each time? Do you see why the "slide loop" goes from $i-1$ down to *Right*? It would probably be a good idea for you to implement the algorithm in Pascal and test it to make sure it actually sorts the numbers.

The advantage of the binary search is not felt until the number of numbers in the array gets over 10, or so. In any case, as we saw with the analysis of the binary search earlier, it takes about $\lceil \log_2(N+1) \rceil$ "looks" into the array to find the location of a particular element. With the insertion sort we are only looking in that portion of the array to the left of the ith element. In other words, when we are searching for the place to insert A_i, it will take us about $\lceil \log_2 i \rceil$ comparisons. The total number of comparisons required will thus be on the order of:

$$\log_2 2 + \log_2 3 + \log_2 4 + \ldots + \log_2 N.$$

It's beyond our purposes to determine the sum of this series, so let's just resort to using some advanced mathematics on the problem. Don't worry about how the math is done. An approximation for the sum of this series is:

$$k(N \log_2 N - N)$$

where k is a constant. Remember we discard the lower degree terms of the formula and the constant. Remember also that it isn't important that the logs are to the base 2. Therefore, we conclude that the binary search version of the insertion sort is $O(N \log N)$.

Take a look at figure 2.2. Do the times reported there agree with our conclusion? Surely the binary insertion sort is considerably faster than the linear insertion sort, but that's not the question. Does it seem to be $O(N \log N)$? Notice that when we double the number of numbers in the array, the time required to sort the array is about quadrupled. That's not $O(N \log N)$, that's $O(N^2)$! What did we do wrong?

Our calculations are not in error; the mathematics is correct. What we did wrong was to only consider comparisons. We have significantly reduced the number of comparisons by replacing the linear search with a binary search, but we have not reduced the number of times elements of the array have to be moved around. In fact, the number of assignments of elements of the array is exactly the same as before. Remember we said earlier that we were going to stick with comparisons for awhile. We have reached a point where the number of assignments outweighs the number of comparisons by such a degree that the time required for the sorting to be accomplished depends primarily on the assignments, not on the comparisons.

Let's look at assignments. In particular, let's look at the number of times an element of the array is moved. Here's the algorithm again, but we have left out the "search" part since no assignments of array elements take place within it.

```
loop for i going from 2 to N
    store Aᵢ in Temp
    { search for place to insert Temp }
    loop for j going from i−1 down to Right
        store Aⱼ in Aⱼ₊₁
    store Temp in A_Right
```

The outer loop is executed $N - 1$ times. Each time through there are two assignments, one at the top and one at the bottom. The "slide" part consists of sliding the elements larger than *Temp* over one position. If the array is in a random order, the number of "slides" will average out to about half the value of i. Thus, the total number of assignments will be about:

$$2\tfrac{1}{2} + 3 + 3\tfrac{1}{2} + 4 + 4\tfrac{1}{2} + \ldots + (2 + \tfrac{N-1}{2}).$$

As before, we can find this sum by writing the series down in reverse order, adding vertically then horizontally, and dividing by two. This results in a sum of:

$$\frac{(N-1)(\tfrac{N}{2} + 4)}{2} = \frac{N^2 + 7N - 8}{4}.$$

Now we conclude that if we count assignments, the algorithm is $O(N^2)$. It's interesting to note that the number of assignments done during the linear insertion sort is exactly the same as the number done during the binary insertion sort. Both algorithms are $O(N^2)$ when we consider assignments.

When we look at comparisons, the binary insertion sort is $O(N \log N)$. When we look at assignments, the binary insertion sort is $O(N^2)$. Which should we use for our conclusion? As the size of N increases, the number of assignments will be the determining factor in the speed of the algorithm—since N^2 grows much faster than $N \log N$—so we conclude that the binary insertion sort is $O(N^2)$.

Sorting Algorithms So Far

It would not be surprising to hear a few complaints about now. Every algorithm we have analyzed is $O(N^2)$! Looking back at figure 2.2, it's clear that these three algorithms are not equally fast. The binary insertion sort is still much faster than the others—at least for random data. When we say that two algorithms are both $O(N^2)$, we are not saying that they run at the same speed. Remember that we dropped off the constant in front. The constant for the bubble sort is much larger than the constant for the binary insertion sort so the binary insertion sort runs much faster. However, it is still the case that when the number of numbers in the array is doubled, the time the sort requires to get the array in order is quadrupled.

There are faster sorting algorithms. Let's now look at the heap sort, allegedly a "better" algorithm than any of these $O(N^2)$ algorithms.

The Heap Sort

The heap sort uses quite a different approach than the bubble sort or the insertion sort. Rather than viewing an array as a linear sequence of numbered cells, we can view an array as a structure known as a *tree*—so called because it looks like an upside-down tree or like a family tree. It's worth noting that we are not really working with a tree. The array is not being changed in any way at all. We are just thinking of the array as a tree. "Real" binary trees are data structures discussed in detail in chapters 7 and 8..

Tree Notation

Let's consider some of the terminology we'll use to talk about trees. When we view the array as a tree, we will call the cells *nodes*. In figure 2.5, the nodes of the array are drawn in layers, with one node on the first layer, two on the next, four on the next, and so on until we run out of nodes. We connect the nodes so that each node is connected to one on the level above, which is called its *parent*, and at most two on the level below, which are called its *children*. A tree like this whose nodes have at most two children is called a *binary tree*.

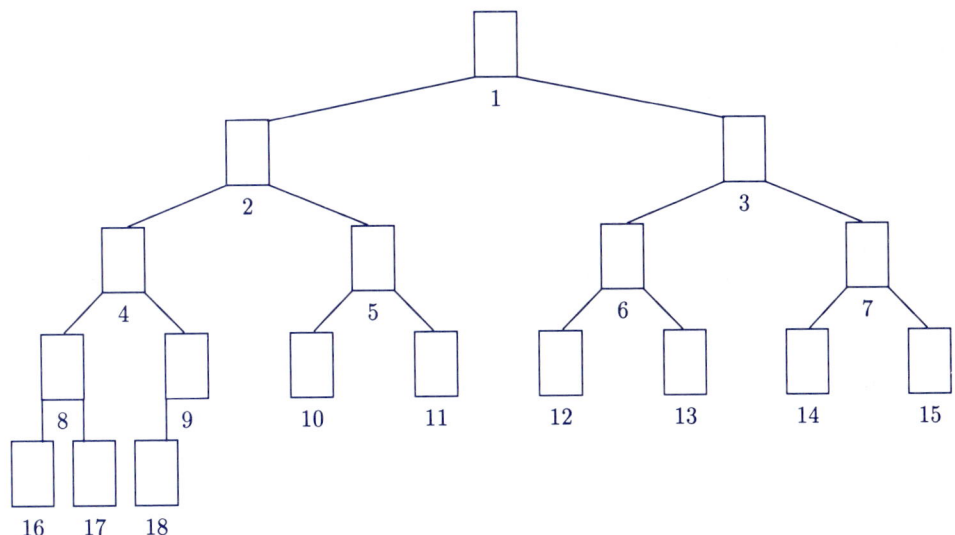

Figure 2.5 An Array Viewed as a Binary Tree

Note that the only node that does not have a parent is the node corresponding to the first cell of the array, A_1. We call this node the *root node*, since it's like the root of the tree. Also note that some nodes have only one child, and some have no children at all. A node with no children is called a *leaf*.

It is easy to find which node is the parent of a given node, and which nodes (if they exist) are its children. The parent of the node A_i is $A_{i \text{ div } 2}$, for $i > 1$. The children of the node A_i are A_{2*i} and A_{2*i+1}, as long as these indices are not bigger than N.

A *subtree* of a tree is the collection of all the nodes starting at a given node and including all the descendants of that node (i.e., its children, its children's children, etc.). The first node in the collection is called the *root node for the subtree.* For example, the subtree with root node 3 in figure 2.5 consists of the nodes numbered 3, 6, 7, 12, 13, 14 and 15.

A Heap

We call a tree or a subtree a *heap* if every node in the tree (or subtree) contains a value larger than or equal to those of both its children. A subtree which is a leaf is considered a heap by default.

Making a subtree into a heap is the key to the heap sort. If the entire tree is a heap, then the root node contains the largest value in the array. We can exchange the contents of the first element with that of the last element and know that the largest element is in the right place. Doing this will, of course, mess up the heap structure of the entire tree. However, if we simply ignore the last element—it is in the right place, after all—then we can continue to work on the remainder of the array.

Thus, we need a routine that will turn a subtree into a heap. We'll call this routine *Heapify.* For reasons that will become clear in a moment, we will always assume, as a precondition, that when *Heapify* starts, the subtrees of the tree being "heapified" are already heaps. That is, whenever we call *Heapify* to turn a subtree into a heap, we must know that its children are already heaps. Before you conclude that we can never get started, remember that a leaf is a heap by default.

We'll return to the routine that does the sorting in a moment. Let's first look at *Heapify.*

The routine can be written in several ways. It is especially elegant when viewed recursively. Besides, viewing it recursively will give us an opportunity to analyze a recursive algorithm.

Let's think about how a subtree can be turned into a heap. You know that the two children of the tree being heapified are heaps, and you can examine the data contained in these two nodes. If either data item is larger than the data item in the root node, exchange the data in the root with the data in the larger child and heapify that child. There's the recursion; *Heapify* calls itself to turn the child into a heap. The other child will remain a heap and since we choose the child with the larger data, the entire subtree becomes a heap. This analysis results in the following algorithm for *Heapify*:

START OF Heapify(A, Start, Stop)
Passed by value: Start, Stop
Passed by reference: A, an array with at least Stop elements
Precondition: The subtrees with root nodes 2*Start and 2*Start + 1 are heaps.
Postcondition: The subtree with root node Start is a heap.

store 2 * Start in Child
if Child ≤ Stop
    then
        if Child < Stop and $A_{Child} < A_{Child+1}$
            then
                store Child + 1 in Child
        if $A_{Start} < A_{Child}$
            then
                call Swap(A_{Start}, A_{Child})
                call Heapify(A, Child, Stop)

END OF Heapify

Every recursive algorithm must have a non-recursive case where no recursion is required. Where is the non-recursive case for this algorithm? The non-recursive case occurs when Child gets bigger than Stop. When that happens, the routine simply does nothing.

Now that we have a module which will heapify any subtree, including the whole tree, we can use it to sort the array. (Remember this routine will heapify a tree which consists of array elements from one point in the array through another point as long as the two children of the tree being heapified are already heaps.)

The heap sort sorts the tree by first turning the entire tree into a heap. Then the data in the root node is exchanged with that in the last node in the array. Ignoring the last cell from now on, we can heapify the tree again, this time bringing the "next-to-the-largest data" into the root. This data can be exchanged with the data in node number $N - 1$ and the process continues.

The entire tree is turned into a heap by starting with the element with the largest index that possibly is not a heap. Since all the leaves are heaps by default, the last (possible) non-heap would be the last node which has a child: node number $N \div 2$. As we work our way backwards from this point, heapifying all the subtrees as we go, the entire tree becomes a heap.

A refined version of the algorithm would look like the following—assuming we have Heapify(A, Start, Stop) which turns the subtree from Start through Stop into a heap:

```
START OF HeapSort(A, N)
Passed by value: N
Passed by reference: A
Postcondition: The array is in ascending order.

loop for i going from N ÷ 2 down to 1
    call Heapify(A, i, N)
loop for i going from N down to 2
    call Swap(A₁, Aᵢ)
    call Heapify(A, 1, i−1)

END OF HeapSort
```

Our goal in this chapter is not to discuss the heap sort algorithm but to analyze it. You should think about the algorithm some more, make sure you understand, implement it in Pascal and test it before you go on. We'll leave this for the exercises.

Analysis of the Heap Sort

This is going to take more work, but we have laid the foundation for what we need to do. First we have to decide whether to count comparisons or assignments. We would normally attempt to count whichever requires the majority of the time. But what if we don't know which of the two requires the most time? Which should we count? Nothing prevents us from counting both!

Let's analyze the heap sort and estimate the total number of comparisons and assignments that are required.

The main routine calls the *Heapify* subroutine several times. There are two independent loops which call *Heapify*. The total number of comparisons and assignments will be the sum of the number required in each loop; thus, we can count each loop separately.

If we can count the numbers of comparisons and assignments required inside *Heapify*—based on the values of *Start* and *Stop*—we will be able to find the total we want because we know how many times *Heapify* is called and with what parameters. So, let's look at *Heapify*.

Consider figure 2.6. Recall that each subtree is a heap and that only the data in position *Start* is (possibly) out of place. The algorithm is called and calls itself until it finds the right place for the original root node, swapping elements "up" until both descendants of the current node are larger than the original root node or until it gets to *Stop*. How many calls will it have to make? The answer to that is related to the number of "levels" in the tree between

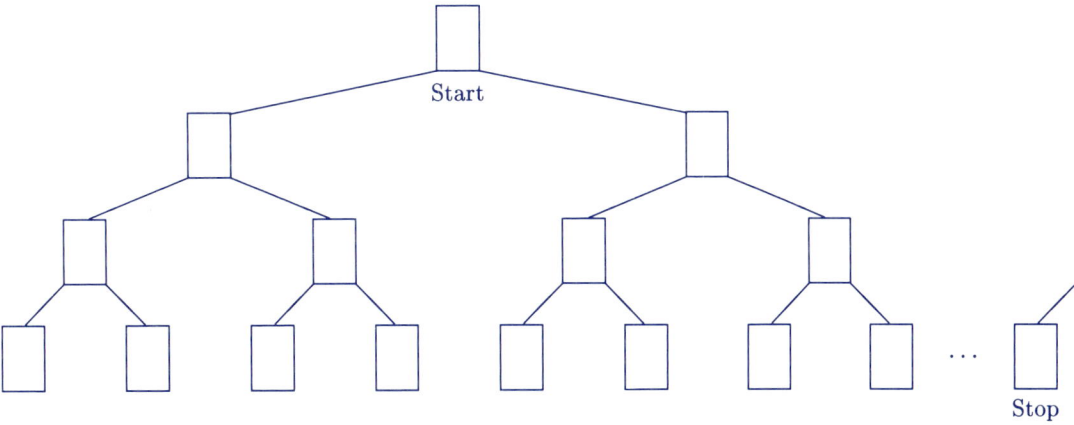

Figure 2.6 A Subtree Sent to Heapify

Start and *Stop*. Suppose, for example, that *Start* equals 20 and *Stop* equals 95. The nodes in this subtree on the level below A_{20} are numbered 40 and 41. The nodes on the next level are 80, 81, 82 and 83. The next level below this one would contain nodes numbered 160 through 167. Since 95 is less than 160, we'll not have to look below the level containing the 80, 81, 82 and 83. Thus, there are only two levels between A_{20} and A_{95} that will have to be searched, not counting the node A_{20} itself. Thus, counting the original call, *Heapify* will be called at most three times.

As another example, how many calls will be made if *Start* originally equals 1000 and *Stop* equals 9000? At most four: the original call, possibly a call to the level containing nodes numbered 2000 and 2001, possibly a call to the level containing nodes numbered 4000, 4001, 4002 and 4003, and possibly a call to the level containing nodes numbered 8000, 8001, 8002, 8003, 8004, 8005 and 8006.

We conclude that we will have to make a maximum of one additional call if *Stop* is bigger than twice *Start* but smaller than four times *Start*. A maximum of two additional calls have to be made if *Stop* is at least four times *Start* but less than eight times. The number of calls depends on the *ratio* of *Stop* to *Start*. The maximum number of calls is one plus the greatest integer contained in the logarithm to the base two of this ratio. That is, divide *Stop* by *Start* and take the log to the base 2 of the quotient, then add 1 because we always make the first call. Since this will likely be a real number, while we want an integer—we are counting calls, after all—we will then take the greatest integer contained in the result.

Expressed as a formula, the maximum number of calls that we have to make becomes:

$$1 + \lfloor \log_2 \frac{Stop}{Start} \rfloor.$$

The '$\lfloor \ldots \rfloor$' means the greatest integer, also known as the "floor" function. It's the counterpart to the ceiling function discussed earlier.

In algebra we learned that

$$\log_2 \frac{Stop}{Start} = \log_2 Stop - \log_2 Start.$$

Since we are going to throw out the lower order terms anyway, let's throw away the 1 and the negative term and only consider the positive term. Let's also ignore the difference between the integer and the real value. We can be confident that the number of calls is smaller than $\log_2 Stop$—often considerably smaller.

Now that we have an estimate of the number of calls, we can estimate the number of comparisons and assignments. On each call it makes at most three assignments—each swap requires three assignments—and two comparisons. If we make C calls, we will make at most $2C$ comparisons and $3C$ assignments.

We have the estimate we are looking for. The total number of assignments and comparisons required by Heapify cannot exceed $5L$ where $L = \lfloor \log_2 Stop \rfloor$.

The real value ($\log_2 Stop$) can be used since the integer value ($\lfloor \log_2 Stop \rfloor$) is only a little smaller than the real value. We conclude that the total number of comparisons and assignments made each time Heapify is called from Heap Sort is smaller than

$$5 \log_2 Stop.$$

Looking back at the main routine, we see that Heapify is called in the first loop $N/2$ times with Stop equal to N each time. Thus, the first loop will require less than $\frac{5N}{2} \log_2 N$ comparisons and assignments.

The second loop calls Heapify $N-1$ times with Stop equal to N, $N-1$, $N-2$, $\ldots$, 2. There are three more assignments required by the additional swap, so each time through this loop the total number of assignments and comparisons becomes:

$$3(N-1) + 5(\log_2 N + \log_2(N-1) + \ldots + \log_2 2).$$

As we saw earlier—when we worked on the insertion sort with a binary search—the sum of the series in the parentheses can be approximated by:

$$k(N \log_2 N - N)$$

where k is a constant. Thus, the total number of comparisons and assignments required by the second loop is approximately:

$$3(N-1) + 5k(N \log_2 N - N).$$

Dropping the low-order terms and the coefficients, each of the two loops requires $N \log N$ comparisons and assignments. If we add these two results together, we get $2N \log N$, but since we drop the constant in front, we still have $N \log N$. The entire algorithm is thus $O(N \log N)$. This is the first algorithm we have seen which is better than $O(N^2)$. As you can see from figure 2.2, the heap sort is much faster than the bubble, selection and insertion sorts, and it gets even better, by comparison, as N gets larger.

Examining figure 2.4, we note that even when the array is already sorted, the heap sort gets the job done almost as fast as before. The heap sort has the interesting property that the time required for the sort is about the same regardless of the original ordering of the elements. It's an unsolved problem in computer science to find both the best case and the worst case performances of the heap sort algorithm.

2.6 Orders of Magnitude, Graphically

Figure 2.7 illustrates the difference between the orders of magnitude of the functions we have been discussing as well as other functions. The function $f_1(N)$ is a function that is $O(1)$. (Yes, such algorithms do exist. Consider the time required to find the *smallest* element in an ordered list.) The function $f_2(N)$ is $O(\log N)$, $f_3(N)$ is $O(N)$, $f_4(N)$ is $O(N \log N)$, $f_5(N)$ is $O(N^2)$ and $f_6(N)$ is $O(2^N)$. It is clear that for large values of N, the difference between the growth rates becomes more and more significant.

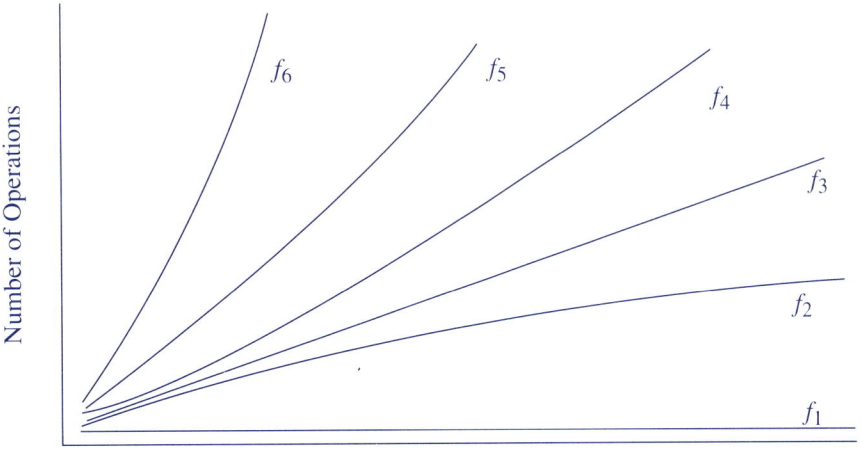

Figure 2.7 A Graph of Different Orders of Magnitude

2.7   Stability of Sorting Algorithms

A sorting algorithm is called *stable* if the relative position of two array elements with equal sorting keys is left unchanged by the algorithm. For example, if A_4 and A_9 have equal contents, then after the array is sorted the final position of the contents of A_4 will be before the final position of the contents of A_9. When sorting arrays that contain just numbers, the notion of stability seems meaningless—it doesn't matter which of two equal numbers is in a cell. However, sorting numbers in arrays is only an example of the real sorting that is done. The normal situation is to sort records, not numbers. In such a case the things that are being rearranged are not just numbers but entire records containing diverse data. With this in mind we can see the importance of using stable sorting algorithms. Suppose, for example, we have a collection of student records sorted into alphabetical order by the students' names. Then suppose we want to rearrange the records into descending order by grade point average (GPA). There will likely be several students with the same GPA and it would be better if all the students with the same GPA remained in alphabetical order. Hence, a stable sorting algorithm should be used.

Let's look at a couple of the algorithms we've discussed and ask if they're stable.

The Bubble Sort

First the bubble sort. Is it stable? Imagine an array containing cells with equal numbers. Are these two ever swapped? No. The algorithm only does an exchange if the number in one cell is greater than the number in the next cell. The bubble sort is stable.

The Insertion Sort

Is the insertion sort stable? When we used a linear search we stopped searching for the place to insert the new element as soon as we encountered an element that was smaller than or equal to the value stored in *Temp*. That means that if we encountered an element that was equal to the current element being inserted, it is not "slid" over, which keeps the relative positions of the equal elements the same. In other words, the linear insertion sort is stable.

How about the binary insertion sort; is it stable? Look back at the algorithm. If the same value exists in the array in more than one place, can it happen that one which was originally to the left of another ends up being to the right? In order to answer this question, you will need to look carefully at how the binary search works. We stored the value of *Right* in *Place*. Why? You should trace the algorithm using an array that contains several cells with equal values and watch what happens to *Right*. We'll leave the rest of this for the exercises.

The Heap Sort

While the heap sort is more efficient than the others, it is also more complicated and therefore harder to follow. Since it only takes one example to demonstrate that an algorithm is not stable, while it requires a proof to show that it is stable, let's try to find an example where two cells with equal values get their original relative order reversed.

Let's start with a very simple case and see if we can find a counterexample. Suppose the array has only three cells and the original values in the array are, in order, 50, 100 and 100. When the array is turned into a heap the first time, the 100 in position 2 is swapped with the 50 in position 1. Then the second loop starts off by swapping the element in position 1 with the element in position N (3). The two 100s are swapped and the 100 that originally was in position 2 is left in position 3, thus demonstrating that the heap sort is not stable.

2.8   Summary and Review

- This chapter concentrated on measuring the efficiency of algorithms.

- We introduced the concept of *order of magnitude* and explained how we can use it to compare algorithms. We introduced the "Big-O notation" to indicate the order of magnitude of an algorithm.

- We calculated the order of magnitude for two searching algorithms as well as the order of magnitude of several sorting algorithms.

- When attempting to determine the order of magnitude of an algorithm, it is important to count the action that becomes the major factor in determining the time required by the algorithm as N gets larger. We determined that the binary insertion sort is $O(N \log N)$ when we only look at comparisons, but is $O(N^2)$ when we consider assignments.

- We determined that the heap sort is $O(N \log N)$ when the numbers are arranged randomly as well as when the numbers are already in ascending order. The heap sort is an excellent algorithm to use in a wide variety of cases.

- We introduced the notion of "stability" for sorting algorithms and showed that the bubble sort and the linear insertion sort algorithms are stable. The stability of the binary insertion sort was left as an exercise. We found a quick counterexample to demonstrate that the heap sort algorithm is not stable.

2.9   Exercises

1. Trace the binary search algorithm on an array with N equal to a power of two to verify that the correct formula is Maximum Looks = $\lceil \log_2(N+1) \rceil$ rather than Maximum Looks = $\lceil \log_2 N \rceil$.

2. Rewrite the binary search algorithm so that it's recursive.

3. In an attempt to improve the bubble sort, it has been suggested that successive passes should go in alternate directions. In other words, the first pass would go from 1 though $N - 1$, exchanging elements when a larger one is found; the second pass would go from $N - 2$ down through 1, exchanging elements when a smaller one is found. Write an algorithm for this sorting algorithm. Determine the order of magnitude of this method. Is it more efficient than the original bubble sort?

4. A problem that is related to the sorting problem is the problem of finding the *median* value in a collection of values. The median value is defined as that value such that there as many values smaller than (or equal to) it as there are larger than (or equal to) it. Since there might be an even number of numbers in the collection, there could be two values that fall in the middle, in which case we'll not care which is called the median. In the collection: $56, 78, 13, 81, 54, 56, 51, 99$ and 13, the median is 56. Solve the problem of finding the median of a collection of numbers. Turn your solution into an algorithm. Clearly this can be done by simply sorting the N numbers and then looking at the element with index $N/2$. Can you find a more efficient solution?

5. The selection sort works as follows: First, locate the largest element in the array. Swap this value with the one in position N. Next locate the largest element in the array from 1 through $N - 1$. Swap this value with the one in position $N - 1$. Continue finding largest values and swapping until you work your way backwards to the top of the array.

   Write an algorithm for the selection sort. If possible, find an algorithm that makes the sort a stable sort. Determine the order of magnitude of the selection sort.

6. Write a complete Pascal program that implements and compares sorting algorithms. Your program should allow the user of the program to choose the initial arrangement of the numbers. He might choose them to be in ascending order, descending order or random order. You might also want to allow the user to enter the numbers himself so as to test the sorting routines with a particular collection of numbers. However, so as to permit the routines to sort large amounts of numbers, make the user entry an option. Then, allow the user to choose which sorting algorithm to use to sort the numbers. You should implement the bubble sort, both versions of the insertion sort and the heap sort. If you worked exercise 4, you should

implement the selection sort as well. Run the program and estimate the amount of time that the various algorithms take to sort arrays with different initial arrangements and different sizes. Check to see if the times you get are consistent with the conclusions reached in this chapter.

7. Is the binary insertion sort stable?

8. Can you make the heap sort stable by modifying the relational operators in *Heapify*? For example, *Heapify* chooses $Child + 1$ if $A_{Child+1}$ is greater than A_{Child}; would it make any difference if we changed that to "greater than or equal"? Would the algorithm still get the array sorted? If so, would the algorithm then be stable?

9. In the second loop in the main routine of *Heap Sort*, we always swap A_1 and A_i regardless of whether A_1 is greater than A_i or not. If we added a test here and only did the swap when the two values were out of order, would the algorithm still get the numbers sorted? If so, would it then be stable?

10. If the numbers in the array being sorted are already arranged in ascending order, what is the order of magnitude of the bubble sort? Answer the same question for the insertion sort, the binary insertion sort, the selection sort and the heap sort. Look at the table in figure 2.4 and see if you can guess the order of magnitudes of the Shell sort and the quicksort.

11. If the numbers in the array being sorted are already arranged in descending order, what is the order of magnitude of the bubble sort? Answer the same question for the insertion sort, the binary insertion sort, the selection sort, and the heap sort.

Chapter 3

Data Structures: Stacks and Queues

> Garbage In, Garbage Out.
> — Ed Norton

3.1   Overview of the Chapter

This chapter will present an introduction to the notion of a data structure. Two particular data structures, stacks and queues, will be used to illustrate what data structures are and how they are used. These two data structures will be discussed informally at first. We'll not be concerned with how they're implemented until after we have completed the algorithms that utilize them. In this chapter we will implement them with arrays. In later chapters, we will implement them with linked lists.

3.2   Introduction

In chapter 1 we broke the programming process down into five steps, which we called the FIVE + STEPS of programming (see page 2). However, the truth is that programming amounts to more than this. There is more going on than just writing algorithms and implementing them in some language. These FIVE + STEPS don't completely describe the process. What's missing is the major topic of this book: *data structures*.

When you are working on the solution to a problem and turning that solution into an algorithm, you have to be concerned with the data the problem involves, and you have to make decisions as to how those data are going to be stored and accessed by your program. With this in mind, the FIVE + STEPS might be restated as in figure 3.1.

1. Define the problem.

2. Find a solution to the problem, choosing appropriate ways to represent and access the data involved.

3. Design the data structure(s), and write an algorithm for the solution.

4. Code the algorithm in some computer language, implementing the data structure(s) in appropriate ways.

5. Test and debug the program.

+ Document continuously.

Figure 3.1 The Revised FIVE + STEPS of Programming

A data structure is more than just data or a data type. Data structures are characterized by the way the data are accessed, not just by the manner in which the data are stored. A data structure is a collection of data that is organized in a manner that makes certain methods of accessing the data possible. A data structure is a way of implementing an *abstract data type*.

Let's look at a problem that needs a data structure for its solution.

3.3   Expression Evaluation

Our problem can be stated simply:

Write a routine that will evaluate an arithmetic expression.

As is often the case with the first statement of a problem, this leaves a lot unstated, and we need to refine it. Let's work on the problem definition.

What we want is a routine that will take an expression and find its value. Here's a simple expression:

$$3 + 4 * 5.$$

The value of this expression is 23. The computer has a built-in routine that will get the correct result. What we want to do is duplicate that routine ourselves. Please notice it's not as simple as just looking at the characters from left to right and applying operators. The precedence rules state that the multiplication has to be done before the addition. The evaluation is not taking place from right to left, or from left to right; consider:

$$3 * 4 + 5$$

where the operation on the left, the "*," is evaluated before the operation on the right, the "+."

In fact, this is a not a trivial problem. Find the value of the following expression before you read on.

$$((9 + 3 * (8 - 3))/4) - 6.$$

Did you get 0? Notice that we could not have expressed this without using the parentheses. They are necessary because of the "precedence" of the arithmetic operators.

It turns out that the problem of precedence and the use of parentheses complicates the problem of expression evaluation beyond what we'd like to pursue for now. Instead, we will look at evaluating expressions in a somewhat simpler form. The data structures we develop in so doing can be applied later to a solution of our original problem.

Prefix and Postfix Notation

Let's look at a different way of writing expressions. The above notation is called "infix" notation because the operators are *between* the operands. There are two other well-known notations: prefix and postfix. As you could guess from the names, with prefix notation the operators *precede* the operands, while with postfix notation the operators *follow* the operands.

Prefix notation was invented by the Polish mathematician/logician Jan Lukasiewicz and is also known as *Polish notation*. Postfix notation is therefore known as *Reverse Polish Notation*. Hewlett-Packard calculators are famous for their use of Reverse Polish Notation, known as "RPN."

The infix expression "$3 + 4 * 5$" becomes "$+ 3 * 4\,5$" in prefix, and "$3\,4\,5 * +$" in postfix.

Look again at the prefix expression "$+ 3 * 4\,5$." What does that mean? The "$+$" means we are supposed to add two things together, but what two things? The "3" must be one of the two, but what's the second? The result of "$* 4\,5$," of course. The two operands are the "3" and the "$* 4\,5$."

Postfix notation is similar, but works in the opposite way. We encounter the operands first, and then the operators. Whenever we come to an operator, we are supposed to apply it to the last two operands we saw. Are a postfix expression and the equivalent prefix expression the same symbols written in the reverse order? Look at the prefix and postfix equivalents for "$3 + 4 * 5$" if you're not sure of the answer to this question.

Take a moment and convert the infix expressions "$3 * 4 + 5$" and "$(3+4) * 5$" to both prefix and postfix before going any further.

Notice that we can totally avoid the need for parentheses and the problems of precedence by using either prefix or postfix notation. That's the great advantage of prefix and postfix; we don't have to worry about the precedence of the operators and, therefore, don't have to use any parentheses. If you're familiar with a calculator that uses RPN, you'll remember that there are no keys marked "(" or ")" or "=."

For the time being, then, we'll confine ourselves to the evaluation of postfix expressions. In the exercises, you'll be asked to apply the methods we develop to evaluating prefix and infix expressions, and to converting from infix to postfix or prefix.

So, our problem definition becomes:

> Write a routine that will accept a string of characters representing a postfix expression, evaluate the expression and return the value.

Let's also agree to restrict ourselves to the four arithmetic operations: addition, subtraction, multiplication and division. (We omitted exponentiation.) For these four operations, let's use the familiar four operators: "+," "−," "*" and "/."

Solve the Problem

Now we can proceed to the second step: solving the problem, and choosing appropriate ways to represent the data. Let's continue by looking at a simple postfix expression:

$$3\,4\,5 + *.$$

The key to the solution is realizing that we need to store away the operands until they are needed, and then retrieve them in such a manner that the ones most recently stored are retrieved first. That is, the first operand in the string, the 3, is stored away somewhere. Then the second operand, 4, and the third, 5, are put somewhere. When we come to the "+" operator, we have to retrieve the last two operands and add them together, getting 9. Then we have to put this result somewhere, and move on down the string. Since we now come to another operator, the "*," we retrieve the last two operands and apply the operator; i.e., we multiply the 3 times the 9 to get 27, our final value.

What we need, then, is a way of storing the values of the operands away somewhere and getting them back in the reverse order. Such a data structure exists and is known as a *stack*.

A Stack

Perhaps the easiest way to envision a stack is to think about the spring-loaded devices used in cafeterias to hold plates. The tension in the spring is set in such a manner that as plates are put in, only the topmost plate can be removed from the stack of plates. Each time a plate is removed, the remaining plates rise up a little; each time a plate is put on the stack, it drops just a little. Stacks are also commonly called "*LIFO*" devices; "LIFO" stands for "last in, first out."

A stack is just what we want for the operands of a postfix expression. We want to be able to get the most recently seen operands first—last in, first out— and then those that were seen earlier.

Given a stack, we will use the word *push* to indicate putting something on the stack, and the word *pop* to indicate removing whatever is on the top of the stack. Now let's try expressing our solution using the notion of a stack and the concepts "push" and "pop."

> Work your way down the string. Whenever you encounter an operand, push it onto a stack. Whenever you encounter an operator, pop two operands off the stack, apply the operator, and push the result onto the stack. When you get to the end of the string, the value on top of the stack is the value of the expression.

Perhaps the expression we used before is too simple. Let's try a slightly more complicated postfix expression:

$$7\ 4\ 2 + 8\ 2\ / * +.$$

What is the value of this expression? Figure it out before you read further.

Now try our solution. Look at the elements in the string from left to right. Whenever you encounter an operand, push it onto a stack. The first three things we encounter are operands, so they get pushed. When we come to the first "+," the stack will look like:

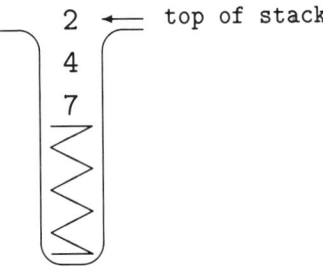

We then pop the 2 and the 4 off the stack, add them together and push the result, 6, onto the stack.

Now the stack looks like:

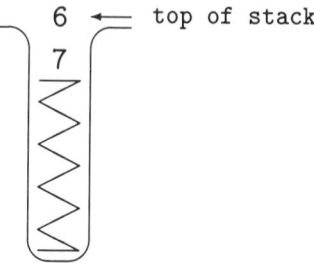

Next, we move along the string, encountering operands 8 and 2, which simply get pushed. When we come to the "/" operator, the stack will look like:

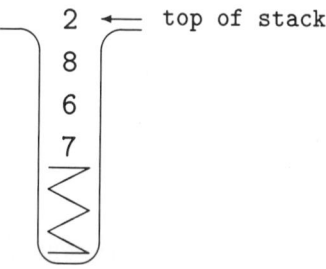

The operator is a "/" which indicates we need to divide. We pop the top two elements off the stack, 2 and 8, divide the 8 by the 2, and push the result, 4, onto the stack. (We must be careful to divide the 8 by the 2, not the other way around.) Now the stack looks like:

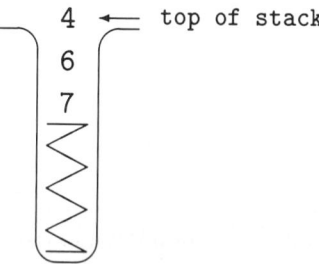

Upon encountering the operator "∗," we pop the 4 and 6 off the stack, multiply them together, and push the result, 24, onto the stack.

Now it looks like:

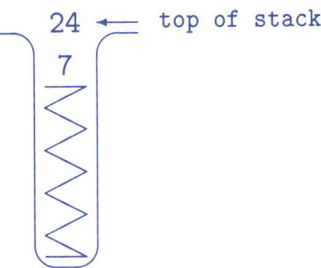

The final character in the string is another operator, a "+." We pop off the two operands, add them together and push the result, 31, onto the stack. Since we are now at the end of the string, the element on top of the stack is the value of the expression. This element is popped off and returned as the value of the routine. Did you get 31?

Let's look at our solution expressed as an algorithm:

```
loop while not at the end of the string
        if the next element on the string is an operand
            then
                    push it onto the stack
            else
                    if that element is an operator
                        then
                                pop two elements off the stack
                                perform the indicated operation on them
                                push the result onto the stack
pop an element off the stack, and return it
```

3.4   The Notion of an Abstract Data Type

Before we continue with the refinement of the expression evaluation algorithm, we need to look at the concept of an *Abstract Data Type*, or *ADT*. An abstract data type is a collection of operations defined on some data. There is no attention given to how the operations will be implemented on the computer. An ADT just indicates what operations are necessary to be performed on the data. In the current example, we saw that two of the basic operations that are required for a stack are those of a push and a pop. As we will see, there are other operations in the ADT of a stack, but the main point here is that the concept of a stack is an *abstract* data type. When you think about a stack, you don't need to think about whether the stack is an array, a linked list, or something else. Indeed, as we shall see, you can complete the algorithm for the solution to the expression evaluation problem without ever considering how the stack will be implemented.

It should be mentioned that this notion of abstraction makes things easier to work with, not harder. There is a tendency for people to think that when something is "abstract," it is theoretical, and then that theoretical things are harder to understand than concrete things. In actuality, the goal is just the opposite. When we think about an abstract data type, we can ignore the details of how the type will be implemented later, and concentrate on the important operations that define the type.

The goal in defining an abstract data type will always be to just define those operations that are necessary in order for the data type to do what it has to do.

3.5   A Stack as an Abstract Data Type

We need to consider this notion of a stack and see it as an abstract data type. We need to see what operations are fundamental to the concept. That is, we need to define the fundamental operations for the abstract data type stack.

First, since we want to know what's on the stack at all times, we need to be able to guarantee the stack is empty to begin with. We will need a routine that initializes a stack. Let's call it *InitStack*.

We have already seen the need for *Push* and *Pop*. Are there other routines that we will need?

What happens if the postfix expression is not a valid expression? The most serious thing that could happen would be for us to attempt to pop something off the stack when there's nothing on it. We need a way of telling whether or not the stack is empty before we attempt a pop. Let's assume that there is a function called *EmptyStack* that will tell us whether or not the stack is empty. We can call this function before we do a pop.

We have to worry about "stack overflow" too. This can happen when we try to push something onto a stack that won't hold any more elements. Even though this is really an implementation problem, there is always a limit on the size of the stack. For this reason we'll need a function *FullStack* to tell us whether or not the stack is full.

These five operations characterize a stack. We can make use of a stack in the current problem and in future problems as long as we have these five routines available. Let's repeat them for the record:

- **InitStack** A routine that initializes a stack to empty.

- **EmptyStack** A Boolean-valued function that returns **true** if a stack is empty and **false** otherwise.

- **Push** A routine which puts an element onto the top of a stack.

- **Pop** A routine which removes the top element from a stack.

- **FullStack** A Boolean-valued function that returns **true** if a stack is full and **false** otherwise.

These five operations define the abstract data type of a stack.

Notice that we have *not* said anything yet about how the stack is to be implemented. That's the whole point. We can work with the abstract data type of a stack and worry later about how to implement it.

We do, however, need to look at the five routines more closely and decide what sort of routines they are going to be. *EmptyStack* and *FullStack* are Boolean-valued functions. Will they require any parameters? Yes, the stack. We'll send the stack to them and have them send back *true* or *false*.

InitStack will be a procedure with one parameter, the stack. We'll send the stack to *InitStack* to initialize it.

That leaves *Push* and *Pop*. Since *Pop* returns a value, it might make sense to treat it as a function. However, the stack will have to be sent to *Pop*, and it will get changed by the routine. If we were to write *Pop* as a function, it would have a side effect. Since we want to avoid side effects, let's treat both *Push* and *Pop* as procedures. (Passing a parameter by reference to a function and changing the value of the parameter inside the function is only one example of a side effect. In more general terms, a side effect is any action that is transparent. The use of global variables is another example. Programming that allows side effects is considered bad style because it makes the program very hard to maintain.)

Refinement of the Algorithm

We intend to finish the postfix expression evaluation problem all the way to the code level. Before we can get that far, though, we must give some more thought to the problem definition.

In the examples above, we used single-digit numbers, and in the case of division, we purposely chose numbers that divided evenly. We would like our expression evaluator to be able to handle real numbers (positive, negative or zero). That introduces the problems of distinguishing one operand from another and between a minus sign that marks a number as negative and the subtraction operator.

We will agree to put a space between our operands; if a plus or minus sign directly precedes a digit, then the number is signed, either positive or negative. If a space follows a plus or minus sign, then the operator designates addition or subtraction, respectively.

Let's make it a precondition that the string we are processing contains only digits, periods, spaces and the four characters: "+," "−," "*" and "/." Another precondition is that the string represents a well-formed postfix expression.

Even though we're making it a precondition that the string is a well-formed postfix expression, we should do our best to write it in such a manner that the procedure will not crash if sent an invalid expression. That means we won't do any error checking, nor will the routine be expected to return a reasonable result, but we should take some action rather than let the program crash.

Our problem statement becomes:

Write a routine that will accept a string of characters representing
a well-formed postfix expression, evaluate the expression and return
the value. The operands are digit strings with an optional leading
plus or minus sign and an optional single decimal point embedded
between two digits. All operands and operators will be separated
by spaces. The only characters in the string will be digits, periods,
spaces and the four characters: "+," "−," "*" and "/."

Should the routine be a function or a procedure? Since it returns a value, it
could be treated as a function. It also performs a complicated task, so it could
be a procedure. It seems to be a close call; we could decide either way. Let's
choose to make it a procedure. An algorithm for our solution—using the draft
algorithm developed above—would look like:

```
START OF PostEval(Exp, Val)
Passed by value: Exp
Passed by reference: Val
Preconditions: Exp is a string containing only digits, periods,
               spaces and the four characters: "+," "−," "*" and "/"
               and represents a well-formed postfix expression.

call InitStack(Stack)
store 1 in i
loop while i ≤ length of Exp
    if Exp_i is a digit or Exp_i is a "+" or "−"
                and Exp_{i+1} is a digit
        then
            call GetOperand(Exp, i, Op)
            call Push(Stack, Op)
        else
            if Exp_i is "+," "−," "*" or "/"
                then
                    call Pop(Stack, Op2)
                    call Pop(Stack, Op1)
                    when Exp_i is
                        "+,"   call Push(Stack, Op1 + Op2)
                        "−,"   call Push(Stack, Op1 − Op2)
                        "*,"   call Push(Stack, Op1 * Op2)
                        "/,"   call Push(Stack, Op1 / Op2)
        add 1 to i
call Pop(Stack, Val)

END OF PostEval
```

The procedure *GetOperand* will take the expression *Exp* and the current position of the index *i*. It will start at *i* and find a real value contained in the expression from that point on. The index *i* will be advanced to the space following the operand—consequently *i* will have to be passed by reference to *GetOperand*—and the value of the operand will be put in *Op*. We leave the writing of *GetOperand* as an exercise.

Pascal Code for `PostEval`

The algorithm is easy to implement in Pascal. Notice that we are treating the expression as a **record** and using the length of the string as one field of the record. Here is the declaration for `ExprType`:

```
const
  MAXLEN = 80;
type
  ExprType  = record
        Str : packed array[1 .. MAXLEN] of char;
        Len : integer
      end;
```

And the procedure itself is on the next page.

```
procedure PostEval(Expr : ExprType; var Val : real);

{  This procedure evaluates a postfix expression.          }
{  Precondition:  The postfix expression is well-formed.   }

var
  i              : integer;
  S              : Stack;
  Op, Op1, Op2 : real;

begin
  InitStack(S);
  i := 1;
  while i <= Expr.Len do
    begin
      if (Expr.Str[i] in ['0' .. '9']) or
         (Expr.Str[i] in ['+', '-']) and (i < Expr.Len) and
         (Expr.Str[i+1] in ['0' .. '9'])
        then
          begin
            GetOperand(Expr, i, Op);
            Push(S, Op)
          end
        else
          begin
            if Expr.Str[i] in ['+', '-', '*', '/']
              then
                begin
                  Pop(S, Op2);
                  Pop(S, Op1);
                  case Expr.Str[i] of
                    '+' : Push(S, Op1 + Op2);
                    '-' : Push(S, Op1 - Op2);
                    '*' : Push(S, Op1 * Op2);
                    '/' : Push(S, Op1 / Op2)
                  end
                end;
            i := i + 1
          end
    end;
  Pop(S, Val)
end;
```

You should ask yourself about the evaluation of the Boolean expression in the first ⟨*if statement*⟩; i.e., the expression:

```
(Expr.Str[i] in ['0' .. '9']) or
(Expr.Str[i] in ['+', '-']) and (i < Expr.Len) and
(Expr.Str[i+1] in ['0' .. '9'])
```

Clearly we want the **and** parts of the expression evaluated before the **or**. Do we need extra parentheses or will Pascal do what we want? The precedence of the **and** is higher than the precedence of the **or** so it will work correctly. The **and** is considered a "multiplying" operator, as with the * and /, while the **or** is considered an "adding" operator, as with the + or -. As always, you can add parentheses whenever you're not sure.

Notice that this version assumes that the expression is a valid postfix expression and does not call the functions `EmptyStack` and `FullStack`. You should make the necessary modifications to it so that if the expression has too many operands or too few operators, or if the expression is too long, some appropriate action will be taken rather than just letting the program crash. We leave this as an exercise.

Implementation of a Stack

We have written the procedure `PostEval` without regard to how the routines for `Push`, `Pop`, `InitStack`, `EmptyStack` and `FullStack` will look. Indeed, we have not even decided how to implement a stack in Pascal. The point is, a stack is a data structure, an *abstract* data type, not just a data type. We have to implement it somehow, but not before we are able to write the rest of the program. Of course, you could have decided how to implement the stack before you wrote the procedure, but you don't have to.

The time has come for us to implement a stack in Pascal. We now have to figure out what to use for a stack. The only things we have at our disposal are simple variables, arrays and records. Which of these can we use? Since all accessing of data to a stack occurs at the "top" of the stack, we need a way to be able to keep adding data to the stack and always know which element was added last. You might think of using an array like the stack of dishes referred to earlier—moving every element up or down as new elements are removed or added. The time involved to do all the shifting would make the algorithm too inefficient, but an array can still be used. What we can do is leave the bottom of the stack in the first position of the array and add and remove elements to the array at a position determined by an index variable that indicates the "top" of the stack.

It would also be nice to add as many elements to the array as we want, making it as big as necessary. But, of course, we cannot. The size of the array has to be indicated in advance, not while the program is running.

To get around this, we can declare the array to be big enough to hold the maximum number of things that will be on the stack at one time. And we will have to be able to keep track of where we put the last element. A record is just right to hold both the array and the location of the last element pushed onto the stack. The field variable `Top` will be an integer that "points" at the element currently on top of the stack. The field `List` will be the array itself.

Here are the declarations we need for the stack:

```
const
  MAXSTACK = 100;
type
  Stack = record
      List : array [1 .. MAXSTACK] of real;
      Top  : integer
    end;
```

Whenever we do a `Push`, we add 1 to the value of `Top` and place the new element at the location indicated by `Top`.

Whenever we do a `Pop`, we store the element pointed at by `Top` in the parameter we're passing back and then subtract 1 from `Top`.

`EmptyStack` is easy. If the value of `Top` is zero, the stack is empty; otherwise, it's not.

`InitStack` is also easy. All we have to do to initialize a stack is set the `Top` to zero, and the stack is initialized to empty.

`FullStack` is similar to `EmptyStack` but depends on the constant `MAXSTACK`.

Here are two of the routines in Pascal. We'll leave the other three for you to write.

```
procedure Push(var S : Stack; Val : real);

{ This procedure pushes Val onto the top of stack S.  }

begin
  S.Top := S.Top + 1;
  S.List[S.Top] := Val
end;
```

```
function EmptyStack(S : Stack) : Boolean;

{ This function determines whether or not a stack, S, is empty.  }

begin
  EmptyStack := S.Top = 0
end;
```

We'll leave the postfix expression evaluation problem at this point. You should complete the three missing stack routines, write test routines for these five, write an algorithm and the code for *GetOperand*, test it and then put all the pieces together with a main program that allows you to enter a postfix expression and see its value.

We introduced the expression evaluation problem in order to introduce you to the notion of a data structure, and to the data structure called a stack. In the exercises, you'll have an opportunity to use stacks to evaluate prefix and infix expressions, and to convert from one form to another. Now let's look at another problem that requires a data structure for its solution.

3.6   Simulation of a Single Server

As is our custom, we start with a problem. In this section, the problem we will solve will be simulating a single server (a bank teller) working at a bank with people lining up waiting for service. The situation happens many times in the real world and is familiar to us all. We often line up at post offices, banks, grocery stores, etc. We want to design a simulation of what is happening. Of course, real world problems are more complicated than one server and one line, but we'll start with this simplified version.

Define the Problem

To make the problem more interesting, imagine that the manager of a small bank has one teller. The teller can only serve one customer at a time, and if other customers come in while the teller is busy, they have to wait in line. Suppose the owner of the bank—let's call her Ms. Pinch-Penny—notices that there are often several people waiting in line and wonders if it would be a good idea to hire another teller. After all, if people spend too much time waiting in line, they might decide to transfer their business to another bank. Ms. Pinch-Penny cannot hire another teller until she's sure that the expense would be justified. She also cannot afford to sit at a desk with a stop-watch, timing the arrivals and departures of customers. Let's suppose Ms. Pinch-Penny asks us to write a program for her that will allow her to *simulate* the situation, determining how much time customers have to wait and how much time the teller is idle (not waiting on a customer). Let's suppose Ms. Pinch-Penny knows the average time customers take once they get to the teller and the average arrival time between customers.

We want to write a program that allows a user to enter the average service time for a customer and the average time between the arrival of customers. The program should simulate a single server and people waiting in line, print a summary that indicates the average time each customer had to wait in line, and display the total amount of time each day that the teller was idle.

This amounts to a definition of the problem. We can turn to the solution.

Solve the Problem

As we saw at the beginning of this chapter, the solution to a problem involves determining how to handle the data involved; i.e., choosing appropriate data structures. The primary data structure needed for this problem is one that will handle the simulation of the people waiting in line. Can we use a stack? No. A stack is a "LIFO" structure. People waiting in line are not served in "last in, first out" manner; they are served in a "first in, first out" manner. Those people waiting in the line the longest are supposed to be served before those who came later. We need a "FIFO" structure. Such a structure is known in computer science, and also in many countries around the world, as a *queue*.

A Queue as an Abstract Data Type

Before we continue with the solution to the simulation of a single server, let's discuss queues. Unlike a stack, a queue has two ends, a *head* and a *tail*. New elements are always put on the queue at the tail. When an element is removed from the queue, it is taken from the head of the queue. While the terms "push" and "pop" could be used for the actions of putting things on and removing things from a queue, they are normally reserved for stacks. Instead, let's use the terms "enqueue" to indicate putting something on a queue and "dequeue" for removing something from it.

As with stacks, we will have three more operations: "InitQueue," "EmptyQueue" and "FullQueue." These five operations completely characterize a queue; i.e., by defining these five operations, we define an abstract data type of a queue. Let's look at them in more detail.

- **InitQueue** A routine that initializes a queue.

- **EmptyQueue** A Boolean-valued function that returns *true* if a queue is empty and *false* otherwise.

- **FullQueue** A Boolean-valued function that returns *true* if a queue is full and *false* otherwise.

- **EnQueue** A routine which puts an element onto the queue at the tail.

- **DeQueue** A routine which removes the element from the head of the queue.

InitQueue will be a procedure with one parameter passed by reference, the queue. We'll send the queue to *InitQueue* to be initialized to empty. *EmptyQueue* and *FullQueue* will be Boolean-valued functions similar to *EmptyStack* and *FullStack*.

DeQueue and *EnQueue* will be treated as procedures even though *DeQueue* returns a value. Both procedures will have the queue sent to them and changed. *DeQueue* will return the element removed from the queue via a parameter passed by reference. An element to be added to the queue will be passed by value to *EnQueue*.

Write an Algorithm

We turn now to the development of an algorithm that will handle the simulation. We must decide on the basic structure of the program; there are essentially two ways we can handle it. We can write it by watching for something to happen and, when something does happen, determine what time the event happened and update everything at that point. This way of simulating things is known as *event-driven simulation*. The alternative is known as *time-driven simulation*. With time-driven simulation, a big loop controls everything. The body of the loop is executed once for every "tick" of a clock. Every time around, the program would do whatever is necessary to update things and would check to see if something happened. When something happens, the program would update whatever was necessary at that time. The clock can be made to "tick" as often as desired. You can design it so that each iteration of the big loop represents a second, a minute, an hour, or whatever time interval is appropriate.

Let's agree to write our algorithm as a time-driven simulation, with each iteration of the loop representing one minute of time. A high-level algorithm for our simulation would look like:

```
initialize necessary variables
loop once every minute
    if a customer arrives
        then
            process an arrival.
    if the teller is busy,
        then
            subtract one minute from the time remaining
                until the current customer is finished.
            if the teller finishes serving a customer
                then
                    process a departure
        else
            add one minute to the total idle time.
    if the teller is idle and the queue is not empty
        then
            process the start of serving a new customer.
```

This would handle the regular working hours for the teller, but what should happen if the teller is waiting on someone at closing time or there are still people in line at closing time? Another loop will allow the people in the bank to get served too.

loop while there are still customers in the bank
        subtract one minute from the time remaining
                until the current customer is finished.
        if the teller finishes serving a customer
                then
                        process a departure
                        if the queue is not empty
                                then
                                        process the start of serving a new customer
calculate and display the results

Let's start thinking about what data we want to gather. We will want to know how many customers were served, what the average time in the bank was for the customers, the total amount of time the teller was not waiting on a customer, the maximum queue length and the average queue length.

We can start identifying some variables we'll need. Each time the teller starts serving a customer, we'll call a function that will return a service time for that customer. This function will have to be written in such a manner that the average time it returns corresponds to the average time entered by the user. The time returned by the function can be assigned to a variable that we'll use for the time remaining for that customer. Let's call that variable *CurrentServiceTime*. Whenever *CurrentServiceTime* is greater than zero, the customer at the teller's window is still being helped, and the teller is not idle. When this variable equals zero, the teller is free. If the queue is not empty, the teller can start helping another customer. If the queue is empty, the teller is idle.

We'll also need variables for the total idle time (we'll add 1 to this variable every time through the loop that the teller is idle), a variable for the number of customers (we'll add 1 to this variable every time a customer arrives), a variable for the total time spent by customers in the bank (we'll add the time spent by each customer to this variable each time someone leaves the bank), a variable for the current queue length and a variable for the maximum queue length. Since a customer can arrive, get put on the queue and get taken off the queue all in the same iteration of the loop, let's not add the current queue length to the accumulated queue length when a customer arrives. Let's add it at the end of the big loop. Similarly, let's check to see if the new queue length is greater than the previous maximum queue length at the end of the big loop, not when we process an arrival.

These variables help us with several of the steps in the above algorithm. Let's rewrite the algorithm using the variables.

START OF Single Server Simulation

initialize
loop once every minute
    if a customer arrives,
        then
            process an arrival.
    if CurrentServiceTime > 0
        then
            ·   subtract 1 minute from CurrentServiceTime
                if CurrentServiceTime = 0
                    then
                        process a departure
            else
                add 1 minute to TotalIdleTime.
    if CurrentServiceTime = 0 and the queue is not empty
        then
            process the start of serving a new customer.
    if the QueueLength is longer than MaximumQueueLength
        then
            store the QueueLength in MaximumQueueLength
    add QueueLength to AccumulatedQueueLength
loop while CurrentServiceTime > 0
    subtract 1 minute from CurrentServiceTime
    if CurrentServiceTime = 0
        then
            process a departure
            if the queue is not empty
                then
                    process the start of serving a new customer
calculate and display the results

END OF Single Server Simulation

Arrivals and Service Times

We need a couple of functions that will determine whether or not a customer arrives each minute and the time that each customer takes to get served.

Both of these functions can be written in a fairly straightforward manner if we can assume the existence of a random number generating function that will return a pseudo-random real number between 0 and 1. This is the customary way of working with pseudo-random number generation.

Here's a function that does the job:

```
function Random : real;

{  This function returns a pseudo-random real number     }
{  between 0 and 1.  Seed is a global integer variable.  }

const
  MULTIPLIER = 40;
  INCREMENT  = 3641;
  MODULUS    = 729;

begin
  Seed := (Seed * MULTIPLIER + INCREMENT) mod MODULUS;
  Random := Seed / MODULUS
end;
```

Every time `Random` is called, it will return a `real` value between 0 and 1. It will return 729 different `real`s before it starts to repeat. (A different choice of the values 729, 40 and 3641 will cause different numbers to be returned before it starts to repeat, but these values do need to be chosen with care.) `Random` depends on a `integer` global variable, `Seed`, that will have to be declared and initialized in the main program. If the same initial value is given to `Seed` each time the program is run, the simulation will use the same sequence of numbers. When a different `Seed` is used, a different sequence is generated.

We wrote this function so it would work on any compiler, and so we wouldn't have to spend much time discussing it. As a result, it isn't the best random number generating function. Even though this function will work, there's a good chance that the system you're working on has a better one. Either use the one above or use the one on your system. The better the random number sequence you use, the better the results of this simulation. We'll spend a lot more effort on random number generation in a later chapter. For the remainder of this section we'll assume we have access to a function called `Random` that returns a pseudo-random real number between 0 and 1.

Arrivals

Now that we can assume the existence of a random number generator, how can we tell when a customer arrives? If we let the user—Ms. Pinch-Penny—enter the average time between arrivals when the program starts, we should be able to write a function that will tell us when a customer arrives. The function should accept the average time between arrivals and return either true or false depending on whether or not a customer has arrived. The program will call this function once every minute. Suppose, for example, that the average time between arrivals is two minutes. Then every other time we call this function— on the average—it should return true. Similarly, if the average time between arrivals is five minutes, then the function should return true about one-fifth of the time it's called and false about four-fifths of the time. Let's name the function *Arrival*.

An easy way to write this function is to call Random to obtain a number between 0 and 1. If this number is less than $1/N$—where the average time between arrivals is N minutes—then return true, otherwise, return false. In other words, the function should return true whenever the random number is less than the reciprocal of the average time between arrivals and false otherwise. We'll leave the details for you to complete.

Service Times

Ms. Pinch-Penny is allowed to enter the average time it takes a customer to get served. We can write a function that will return a positive integer with the property that if the function is called a large number of times, the average of the numbers returned will be approximately equal to the average service time. Let's call this function *ServiceTime*. The average service time should be sent to the function as a parameter. The question is, how do we get the proper values sent back?

Leaving the mathematical details and explanations aside, let's look at a particular situation to see how this can be accomplished. Suppose the average service time, *AvgServeTime*, is ten minutes and we call the function 100 times. Consider the following sequence of numbers:

20	3	2	12	1	8	14	21	24	4
21	9	6	1	2	3	7	8	36	14
5	4	1	9	28	1	5	15	8	14
46	3	14	2	10	18	1	8	23	3
9	7	6	1	1	1	16	2	10	15
3	15	28	7	7	17	24	25	9	2
10	6	11	10	8	5	9	13	10	7
4	5	7	9	2	18	6	15	4	13
3	8	12	7	1	6	2	12	14	5
7	1	15	2	1	6	4	19	11	4

The arithmetical average of this set of numbers is 9.51. Notice that the numbers are not between 1 and 20, but between 1 and 46. This approximates what happens in the real world. Many customers take only a minute or two to get their banking done while a few take much longer. The overall average, though, is about ten minutes.

The numbers in the above table were generated by calling the following function 100 times.

```
function ServiceTime(AvgServTime : integer) : integer;

{  This function returns a random service time.  The times     }
{  returned over a long time interval will average to AvgServTime.  }

var
  i    : integer;
  Temp : real;

begin
  i := 0;
  Temp := 1/AvgServTime;
  repeat
    i := i + 1
    until Random < Temp;
  ServiceTime := i
end;
```

Pretend that `AvgServTime` is 10, and trace the function. The **repeat** loop will always be executed at least once. If the first random number returned is less than 1/10, the loop will be exited and the function will return 1. If the first random number is not less than 1/10, but the second one is, the function will return 2. If the first two numbers are not less than 1/10, but the third one is, the function will return 3. The loop will be executed and i incremented until a random number less than 1/10 is returned by the random number generator.

It easy to see that the function will return 1 about one-tenth of the time. How often will it return 2? In order to return a 2, the loop will have to be executed exactly twice. That is, a random number greater than 1/10 will have to be returned by `Random` the first time and a random number less than 1/10 the second time. That will happen about $9/10 \times 1/10$ of the time. Therefore, it will return a 2 about 9/100 of the time. Similarly, it will return a 3 about 81/1000 of the time ($9/10 \times 9/10 \times 1/10$). It can be shown that the average value of this function will be 10. Such a demonstration is beyond us here so we'll not proceed any further with the discussion.

You should type this function in and write a test routine that calls it several times—printing the values returned and averaging them—until you're convinced that it does what we want.

Routines Called by the Main Program

There are three routines that are called by the main routine: *ProcessArrival*, *ProcessDeparture* and *ProcessStartService*. Let's think about what each of these will have to do.

ProcessArrival

Every time a new customer arrives, we'll have to put the customer onto the queue. Since the queue will then be one element longer, we will want to add 1 to the length of the queue. We also want to count the total number of customers; we can add 1 to the number-of-customers counter at this point. Before we can go any further, we have to decide what to put on the queue. We won't need the customer's name or know which customer it is. What we will need to know later is at what time the customer arrived. Thus, all we need to put on the queue is the arrival time. The parameters to this procedure are the queue, the arrival time, the current queue length and the number-of-customers counter. As an algorithm, this will look like:

> START OF *ProcessArrival*(*Queue, ArrivalTime, QLen, NumCust*)
> *Passed by value: ArrivalTime*
> *Passed by reference: Queue, QLen, NumCust*
>
> *call EnQueue*(*Queue, ArrivalTime*)
> *add 1 to QLen*
> *add 1 to NumCust*
>
> END OF *ProcessArrival*

ProcessDeparture

By "departure" we mean a customer leaving the bank. Be sure you see that this means the customer has just finished being served, and that this is *not* when the customer is removed from the queue. Customers are removed from the queue when they step up to the teller's window; i.e., when *ProcessStartServing* is called. What does happen when a customer leaves the bank? What do we have to do to process the departure?

After thinking about it for awhile, you'll realize that all we need to do at this point is to update the accumulator that is keeping track of the total number of minutes each customer is in the bank. This total will be divided by the number of customers later to determine the average time each customer was in the bank. How long was the departing customer in the bank? That number is just the difference between the current time and the time he arrived. Thus, the algorithm for *ProcessDeparture* will look like:

START OF ProcessDeparture(CurrentTime, ArrivalTime, AccumulatedTime)
Passed by value: CurrentTime, ArrivalTime
Passed by reference: AccumulatedTime

add CurrentTime - ArrivalTime to AccumulatedTime

END OF ProcessDeparture

ProcessStartService

This routine is called whenever the teller is idle and the queue is not empty.
What has to be done? An arrival time has to be taken off the queue and saved
so we can use it later in *ProcessDeparture*. Since the queue is then one shorter,
we'll need to subtract one from the queue length. And, since the person who
was in the queue is now going to get served, we need to determine how long
the service will take and store this number in the current service time. This
number is determined by calling our function ServiceTime. The algorithm is
easy:

START OF ProcessStartService(Queue, QLen, CurrServTime,
                          ArrivalTime, AvgServTime)
Passed by value: AvgServTime
Passed by reference: Queue, QLen, CurrServTime, ArrivalTime

store ServiceTime(AvgServTime) in CurrServTime
call DeQueue(Queue, ArrivalTime)
subtract 1 from QLen

END OF ProcessStartService

The Main Routine

With these subroutines completed, the main routine is easier to write. The
queue has to be initialized, several variables need to be initialized to zero and
the two values will have to be entered by Ms. Pinch-Penny. The algorithm will
look like the following:

```
store 0 in CurrentServiceTime
store 0 in AccumulatedTime
store 0 in NumberOfCustomers
store 0 in IdleTime
store 0 in MaxQueueLength
store 0 in QueueLength
store 0 in AccumulatedQueueLength
call InitQueue(Queue)
display "Enter the average time between arrivals"
accept AverageTimeBetweenArrivals
display "Enter the average service time"
accept AverageServiceTime
```

This can be considered part of the main routine or a separate routine called by the main routine. You decide how to implement it. The main loop can be a *loop for*:

```
loop for Time going from 1 to NumberOfMinutesInDay
    if Arrival(AverageTimeBetweenArrivals)
        then
            call ProcessArrival(Queue, Time, QueueLength, NumberOfCustomers)
    if CurrentServiceTime > 0
        then
            subtract 1 from CurrentServiceTime
            if CurrentServiceTime = 0
                then
                    call ProcessDeparture(Time, ArrivalTime, AccumulatedTime)
        else
            add 1 to IdleTime.
    if CurrentServiceTime = 0 and not EmptyQueue(Queue)
        then
            call ProcessStartService(Queue, QueueLength, CurrentServiceTime,
                                     ArrivalTime, AverageServiceTime)
    add QueueLength to AccumulatedQueueLength
    if QueueLength > MaxQueueLength
        then
            store QueueLength in MaxQueueLength
```

Then the loop that empties the queue—in case there are still customers in the queue after the bank closes—will look like:

```
loop while CurrentServiceTime > 0
    add 1 to Time
    subtract 1 from CurrentServiceTime
    if CurrentServiceTime = 0
        then
            call ProcessDeparture(Time, ArrivalTime, AccumulatedTime)
            if not EmptyQueue(Queue)
                then
                    call ProcessStartService(Queue, QueueLength,
                        CurrentServiceTime, ArrivalTime, AverageServiceTime)
```

And, finally, we will need to:

```
calculate and display the results
```

Calculate and Display Results

Most of the work has been done. All of the data have been collected, and only some calculating—such as determining the average time each customer was in the bank by dividing the total time the customers were in the bank by the number of customers—and displaying the results on the screen remain. To insure that you are really following what's being done here, we'll leave it for you to determine what calculations need to be done and how the results should be displayed.

3.7   Implementing the Algorithms

Other than the implementation of the queue itself, all of the above should be straightforward to implement in Pascal. There's no new Pascal required. We'll leave the writing of the code for you.

Implementation of the Queue

That leaves just the queue itself. How do we implement a data structure that has the operations EnQueue, DeQueue, InitQueue, EmptyQueue and FullQueue? As with the stack, we don't have a lot of choice at this point. The only things we know about that might work are arrays. So, how could we use an array to implement a queue? Clearly we need to keep track of two indices for the queue rather than the one we used for a stack since the queue has a head and a tail. It might seem simple at first glance to keep track of two pointers, call them the Head and the Tail, and just increment them each time something is added or removed from the array. However, that won't work unless we are willing to use an extremely long array. Since both pointers keep growing as elements are added and removed, the entire queue continues to "creep" to the right of the array. After only a short time, all the spaces in the first part of the array have been used—and will never be used again—and the portion of the array that is actually holding the queue has moved to the right. See figure 3.2.

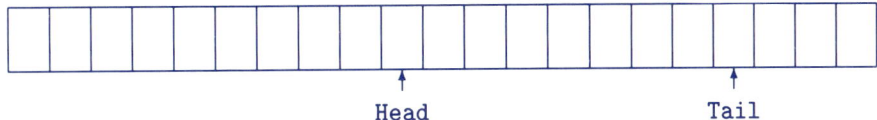

Figure 3.2 A Poor Implementation of a Queue

It is clear that we cannot afford to continually slide the queue back to the left; that would take far too much time. So, what can we do? The trick is to tie the two ends of the array together and use the front part of the array over again. As elements are added to the queue, the `Tail` moves to the right. As elements are removed, the `Head` moves to the right also. When either `Head` or `Tail` reaches the end of the array, it simply jumps back to the front of the array and the program can continue. See figure 3.3.

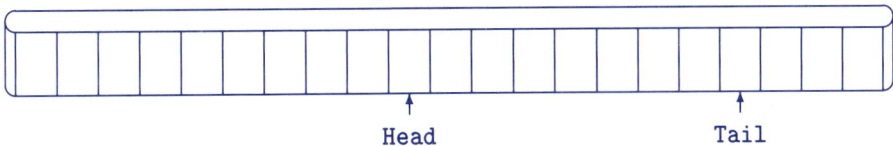

Figure 3.3 A Better Implementation of a Queue

`Head` and `Tail` will each point at some element in the array. Before we can add an element, we'll need to add one to the value of `Tail`. Similarly, after we remove an element, we'll add one to the value of `Head`. In both cases we should watch for the special situation when the end of the array is reached.

Let's use the **record** data type of Pascal to hold the array and these two pointers. Let's use a constant for the length of the array. The definitions would look like:

```
const
  MAXQUEUE = 50;
type
  Queue = record
    List      : array [1 .. MAXQUEUE] of integer;
    Head, Tail : integer
  end;
```

Because we remember that we have to jump back to the beginning of the array when we reach the end, the codes for EnQueue and DeQueue are straightforward.

```
procedure EnQueue(var Q : Queue; Element : integer);

{  This procedure places a new element at the tail of a queue, Q.  }

begin
  Q.Tail := Q.Tail + 1;
  if Q.Tail > MAXQUEUE
    then
      Q.Tail := 1;
  Q.List[Q.Tail] := Element
end;
```

```
procedure DeQueue(var Q : Queue; var Element : integer);

{  This procedure removes an element from the head of a queue, Q.  }

begin
  Element := Q.List[Q.Head];
  Q.Head := Q.Head + 1;
  if Q.Head > MAXQUEUE
    then
      Q.Head := 1
end;
```

That leaves InitQueue, EmptyQueue and FullQueue. If both Head and Tail point at the same location in the array, the element being pointed at would be considered *in* the queue, so that cannot be the condition of either a full queue or an empty queue. Consider a queue with one element, as in figure 3.4.

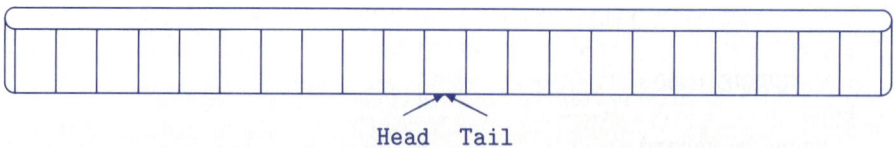

Head   Tail

Figure 3.4 A Circular Queue With One Element

After we remove that element, what would be the relative positions of Head and Tail? Tail would be one less than Head, and that tells us how to write EmptyQueue:

```
function EmptyQueue(Q : Queue) : Boolean;

{ This function determines whether or not the queue Q is empty. }

begin
  EmptyQueue := Q.Tail + 1 = Q.Head
end;
```

But wait. That cannot always be right. What happens when `Head` and `Tail` are at the end of the array? There is one situation where the queue is empty, but `Tail + 1` is not equal to `Head`. That happens when `Head` equals 1. Then `Tail` will equal `MAXQUEUE`. The correct version of `EmptyQueue` will have to consider that also:

```
function EmptyQueue(Q : Queue) : Boolean;

{ This function determines whether or not the queue Q is empty. }

begin
  EmptyQueue := (Q.Tail + 1 = Q.Head) or
                (Q.Head = 1) and (Q.Tail = MAXQUEUE)
end;
```

Notice once again the importance of the precedence between and and or. This works as is because and has a higher precedence than or.

Now that we are sure how to determine when a queue is empty, we can see how to write InitQueue:

```
procedure InitQueue(var Q : Queue);

{ This procedure initializes the queue Q to empty. }

begin
  Q.Head := 1;
  Q.Tail := MAXQUEUE
end;
```

That leaves `FullQueue`. As the queue grows and shrinks, `Tail` chases `Head` along (and around) the array. We might be tempted to say that when `Tail` comes to within one array element of `Head`, the queue is full. But remember, that's just the condition we have stated for an *empty* queue. We have to stop *two* elements short of `Head`. We'll leave it to you, bearing this in mind, to write `FullQueue`.

As long as the array is big enough to hold the longest possible queue, everything will work just fine. The major disadvantage of this implementation is having to decide in advance how big to make the array. If you choose a number for MAXQUEUE that is too small, the Head and the Tail will come together and the queue will be full. To allow enough room to guarantee that the queue won't overflow means wasting quite a bit of memory. In chapter 6 we'll use an implementation that solves this problem.

Sample Runs

Here are a couple examples of what the output of the program should look like. In the first example, we entered 10 for the average time between arrivals and 10 for the average service time. For the second example, we entered 10 and 8. For the third, we entered 5 and 6.

```
Run 1:

Enter the average time between arrivals: 10
Enter the average service time: 10

The number of customers was 47.
The average time each customer spent in the bank was 112.79 minutes.
The maximum queue length was 18.
The average queue length per minute was 8.51.
The total idle time was 1 hour(s) and 12 minute(s).
Customers were in the bank for 9 hour(s) and 40 minute(s).



Run 2:

Enter the average time between arrivals: 10
Enter the average service time: 8

The number of customers was 65.
The average time each customer spent in the bank was 12.32 minutes.
The maximum queue length was 4.
The average queue length per minute was 0.91.
The total idle time was 1 hour(s) and 58 minute(s).
Customers were in the bank for 8 hour(s) and 3 minute(s).
```

Run 3:

```
Enter the average time between arrivals: 5
Enter the average service time: 6

The number of customers was 88.
The average time each customer spent in the bank was 37.26 minutes.
The maximum queue length was 13.
The average queue length per minute was 4.02.
The total idle time was 0 hour(s) and 35 minute(s).
Customers were in the bank for 9 hour(s) and 43 minute(s).
```

Notice that, contrary to what you might have guessed, when the average time between arrivals and the average service time are about the same, the queue can still get—and stay—quite long, and the time that each person spends standing in line is unacceptable. After running the program a few times, Ms. Pinch-Penny would have to conclude that if the average service time is about the same as the average time between arrivals, her customers will spend too much time standing in line and, therefore, might transfer their accounts to another bank. You should play with your program, running it several times with different values. Try to see what values for the average service time and average time between arrivals cause the average queue length and the average time each customer spends in the bank to become unacceptable.

Considerable time has been spent doing research with programs just like this. It's an active area of interest in computer science and much more can be done than what we have done. The `ServiceTime` function could be improved upon, for example, and we'll suggest an improvement in the exercises. A simple extension—we'll also leave that for the exercises—is to have one queue but more than one teller. The algorithm and the code can be modified without much trouble to allow this situation. Indeed, you could write the program to add tellers when the queue reaches a certain length and see how many tellers are needed.

3.8   Summary and Review

- We expanded on the FIVE + STEPS of programming by adding data structures to steps 2 and 3. We saw that not only does a programmer have to develop an algorithm that describes the solution to the problem, but she also has to choose appropriate data structures to represent the data.

- Data structures as abstract data types were introduced. We used the examples of stacks and queues to illustrate abstract data types. We saw that they could be discussed as abstract data types without regard to how they were implemented. We defined an abstract data type as a collection of operations on some data. By defining these operations, we define an abstract data type.

- We learned about prefix and postfix arithmetic expressions.

- We defined the ADT stack entirely in terms of five operations: *Push*, *Pop*, *InitStack*, *EmptyStack* and *FullStack*. As long as we can count on having these five operations, we can do everything we need to do with a stack. To emphasize the abstract nature of a data structure, we developed a complete solution to a problem regarding evaluating postfix expressions, and we never thought about what the stack really looked like until we had the program finished except for the five routines: `Push`, `Pop`, `InitStack`, `EmptyStack` and `FullStack`. We implemented the stack using `records` and `arrays`. We indicated that another implementation will be developed in chapter 5.

- The ADT queue was introduced in a similar manner. We used a queue to simulate people coming to a small bank with only one teller. People had to stand in line (a queue) and wait if the teller was busy. As before, we completely solved the problem with an abstract queue, using only the five operations: `EnQueue`, `DeQueue`, `InitQueue`, `EmptyQueue` and `FullQueue`. We implemented the queue with a combination of a `record` and an `array`. We saw that a simple array would not work well so we tied the two ends of the array together to make a circular array.

- While working on the simulation problem, we saw how a pseudo-random number generator can be used to write functions that tell whether or not a customer arrived at the bank each minute, and how long it will take each customer to get served.

- We discussed the precedence of **and** and **or** in Pascal. The **and** operator has the same precedence as * and /, and the **or** operator has the same precedence as + and -.

3.9 Exercises

1. Write an algorithm and the corresponding code that will evaluate an expression in prefix notation.

2. Write the algorithm and code for *GetOperand*. Test the code before using it in the main program.

3. Write and test the Pascal procedures `Pop`, `InitStack` and `FullStack`.

4. Notice that the ⟨*while statement*⟩ on page 52 looks like a *loop for*. The index i starts at 1 and is incremented by one at the bottom of the loop each time through. Could the ⟨*while statement*⟩ be replaced by a ⟨*for statement*⟩? Explain your answer.

5. Finish the code for the postfix expression evaluation program. Design and implement a collection of test data to try on your program. Make sure you try expressions that are not valid to see what your program will do. Make the necessary modifications to `PostEval` to keep the program from crashing in the case of an invalid postfix expression, or in case it's too long.

6. Write the algorithm and the code for a procedure that converts a valid prefix expression to postfix.

7. Write the algorithm and the code for a procedure that evaluates a valid infix expression. To make the problem simpler, assume that the expression is *fully parenthesized*. That is, every operator in the expression is accompanied by a pair of parentheses. (Hint: You may wish to consider two stacks: one for the operands and one for the operators.)

8. Write the algorithm and the code for a procedure that converts a valid infix expression to postfix.

9. Finish the algorithm for *Arrival* as described on page 60. Write and test the functions `Arrival` and `ServiceTime` (from page 61). You will need to implement a function that returns a pseudo-random real number between 0 and 1. Use the function that comes with your compiler if there is one, or write your own similar to the one in the chapter.

10. The function we wrote for `ServiceTime` is not entirely satisfactory. Even though it will generate a sequence of service times with the given average, there will be more 1s than 2s, more 2s than 3s, and so forth. A better function might return fewer 1s and 2s than 3s and 4s, more 3s and 4s than 5s and 6s, etc., but still return numbers which average out to what we want. If you know some elementary probability and statistics, you'll be familiar with the normal distribution and maybe with the Poisson distribution. It is possible to write functions similar to our `ServiceTime` function that return numbers distributed according to either a normal

distribution or a Poisson distribution with a given mean and standard deviation. This problem and related problems are discussed in chapter 12. Look through chapter 12 to find the discussion of the normal and Poisson distributions, and use the information you find to rewrite `ServiceTime`.

11. Write the Pascal code for `ProcessArrival`, `ProcessDeparture` and `ProcessStartService`.

12. Finish and test the code for a complete program that simulates a single server queue. You will need to complete the portion of the program that calculates and displays the results.

13. On page 69 we mentioned the precedence of **and** and **or**. Is it clear that it matters? Suppose that **or** had a higher precedence than **and**, and suppose we left off the extra parentheses. What would be the result?

14. Write the algorithm and the code for the function `FullQueue`.

15. Modify the algorithm and the code for the queue simulation as suggested on page 71 to allow multiple tellers and one queue.

16. We viewed the Bank Teller problem solution as a time-driven simulation. The program had two major loops with both loops getting executed once per minute. We could have written the problem as an event-driven simulation instead. In fact, the second loop could easily have been written as an event-driven simulation since only one thing of note happens each time the body of the loop is executed: a customer leaves the bank. Rewrite the second loop so that each iteration of the loop occurs when a customer is finished being served.

17. An important problem that arises in mathematics and other areas is the need to convert a numeral from one base to another. For example, the numeral 179 (base ten) becomes 1011 0011 (base two). One method to perform the conversion involves repeatedly dividing the number by two, each time recording the remainders and replacing the number by the quotient, until the quotient is zero. The problem with this method—if there is one—is that the binary digits are generated in the wrong order; i.e., the units bit is the first remainder, the twos bit is next, etc. To handle this difficulty, you could push the remainders one at a time onto a stack and pop them off later to form the desired numeral. Turn this description of the solution into a complete algorithm, treating the stack as an abstract data type. Implement your algorithm in Pascal, using an array for the implementation of the stack.

18. The method in exercise 17 can be used to convert a numeral from any base to another. Using the letters from A through Z to represent digits larger than 9 in bases larger than 10 would allow us to express numerals in bases up to 36. Rewrite your algorithm from that exercise to allow a user to convert a numeral from any base between 2 and 36 to any other

base between 2 and 36. The user should be allowed to enter the two bases and the numeral. Implement your algorithm in Pascal. Notice that you will have to allow the user to enter the numeral as a string of characters, not as an integer.

Chapter 4

Dynamic Memory Allocation

A chain is only as strong as its weakest link.
—Anonymous

4.1 Overview of the Chapter

In this chapter we'll introduce dynamic variables and *pointers*. We will discuss *linked lists* and the algorithms needed to maintain an ordered list of data using a linked list. We'll introduce the Pascal syntax used to implement dynamic variables.

As an example, we will write a program that maintains a file of alphabetically ordered words such as a spelling checker program might use. We'll introduce doubly linked and circularly linked lists as examples of more complex data structures. We'll write a simple adventure game as an illustration of these more complicated linkages.

4.2 Introduction

In the last chapter we implemented stacks and queues using arrays and records. We had to be careful about choosing the size of the array so that the stack or queue could be as large as the application required. When we implemented the queue, we had to make the array circular, which meant that the array only needed to be as large as the number of people in the queue at any one time, rather than equalling the total number of people served by the teller.

An array is a useful data type, but it has one important limitation: in most programming languages, including Pascal, its size has to be determined before the program is compiled. In implementing a stack or a queue, we would like to have a way of storing the data that can grow or shrink as the stack or queue does.

This limitation is true of any Pascal type we have studied so far. Whenever something is to be stored in a variable, that variable has to be declared in advance by the programmer, who has to determine what the needs of the application are before the program is even compiled. We are now ready to introduce a way for the program *itself* to create variables and destroy them as needed. Of course, it's the programmer who instructs the program to do this, but she need not know in advance how many variables might be needed when the program is run. These kinds of variables are called *dynamic variables*.

4.3   Dynamic Variables

Consider what we mean by the term "variable." It refers to a location in memory where some value can be stored. The amount of memory set aside (or *allocated*) for this variable depends on the data type of the variable: a few bytes for integers or reals, much more for complex data types. The system keeps track of the location of the variable by its *address*. We think of the address as a numerical value that "points to" the corresponding variable.

Now this numerical value is something which could itself be stored in a variable. That is, we could have a variable that stores an address, and that address is the location of a conventional variable. We call such a variable (one that holds an address) a *pointer* variable. We call the variable to which the pointer points a dynamic variable.

The memory used by a dynamic variable is allocated and deallocated as required by the program. When memory is allocated, the address of the location is stored in a particular pointer variable. When the memory is deallocated, the value stored in the pointer variable becomes undefined. In our algorithms, we'll call a procedure, *Allocate*, to allocate memory for a dynamic variable, and we'll pass as a parameter the pointer variable associated with it. For example, if P is a pointer variable, then *call Allocate(P)* will set aside an area of memory and place its address in P. For short, we will use the symbol $P^\wedge$ for "the dynamic variable to which P points."

Similarly, we will call *Deallocate(P)* to return the space set aside for $P^\wedge$ to the storehouse of available memory and to make the contents of P undefined.

All this might be easier to understand pictorially. Figure 4.1 shows a pointer variable P, whose contents are undefined.

P

Figure 4.1 The Undefined Pointer P

Figure 4.2 represents the situation after a call to *Allocate(P)*. The variable P now has a value (namely the address of $P^\wedge$), but $P^\wedge$ itself is undefined.

Now let's *store 3 in $P^\wedge$*.

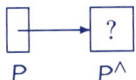

Figure 4.2 After *call Allocate (P)*

Figure 4.3 shows the result.

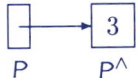

Figure 4.3 After *store 3 in $P^\wedge$*

Finally, figure 4.4 shows the result of *call Deallocate(P)*.

Figure 4.4 After *call Deallocate(P)*

As another example, consider the following sequence of statements. Draw diagrams like those in figures 4.1–4.4 to represent these steps.

call Allocate(P)
call Allocate(Q)
store 3 in $P^\wedge$
store $P^\wedge + 1$ in $Q^\wedge$
call Deallocate(Q)
store P in Q

Compare your diagrams to those in figure 4.5. As we discuss dynamic variables and the data structures we build with them, drawing diagrams like these will help you to understand the discussion.

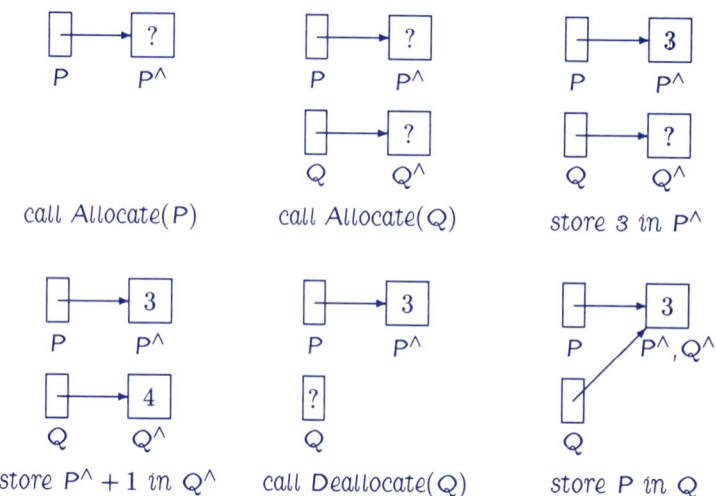

call Allocate(P)   call Allocate(Q)   store 3 in P^

store P^ + 1 in Q^   call Deallocate(Q)   store P in Q

Figure 4.5

4.4   Linked Lists

To see how we use dynamic variables to build data structures, recall that a dynamic variable can be a record with fields of various types. Imagine that one of those fields is a pointer, which points to another record, one of whose fields is a pointer, and so on. The records would be "linked" together to form a *linked list*. In fact, more than one field in the record can be a pointer, so that a given record can be linked to more than one other record. Various other data structures can be built in this fashion.

Let's consider the simplest such structure, a linear singly linked list, which is what the name "linked list" usually refers to. Each element of the list is called a *node*. A node is a record that we can think of as containing two parts: the data part and a pointer that points to another node. Let's say that we have a pointer variable P that points to such a node. The node itself would be $P^\wedge$. The data part could be $P^\wedge.Data$ and the pointer field could be $P^\wedge.Ptr$. In figure 4.6, the pointers are drawn as arrows, and each node is a box with two compartments: one for the data and one for the pointer.

The very first pointer is not part of a node, but it exists on its own. It's called the *head*. The pointer in the last node is drawn differently to indicate that there are no more nodes following it. When we implement the list with pointers, the pointer in the last node will have to have a special value so that we know it doesn't point to anything. Note that there is a difference between a pointer with an undefined value and a pointer that doesn't point to anything. The latter type of pointer is said to contain the value *nil*. In our figures, we'll use the symbol ⊣ for the *nil* pointer.

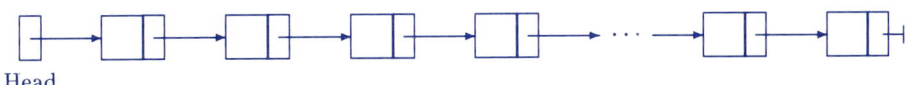

Head

Figure 4.6 A Linked List

Occasionally there is another stand-alone pointer that points *to* the last node in a linked list; this pointer is the *tail*. We are not showing a tail pointer in these figures.

Inserting and Deleting Nodes

Before, when we implemented lists with arrays, inserting or deleting items involved a good deal of moving values around. To insert a value into an array, you have to move existing array elements aside to make room for it. To delete an item from an array you have to slide the rest of the elements over to take up the empty space.

One of the main advantages of using pointers to implement lists is that insertion and deletion can be accomplished just by moving a few pointers; the data itself doesn't move.

Let's say you want to insert a node between nodes A and B (figure 4.7). After allocating space for a new node and assigning a value to the data part, you would set its pointer equal to A's pointer (since A's pointer points to B), and then make A's pointer point to the new node.

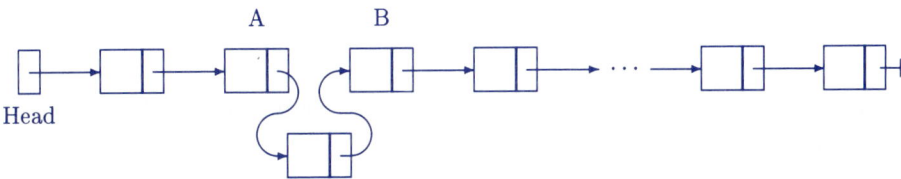

Head

Figure 4.7 Inserting a Node into a Linked List

If node B lies between nodes A and C and you want to delete it, simply point A's pointer at C and deallocate B (figure 4.8).

Inserting and deleting get a little tricky in some cases, but this gives you the general idea. Usually the list is maintained in some particular order; this is normally ascending order based on some key field. When we want to insert or delete nodes in the middle of the list, we'll have to find the place in the list to do the deletion or insertion. This involves searching the list from the beginning to find a key of a particular value.

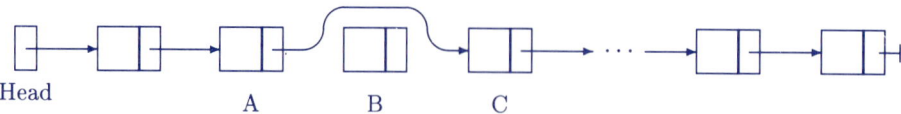

Figure 4.8 Deleting a Node from a Linked List

In short, we wish to write algorithms for the following routines:

- *search* the list for a particular data value, called a *Key*,

- *insert* a value into the list in the proper place if it's not already there, and

- *delete* a value from the list if it's there.

Linked Lists as Parameters

Before we get to the details of these algorithms, we should think about how we might pass linked lists to these routines. Although the search routine will not change the list, the insert and delete routines usually will, so the lists should be passed by reference in the latter two cases. But what does it mean to pass a linked list as a parameter at all?

It may seem strange at first, but all we need to pass is the pointer to the first node in the list, namely *Head*. This parameter can be passed either by value or by reference; in fact it will be passed by value to the search routine and by reference to the insert and delete routines. The important thing to remember, though, is that passing *Head* effectively passes the entire list, since access to each node is through the pointer pointing to it. Once we have *Head*, we have *Head^.Ptr* and then *Head^.Ptr^.Ptr* and so on. Once we have *Head*, we have the entire list.

In addition to *Head*, we will have to pass other parameters to the routines. We'll pass the key value involved in the routine (whether we're searching for it, inserting it or deleting it), and we will also pass back a Boolean value to indicate whether or not the given operation was successful. We'll write a recursive algorithm that searches the list (we'll make it a Boolean-valued function, *InList*) and iterative algorithms for *Insert* and *Delete*. There's a reason for not writing *Insert* and *Delete* recursively that we'll discuss briefly later in this chapter and expand upon in chapter 5.

The *InList* Algorithm

The parameters to be passed to *InList* are *Head* and *Key*. The function will return a Boolean value indicating whether or not the search was successful.

Recall that the list is in order, and think about how *InList* should work. If *Head* is *nil*, or if the key in the first node is greater than *Key*, then *Key* isn't in the list. If the key in the first node is equal to *Key*, then the search is successful. If none of these possibilities occur, then we must continue the search on the rest of the list. We can simply call *InList* recursively, passing a pointer to the next node in the list. Here's the algorithm:

```
START OF InList(Head, Key)

if Head = nil or Head^.Data > Key
    then
        return false
    else
        if Head^.Data = Key
            then
                return true
            else
                return InList(Head^.Ptr, Key)

END OF InList
```

The *Insert* Algorithm

The parameters to be passed are *Head*, *Key* and a Boolean value *Successful*. Let's say that we want to prevent duplicate entries in the list. If *Key* equals a value already in the list, it will not be inserted, and *Successful* will be returned set to *false*. *Head* must be passed by reference since it might be changed. The same is true for *Successful*, but *Key* should be passed by value.

If the list is empty, or if the key in the first node is greater than *Key*, then the insertion takes place at the beginning of the list. Otherwise, we loop until we either find the place to do the insertion or find a value equal to *Key*. Here is a high level algorithm for *Insert*:

```
START OF Insert(Head, Key, Successful)
Passed by value: Key
Passed by reference: Head, Successful

if Head = nil or Head^.Data > Key
    then
        create a new node
        insert the node at the beginning of the list
        store true in Successful
    else
        look further down the list for the place to insert Key

END OF Insert
```

Creating a new node involves calling the *Allocate* procedure and storing *Key* in the new node's key data field. Inserting it at the beginning of the list involves setting two pointers—*Head* and the new node's pointer. The new node's pointer should first be set equal to *Head*, then the pointer to the new node is stored in *Head*.

Looking further down the list for the right place to do the insertion is a little tricky. The reason is that when you find a node containing a *Data* field greater than *Key*, you have already passed the node whose pointer you will have to change. This means you'll have to set up a pointer, sometimes called a *trailer*, that points to the node previous to the one you're examining. We'll call this pointer *Prev*.

Here's a refined version of the algorithm. It is a good idea to draw yourself some diagrams similar to figures 4.6–4.8 and follow the steps of the algorithm. Even people who have experience with pointers can find these steps confusing— forming a good visual image of the process helps a great deal.

```
START OF Insert(Head, Key, Successful)
Passed by value: Key
Passed by reference: Head, Successful

store true in Successful
if Head = nil or Head^.Data > Key
    then
        call Allocate(P)
        store Key in P^.Data
        store Head in P^.Ptr
        store P in Head
    else
        store nil in Prev
        store Head in P
        loop while P ≠ nil and P^.Data < Key
            store P in Prev
            store P^.Ptr in P
        if P ≠ nil and P^.Data = Key
            then
                store false in Successful
            else
                create a new node pointed at by Prev^.Ptr


END OF Insert
```

Notice we used a *loop while* to save a step, and we used *Prev* to keep track of the node that contains the pointer to the place where *Key* is being inserted. It's the pointer in this node that has to be changed. Only by carefully reading this algorithm and tracing it on a particular linked list, inserting elements in various places in the list, will you appreciate all the details. Notice also that we stored *true* in *Successful* once at the start of the routine, changing it to *false* if the insertion did not take place.

The last part of the algorithm to take care of involves creating the node pointed at by *Prev^.Ptr*. That process is just the same as creating a node pointed at by *Head*, which is done in the first part of the algorithm. In fact, we could make that a separate module, and pass it the right pointer as a parameter. Consider the following algorithm:

```
START OF MakeNewNode(P, Key)
Passed by value: Key
Passed by reference: P


call Allocate(Temp)
store Key in Temp^.Data
store P in Temp^.Ptr
store Temp in P


END OF MakeNewNode
```

With this module in hand, we can finish the *Insert* algorithm:

```
START OF Insert(Head, Key, Successful)
Passed by value: Key
Passed by reference: Head, Successful


store true in Successful
if Head = nil or Head^.Data > Key
    then
        call MakeNewNode(Head, Key)
    else
        store nil in Prev
        store Head in P
        loop while P ≠ nil and P^.Data < Key
            store P in Prev
            store P^.Ptr in P
        if P ≠ nil and P^.Data = Key
            then
                store false in Successful
            else
                call MakeNewNode(Prev^.Ptr, Key)


END OF Insert
```

The *Delete* Algorithm

The parameters we will pass to *Delete* are the same as those passed to *Insert*. (In fact, they are passed the same way.) In addition to setting the Boolean parameter to *true*, we reroute some pointers and deallocate the node. Here's the algorithm for *Delete*:

```
START OF Delete(Head, Key, Successful)
Passed by value: Key
Passed by reference: Head, Successful

if Head = nil or Head^.Data > Key
    then
        store false in Successful
    else
        store nil in Prev
        store Head in P
        loop while P ≠ nil and P^.Data < Key
            store P in Prev
            store P^.Ptr in P
        if P = nil or P^.Data > Key
            then
                store false in Successful
            else
                store true in Successful
                if Prev = nil
                    then
                        store P^.Ptr in Head
                    else
                        store P^.Ptr in Prev^.Ptr
                call Deallocate(P)

END OF Delete
```

4.5   Orders of Magnitude

In chapter 2 we examined the notion of order of magnitude. We determined that a linear search is $O(N)$ and that a binary search is $O(\log N)$. How do these conclusions compare to the order of magnitude of searching a linked list? Since the search of a linked list is just a linear search, i.e., we start at the head and look at nodes until we either find the key or come to the end of the list, the search of a linked list is $O(N)$.

While we're at it, let's examine the insertion and deletion routines. What is the order of magnitude of an insertion into an unordered array? That's easy. You just put the new element on the end of the array; that's $O(1)$. If, on the other hand, you needed to guarantee that there were no duplicates before the new element was inserted, you would have to search the entire array, making it $O(N)$. A deletion would be similar: you would have to find the element to delete, using a linear search, and then, probably, replace the deleted element with the element in the last position. The search portion would require the most work, making the deletion $O(N)$.

How about the order of magnitude of insertion into an ordered array? It would be necessary to first search for the place to do the insertion, that's $O(\log N)$. After finding the correct place, those elements larger than the one being inserted would have to be moved to the right to make room for the new element. When we looked at the insertion sort we saw that it was necessary, on the average, to move about half of the elements. The moving takes longer than the search. That makes a single insertion $O(N)$. In the case of a deletion, it would still be necessary to do the search as well as the move—this time moving the items the other way to fill the hole—so a deletion is also $O(N)$.

Inserting an element into a linked list requires a linear search to find the place to do the insertion. The insertion itself requires only modifying a few pointers, but the entire process is going to be $O(N)$. Similarly, to delete an element from a linked list would require the same search, making it $O(N)$ as well.

Thinking about linked lists this way makes it seem that we haven't accomplished anything. Indeed, the search routine is even slower than for a binary search. Two things can be said. First, even though insertions into a sorted array and a linked list both are of $O(N)$, the linked list insertion will likely be faster since few things have to be moved.

Secondly, and more importantly, the advantage of a linked list was never expected to be an improvement in the speed of the routine. The whole point is the dynamic allocation of memory that is possible with a linked list. With arrays, we are always faced with the need to determine in advance how many cells are going to be required and the resultant possibility of wasting a great deal of space. With linked lists, we can always allocate just as much memory as we need.

Computer programming often involves wrestling the tradeoffs between saving time versus saving space. A linked list is a space-saving data structure, not necessarily a time-saving one. In chapters 7–9 we'll discuss binary trees and will see that they allow us to save both space and time when compared to arrays and linked lists.

4.6   Pointers in Pascal

The job of a pointer in Pascal is to *reference* or *point to* a dynamic variable, which is of some type, such as `integer`, `real`, `array` or other supplied or user-defined type.

For example, if we wanted a program to be able to create a dynamic variable of type integer, we could define a type IntegerPointer as follows:

```
type
    IntegerPointer = ^integer;
```

Note the "^" before the word integer. In English, we would say that any variable of type IntegerPointer is a pointer that points to a dynamic variable of type integer. Variables of this type are declared in the usual way:

```
var
    P : IntegerPointer;
```

The dynamic variable to which P points is referred to in the program as "P^." That is, once P is declared as a variable of type IntegerPointer, P^ is a variable of type integer that can be created by the program. It then can be assigned, displayed and compared the same as any other integer. Notice the difference between the "^" before the type identifier and the "^" after the pointer variable. "^integer" means "pointer to an integer," and "P^" means "the integer to which P is pointing."

new and dispose

Declaring P as a pointer variable doesn't by itself create the dynamic variable to which it points. We allocate space for dynamic variables in Pascal through the use of the new procedure. This procedure accepts a pointer variable as its single parameter and actually creates a dynamic variable of the type to which this variable points. For example,

```
new(P)
```

has the effect of creating a dynamic integer variable pointed to by P; that is, it creates P^. Before invoking the new procedure, P^ is undefined.

Just as the new procedure allocates memory space to be occupied by a new dynamic variable, the dispose procedure deallocates that space so that it again becomes available to the system. In other words,

```
dispose(P)
```

releases the memory occupied by the dynamic variable P^ to the storehouse of available memory and renders P^ undefined.

The nil Token

Pointer variables are assigned their values in one of three ways. The first is via the new procedure, where the "thing the pointer points to" is a brand-new dynamic variable of the appropriate type, as yet containing an unpredictable value.

The second way is by a simple assignment statement involving another pointer of the same type. If, for example, P and Q are both pointers of type ^integer, then the simple assignment Q := P makes Q point to the same integer variable that P does. In other words, Q^ is now the same dynamic variable as P^ is, and the statement dispose(P) would render Q^ undefined as well as P^.

The third way for a pointer variable to acquire a value is by assigning it the special value called nil. The assignment

```
P := nil
```

is equivalent to saying "let P point to nothing." If P has the value nil, then it is an error to refer to P^.

More Examples of Syntax

All this may seem confusing, so let's look at some examples. Consider the following definitions and declarations:

```
type
  IntegerPointer = ^integer;
  CharPointer    = ^char;
var
  P, Q : IntegerPointer;
  R    : CharPointer;
  i    : integer;
```

Now P and Q are pointers to integers, and R is a pointer to a char. They are *not*, however, integers and chars themselves. P and Q could never be used in an arithmetic expression, but P^ and Q^ could be, if these variables had been created by the new procedure.

There is no order to pointer variables, so it never makes sense to compare them using the relational operators < and >, but you *can* compare them for equality or inequality using = and <>. Note that if P = Q then P^ must be the same as Q^ because P and Q point to the same integer variable. P^ could be the same as Q^ without P being equal to Q, though, since two different integer variables can have the same value.

Assuming that the corresponding dynamic variables have been created with the **new** procedure, the following statements would be valid:

```
P^ := i

P := Q

R^ := 'a'

writeln(R^)

i := P^ + Q^

P := nil

if P <> Q
   then
       ...
```

The following statements would *not* be valid:

```
i := P + Q            { P and Q are not integers }

P := R                { P and R are not the same type }

writeln(P)            { pointers cannot be displayed }

nil := P              { nil is not a variable }

if P < Q
   then
       ...            { pointers are not ordered }
```

You must be careful how you use the procedure **new**. For example, the statements

```
new(P);
new(Q);
P^ := 3;
P := Q
```

would be legal, but the dynamic variable created by the first **new** would be lost. It would still hold the value 3, but you'd never be able to "find" it, because nothing points to it any more. Many programmers use the term *garbage* for such memory space that is allocated but unusable. Consider also the following statements:

```
new(P);
Q := P;
P^ := 3
```

If we then display Q^, we will see the value 3, since Q points to the same place P does. You can see that it will be important to keep track of where pointers are pointing and what's stored there.

Linked Lists in Pascal

As we mentioned before, the real advantage of dynamic variables occurs not when they are simple types, as in the above examples, but when they are records, one of whose fields is itself a pointer. Let's look at the Pascal syntax used to build a linked list. Assume that there is some type called DataType that will be used to store the data in each node of the list. We would define the type needed to construct the linked list as follows:

```
type
  DataType = ... ;
  NodePointer = ^Node;
  Node = record
      Data : DataType;
      Ptr  : NodePointer
    end;
```

Notice that the Node type is undefined when it is first mentioned in the definition NodePointer = ^Node. Pascal allows this kind of definition as long as the as-yet-undefined type is defined in the same ⟨type definition part⟩. If it weren't allowed, then we couldn't define a Node, because one of its fields is of type NodePointer. We would have the problem of "which comes first, the pointer or the node?"

As with any record, the fields of a variable of type Node are referred to in the program by the record identifier, a period, and the field name. Let's say that we declare a variable P of type NodePointer, and create a new node with the new procedure. Then P^.Data is a variable of type DataType, and P^.Ptr is a variable of type NodePointer.

With these definitions in mind, it is a simple matter to convert the algorithms for InList, Insert and Delete into Pascal code. Let's consider an application for which these modules would be useful.

4.7   A Linked List Application

You have probably seen a program that checks the spelling of the words in a file. A program like this compares the words in the file with those in another file, usually called the "dictionary" file. Imagine that the dictionary file is a textfile that stores the words alphabetically and in uppercase. Our goal is to write a program to maintain this dictionary file. It should allow you to search the list for a particular word, add words to the file, delete words from the file and display a listing of the words in the file.

We can have the program read the file into a linked list, so we don't have to worry about the maximum number of words in the dictionary. Naturally, there are limitations on the memory capacity in any implementation, but we won't concern ourselves with that problem here.

It's important for you to understand that the dictionary file is an ordinary textfile, not a linked list. It is a file of `chars` arranged in lines, as every textfile is. We are choosing to take the information in the file, namely the dictionary words, and place each one into a node of the linked list, building the list as we go. At the conclusion of the program we will traverse the list from beginning to end, writing out to the file the word stored in each node. We could read the words into an `array` instead; that wouldn't affect the way the words are stored in the file. The advantage of using a linked list is that we need do not need to know in advance how many words the dictionary contains; our data structure can expand to the required size.

None of the pointers in the list are written to the file; indeed, pointers can never be written to a file or even to the screen. A pointer is the address of a place in memory. It doesn't make sense to save the value of pointers in a file since the next time the file is read, the data will probably be put somewhere else. It similarly is never necessary for the user of a program to see the value stored in a pointer, only that to which the pointer is pointing.

The Problem

Our problem is to write a program to read a dictionary file into a linear, singly linked list and allow searches, insertions and deletions to be performed on the list while it is in memory. The list can also be displayed on the screen. When the user elects to quit, he has the option of saving the changes or exiting without saving.

We will assume that the maximum word length is 20 characters, and that the words are stored in the file in uppercase, one word per line. There are to be no duplicates in the file, so if the user attempts to insert a word that is already there an error message will result.

After reading the dictionary file into the linked list, the program will display a menu like the following:

```
Please select a letter and press Return:

        (S)earch the list for a word
        (I)nsert a word in the list
        (D)elete a word from the list
        (P)rint the list on the screen
        (Q)uit without saving the changes
        (E)xit and save the changes

    Your choice:
```

If one of the first three choices is made, the program should prompt for the key word, accept the word and convert it to uppercase before going on.

The Modules

Here's a high-level algorithm for the main program module:

START OF DictionaryBuilder

read file into linked list
store false in both Quit and Exit
loop
    display and process main menu choices
    until Quit or Exit is selected
if Exit is selected
    then
        write the linked list to the file

END OF DictionaryBuilder

Given this high level algorithm, it looks like the modules we'll need are *ReadFile, MainMenu* and *WriteFile*. The *MainMenu* module will display the available choices for the user, accept the choice and call the corresponding subroutine. We'll write the algorithms for *ReadFile* and *WriteFile* first, then concentrate on the main part of the program.

The *ReadFile* Module

The *ReadFile* module will read the words in the dictionary file one by one, constructing the linked list as it goes along. We will pass the textfile by reference (the only way a file can be passed), and the head of the linked list by reference as well, since it's being changed and passed back.

The module should be able to handle the case where the list is empty; in this case, *Head* should be passed back as *nil*. In the general case, there will be at least one word in the list and the module will start by creating the first node in the list, and continue adding nodes to the end of the list until there are no more words in the file. Notice that we are not going to use our *Insert* routine to add words to the list. Since we know in advance that the words in the file are stored in alphabetical order, it would take a lot of extra time to search through the entire list every time to insert the new word on the end of the list.

Adding a node to the end of a linked list only involves rerouting the pointers of the last node, so it will be necessary to have a pointer that points to the last node. We'll call this pointer *Tail*. The main loop of the module will create a new node, set its pointer to *nil*, fill its data field with the next word in the file and reroute the appropriate pointers. Here's what the algorithm looks like:

```
START OF ReadFile(DictFile, Head)
Passed by value: none
Passed by reference: DictFile, Head

prepare DictFile for reading
store nil in Head
loop while not at end of DictFile
    if Head = nil
        then
            call Allocate(Head)
            store Head in Tail
        else
            call Allocate(Tail^.Ptr)
            store Tail^.Ptr in Tail
    read next dictionary word into Tail^.Data
store nil in Tail^.Ptr

END OF ReadFile
```

The *WriteFile* Module

The *WriteFile* module is very simple. We pass it the textfile by reference, and the head of the list by value. We start by preparing the file for writing. The main part of the module is a *loop while* that writes a word to the file and advances *Head*, stopping when *Head* becomes *nil*. Since *Head* is passed by value, we haven't lost the head of the original list.

START OF WriteFile(DictFile, Head)
Passed by value: Head
Passed by reference: DictFile

prepare DictFile for writing
loop while Head ≠ nil
    write Head^.Data to DictFile
    store Head^.Ptr in Head

END OF WriteFile

The MainMenu Module

What parameters should be passed to the main part of the program? We don't have to pass the textfile, since the words have been read into the linked list. Of course, we have to pass the list by passing Head, and it should be passed by reference. Also, if we want the calling routine to know when Quit or Exit is selected, we should pass these Boolean variables by reference as well. In that case a refined DictionaryBuilder algorithm would be:

START OF DictionaryBuilder

call ReadFile(DictFile, Head)
store false in Quit and Exit
loop
    call MainMenu(Head, Quit, Exit)
    until Quit or Exit
if Exit
    then
        call WriteFile(DictFile, Head)

END OF DictionaryBuilder

The MainMenu module displays the choices shown on page 92 and accepts the user's choice. If one of the first three choices is selected, the user is asked to enter a key word. We'll write a subroutine named EnterWord that is called in these cases to accept the word and convert it to uppercase.

The algorithm for MainMenu is on the next page.

```
START OF MainMenu(Head, Quit, Exit)
Passed by value: none
Passed by reference: Head, Quit, Exit

loop
    display menu for user
    accept Choice
    until Choice is valid
if Search, Insert or Delete is selected
    then
        call EnterWord(Key)
when Choice is
    Search : call SearchList(Head, Key)
    Insert : call InsertInList(Head, Key)
    Delete : call DeleteFromList(Head, Key)
    Print : call Display(Head)
    Quit : store true in Quit
    Exit : store true in Exit

END OF MainMenu
```

The Subprograms within *MainMenu*

The routine for *Display* is very similar to *WriteFile*, except that the data are displayed on the screen rather than written to the file. The modules *SearchList*, *InsertInList* and *DeleteFromList* call *InList*, *Insert* and *Delete*, respectively, and display a message to the user as to whether the action was successful. For example, here is the algorithm for the *SearchList* module:

```
START OF SearchList(Head, Key)
Passed by value: Head, Key
Passed by reference: none

if InList(Head, Key)
    then
        display "The word is on the list."
    else
        display "The word is not on the list."

END OF SearchList
```

We'll leave the algorithms for *EnterWord*, *InsertInList* and *DeleteFromList* as exercises.

4.8   Coding the Modules

Let's start with the following definitions and declarations:

```
const
    MAXWORDLEN = 20;

type
    CharArray = packed array [1 .. MAXWORDLEN] of char;
    String    = record
            Str : CharArray;
            Len : integer
        end;
    Pointer   = ^Node;
    Node      = record
            Data : String;
            Ptr  : Pointer
        end;

var
    Quit, Exit : Boolean;
    DictFile   : text;
    Head       : Pointer;
```

The best modules to start coding are ReadFile and Display, since having the linked list in memory is essential to the other modules. Coding these two modules will allow you to write a test program that simply reads a short test file into a linked list and displays the list on the screen. The code for ReadFile is on the next page.

```
procedure ReadFile(var DictFile : text;
                   var Head : Pointer);

{ This procedure reads the words from DictFile      }
{ into a singly linked list.                        }

var
   Tail : Pointer;
   i       : integer;

begin
   reset(DictFile);
   Head := nil;
   while not eof(DictFile) do
      begin
         if Head = nil
            then
               begin
                  new(Head);
                  Tail := Head
               end
            else
               begin
                  new(Tail^.Ptr);
                  Tail := Tail^.Ptr
               end;
         Tail^.Data.Len := 0;
         while not eoln(DictFile) do
            begin
               Tail^.Data.Len := Tail^.Data.Len + 1;
               read(DictFile, Tail^.Data.Str[Tail^.Data.Len])
            end;
         readln(DictFile);
         for i := Tail^.Data.Len + 1 to MAXWORDLEN do
            Tail^.Data.Str[i] := ' '
      end;
   Tail^.Ptr := nil
end;
```

Notice that after each word is read from the file, the remainder of the defined length of the string is padded with spaces. When we test strings for equality in Pascal, they are compared along their entire defined lengths, not just their actual lengths. If we didn't pad with spaces, the garbage in the remainder of the strings would affect the comparisons.

The `Display` procedure can be coded directly from the *WriteFile* algorithm, since the only difference is whether the words go to the screen or the file. Here is the code:

```
procedure Display(Head : Pointer);

{ This procedure displays on the screen         }
{ the data from each node of the list.          }

begin
   while Head <> nil do
      begin
         writeln(Head^.Data.Str : Head^.Data.Len);
         Head := Head^.Ptr
      end;
   writeln;
   write('Press Return to continue: ');
   readln
end;
```

The test program for these two procedures should consist of the definitions and declarations mentioned previously, the code listed above and the following main program block:

```
begin
   ReadFile(DictFile, Head);
   Display(Head)
end.
```

You should put these pieces together and run the program, using a short dictionary file created with the text editor. You should be aware that on some systems, the consequences of making mistakes in dealing with pointers can be quite unpredictable, and even disastrous. It is very important to trace through any algorithm or code that deals with pointers, using diagrams like those in figures 4.6–4.8.

WriteFile and MainMenu

Once `ReadFile` and `Display` have been written and tested, the next to be written are the `WriteFile` and `MainMenu` procedures. Again, `WriteFile` is very similar to `Display`, except that the word in each node is written to the dictionary file rather than the screen. We'll leave the code to be written as an exercise.

The code for the statement part of the `MainMenu` part of the program follows.

```
begin
   repeat
      writeln;
      writeln('Please select a letter and press Return:');
      writeln;
      writeln('                    (S)earch the list for a word');
      writeln('                    (I)nsert a word in the list');
      writeln('                    (D)elete a word from the list');
      writeln('                    (P)rint the list on the screen');
      writeln('                    (Q)uit without saving the changes');
      writeln('                    (E)xit and save the changes');
      writeln;
      write('       Your choice: ');
      readln(Choice);
      Choice := Upper(Choice)
   until Choice in ['S', 'I', 'D', 'P', 'Q', 'E'];
   if Choice in ['S', 'I', 'D']
      then
         EnterWord(Key);
   case Choice of
      'S' : SearchList(Head, Key);
      'I' : InsertInList(Head, Key);
      'D' : DeleteFromList(Head, Key);
      'P' : Display(Head);
      'Q' : Quit := true;
      'E' : Exit := true
      end
end;
```

Of the modules that MainMenu calls, only Upper hasn't been mentioned. This is a function to convert lowercase letters to uppercase. It will be used in EnterWord, and we used it in MainMenu so that the user can enter the Choice in either upper or lowercase. It is immediately converted to uppercase. The easiest way to do this is with the ord and chr functions. Here is the code for Upper:

```
function Upper(Ch : char) : char;

{  This function converts lowercase letters to uppercase.  }
{  Other characters are unchanged.                         }

begin
   if Ch in ['a' .. 'z']
      then
         Upper := chr(ord(Ch) + ord('A') - ord('a'))
      else
         Upper := Ch
end;
```

Finishing the Program

At this point you should write the statement part of the main program, following the algorithm on page 95, and assemble the pieces you have written so far. The procedures `SearchList`, `InsertInList`, `DeleteFromList` and `EnterWord` and the function `Upper` are to be contained within `MainMenu`. Type in only the procedure headings and a **begin** and an **end** for those procedures that you haven't yet written.

We'll leave it as an exercise for you to compile and run the program to test the `MainMenu` section and the `WriteFile` section. Then write the remaining parts of `MainMenu`, testing as you go.

An Implementation Warning

There are some difficulties you might encounter in implementing some of these routines. For example, consider this part of the *InList* algorithm:

if Head = nil or Head^.Data > Key
    then
        return false
    else
        . . .

You might code this as follows:

```
if (Head = nil) or (Head^.Data.Str > Key.Str)
   then
      InList := false
   else
         .  .  .
```

The problem arises because there are different ways for a compiler to evaluate the compound Boolean expression. One method is to evaluate both parts of the expression, and return "true" if at least one part is true. Another method is to evaluate the first part only, and if it's true, return "true" and don't bother evaluating the second part. If the first part is false, the second part is evaluated and its value returned. Only if the first part is false is the second part evaluated. This latter method is called *short-circuit evaluation.*

If your compiler doesn't use short-circuit evaluation, then it will evaluate `Head^.Data.Str > Key.Str` even when `Head = nil` is true. But in Pascal, any reference to `Head^` is an error when `Head` is the `nil` pointer. This will cause a run-time error on many systems.

To be on the safe side, you shouldn't assume that your compiler uses short-circuit evaluation—write the code so that the program will run regardless of which method is used. One way to code the above part of *InList* is to use nested ⟨*if statement*⟩s:

```
if Head = nil
   then
      InList := false
   else
      if Head^.Data.Str > Key.Str
         then
            InList := false
         else
            ...
```

This problem with the implementation of 'or' is called "the **or** problem." There is a corresponding problem with the implementation of 'and', known as "the **and** problem."

The *Insert* and *Delete* algorithms each contain an *or* similar to the one we just discussed, and the fix is just as easy as this one. But they also contain a more difficult instance of the **and** problem: the *and* in the *loop while.*

Consider these steps from the algorithm for *Insert*:

store nil in Prev
store Head in P
loop while P ≠ nil and P^.Data < Key
    store P in Prev
    store P^.Ptr in P
...

Suppose you implement these three steps as:

```
...
  Prev := nil;
  P  := Head;
  while (P <> nil) and (P^.Data < Key) do
      begin
          Prev := P;
          P  := P^.Ptr
      end;
...
```

If you are trying to insert a new word that comes at the end of the list, P will become nil before a node containing a name greater than Key is encountered. Thus, the compound Boolean expression:

```
(P <> nil) and (P^.Data < Key)
```

will be evaluated. If your compiler does not use short- circuit evaluation, it will attempt to determine whether or not P^.Data < Key even though P is nil. This is an error and will cause many programs to crash. (We have to say "many" rather than "all" since what the compiler does upon encountering such an error is not specified by the Standard.)

The "fix" is not trivial. You would be well-advised to try to fix it yourself before reading on.

We "fixed" the problem by rewriting the algorithm slightly. Rather than use the test:

```
(P <> nil) and (P^.Data < Key)
```

which has the "and problem"; we use a *loop while* containing a test that looks at the pointer field and the data field of P at the same time. We place the loop right after the first *if...then* where we know for sure that P is not nil.

We incorporated the routine `MakeNewNode` that actually allocates the space for the new node. Here's our code. Compare it to the algorithm on page 85 to see the changes we made:

```
procedure Insert(var Head : Pointer;
                          Key : String;
            var Successful : Boolean);

var
  P, Prev  : Pointer;

  procedure MakeNewNode(var P : Pointer; Key : String);

  var
    Temp : Pointer;

  begin
    new(Temp);
    Temp^.Data := Key;
    Temp^.Ptr := P;
    P := Temp
  end;
```

```
begin {  Insert  }
  Successful := true;
  if Head = nil
    then
      MakeNewNode(Head, Key)
    else
      begin
        Prev := nil;
        P  := Head;
        while (P^.Ptr <> nil) and (P^.Data.Str < Key.Str) do
          begin
            Prev := P;
            P  := P^.Ptr
          end;
        if P^.Data.Str = Key.Str
          then
            Successful := false
          else
            if P^.Data.Str < Key.Str
              then
                MakeNewNode(P^.Ptr, Key)
              else
                if Prev = nil
                  then
                    MakeNewNode(Head, Key)
                  else
                    MakeNewNode(Prev^.Ptr, Key)
      end
end;  {  Insert  }
```

As we said earlier, even if you are using a compiler that uses short-circuit evaluation of Boolean expressions, you should write the code so that it won't crash on a system that doesn't. It's not always possible to predict whether or not the code might be transported to such a system in the future. If you decide not to follow our advice in this regard, at least study the above example so if you are asked to write code that runs correctly on a system that doesn't use short-circuit evaluation, you'll know how.

The *Insert* algorithm is interesting in that it contains one occurrence of the **or** problem and two occurrences of the **and** problem.

4.9   Iteration vs. Recursion

On page 82, we said that we had a reason for writing *Insert* and *Delete* iteratively rather than recursively. As a matter of fact, when we wrote the first draft of this text, we wrote them both recursively. The recursive routines are shorter, and probably easier to understand. We wrote test routines for them and used a text editor to create small sample files for them to run on. The routines worked fine and all the tests we ran were passed without any problem. Why then did we decide to rewrite them as iterative routines?

After completing the first draft, we assigned the completion of the program for one of our classes as an exercise. As part of the assignment, we put together a "real" dictionary file with hundreds of words and gave this file to the students in the class to use on their programs. Their programs worked fine on the test files they created but crashed when given our files. Neither **Insert** nor **Delete** would allow them to get past the first 100 words or so.

When a recursive routine calls itself, it has to be able to come back to where it is, and continue from that point when the recursive call is completed. In order to be able to continue from that point, all of the values of the local variables and the value parameters have to be "remembered" somehow so that when the call is completed, the old values can be restored. As long as the number of recursive calls was small, as it was in the test cases, the computers had enough memory to keep track of everything and restore the values when the recursive calls were completed. On long lists, however, the computers did not have enough memory to put the needed multiple copies of everything away somewhere and get it back when the call was completed. In short, the computers ran out of memory doing the many levels of recursive calls that were asked for.

There are two lessons to be learned from our experience. The first is that recursion uses a lot of memory, especially when a recursive routine utilizes local variables. When you encounter a situation where you expect to need many levels of recursion, then you should look for an iterative solution rather than a recursive one. In chapter 5, we'll look more closely at where the computer actually stores the values of the local variables and value parameters. You probably have already guessed the answer: on a stack.

The second lesson—and the main reason we added this section rather than just replacing the recursive routines with iterative routines and omitting the entire discussion—is to illustrate that even experienced programmers can write code containing errors. Moreover, these errors can remain in the program even though they are carefully tested. No amount of testing can ever prove that a program is correct. Testing only reveals bugs; it does not prove that they don't exist.

The *InList* routine on page 83 was written recursively, and for the same reasons that *Insert* and *Delete* were re-written iteratively, *InList* should be re-written. We'll leave it as an exercise to re-write *InList*.

Tail Recursion

The *InList* routine will prove easier to re-write iteratively than did either *Insert* or *Delete*. *InList* has one recursive call, and that call is at the end of the routine. Such a recursive routine is called "tail recursive." Essentially, a tail recursive routine is using recursuion at its end to get the routine to repeat itself. Thus, the recursive call can be replaced by a loop. While it is often the case that a routine is easy to write "tail-recursively," it will be more efficient and less likely to run out of memory if it's coded as an iterative routine.

4.10   Circularly Linked Lists

Linear singly linked lists are the simplest examples of the kinds of linkages that can be set up using pointers. A *circularly* linked list is easy to create; instead of making the last node's pointer be `nil`, make it point back to the first node. In this case, the list has no first or last node as such—the list is more like a ring. The list can be accessed by an external pointer pointing to any node.

If the list holds data elements in order, then there is an advantage to pointing the external pointer, say `Tail`, at the *last* node. This pointer functions as a `Head` pointer as well; in fact, `Tail^.Ptr` points to the beginning of the list. This means that with only one external pointer, you can easily access both the beginning and the end of the list.

Consider a circularly linked list whose nodes are ordered words like those in the `DictionaryBuilder` program. Let `Tail` be a pointer that points to the last node. How would you code the procedure `Display` so that the contents of each node is displayed once? How about:

```
procedure Display(Tail : Pointer);

{ This procedure displays each node in a circularly  }
{ linked list, ending with Tail.                     }

var
   P : Pointer;

begin
   P := Tail;
   if P <> nil
      then
         repeat
            P := P^.Ptr;
            writeln(P^.Data.Str : P^.Data.Len)
            until P = Tail
end;
```

Trace through this routine using figure 4.9. Remember also to consider the cases where the list has no elements at all and where it has only one element.

Figure 4.9 A Circularly Linked List

4.11   Doubly Linked Lists

A linear singly linked list is like a sequential file in the sense that you can go forward one element at a time, but to go backwards you have to go all the way back to the beginning. A *doubly linked* list is a bit more complicated. Instead of one pointer per node, a doubly linked list has two pointers: one points at the *next* node in the list and the other points at the *previous* node. The advantage of using the double linkage is that the list can be traversed either forward or backward.

We have seen one example already where the ability to traverse the list backward would be helpful. In writing the algorithm for *Insert*, we had to use a trailer pointer *Prev* to enable us to go backward one node. As another example, consider a word processing program where each line in the document is stored as a node in a linked list. In order to be able to scroll forward and backward, it would make sense that the list be doubly linked.

Figure 4.10 shows how the pointers are set up in a typical doubly linked list.

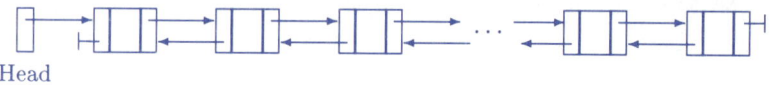

Head

Figure 4.10 A Doubly Linked List

The disadvantage of using the double linkage is that the pointer manipulations are a bit more complicated. To insert a node after a typical node in the list, for example, you would have to create the new node and take care of four pointers—the new node's two and the two that end up pointing *to* the new node. To delete a typical node, you have to reroute the two pointers to the node and dispose of it.

4.12   An Adventure Game

To illustrate doubly linked lists, we'll write the algorithms and some of the code for a simple adventure game. Here's the way it will work: Imagine the user falls

down a long mine shaft into an underground chain of caves. The rubble that
falls in after him seals the mine shaft, so there is no escape that way.

In each cave, the user meets a creature guarding some treasure, and a tunnel
leading to another cave. The object is to find the exit to the chain of caves
and escape with as much treasure as possible. The user has attributes such
as strength, intelligence and stamina, and each creature has attributes such
as power, anger and agility. These attributes will be stored as integers on a
scale from 1 to 100. When the user meets a creature, he is given a choice
of actions such as fighting the creature, escaping from the creature or trying
to steal its treasure. The outcome of a particular action will depend on a
combination of the user's and creature's attributes. For example, fighting the
creature might decrease the user's stamina and increase the creature's anger.
The actual numeric details will be left to you.

Once the user has completed his action, he is given a choice of directions to
move (ahead or back), or to quit the game. If the user chooses to move ahead,
he may find the exit, or, more likely, he'll find another cave with a different
creature. If the user chooses to move back, he'll either encounter a creature
he's seen before, or he'll come to the first cave, which is a dead end. The game
continues until the user finds the exit, runs out of stamina or quits.

Choosing Data Structures

The main data structure for this program is a doubly linked list that will represent the chain of caves. Each node will be a record that holds information
about the name and attributes of the creature in that cave and pointers forward
and back to adjacent caves. When the user goes forward into a new cave, the
program will create a new node, randomly choose a name for the creature and
assign values to its attributes, and set up its pointers. The forward pointer
of the new node will be set to *nil* and the backward pointer will point to the
previous node. In the first node, the backward pointer will be *nil*, to represent
the dead end. The character in the adventure (the user) will be represented by
a record which simply contains his attributes.

The *CaveWalker* Algorithm

Here is a high-level algorithm for the main program:

START OF CaveWalker

display an introductory message for the user
initialize the character, the first cave, and other variables
        such as the odds of finding the exit
loop
    display the name of the current creature
            and the current status of the character
    accept and process the character's action
    if the character has any stamina left
        then
                accept and process the character's move
    until the exit is found, or the character quits, or
            the character runs out of stamina
display a concluding message for the user

END OF CaveWalker

We can create the following modules to be called by the main program:

- *Introduce* will display an introductory message.

- *Initialize* will initialize variables, create the first creature along with its attributes and give the character his initial attributes.

- *DisplayStatus* will display the name of the creature in the current cave and the attributes of the character.

- *GetAction* will prompt the user for his choice of action, accept his response and do any necessary error checking.

- *ProcessAction* will determine the outcome of the action and change the creature's and character's attributes accordingly.

- *GetMove* will ask the user to move forward, backward or quit. It will also do appropriate error checking.

- *MakeMove* will go to the next node in the list, either forward or back, creating a new node if the character goes forward from the last node.

- *Conclude* will display the results of the game, showing the character's attributes at the end.

Using these modules, but leaving off the parameters for now, the algorithm for the main program can be written as follows:

START OF CaveWalker

call Introduce
call Initialize
loop
 call DisplayStatus
 call GetAction
 call ProcessAction
 if the character has any stamina left
  then
   call GetMove
   if Quit has not been chosen
    then
     call MakeMove
 until exit is found, quit is chosen or
   the character runs out of stamina
call Conclude

END OF CaveWalker

We'll concentrate on the modules that involve creating and moving through the doubly linked list, leaving you to fill in the details for the other modules. In what follows, we'll assume these definitions:

```
const
   MAXNUM = 100;
   MAXLEN = 10;

type
   CharArray = packed array[1 .. MAXLEN] of char;
   Character = record
         Strength,
         Stamina,
         Intelligence,
         Treasure       : [1 .. MAXNUM]
      end;
   CavePtr   = ^Cave;
   Cave      = record
         Name      : CharArray;
         Power,
         Anger,
         Agility,
         Treasure : [1 .. MAXNUM];
         Ahead,
         Back      : CavePtr
      end;
```

The *Initialize* Module

This module should create the first cave and give the character his attributes.
Creating a cave involves choosing a name for the creature and assigning attributes to it. Since this will have to be done whenever the user enters a new
cave, we could write a module called *Create* that does this. *Create* will have to
pass back only the pointer to the new node. Once the node is created, *Initialize*
should then set both of its pointers to *nil*. Here's a high-level algorithm for
Initialize:

```
START OF Initialize(CavePointer, Character, etc.)
Passed by value: none
Passed by reference: all variables

initialize miscellaneous variables
call Create(CavePointer)
store nil in CavePointer^.Ahead and in CavePointer^.Back
initialize the attributes of Character

END OF Initialize
```

The *Create* procedure calls *Allocate* to create a node and assigns values to its fields. To create a name for the creature, you can simply have the routine generate a string of randomly chosen characters. You might choose lowercase letters then call **Upper** to convert the first letter to uppercase. If we leave this to another procedure, say *GetName*, then *Create* would be:

```
START OF Create(CavePointer)
Passed by value: none
Passed by reference: CavePointer

call Allocate(CavePointer)
call GetName(CavePointer^.Name)
store random integers between 1 and 100 in:
        CavePointer^.Power, CavePointer^.Anger,
        CavePointer^.Agility and CavePointer^.Treasure

END OF Create
```

The *MakeMove* Module

We pass to this procedure a letter indicating the move to be attempted (*A* for ahead and *B* for back), the odds against finding the exit, and a pointer to the current cave. It will pass back a Boolean value indicating whether or not the character has found the exit; otherwise, it will advance the pointer to the appropriate cave, creating one if necessary. Here is the algorithm for *MakeMove*:

```
START OF MakeMove(Move, Odds, Current, Found)
Passed by value: Move, Odds
Passed by reference: Current, Found

if Move is Back
    then
        if Current^.Back is nil
            then
                display dead-end message
            else
                store Current^.Back in Current
    else
        if Current^.Ahead is nil
            then
                if a random number is less than 1 / Odds
                    then
                        store true in Found
                    else
                        call Create(Next)
                        store Next in Current^.Ahead
                        store nil in Next^.Ahead
                        store Current in Next^.Back
        store Current^.Ahead in Current

END OF MakeMove
```

With the groundwork we have laid, you should be able to write the remaining algorithms and the code for the program. These exercises will ask you to complete the program and write some modifications.

4.13   Summary and Review

- We introduced dynamic variables, a way for the program to allocate memory at run time rather than when the program is compiled. This is done using pointers.

- When a pointer points to a record variable, and one or more of the fields of the record is another pointer of the same type, these variables can be linked together to form various data structures. The simplest such structure is a linear linked list.

- We developed algorithms for inserting and deleting items from a linked list, and for searching through a linked list for a particular value.

- We learned about pointers in Pascal. The dynamic variables are accessed through pointers of the appropriate type.

- The **new** and **dispose** procedures allocate and deallocate memory to be used by dynamic variables.

- Pointers can be given the value **nil**, which means they don't point to any dynamic variable.

- Using the algorithms mentioned above, we developed a program using a linked list to maintain a file of words in alphabetical order.

- We introduced circularly linked lists; these are linear linked lists where the last node's pointer points to the first node.

- We introduced doubly linked lists. These have two pointers per node: one points to the next node and the other points to the previous node.

- We described a simple adventure game which could be implemented with a doubly linked list, and developed the algorithms which deal with moving through the list and creating new nodes.

4.14   Exercises

1. Re-write the algorithm for *InList* on page 83 to make it an iterative routine rather than a tail recursive routine.

2. Write a test program for the `ReadFile` and `Display` procedures with the main program block given on page 99. Use your text editor to create a dictionary file consisting of uppercase words of 20 characters or less, one word per line. Compile and run the test program.

3. Code the `WriteFile` module and add it to the test program in the previous exercise. Compile and test the program. Then add the procedure headings for `EnterWord`, `SearchList`, `InsertInList` and `DeleteFromList`. Write simple procedure blocks such as

```
begin
    writeln('EnterWord procedure')
end;
```

   for each of the procedures and compile and test the program.

4. Write the algorithm and the code for the `EnterWord` procedure. Add it to the program from the previous exercises and compile and test it.

5. Write algorithms for the *InsertInList* and *DeleteFromList* modules. How should the parameters be passed to these modules? Write the code for these modules and finish writing the program from the previous exercises.

6. Write the algorithm and the code for a module that reads a file of words, such as the Dictionary file, into a circularly linked list such as the one in figure 4.9. Use the `Display` procedure from page 107 in a test program for the module.

7. Write a complete program that solves the following problem, known as the Josephus Problem:

   > A group of soldiers is surrounded by an enemy force. There is only one horse, and the soldiers have to decide how to pick a volunteer who is to take the horse and try to get through the enemy lines and get help. In order to choose one soldier, they agree to stand in a circle and alternately eliminate every other soldier until only one is left. The one that is left is elected to go try to get help.

   The problem is to write a program that represents the circle of soldiers—a circular list seems obvious—and allows every other soldier to be eliminated until there is only one left. The program should accept the original number of soldiers. The output should be the soldier numbers as they are eliminated from the circle and the number of the soldier who is chosen to go for help.

8. As a modification to the problem in exercise 7, instead of having every other soldier eliminated from the list, have every nth soldier eliminated. The input should be the initial number of soldiers and the value of n. The output should be the same as before.

9. Consider the Josephus Problem discussed in the two previous exercises. Suppose you know the value of n, and suppose you know that there is a way to succeed in getting past the enemy soldiers, and, thus you want to be chosen. Where would you stand in the circle?

10. Write algorithms for inserting and deleting nodes from a doubly-linked list. What parameters should be passed to these modules?

11. Write an algorithm for a procedure that deletes the Nth node from a doubly-linked list, if it exists. The procedure can call the routine from the previous exercise to actually delete the node.

12. Write algorithms for the remaining modules from the CaveWalker program: *DisplayStatus*, *GetAction*, *ProcessAction* and *GetMove*. The attributes of the user and creature, the actions of the user, and the results of these actions are up to you.

13. Write the code for the CaveWalker program using the algorithms from the chapter and the previous exercise. Remember to add the Introduce and Conclude procedures.

14. Modify the CaveWalker program so that the first cave has *two* tunnels with no dead ends. In other words, the user has been deposited in the middle of the chain of caves, rather than at one end.

15. Devise and implement a method for the user to have the option of stopping the Cave Walker game and saving everything in a textfile, so that at a later time he can take up where he left off. You will have to think of a format for the data in the textfile and a way of determining which cave the user was in when the game was stopped. You might also want to store the current value of the random number seed. At the beginning of the game, the user should have the choice of beginning a new game or continuing an old one.

Chapter 5

Stacks, Revisited

I'll have a short stack
and a side of bacon.
— Tim Wilson

5.1 Overview of the Chapter

In this chapter we will implement a stack as a linked list and use this implementation for the program that evaluates a postfix expression. We'll introduce another problem, that of solving a maze, that uses a stack for its solution. We'll also discuss how recursive routines use stacks.

5.2 A Stack as a Linked List

The previous chapter developed most of the tools that we need to implement a stack as a linked list. Let's think about what is needed for a stack and how a linked list can be used. First, remember that everything that happens to a stack happens at the top of the stack; we push elements onto the top of the stack and pop them off the top. To see if a stack is empty, we only need to see if there is something on the top; to initialize a stack, we simply make sure there is nothing on the top. All of this can easily be done to a linked list. The pointer to the head of the list becomes a pointer to the top of the stack, a Push becomes an insertion at the head of the list, and a Pop is nothing other than a deletion of the element at the head of the list. A stack is initialized by setting the head pointer to nil, and the function EmptyStack needs only to check to see if this pointer equals nil.

The biggest problem is deciding what names to give things. When we used an array to implement a stack, the record containing the array and the pointer to the element at the top of the stack became the stack. Whenever we needed to pass the stack to a subroutine, the entire record was passed.

119

With a linked list implementation, it's not as clear what constitutes the stack itself. Is the first pointer the stack, or is the entire linked list the stack? Conceptually at least, the latter is probably closer to how we imagine the stack. However, when we pass the stack to a subroutine, what do we pass? We don't need to pass the entire list—indeed, it's not clear how the entire list could be passed. All we need to pass is the pointer to the first node in the list. For this reason, and so that the changes to the existing code are minimized, we'll define the type `Stack` as a pointer to a node of the list.

That is, our type definitions for a `Stack` become:

```
type
  Stack     = ^StackNode;
  StackNode = record
        Data : ElementType;
        Ptr  : Stack
     end;
```

where `Data` is of type `ElementType` because we haven't decided yet what we are putting on the stack.

Postfix Expression Evaluation

In chapter 3 we developed a complete Pascal program that evaluated a postfix expression entered by the user. If you now modify the ⟨*type definition part*⟩ to include the type definitions above and replace the routines for `Push`, `Pop`, `InitStack` and `EmptyStack` with the following routines, the program will run as before with no other changes required. Notice that `ElementType` becomes `real` since this program put `real` values onto the stack. Notice also how similar the following routines are to the linked list routines from the previous chapter.

```
procedure Push(var S : Stack; Val : real);

{  This procedure pushes Val onto the stack S.  }

var
  P : Stack;

begin
  new(P);
  P^.Data := Val;
  P^.Ptr := S;
  S := P
end;
```

```
procedure Pop(var S : Stack; var Val : real);

{  This procedure pops an element off the top of stack S.  }

var
  P : Stack;

begin
  P := S;
  Val := S^.Data;
  S := S^.Ptr;
  dispose(P)
end;
```

```
procedure InitStack(var S : Stack);

{  This procedure initializes stack S.  }

begin
  S := nil
end;
```

```
function EmptyStack(S : Stack) : Boolean;

{  This function determines whether or not stack S is empty.  }

begin
  EmptyStack := S = nil
end;
```

The fifth stack routine, FullStack, is a special case. When we implemented the stack as an array, the possibility that the stack might fill up is a real problem because the array has a maximum size. We had to decide the array size based on our estimate of the maximum stack size. When we implement the stack as a linked list, it's not clear that we have a problem, since the list can expand as needed to accomodate the stack.

In any implementation there is a finite amount of memory, so an attempt to allocate memory for a dynamic variable could fail with unpredictable consequences. Since Standard Pascal gives us no way to determine how much memory is available, it's impossible to protect against this kind of situation. Particular implementations, however, may provide some nonstandard alternative.

Aside from the problem of the full stack, then, we have modified the expression evaluation program to implement the stack as a linked list. This modification was very easy to accomplish because we treated the stack as an abstract data type. The only routines that we allowed for the stack were the basic ones. We did not allow any routines that examined the bottom element of the stack or that counted the number of elements in the stack. Had we allowed such routines, the modification could not have been handled so easily. We would have had to look carefully through all the code to see where these "other" operations were performed. The code then would have become hard to maintain.

The important lesson here is to treat data structures as abstract data types and not to allow yourself to take liberties with their implementation. You should write and run the program after replacing the original type definitions with the one on the previous page and the earlier stack routines with these four.

5.3   A Mazing Problem

Let's now turn to another problem that uses a stack for its solution. This problem needs a stack too, and we'll use our linked list implementation for its solution.

Suppose you need to determine whether or not a particular maze can be solved. We'll think of the maze as composed of tall thick green hedges surrounding numerous paths. There will be a single entrance to the maze and a place where we want to get: the goal. On the computer, a maze will be a two-dimensional array of characters such as:

```
HHHHHHHHHHHHHHHHHHHHHHHHHHHHHHHHHHHHHHHHHHHHHH
H       H      H            H H         H     H
H HHHHHHH HHHHH H H HHHHHHHHHH H HHHHH HHH   HHH H
H H     H H   H H H H              H H   H  H H    H H
H H HHHHH HHH H H HHH HHHHHHHH H H H HHHHH HHH HHH
E         H       H H H GH H        H H    H H    H
HHH HHHHHHH HHHHHHHHH H H HH H HHHHHHH H HHH HHHHH
H H       H H        HH HH H H H      H   H      H
H HHH HHHHH HHHHHHHHH H HH H H H HHHHH HHHHH HHH H
H   H H  H H H         H      H H       H H H
HHH H H HHH H H HHH HHHHH HHHHHHHHHH H HHHHHHH H H
H H    H H H H H H H           HH   H H H       H H
H   H    H      H      H H H H     H   H   H H H    H
HHHHHHHHHHHHHHHHHHHHHHHHHHHHHHHHHHHHHHHHHHHHHHHHHH
```

where each 'H' represents the hedge, the 'E' represents the entrance to the maze, the 'G' represents the goal position—think of it as a chest where some gold is hidden—and the blanks represent the paths between the hedges. We'll store the maze in a textfile—a file that you may have to create—and will input the maze from the textfile.

We'll assume we know the location of the entrance but not the location of the gold. The question to be answered is, "Is there a path to the gold?"

At first glance this problem might seem quite difficult but having a stack around should make a solution easy to follow. Imagine walking through the maze. After each step you take, look around in all four directions. If there is only one place to go next, just go there. If there are two or more possibilities, choose one of them to try next and put (push) the other(s) onto a stack. Whenever you come to a dead end, take (pop) an untried place off the stack and go there. If you reach a dead end and the stack is empty, you will have tried all the possible places and will know that the maze cannot be solved. Notice that a stack as a LIFO structure is appropriate for the solution. You would not want to go all the way back to the entrance and start over every time you reach a dead end.

This solution is fairly easy to turn into an algorithm, but there are a couple of details to keep in mind. First, which initial location should we push onto the stack? If we push the location of the entrance, the algorithm might cause us to wander around looking at places that are not inside the maze—actually, we would likely get a "subscript out of range" error. Let's start with the first blank location *inside* the maze.

The solution contains a loop, since we keep taking steps until we either reach the gold or run out of possible paths. In this case, we don't know in advance how many steps we'll have to take, but we can assume there will always be at least one blank space to try, and we will always take at least one step. Thus we decide to use a *loop until*.

What will be the terminating condition for the loop? Surely we will quit when we find the gold or when there are no more paths to try. Next, how do we decide which one of the four possible directions to go and which to push onto the stack? An easy way to handle this is to push all those that have not yet been tried onto the stack—in any order we like—and every time through the loop, pop off whichever location is on top of the stack. Of course, the order in which we push the untried directions onto the stack will have an effect on the eventual path found (if there are several possible ways to get to the gold) and on the number of dead ends we encounter before finding one of the paths. Since we are only interested in discovering whether or not a path to the gold exists, we won't worry about the order the untried directions are pushed onto the stack.

Here is an algorithm for the solution we have been discussing:

Start with the first path location inside the entrance
Push the row and column of this location onto a stack
loop
    Pop a row and column off the stack
    Step to that location, mark it as having been tried, and look
        at each of the four possible places you could go next
    Push each of these that are empty onto the stack, continue
    until either you find the gold or the stack becomes empty
if you found the gold
    then
        display a message saying that the maze can be solved
    else
        display a message saying that the maze cannot be solved

How could we "mark" a location as having been tried? Easy; just put a dot (.) there. How do we tell if the gold has been found? If a new location that we look at contains the 'G', then we know we have found the gold and we can use a Boolean variable, say *Found*, to keep track. After the loop terminates, we can display the maze. The spaces marked with a '.' will show where we went.

Should we push row and column numbers separately or together? It could be done either way, of course. Since it will give us another example of using **records** in Pascal, let's agree to push and pop locations in the maze as pairs of coordinates.

With these things in mind, our algorithm becomes:

Push the StartPair onto the stack
loop
    Pop a Row and Column off the Stack
    store a dot in Maze(Row, Column)
    if Maze(Row + 1, Column) is empty and not a 'G'
        then
            Push that pair onto the stack
        else
            if Maze(Row + 1, Column) is a 'G'
                then
                    store true in Found
    if not Found and Maze(Row, Column + 1) is empty and not a 'G'
        then
            Push that pair onto the stack
        else
            if Maze(Row, Column + 1) is a 'G'
                then
                    store true in Found
    if not Found and Maze(Row − 1, Column) is empty and not a 'G'
        then
            Push that pair onto the stack
        else
            if Maze(Row − 1, Column) is a 'G'
                then
                    store true in Found
    if not Found and Maze(Row, Column − 1) is empty and not a 'G'
        then
            Push that pair onto the stack
        else
            if Maze(Row, Column − 1) is a 'G'
                then
                    store true in Found
    until either Found or the stack is empty
if Found
    then
        display a message saying that the maze can be solved
    else
        display a message saying that the maze cannot be solved
Display the maze

The steps where the decision is made for each of the four locations are the same. We could avoid repeating them by writing another module, say *CheckAndPush*, that checks to see if the location contains the gold or is empty. It would set *Found* to true if the gold has been found and push the location onto the stack if it is empty. Assuming the existence of such a routine, the above algorithm would look like:

```
call Push(Stack, StartPair)
loop
    call Pop(Stack, Pair)
    store a dot in Maze(Pair.Row, Pair.Column)
    call CheckAndPush(Pair.Row + 1, Pair.Column, Stack, Found, Maze)
    if not Found
        then
            call CheckAndPush(Pair.Row, Pair.Column + 1, Stack, Found, Maze)
    if not Found
        then
            call CheckAndPush(Pair.Row − 1, Pair.Column, Stack, Found, Maze)
    if not Found
        then
            call CheckAndPush(Pair.Row, Pair.Column − 1, Stack, Found, Maze)
    until either Found or the stack is empty
if Found
    then
        display a message saying that the maze can be solved
    else
        display a message saying that the maze cannot be solved
Display the maze
```

5.4   Pascal Implementation of Maze Algorithm

The code for this program follows directly from the algorithm, but we do have to make a decision about the data structures. We decided to push and pop the location in the maze as a pair consisting of a row number and a column number. In Pascal, such a pair can be defined as a record with two `integer` fields:

```
type
  Pair = record
         Row, Column : integer
       end;
```

And then, following the definition given earlier in this chapter for a stack, we would have:

```
type
  Pair = record
         Row, Column : integer
       end;
  Stack = ^StackNode;
  StackNode = record
         Data : Pair;
         Ptr  : Stack
       end;
```

The code for Push, Pop, EmptyStack and InitStack will be nearly identical to the earlier versions. The only difference will be the type name of the parameter being either Pushed onto or Popped off the stack. We'll leave the code for these routines as exercises.

The main program will have to get the maze from the file and will have to call the routine that attempts to solve the maze. We'll leave the main routine and the routines that get the maze from the file, as well as a routine that displays the maze, for the exercises. We should, however, make some decisions about the maximum size of the array. Let's agree to make the array at most 23 rows by 65 columns. This will allow it to fit nicely on most terminal screens. Naturally the array will be an array of char. Thus, the above type definitions can be expanded to include:

```
const
  MAXROWS = 23;
  MAXCOLUMNS = 65;
type
  MazeType  = array [1 .. MAXROWS, 1 .. MAXCOLUMNS] of char;
  Pair = record
         Row, Column : integer
       end;
  Stack = ^StackNode;
  StackNode = record
         Data : Pair;
         Ptr  : Stack
       end;
```

Let's look at the procedure that attempts to solve the maze, SolveMaze. First, as always, we'll examine the parameters. What do we send to SolveMaze? The maze itself has to be sent, but should it be passed by value or by reference? We will want to mark the places where we walked and be able to display the

maze with these places marked, so we will pass the maze by reference. (Indeed, we might have passed it by reference even if we didn't want it changed. Why?)

What else will we need to pass? SolveMaze will have to know the starting location so the first position can be pushed onto the stack. We'll send it as a Pair. Should it be passed by value or by reference? It should be passed by value, since it's not being changed.

How about the stack; should we pass it from the main routine to SolveMaze? No, the stack is not needed in any higher level routines and can just be a local variable inside SolveMaze. The procedure declaration heading line will thus be:

```
procedure SolveMaze(var Maze : MazeType; StartPair : Pair);
```

For local variables, we'll need a stack, a place to put the pair we pop off the stack each time through the loop, and a Boolean variable that will keep track of whether or not the gold has been found:

```
var
  S     : Stack;
  Pr    : Pair;
  Found : Boolean;
```

The statement part is mostly an implementation of the algorithm. We do have to initialize the stack as well as Found, of course. We'll write the code assuming the existence of CheckAndPush, which we'll leave for the exercises. Here's our code:

```pascal
procedure SolveMaze(var Maze : MazeType; StartPair : Pair);

{ This procedure determines whether there is a solution to a maze. }

var
  S     : Stack;
  Pr    : Pair;
  Found : Boolean;

begin
  InitStack(S);
  Found := false;
  Push(S, StartPair);
  repeat
    Pop(S, Pr);
    with Pr do
      begin
        Maze[Row, Column] := '.';
        CheckAndPush(Row - 1, Column, S, Found, Maze);
        if not Found
          then
            CheckAndPush(Row + 1, Column, S, Found, Maze);
        if not Found
          then
            CheckAndPush(Row, Column - 1, S, Found, Maze);
        if not Found
          then
            CheckAndPush(Row, Column + 1, S, Found, Maze)
      end
    until Found or EmptyStack(S);
  if Found
    then
      writeln('The maze can be solved.')
    else
      writeln('The maze cannot be solved.');
  DisplayMaze(Maze)
end;
```

Notice that we used a ⟨*while statement*⟩ to save some typing. We are sending Found to CheckAndPush. Will we pass it by value or by reference?

The order in which we call CheckAndPush will not affect the determination of whether or not a solution to the maze exists, but will affect the number of dead ends that are reached while trying to find the gold. It could also affect which path is found if there are several paths to the gold. We usually write an algorithm to handle the general case, but a given algorithm may not work best in a particular instance. You should rearrange the calls to `CheckAndPush` and run the program on various mazes to see what happens.

Sample Run

Before you can run this program, you will have to create a maze yourself using a text editor. Remember that the maximum number of rows (according to the decisions we made above) is 23 and the maximum number of columns is 65. You might want to start with simpler mazes, or allow the file to contain the actual number of rows, columns and the location of the first step. When we wrote the program, we started with a maze containing 14 rows and 50 columns, and we put the 'E' in row 6 column 1. (That meant we used a starting location of (6, 2) since the first step into the maze had to be inside.) Here is a sample run from our program. We printed a short introduction, read the maze from the file and displayed it:

```
This program reads a maze from a file, displays it and
checks to see if it can be solved.  Press RETURN.


HHHHHHHHHHHHHHHHHHHHHHHHHHHHHHHHHHHHHHHHHHHHHHHHHH
H       H     H           H H           H     H
H HHHHHHH HHHHH H H HHHHHHHHHH H HHHHH HHH   HHH H
H H     H H   H H H H             H H   H   H H   H H
H H HHHHH HHH H H HHH HHHHHHHH H H H HHHHH HHH HHH
E         H         H H H GH H       H H   H H   H
HHH HHHHHHH HHHHHHHHH H H HH H HHHHHHH H HHH HHHHH
H H       H H         H H H H H       H   H     H
H HHH HHHHH HHHHHHHHH H HH H H H HHHHH HHHHH HHH H
H   H H   H H H         H       H H   H         H H H
HHH H H HHH H H HHH HHHHH HHHHHHHHHH H HHHHHHH H H
H H   H H H H H H H           HH   H H H         H H
H   H   H     H     H H H H     H   H   H H H   H
HHHHHHHHHHHHHHHHHHHHHHHHHHHHHHHHHHHHHHHHHHHHHHHHHHH
```

Then we called `SolveMaze`. After determining whether or not there was a path to the gold, `SolveMaze` printed the appropriate message and exited. The main program then called the routine that displays the maze again:

```
The maze is solvable.

HHHHHHHHHHHHHHHHHHHHHHHHHHHHHHHHHHHHHHHHHHHHHHHHHH
H       H......H............H.H...........H.....H
H HHHHHHH.HHHHH.H.H.HHHHHHHHHH.H.HHHHH.HHH...HHH.H
H H     H.H    H.H.H.........H.H...H...H.H...H.H
H H HHHHH.HHH H.H.HHH.HHHHHHHH.H.H.H.HHHHH.HHH.HHH
E.........H........H.H H.GH.H......H.H...H.H...H
HHH HHHHHHH.HHHHHHHHH.H H.HH.H.HHHHHHH.H.HHH.HHHHH
H H         H.H........H H..H.H.H......H...H....H
H HHH HHHHH.HHHHHHHHH.H HH.H.H.H.HHHHH.HHHHH.HHH.H
H   H H   H.H H......H  ....H.H.....H......H.H.H
HHH H H HHH.H H.HHH.HHHHH.HHHHHHHHHH.H.HHHHHHH.H.H
H H   H H H.H H.H H.H........HH...H.H.H.......H.H
H  H     H....H  ...H H.H.H...H...H...H.H.H...H
HHHHHHHHHHHHHHHHHHHHHHHHHHHHHHHHHHHHHHHHHHHHHHHHHHH
```

The dots indicate which paths were tried. Sure enough, there is a path that leads to the gold. The introduction and conclusion displayed here are deliberately short and boring. You should add your own messages to make it more interesting.

Refinement of the Problem

We could quit here and go on to other problems, but this problem isn't really satisfactorily finished. We did solve the problem we posed; we wrote a program that tells us whether or not a particular maze can be solved. However, if you'll look at the display above, you'll see that we are left inside the maze holding the gold but do not know how to get out! The dots show all the paths that we tried but do not show which path we actually followed. If we want to get out of the maze—taking the gold with us—we have to solve the entire problem again. There must be a better way. Actually, there is a better problem statement. Rather than just determining whether or not there is a path that leads to the gold, we would like to know whether or not such a path exists and, if so, where the path is. A better statement would be:

> Write a program that reads a maze from a file, displays it, determines whether or not there is a path that leads to the goal position, indicates whether or not such a path exists, and, if so, marks the path with a character that will show the path to take. It should then display the maze again.

Let's mark places that do not lead to the gold with dots as before, but mark the actual path, if it exists, with asterisks (*).

We are going to leave this problem as an exercise but will give you a hint that hopefully will lead you to a solution:

Starting at the entrance, push each untried location onto the stack as before. When you pop an untried location off the stack, mark it with a dot, and push it back onto the stack. When you do pop a location off the stack, if there's a dot there, keep poping. When, and if, you do finally reach the gold, those locations on the stack marked with a dot will lead you back out.

This solution, like our earlier one, will involve pushing the places onto a stack and popping a place off every time through a loop. Also, the order in which you push things onto the stack will affect the final path found, if there's more than one solution.

We'll leave it as an exercise to finish a solution (either this one or one of your own), turn it into an algorithm and then implement the algorithm in Pascal.

Example Run

The following shows what the maze could look like after the path to the gold has been marked with asterisks. As before, the dots indicate where we went before we encountered a dead end.

```
HHHHHHHHHHHHHHHHHHHHHHHHHHHHHHHHHHHHHHHHHHHHHHHHH
H        H*******H...........H.H...........H.....H
H HHHHHHH*HHHHH*H.H.HHHHHHHHHH.H.HHHHH.HHH...HHH.H
H H      H*H    H*H.H.H.........H.H...H...H.H...H.H
H H HHHHH*HHH H*H.HHH.HHHHHHHH.H.H.H.HHHHH.HHH.HHH
E**********H*****....H.H H*GH.H.......H.H...H.H...H
HHH HHHHHHH*HHHHHHHHH.H H*HH.H.HHHHHHH.H.HHH.HHHHH
H H        H*H........H H**H.H.H.......H...H.....H
H HHH HHHHH*HHHHHHHHH.H HH*H.H.H.HHHHH.HHHHH.HHH.H
H   H H    H*H H*****..H **..H.H.....H.......H.H.H
HHH H H HHH*H H*HHH*HHHHH*HHHHHHHHHH.H.HHHHHHH.H.H
H H    H H H*H H*H H*H*****....HH...H.H.H.......H.H
H   H      H*****H  ***H H.H.H...H...H...H.H.H...H
HHHHHHHHHHHHHHHHHHHHHHHHHHHHHHHHHHHHHHHHHHHHHHHHHH
```

5.5   Stacks and Recursion

Now that we've had some experience with the notion of a stack, we can explain a little more about what is going on with recursion.

Let's look at the mathematical function factorial as a first example. Here's a recursive definition from mathematics.

Definition:

$$n! \equiv \begin{cases} 1 & \text{, if } n = 0 \text{ or } 1 \\ n \cdot (n-1)! & \text{, if } n > 1 \end{cases}$$

As the definition is recursively applied to 5!, the final value is calculated by the following steps:

$$
\begin{aligned}
5! &= 5 \cdot 4! \\
&= 5 \cdot 4 \cdot 3! \\
&= 5 \cdot 4 \cdot 3 \cdot 2! \\
&= 5 \cdot 4 \cdot 3 \cdot 2 \cdot 1! \\
&= 5 \cdot 4 \cdot 3 \cdot 2 \cdot 1
\end{aligned}
$$

And here's a recursive Pascal function for the factorial function.

```
function Factorial(N : integer) : integer;

{  This function calculates N factorial, recursively.  }

begin
  if (N = 0) or (N = 1)
    then
      Factorial := 1
    else
      Factorial := N * Factorial(N - 1)
end;
```

Let's explain what is happening inside the computer as this function calculates the value of 5!.

Suppose we call `Factorial` from another routine and send it the number 5. The function stores 5 in the parameter N and examines N to see if it's equal to 0 or 1. Since it isn't, the statement in the **else** part is executed. The function will attempt to multiply 5 times `Factorial(4)`. Before this multiplication can be completed, however, the computer will have to know what `Factorial(4)` is. All the current information—including the pending multiplication—gets pushed onto a stack and the program calls `Factorial`. This time it is sent the number 4. Now N equals 4. Since 4 is not equal to 0 or 1, the **else** part is executed once again. This time the program has the computer try to multiply 4 times `Factorial(3)`. And once again the multiplication has to be delayed until `Factorial(3)` is evaluated. Everything is pushed onto the stack and the routine gets called yet another time.

This continues until `Factorial` is called with the value 1. This time it is not necessary to recurse; the value of 1 is returned for `Factorial(1)`. The value of N (2) that was pushed onto the stack is popped off, multiplied by the 1, and the result (2), sent back as the value of `Factorial(2)`. The 3 is popped off the stack, multiplied by the 2 and this result (6) is sent back as the value of Factorial(3). The 4 is popped off the stack, multiplied by the 6 and the result (24) is returned for Factorial(4). Finally the 5 is popped off the stack, multiplied times the 24 and the final result of 120 is sent back to the routine that made the original call.

Let's not worry about how the pending multiplications are delayed; the compiler is able to keep track of the fact that it needs to multiply the returned value by the value popped off the stack. The important thing is the way the computer can use a stack to store the data while the recursive calls are being made.

Combinations

Rather than say any more about factorial, let's look at another function and try to see what happens to the stack. Let's consider the mathematical concept of the number of combinations of n things taken k at a time.

This number represents the number of subsets of size k that can be formed from a set of n elements. Mathematicians use the notation $\binom{n}{k}$ for this function and define it as follows:

Definition:

$$\binom{n}{k} \equiv \begin{cases} 1 & \text{, if } k = 0 \text{ or } k = n, \\ \binom{n-1}{k-1} + \binom{n-1}{k} & \text{, otherwise.} \end{cases}$$

The function can easily be implemented in Pascal:

```
function Combination(N, K : integer) : integer;

{  This function calculates the number of combinations of  }
{  N things taken K at a time, recursively.                }

begin
  if (K = 0) or (K = N)
    then
      Combination := 1
    else
      Combination := Combination(N-1, K-1) + Combination(N-1, K)
  end;
```

This function is more complicated since it involves two recursive calls. To make it a bit easier to follow, let's rewrite Combination to use a local variable in order to separate the two recursive calls. Here is our revised version:

```
function Combination(N, K : integer) : integer;
var
   T : integer;

{  This function calculates the number of combinations of N  }
{  things taken K at a time.                                 }

begin
  if (K = 0) or (K = N)
    then
      Combination := 1
    else
      begin
        T := Combination(N-1, K-1);
        Combination := T + Combination(N-1, K)
      end
end;
```

Every time the function calls itself, the value parameters and local variables are pushed onto a stack. For example, let's suppose that some routine calls Combination, sending it 5 and 2. Since $2 \neq 0$ and $2 \neq 5$, the routine is going to have to call itself and everything gets pushed. Of course, T is undefined at this point, so what it contains is uncertain. Let's assume the values are pushed as a triple: (N, K, T).

We want to visualize how the stack is changing as $\binom{5}{2}$ is calculated. Since T will often be pushed before it has been given a value, we do not know what value actually gets pushed. Whenever a value is pushed that has not yet been defined, we'll display '?'.

When the first recursive call to Combination is about to be made, the stack will contain:

(5, 2, ?)

Now Combination is called and sent 4 and 1 (N-1 and K-1). When Combination starts this time, N equals 4 and K equals 1. Once again $K \neq 0$ and $K \neq N$ so we have to recurse. Before Combination calls itself, the parameters and local variables have to be pushed onto the stack. Now the stack will contain:

(4, 1, ?) (5, 2, ?)

where the top of the stack is to the left. When Combination is called this time, the values of N and K are 3 and 0, respectively. Since K equals 0, no recursion is needed to calculate the return value. Combination just returns the value 1. On the completion of this call to Combination, three values are popped off and T is assigned the returned value of 1. N will be reset to 4 and K reset to 1. The next line of code calls Combination again, sending it N-1 and K. N-1 equals 3 and K equals 1. But before the call is made, everything gets pushed onto the stack once again. The stack will contain:

    (4, 1, 1)   (5, 2, ?)

This time when `Combination` begins, N will equal 3 and K will equal 1. It will be necessary to recurse to determine the value to return. The current values of N, K and T will get pushed and the stack will contain:

    (3, 1, ?)   (4, 1, 1)   (5, 2, ?)

The values sent to `Combination` will be N-1 and K-1, so the new values of N and K will be 2 and 0. No recursion will be needed since $k = 0$ and the value 1 will be returned. When the 1 is returned, the old values for T, K and N will be restored by popping them off the stack, T will be assigned the value 1 and the second call to `Combination` (this time) will be made. The current values will be pushed onto the stack, and it will look like:

    (3, 1, 1)   (4, 1, 1)   (5, 2, ?)

The parameters this time will be 2 and 1, so yet another pair of recursive calls will be needed. Before the first call is made, the current values are pushed and the stack will contain:

    (2, 1, ?)   (3, 1, 1)   (4, 1, 1)   (5, 2, ?)

No recursion will be necessary since K equals 0. The value 1 will be returned and T will be assigned this value. The current values of everything are pushed and the second call made. The stack will contain:

    (2, 1, 1)   (3, 1, 1)   (4, 1, 1)   (5, 2, ?)

On the second call this time, N and K will both equal 1 and no recursion is necessary, the function will return 1. After popping the three values off the stack, it will contain:

    (3, 1, 1)   (4, 1, 1)   (5, 2, ?)

Adding these two values of 1 together, the value 2 will be returned. The stack will contain:

    (4, 1, 1)   (5, 2, ?)

The 2 will get added to the T, producing the value 3, and it will be returned. Upon return, the next three values will be popped off and the 3 will be added to the T, producing 4. Before the 4 is returned, the stack will look like:

    (5, 2, ?)

When the 4 is returned, these three values will be restored to T, K and N. The 4 that is returned will be stored in T. At this point the stack will be empty. Stepping back a bit, remember that we are assuming that some other routine made the initial call of Combination and sent the values 5 and 2. In order to calculate the number of combinations of five things taken two at a time, the function has to add together the number of combinations of four things taken one at a time and the number of combinations of four things taken two at a time. We have just traced it to the point where it has returned the number of combinations of 4 things taken 1 at a time; it now has to calculate the number of combinations of 4 things taken 2 at a time.

The second top-level recursive call to Combination will now get made. The current values of the local variables will be pushed, producing a stack containing:

(5, 2, 4)

and another series of recursive calls will follow.

It is highly likely that we have lost most of our readers by this time and further tracing of the changing of the stack will probably prove futile. For those of you who are still with us, here is a list of stacks that will result from this point on:

```
(4, 2, ?)  (5, 2, 4)
(3, 1, ?)  (4, 2, ?)  (5, 2, 4)
(4, 2, ?)  (5, 2, 4)
(3, 1, 1)  (4, 2, ?)  (5, 2, 4)
(2, 1, ?)  (3, 1, 1)  (4, 2, ?)  (5, 2, 4)
(3, 1, 1)  (4, 2, ?)  (5, 2, 4)
(2, 1, 1)  (3, 1, 1)  (4, 2, ?)  (5, 2, 4)
(3, 1, 1)  (4, 2, ?)  (5, 2, 4)
(4, 2, ?)  (5, 2, 4)
(5, 2, 4)
(4, 2, 3)  (5, 2, 4)
(3, 2, ?)  (4, 2, 3)  (5, 2, 4)
(2, 1, ?)  (3, 2, ?)  (4, 2, 3)  (5, 2, 4)
(3, 2, ?)  (4, 2, 3)  (5, 2, 4)
(2, 1, 1)  (3, 2, ?)  (4, 2, 3)  (5, 2, 4)
(3, 2, ?)  (4, 2, 3)  (5, 2, 4)
(4, 2, 3)  (5, 2, 4)
(3, 2, 2)  (4, 2, 3)  (5, 2, 4)
(4, 2, 3)  (5, 2, 4)
(5, 2, 4)
```

The value returned by the second top-level call is 6.

Finally, the original call to Combination will add together the 4 from the first call and the 6 from the second call and return 10 to the routine that called it in the first place.

While we hope we have removed some of the magic from recursion, we fear we may have replaced it with a lot of confusion. Be assured that you don't have to be able to follow or explain all this yourself. You can simply trust the computer to keep track of everything and produce the correct result.

It should be noted for the record that this is not an efficient way to calculate the number of combinations of n things taken k at a time when n and k get large. This is a beautiful example of recursion and it works very well, but it is *slow!* If you need to use `Combination` for large values of n and k, you should look for a more efficient way to do it.

5.6   Summary and Review

- In this chapter we took a second look at the abstract data type of a stack. Previously we had implemented a stack as an array of records; in this chapter we implemented stacks using linked lists.

- We saw that when an abstract data type is treated as abstract data types, i.e., when only the basic operations of the data type are used to access the data, it is easy to change the way the data type is implemented.

- We introduced a new problem that used a stack—that of deciding whether or not a maze can be solved—and wrote a program that implemented our solution.

- We looked at what happens when a function is called recursively by using a stack to hold data while the recursion is taking place. We saw that whenever a routine calls itself, it pushes all local variables and value parameters onto a stack before it makes the recursive call and pops everything back off the stack when the call is completed.

- We saw that while recursion can make it very easy to write certain routines, there is often a great deal of overhead involved. While recursive routines often are easier to understand and analyze, there are times when an iterative version is just as easy to write. In such cases, the iterative version might be preferred in order to avoid the extra overhead required by the recursion. Also, when there are going to be many levels of recursive calls, an iterative version might be the only one that will actually run.

5.7 Exercises

1. Modify the code for `Push`, `Pop`, `EmptyStack` and `InitStack` from section 5.2 to be used in the maze-solving program.

2. Write the algorithm and the code for the `CheckAndPush` procedure, which checks to see if the location passed to it either contains the gold or is empty. If the location contains the gold, `Found` is set to true. If the location is empty, the coordinates of the location are pushed onto the stack.

3. Write a Pascal procedure, `DisplayMaze`, that displays the maze in a "pretty" manner.

4. Write the algorithm and the code for a complete program that reads the maze from a text file, calls `SolveMaze` to determine whether the maze is solvable, prints the appropriate message, and calls `DisplayMaze` to show the maze and the paths that were tried.

5. Change the order of the calls to `CheckAndPush`, and run the program on a variety of mazes to see how the order of the calls affects the results.

6. Rewrite the `SolveMaze` procedure to solve the refined problem stated on page 131. This version of `SolveMaze` shows an actual path to the gold marked by asterisks.

7. In chapter 2 we worked out a formula for the sum of the integers from 1 through $N-1$. Write a function `Sum` that returns the sum of integers from 1 through `N`, a passed `integer` parameter. Write the function recursively, and trace what happens on the stack when it is passed the value `5`. Write the function using a formula similar to the one in chapter 2 and compare the speed of execution for various values.

8. In the game of chess, the queen can move any number of squares in the same row, column or diagonal on the board. The queen is said to "check" another piece if the queen could move to the square occupied by that piece. It is possible to place eight queens on an 8-by-8 chessboard in such a way that no queen checks another queen. Write a program to find such a placement of queens. Your program should use stacks in a manner similar to the way they are used in `MazeSolver`. You may assume that there is at least one solution to the problem.

9. Rewrite the solution to the previous problem so that it finds a placement of N queens on an $N \times N$ board, if it exists. You should place reasonable limits on the value of N. What is the first value of N to have a solution?

10. In the game of chess, the knight can move to one of eight squares on the board by first moving two squares in one direction (not diagonally), then one square in a perpendicular direction. If the knight is close to

an edge of the board, then some of the eight moves aren't possible. If a knight, starting from a given position on the board, can move to every other square without landing on any square twice, the series of moves is called a "Knight's Tour." Write a program that allows the user to enter the starting position for the knight, and determines whether or not a Knight's Tour is possible. Since this is a big problem, computationally, you might also want to allow the user to enter the number of squares on the side of the board so you can test your program with boards smaller than the normal 8 × 8 board. If a Knight's Tour is possible, the program should display the tour in some meaningful manner.

Chapter 6

Queues, Revisited

The beginning of wisdom
is to call things
by their right names.
—Anonymous; Chinese proverb

6.1 Overview of the Chapter

In this chapter we will implement a queue as a linked list and use this implementation for the program from chapter 3 that simulates people standing in line at a bank. We'll introduce another problem, simulating balls rolling around on a pool table, that uses a queue for its solution. This solution will utilize a different kind of queue, a *priority queue*.

6.2 A Queue as a Linked List

In chapter 4 we developed most of the tools that we need to implement a queue as a linked list. Let's think about what is needed for a queue and how a linked list can be used. First, remember that everything that happens to a queue happens at either the head or the tail of the queue; we put elements onto the queue at the tail and take them off at the head. To see if a queue is empty, we only need to see if there is something at the head; to initialize a queue, we simply make sure there is nothing at the head.

All of this can be done to a linked list, but we do have to make an important decision before we can get very far. We will need two pointers: one for the head of the queue and one for the tail. The head of the linked list will be one of these, but which one?

To answer this question we need to look at the fundamental operations performed on a queue, in particular `EnQueue` and `DeQueue`. An `EnQueue` adds an element to the queue; `DeQueue` removes one. Is it easier to add elements to

the front of a linked list and remove them from the end, or add them at the
end and remove them from the front? Consider figure 6.1.

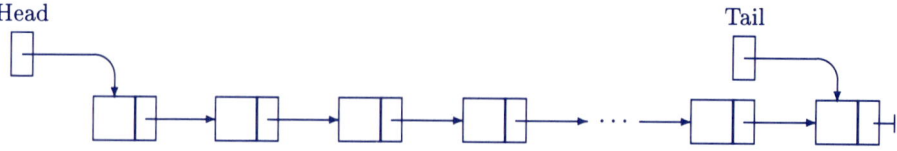

Figure 6.1 A Queue as a Linked List, Version 1

With the head and tail as shown, would it be easy to add an element at the
tail? Would it be easy to remove an element at the head?

Now consider figure 6.2.

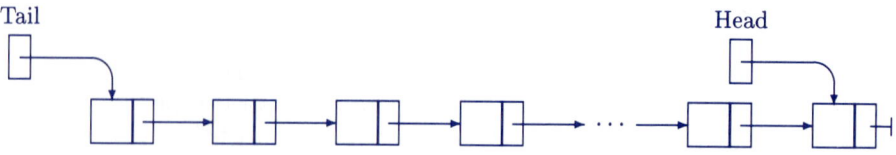

Figure 6.2 A Queue as a Linked List, Version 2

Would it be easy to add an element at the tail and remove an element at
the head?

You should have concluded that both ways of viewing the queue make it
easy to add an element at the point where the tail is pointing. That is, it
doesn't matter whether the tail of the queue is at the front of the list or at the
end.

However, removing an element from the end of a linked list (fig 6.2) is not
easy. The pointer in the node just before the last node has to be changed, and
the head pointer has to be changed to point to this node. We do not have any
easy way to find this node and thus would have to trace down the entire list
to find it every time we call DeQueue. On the other hand, removing a node
from the beginning of a linked list is easy. All we have to do is change the
head pointer to point to the next node and dispose of the old node. Thus, we'll
implement a queue as a linked list like the one in figure 6.1.

The pointer to the head of the list becomes a pointer to the head of the queue; `EnQueue` becomes an insertion at the end of the list. `DeQueue` is just a deletion of the element at the head of the list. A queue is initialized by setting the head and tail pointers to `nil`, and the function `EmptyQueue` needs only to check to see if the head pointer is nil. When `EnQueue` puts an element on a heretofore empty queue, both pointers have to be changed; otherwise, only the tail pointer is changed.

As with stacks, one problem we have is deciding what names to give things. In the case of stacks, we decided just to call the pointer to the top of the stack the stack. However, since queues require two pointers, let's agree to make a queue a record containing the two pointers. Whenever we need to pass the queue to a routine, we'll pass this record.

That is, our type definitions for queues become:

```
type
  QueuePtr  = ^QueueNode;
  QueueNode = record
         Data : ElementType;
         Ptr  : QueuePtr
      end;
  Queue = record
         Head, Tail : QueuePtr
      end;
```

Where `Data` is of type `ElementType` because we haven't decided yet what we are putting on the queue. In actual situations these could be given particular descriptions. Or, to make the programs require fewer changes, we could just define `ElementType` to be the desired type and leave the rest of the program alone. For example, if the data to be stored in the queue are of type `char`, we could just include the definition:

```
type
  ElementType = char;
```

Here are the four fundamental routines needed for the implementation:

```
procedure InitQueue(var Q : Queue);

{  This procedure initializes the queue Q to empty.  }

begin
  Q.Head := nil;
  Q.Tail := nil
end;
```

```
function EmptyQueue(Q : Queue) : Boolean;

{  This function determines whether or not the queue Q is empty.  }

begin
  EmptyQueue := Q.Head = nil
end;



procedure EnQueue(var Q : Queue; Element : ElementType);

{  This procedure puts an element on the tail of the queue Q.  }

var
  P : QueuePtr;

begin
  new(P);
  P^.Data := Element;
  P^.Ptr := nil;
  if EmptyQueue(Q)
    then
      Q.Head := P
    else
      Q.Tail^.Ptr := P;
  Q.Tail := P
end;
```

```
procedure DeQueue(var Q : Queue; var Element : ElementType);

{  This procedure removes the element at the head of the queue Q.  }

var
  P : QueuePtr;

begin
  P := Q.Head;
  Element := Q.Head^.Data;
  Q.Head := Q.Head^.Ptr;
  if EmptyQueue(Q)
    then
      Q.Tail := nil;
  dispose(P)
end;
```

In each of the places where `ElementType` and `Element` appear in these routines, they will have to be modified to agree with the actual data types used in your program, or `ElementType` has to be defined to indicate what we want to store in the queue. Other than that, no changes will have to be made to the program to change the implementation from an array to a linked list.

The program written in chapter 3 that implements a queue as an array can be rewritten to change the queue implementation to a linked list implementation. In so doing, note that only the type definitions and these four routines have to be changed; the remainder of the program is not changed at all. We'll leave the actual changing of the code as an exercise.

6.3 Simulation of Pool Balls

We solved the single server simulation problem with a queue, and the problem solution we developed was *time- driven*. The program went through the big loop that controlled the simulation once each minute. In chapter 3, we mentioned that some simulations can be written as *event-driven* instead. Let's look at another simulation problem, and this time, let's solve it with an event-driven simulation.

Our first problem definition might be:

Simulate a bunch of balls rolling around on a pool table.

While it might be a lot of fun to write a program that did that, it's well beyond our capability at this point. We need to scale things down quite a bit. The hardest thing to simulate would be what happens when two balls hit each other; let's leave that out. Let's just simulate the balls bouncing off the rails of the pool table and falling into the pockets.

A more appropriate problem would be:

> Write a program that simulates a collection of pool balls bouncing
> off the rails of a pool table and falling into the pockets. Allow
> the user to enter the number of balls and the initial positions and
> velocities of the balls. Let the balls bounce off the rails of the table
> until they all fall into pockets.

Event-driven Simulation

The difference between time-driven and event-driven simulations is that with
a time-driven simulation, there is some sort of clock controlling the program,
while with an event-driven simulation, the occurence of events controls the program. Usually a big loop is executed repeatedly. With time-driven simulation,
a particular time interval is selected and every iteration of the big loop represents one of these time intervals. In our bank teller program, the time interval
was chosen as one minute. With event-driven simulation, each iteration of the
loop represents some sort of event taking place.

Using the pool table problem as an example, what would the events be?
We'll define an event to be a ball either striking a rail or falling into one of
the pockets. We'll write the program in such a way that the table will be re-
displayed every time an event occurs; i.e., every time a ball strikes a rail or falls
into a pocket.

Priority Queues

So, what has this to do with queues? How can we use a queue to solve the
problem? In fact, we cannot; a normal queue would not help. What is needed
is something known as a *priority queue*.

A priority queue is a queue where elements are removed from the head of the
queue as before, but elements are placed on the queue in a position depending
on some value, rather than always being placed at the tail. The queue is always
in order based on this value, just like a linked list. The normal situation is for
this value to represent time, and that's what we'll be doing here. We'll place
events on the queue according to the time that they are going to occur, and
whenever an event is taken off the queue, it will be the next event to occur.

Solution of the Problem

To see more precisely how this will help in our problem, consider the following
top-level solution: first we'll determine when each ball is going to hit a rail or
fall into a pocket and then place these events into a priority queue according to
the time the events will take place. Next, we'll remove the element at the head
of the queue, and display the table at the time of that event. If the ball is not
in a pocket, we'll determine when that ball will next hit a rail and place that
event on the queue according to the time the event will happen. This process

will continue until the queue becomes empty. Since it is possible that a ball could bounce forever, never falling into a pocket, we'll probably want the user to input a maximum number of events for the simulation.

We can state our solution more formally by using the fundamental operations on queues that we've been using and writing the solution in an algorithmic form. Here's a first draft:

Initialize the data
For each ball, determine when an event concerning that ball will
*   take place and EnQueue the event on a priority queue*
loop while the queue is not empty and while more events remain
*   DeQueue an event*
*   Recalculate the positions on the table for the time of the event*
*   Redisplay the table*
*   Determine when the next event concerning this ball will occur*
*   EnQueue this event*
Perform any concluding steps

This gets us started, and we can identify several routines that we'll need. In addition to the fundamental queue operations, we'll need:

- a routine that will initialize the data,

- a routine that will determine when a given ball will next be involved in an event,

- a routine that will determine where each ball is located on the table at any given time,

- a routine that will display the table, and

- a routine that will perform any concluding steps.

The first of these—the routine that initializes the data—might be broken into two parts: one part gets the data from a user, and one part initializes the queue. The first part would ask the user how many balls the simulation will work with, and whether the initial positions and velocities of the balls are going to be determined by the user, or randomly by the computer. This part should also ask the user the maximum number of events for the simulation, and, probably, should initialize (to zero) a variable used for the elapsed time as well as a counter for the number of events so far. The second part would consist of a *loop for* that determines the times for the first event for each ball and puts that event on the queue. The time of the event and the ball number will constitute at least part of whatever gets put on the queue, but before we can say what else constitutes the event, we'll have to give some thought to the data structures we'll be needing. We'll do that in a moment.

The next routine will require some thought. How will we be able to determine the time that a given ball will strike a rail or fall into a pocket? We have to solve this problem, but we'll worry about it later.

We can also wait until later to solve the problems of determining where each ball is on the table at any given time and how to display the table. It will be easier to solve these problems after we've made some decisions about the data structures involved.

Data Structures for Pool Table Simulation

Let's think about the data structures we need. Obviously we'll need a priority queue to hold the events. We have to decide what constitutes an event. We'll also need to be able to represent collection of balls on the pool table. That's easily done with an array—an array of balls. Since the size of an array has to be determined in advance, let's agree that there will be a maximum of ten balls on the table. (We could have said sixteen—the normal fifteen plus a cue ball—but by only allowing ten, we can later display each ball by simply displaying its number as a single digit.)

What's a ball? Any ball can be uniquely determined by knowing its position and velocity. The position consists of two real numbers representing an (x, y) coordinate in a rectangular coordinate system—the top of the table. The velocity will also be represented by two real numbers: an x velocity and a y velocity. Thus, a ball can be uniquely determined by four real numbers: x, y, v_x and v_y. The x and y values represent the distance the ball is from the rails. If a ball is next to the left rail, its x value will equal 0; similarly, if a ball is next to the far rail, its y value will be 60. Thus, for any ball, x ranges from 0 to 96, and y ranges from 0 to 60. The velocity components can be positive, negative or zero; however, we won't want both the v_x and v_y to be zero at the same time.

Let's assume the pool table is eight feet long and five feet wide (and let's convert these to 96 and 60 inches for ease of use). Let's assume that the velocity of each ball is between 0 and 100 inches per second. So, for example, a ball might be represented by these four values: $x = 20$, $y = 46$, $v_x = -13.6$ and $v_y = 48.7$. This would mean the ball is currently 20 inches from the left rail, 46 inches from the near rail, is moving to the left at 13.6 inches per second and moving away at 48.7 inches per second. The magnitude of the ball's velocity, v, if needed, can be obtained by use of the Pythagorean theorem: $v^2 = v_x^2 + v_y^2$. In the current example, $v = 50.6$ inches per second. These four numbers would be entered whenever the user enters the initial data on a ball, and the program would have to check to make sure the values are within the proper ranges. If the user decides to have the computer choose the initial position and velocity for a ball, the program can select these four numbers randomly within the proper ranges. In Pascal we can represent these four values quite nicely with a record.

The length and width of the pool table should be treated as constants in the Pascal program; let's call them LENGTH and WIDTH. Similarly, the maximum velocity should be treated as a constant; let's call it MAXVELOCITY. In order to tell whether a ball has fallen into a pocket or not, we'll need to know how large the pockets are. Let's use another constant, called RADIUS, for the radius of the pockets on the table, and set it to 3 inches. We'll use these constants in the program as well as in the algorithms.

That leaves just an event. We have to figure out what constitutes an event. If we assume we have a Boolean-valued function that will tell us whether or not a ball is in a pocket, then all we will need to describe an event will be the number of the ball causing the event and the time the event occurs. Thus, an event can be a record containing two values: the time of the event and the ball number.

That completes the decisions we need to make concerning the data structures. Here are the Pascal type definitions for these data structures:

```
type
  BallType = record
        X, Y, VelX, VelY : real
     end;
  TableType = array [0 .. 9] of BallType;
  EventType = record
        BallNum : [0 .. 9];
        Time    : real
     end;
  Queue = ^QueueType;
  QueueType = record
        Data : EventType;
        Ptr  : Queue
     end;
```

6.4 Algorithms

We'll write some of the algorithms and leave the others as exercises. To finish the algorithms, we'll have to resolve some of the questions posed earlier. Let's start with the routine that determines the time of the next event for a given ball.

TimeOfEvent

Given a particular ball (which means we know its current position and velocity), when will it next strike a rail or fall into a pocket? Suppose, for the sake of an example, that the ball is the same ball used earlier; i.e., suppose the four values are: $x = 20$, $y = 46$, $v_x = -13.6$ and $v_y = 48.7$. Since the ball is traveling to the left, it has to travel 20 inches before it hits the left rail. Since it's also moving toward the far rail, it has to travel 14 inches before it will hit it. The x component of velocity is 13.6 inches/second and the y component is 48.7 inches/second. Thus, it would travel the 20 inches in the x direction in

20/13.6 (1.47) seconds and the 14 inches in the y direction in 14/48.7 (0.29) seconds. Obviously, it will hit the far rail before it hits the left rail. The time until the next event for this ball equals 0.29 seconds. The time of the event equals the current time plus 0.29 seconds. This time and the ball number will have to be placed on the queue.

This discussion results in the following algorithm for a function called *Time-OfEvent*:

> START OF *TimeOfEvent*(*Ball*)
>
> *if* $v_x < 0$
>   *then*
>   store $-x/v_x$ *in* x*Time*
>   *else*
>   *if* $v_x > 0$
>   *then*
>   store $(\text{LENGTH} - x)\,/v_x$ *in* x*Time*
>   *else*
>   store ∞ *in* x*Time*
> *if* $v_y < 0$
>   *then*
>   store $-y/v_y$ *in* y*Time*
>   *else*
>   *if* $v_y > 0$
>   *then*
>   store $(\text{WIDTH} - y)\,/v_y$ *in* y*Time*
>   *else*
>   store ∞ *in* y*Time*
> *return the smaller of* x*Time and* y*Time*
>
> END OF *TimeOfEvent*

We're treating ∞ as a very large value. If either component of velocity is zero, the ball will never reach the corresponding rail and the other time will be smaller. When the algorithm is implemented, all we'll have to do is use a large value for ∞, perhaps `maxint` or `1e10`. Any large value will work.

Recalculate

The procedure *Recalculate* will take the current collection of balls on the table and a time and refigure where each ball will be at that time. To do this, all it will have to do is change each ball's x and y positions to their current positions plus the elapsed time times the respective velocity. In other words, for each ball we'll need to:

$$store\ x\ +\ Time\ *\ v_x\ in\ x$$
$$store\ y\ +\ Time\ *\ v_y\ in\ y$$

where $Time$ is the elasped time since the last event. This routine will also have to change the velocity for a ball that has just hit a rail. If it hits the left rail, the x component of velocity will change to a positive value; if it hits the right rail, it will change to a negative value. A similar thing can be said if it hits the near or far rail. We're not going to simulate the ball having any spin, so we can change the velocity by just reversing the sign of the correct component of velocity.

How about the parameters—what do we need to send to this routine? The array of balls on the table has to be sent (by reference, since the positions of the balls on the table are being changed). The routine will need to know the number of balls, the current time and the event in question. We can pass the time by reference and update it while we're in the procedure. A complete algorithm would look like:

```
START OF Recalculate(Balls, NumBalls, Time, Event)
Passed by value: NumBalls, Event
Passed by reference: Balls, Time

loop for i going from 0 to NumBalls − 1
    if Balls_i is not in a pocket
        then
            store Balls_i.x + (Event.Time − Time) * Balls_i.v_x in Balls_i.x
            store Balls_i.y + (Event.Time − Time) * Balls_i.v_y in Balls_i.y
store Event.BallNum in i
if Balls_i.x = 0 or Balls_i.x = LENGTH
    then
        change the sign of Balls_i.v_x
if Balls_i.y = 0 or Balls_i.y = WIDTH
    then
        change the sign of Balls_i.v_y
store Event.Time in Time

END OF Recalculate
```

This algorithm depends on being able to tell whether a ball is in a pocket or not. A Boolean-valued function, $InPocket$, will do what is needed.

InPocket

We'll leave most of this routine as an exercise but will give a few hints. Since the function will only be called at the time of an event, we'll know that one of the balls is on a rail; i.e., that either the x component of the position equals 0 or 96, or the y component of the position equals 0 or 60. If the y component equals 0 or 60, the ball can be considered to be in a pocket if the x position component is within $RADIUS$ of either end of the table or the center. In other words, for a given ball:

if $y = 0$ *or* $y = 60$
    then
        if $x \leq RADIUS$ *or*
            $LENGTH/2 - RADIUS \leq x \leq LENGTH/2 + RADIUS$ *or*
            $LENGTH - RADIUS \leq x$
        then
            return true
        else
            return false

Similarly, if the ball is on one of the end rails, it can be considered to be in a pocket if it's within $RADIUS$ of the near or far rail. We'll leave the rest of this for the exercises.

Remainder of the Algorithm

The remaining pieces (other than the routines that manipulate the queue) consist of:

- a routine that prints an introduction,

- a routine that initializes the number of balls, the initial positions and velocities, the maximum number of events to simulate, the starting time (0), and the initial number of events (also 0),

- a routine that initializes the queue (starting it off as empty and then putting the first event for each ball on it),

- a routine that displays the table in some attractive manner, and

- a routine that displays some sort of a conclusion.

The first and last of these should be very easy to write. The second is not much harder. It will require some time to get all the details written, but it isn't difficult conceptually. You probably will want to write it so that the user can decide whether the computer is to select the initial positions and velocities randomly or the user is to enter them.

The routine that initializes the queue will call a routine that enqueues the event on a priority queue; we still have to discuss this routine. It also will have to call the routine that determines the time of the event, but we wrote that routine earlier.

DisplayTable

That leaves the routine that displays the table and the balls. We'll leave this one for you, too. It can get tedious to put in all the special characters to represent the rails and pockets—especially in Standard Pascal, where we don't have access to fancy graphing features found in some Pascal compilers today— but it can be done. This book only uses Standard Pascal; if you want to use fancier output routines, you're urged to do so. It is, however, possible to draw a respectable pool table with the usual text characters. Let's look at a couple of examples of pool tables we've drawn. Figure 6.3 shows the table after selecting five balls and positioning them randomly on the table.

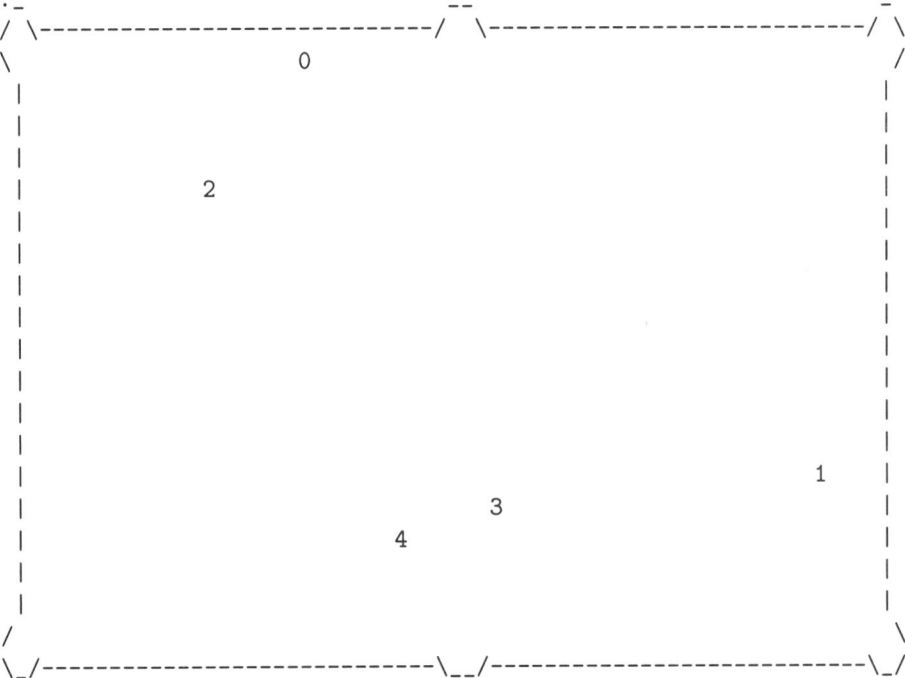

Figure 6.3 Pool Table, Initial Positions of 5 Balls

We allowed the program to simulate 10 events; figure 6.4 shows the table after 10 events. Ball number 0 has fallen in the near side pocket and ball number 4 has just bounced off the left rail.

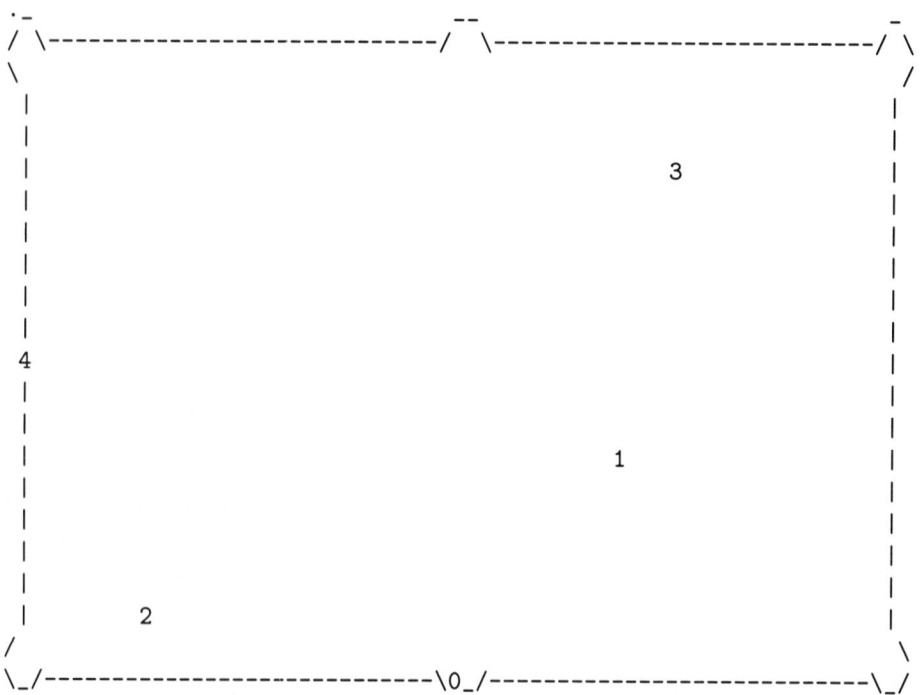

Figure 6.4 Pool Table, Positions after 10 Events

Each pool table we show on the screen is a two-dimensional array of `char`. The complete array has 24 rows and 75 columns. Notice that the pool table itself uses 21 rows and 65 columns of characters. We added some space at the top and on the left for the sake of appearance. The entire array is first filled with space characters, then the rails and pockets are drawn, and finally the position of each ball is determined.

The positions of the balls on the table are determined by taking the (x, y) `real` values, converting them to the appropriate `real` values representing where each ball is on the screen table, and then rounding them off to the nearest `integer` values. For example, if a ball has an (x, y) position of $(0, 0)$, our routine puts it in row 3 and column 10 of the array. (If you think of the normal x, y coordinate system, with the origin at the lower left, this actually flips the table so that what was the bottom of the table now is the top. If that bothers you, you can re-write the formulas that follow or imagine a coordinate system where the origin is at the upper left.) If a ball has an (x, y) position of $(96, 60)$, the routine places it in row 23 and column 74. If we let C stand for the column and R stand for the row, we obtain the two equations: $C = (2/3)x + 10$ and $R = (1/3)y + 3$. Using our earlier example of a ball at $(20, 46)$, our equations convert the 20 to 23.33 and the 46 to 18.33. These two numbers get rounded to 23 and 18, and the ball is placed in the array in row 18, column 23. The routine puts a character in the array equal to the ball number (after converting it to a character, of course). After "drawing" the rails and pockets, and placing all the balls in the array, the array is simply printed on the screen. As we said, this routine is somewhat tedious but worth the trouble to complete. We'll leave its completion for you.

It would be more efficient, of course, to be able to "erase" a ball and redraw it in another position instead of redrawing the entire table. Standard Pascal has no cursor positioning routines we can call on, but most implementations of Pascal have a procedure called `GotoXY` that positions the cursor at a particular place on the screen. If your Pascal implements `GotoXY`, you may wish to incorporate it into your program.

6.5   Implementation of Priority Queue

The only other new things to talk about are the routines that implement a priority queue. After a little thought, you'll realize that three of the four routines are not new at all. A priority queue will get initialized in the same manner as any other queue. We will be able to determine whether a priority queue is empty in the same way we determine whether any other queue is empty, and taking an element off a priority queue will be no different from removing an element from a normal queue. The remaining routine, `EnQueue`, however, is different. We don't just place the new event on the queue at the tail; we have to put the new event on the queue in order according to some key. But this also is not a new problem for us. This is just an insertion into a linked list. Here's the code for `PEnQueue`. You should compare it with the routine we wrote in chapter 4 that inserts a new element into a linked list. The `PEnQueue` stands for "Priority queue EnQueue." Be sure to make the necessary modifications to `MakeNewNode`.

```
procedure PEnQueue(var Q : Queue; Event : EventType);

{  This procedure puts an element on the priority queue Q.   }
{  It is inserted into the queue in order according to the   }
{  time that the event is to occur.                          }

var
  P, Prev : Queue;

begin
  if Q = nil
    then
      MakeNewNode(Q, Event)
    else
      begin
Prev := nil;
P := Q;
while (P^.Ptr <> nil) and (P^.Data.Time < Event.Time) do
  begin
    Prev := P;
    P := P^.Ptr
  end;
if Prev = nil
  then
    MakeNewNode(Q, Event)
  else
    MakeNewNode(Prev^.Ptr, Event)
      end
end;
```

6.6   Summary and Review

- In this chapter we took a second look at the abstract data type of a queue. Previously we had implemented queues using arrays; in this chapter we implemented queues using linked lists.

- We saw that when a data type is treated as an abstract data type, i.e., when only the basic operations of the data type are used to access the data, it is easy to change the way the data type is implemented.

- We introduced a new problem that used a queue, that of simulating balls rolling around on a pool table. We viewed this simulation as event-driven rather than time-driven, as with the bank teller problem.

6.7   Exercises

1. In chapter 3 we discussed a program that used a queue to simulate a single server. We implemented the queue in that program with arrays and records. Modify the program to implement the queue with a linked list.

2. In chapter 3, exercise 15, we suggested a modification that allowed multiple tellers and one queue. Rewrite your program to implement the queue using a linked list instead of an array.

3. In chapter 3, exercise 16, we discussed changing the problem's solution from an event-driven simulation to a time-driven simulation. In that exercise, we only suggested modifying the second loop. Now modify the entire solution to use a time-driven simulation.

4. Complete the algorithm and the code for *InPocket* discussed on page 152.

5. Finish writing the various routines for the pool table simulation program. The remaining pieces are discussed on page 152. These yet-to-be-written pieces include a routine that displays an introduction, a routine that initializes several variables as well as the initial positions of the balls, a routine that initializes the queue and a routine that displays a conclusion.

   You will also need to complete the details on the routine that displays the table, and `MakeNewNode` which is called by `PEnQueue`.

   Add the routines for *InitQueue*, *Dequeue*, *PEnQueue*, *EmptyQueue*; write the necessary code and turn the entire package into a running program.

6. Rewrite the single-server simulation so that the bank customers are placed in the queue according to their service times; i.e., the queue is a priority queue. In this case, the customers will have to be assigned their service times when they enter the bank, rather than when they are dequeued.

   Run the priority simulation and the original simulation with the same inputs. How do the results compare? Can you draw any conclusions?

Chapter 7

Binary Search Trees

> Have a place for everything and
> keep the thing somewhere else.
> This is not advice; it is merely custom.
> — Mark Twain

7.1   Overview of the Chapter

This chapter introduces the concepts of a binary tree. We'll see how a binary tree can be used to provide an efficient way of storing data that is easy to add to, delete from, and search. An important type of tree that is frequently used for storing and retrieving data is a "binary search tree." We'll discuss algorithms and code for routines which insert elements into, delete elements from, traverse, and search a binary search tree. In the next chapter we'll discuss binary trees that are not binary search trees.

7.2   Introduction

The purpose of this chapter is to introduce the binary search tree structure. A binary search tree combines the advantage of dynamic storage allocation inherent in a linked list with the "always in order" property of a sorted array, thus providing the ability to use a binary search. However, searching a linked list for a particular element is slow since you always have to start at the head of the list. A sorted array is often a poor way to hold data since the size of the array needs to be chosen in advance. Additionally, when new elements are added to the array, the existing elements have to be moved down to keep the array in some order. A binary tree has the advantages of both the linked list and sorted array but neither of these disadvantages.

There are many types of trees studied in computer science, such as ternary trees, 2-3 trees, B-trees, etc. We'll only be concerned with binary search trees in this chapter. We'll look at other kinds of binary trees in the next chapter, and we'll look at non-binary trees in chapter 9. We'll not formally define a tree at this point, but informally, a tree is a collection of nodes and pointers to nodes. There is a "root" pointer that points to the first node. Each node contains data and pointers to additional nodes. If each node contains one item of data and two pointers, it's a binary tree. A graph theoretic definition of a tree is in chapter 11, see page 326.

7.3   Statement of the Problem

To illustrate and introduce the nature of a binary tree, we'll solve a data management problem. Since we will be more interested in the techniques than in the problem itself, we'll keep the problem relatively simple. The techniques and the data structure used for the solution of this problem can be used for more complicated problems.

The problem can be stated as follows:

> Write a program that will maintain a database of names. The program should allow us to see the names in alphabetical order, add new names, delete names, search for a particular name and save the database to a text file.

We essentially encountered and solved this problem in chapter 4 when we worked on the dictionary file for a spelling checker program. Because we used a linked list for our solution in chapter 4, the solution can be improved upon. To search the linked list for a particular word, we had to do a linear search through the entire list, starting at the head of the list.

We saw in chapter 2 that an ordered array can be searched with a binary search, and we showed that a binary search is much faster than a linear search. However, you cannot search a linked list with a binary search; you have to start at the head of the list. So, why not use an array? There are two compelling reasons for not choosing an array to hold the words.

First, whenever a new word is added to the array that is to be kept in order, all the words below the place where the new word is to be added have to be moved down to make room for it. In real world problems, these data consist of much more than just words. If an array were used to hold the data, a great deal of time would be spent in moving these data around.

Second, arrays are static. It is necessary to know in advance how much space to set aside for the words. Dynamic allocation of space is a more efficient method than static allocation. We want to be able to add words as needed, and we don't want to have to decide ahead of time how many words are finally going to be stored in the database.

7.4   Binary Trees

All of this leads us to a new data structure, the binary tree. We've seen the term "binary tree" before in chapter 2 when we were working on the heap sort algorithm. In chapter 2 we viewed the array as a binary tree, but an array itself is a linear structure and not a tree at all. Now that we know how to work with pointers, we can construct real binary trees. Figure 7.1 contains a picture of a simple binary tree.

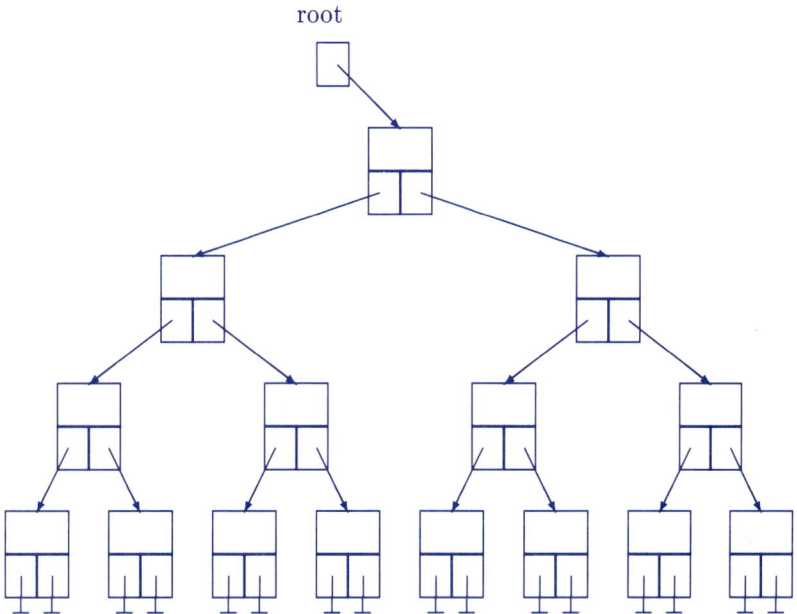

Figure 7.1 A Binary Tree

A binary tree is a collection of "nodes" and "pointers." Every node has two pointers: a "left pointer" and a "right pointer." The non-nil pointers point to other nodes in the tree. There is one special pointer, called the "root," which is not part of a node but just a pointer on its own. If you start at the root and follow either the left pointer or the right pointer at each node, you will eventually come to a nil pointer. If the entire tree is empty, the root is a nil pointer.

It's interesting that a binary tree can be defined recursively. An empty tree is the basis case. In a nonempty binary tree, the root is a pointer to a node that has two pointers, each of which is another (possibly empty) binary tree. Consider this recursive definition:

A binary tree is either:

    1. a nil pointer or

    2. a pointer to a record, two of whose fields are binary trees.

Each node of a binary tree typically contains, in addition to the two pointers, some sort of data. These data can be as simple as a number or string, or something more complicated, such as a record with many fields.

Binary trees are called "binary trees" because each node has two pointers. There are other kinds of trees (ternary trees, B-trees, etc.) which we will not discuss, and for the remainder of this chapter we'll just use "trees" to refer to binary trees.

Tree Notation

The notation used for a tree and its parts comes from real trees and from "family trees." We introduced some of this notation in chapter 2 but it won't hurt to go over it again. For example, if both pointers in a node are `nil`, the node is called a "leaf." The two nodes pointed at by a given node will be called the "children" of the node and the node pointing at a given node will be the "parent" node. Every node will have a parent except one: the node pointed at by the root. We'll call this node "the root node." If the left pointer in a node is not the `nil` pointer, the node it's pointing at is called its "left child." Similarly, a non-`nil` right pointer points at a "right child." The children of a node and the children of these children, etc., are called the *descendants* of the node.

If you start with any node and consider that node and all its descendants, this collection is called a *subtree* of the entire tree. The node you start with is the *root node* of the subtree. The entire tree is considered a subtree of itself.

Additional Notation

Before we continue with the solution to the problem, let's briefly introduce a few more terms that are used in connection with trees.

The *level* of any node in a tree is the number of pointers you have to follow to get to that node. The level of the root node is 1, the children, if any, of the root node have level 2, etc.

The *height* of a tree is the largest number of levels it contains. It might seem contrary to your intuition, but we'll say that a tree with a single node has height 1. The tree in figure 7.1 has height 4.

When a tree has all its leaves on its greatest level, and when all the nodes on lower levels have two non-`nil` pointers, then the tree is *full*. The tree in figure 7.1 is full. The number of nodes in a full tree is always one less than a power of two.

The term *complete* is also used to discuss binary trees, although there is some disagreement among authors as to its definition. The most commonly used definition says that a complete tree has all its leaves on the greatest level or greatest two levels, and the nodes on the greatest level are as far to the left as possible.

The height of a binary tree is related to the number of nodes in the tree. It's easy to see that a tree with N nodes can have a maximum height of N when the tree is essentially a linked list of nodes (see the tree on page 171). It's not much harder to determine the minimum height possible for a tree. The tree in figure 7.1 has 15 nodes which is as many nodes as possible for a tree with height 4; adding one more node to the tree would require putting the new node on level five.

A little work will demonstrate that the maximum number of nodes possible in a tree with five levels is 31 and that the maximum number of nodes possible in a tree with six levels is 63. Turning these around, it can be shown that the minimum height for a tree with N nodes is

$$\lceil \log_2(N + 1) \rceil$$

where $\lceil \ldots \rceil$ is the ceiling function.

A *balanced* tree is a tree with its minimum height. That is, a tree with N nodes whose height is $\lceil \log_2(N + 1) \rceil$ is considered balanced. Such trees are also known as *height-balanced* trees. A tree with 100 nodes could have a height ranging from a minimum of 7 to a maximum of 100. Since we are going to be using trees for searching, it is clearly an advantage to have a tree near its minimum height whenever possible. That is, balanced trees can be searched faster than trees that are not balanced.

The Fundamental Property of a Binary Search Tree

We will assume that the trees we work on will have a "key" field that keeps them in order. While the data part of the node might contain a number of different fields with different sorts of data, there will always be one field containing the key. Then for every node in the entire tree, including the root node, every key field in the right subtree will contain data greater than the key field in the given node. Similarly, every key field in the left subtree will contain data smaller than the key in the given node. A tree that satisfies this property is called a *binary search tree*. We will call this property *the fundamental property of a binary search tree*. Notice that this scheme does not allow two nodes with the same key.

For the remainder of this chapter, when we use the terms "tree" or "binary tree," we'll mean "binary search tree."

From now on we'll simplify the trees we work with. Rather than worry about the data portion containing different fields which have various sorts of data, we'll just let the data portion contain first names. The algorithms we develop will be easy to modify in the more general case where the nodes contain several fields, one of which is the key field.

7.5 Searching a Tree

Let's write an algorithm for a tree search. We will have a particular value, the *Object*, that we want to locate in the tree. The routine should determine whether or not the *Object* is in the tree. The only thing that will be returned is a Boolean value so we can write the routine as a function. Here's a high-level algorithm:

> *Look at the root node. If it is a **nil** pointer, return false. If the Object is there, return true. Otherwise, Search either the left subtree or the right subtree depending on whether the Object is smaller or larger than the data in the root node.*

This strategy will work because of the fact that all the key fields in the left subtree are smaller than the key in the root node of the subtree which, in turn, is smaller than all the key fields in the right subtree. That is, it works because of the fundamental property.

Notice that the above search routine is recursive; the search routine calls itself. Many of our algorithms that deal with trees will be recursive. It turns out that several of them can be written either iteratively or recursively. Those that can be written both ways will be written recursively in the body of the text, and we'll leave the iterative versions for the exercises.

Let's look at a lower-level algorithm. We'll call the function *InTree* so we can refer to the function as a Boolean value. The algorithm becomes:

START OF InTree(Root, Object)

if Root = nil
    then
        return false
    else
        if Object = Root^.Data
            then
                return true
            else
                if Object < Root^.Data
                    then
                        return InTree(Root^.Left, Object)
                    else
                        return InTree(Root^.Right, Object)

END OF InTree

We'll implement this algorithm in Pascal in a few pages. Before we do, we want to look at the problems of inserting a new node into a tree, traversing a tree, saving a tree in a file and deleting a node from a tree.

7.6   Inserting a Node into a Tree

Consider the tree in figure 7.2. First, notice that we have simplified the figure somewhat. In figure 7.1, we drew separate boxes for the pointers. In this, and in subsequent figures, we'll leave these boxes off. When a pointer is the `nil` pointer, we'll just not draw it. Remember that every node has two pointers; if no pointer is shown, it's `nil`.

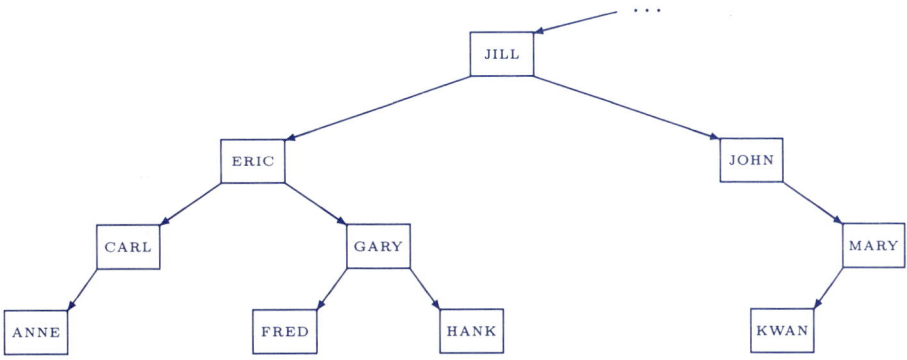

Figure 7.2 Ready to Insert `FRAN`

Suppose you wanted to insert the name `FRAN` into this tree. Where would you put it? Remember that the fundamental property of a binary search tree must be retained.

It might be tempting to try to insert this name *between* the nodes containing `ERIC` and `GARY`, and, in this case, the resulting tree would still satisfy the fundamental property. However, consider the tree in figure 7.3.

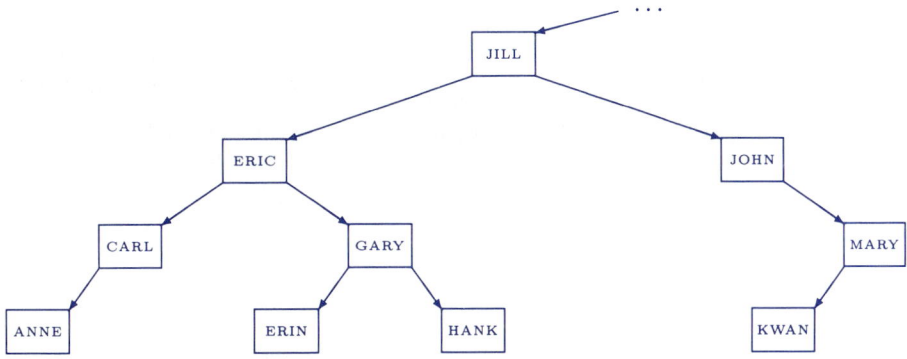

Figure 7.3 Ready to Insert `FRAN`

This tree is identical to the tree in figure 7.2 except for the node on the bottom level which contains `ERIN` instead of `FRED`. Now, if you put `FRAN` between `ERIC` and `GARY`, the resulting tree no longer satisfies the fundamental property. The point is, you cannot just find two nodes on either side of the key to be inserted and put the new node in between them. The only way you can tell the difference between the two trees in the example is to follow pointers until you come to a `nil` pointer. That is, you cannot insert a new node between two existing nodes unless you follow pointers to the bottom of the tree to make sure the insertion at that point would be allowed. Even then, the decision as to where the insertion should be done is not simple. There might be several places along the way where, alphabetically at least, the new node could fit. Moreover, we have not even considered what to do with the pointers in the new node.

Now, consider the tree in figure 7.4. Here we have inserted `FRAN` to the right of `ERIN` and the fundamental property is satisfied.

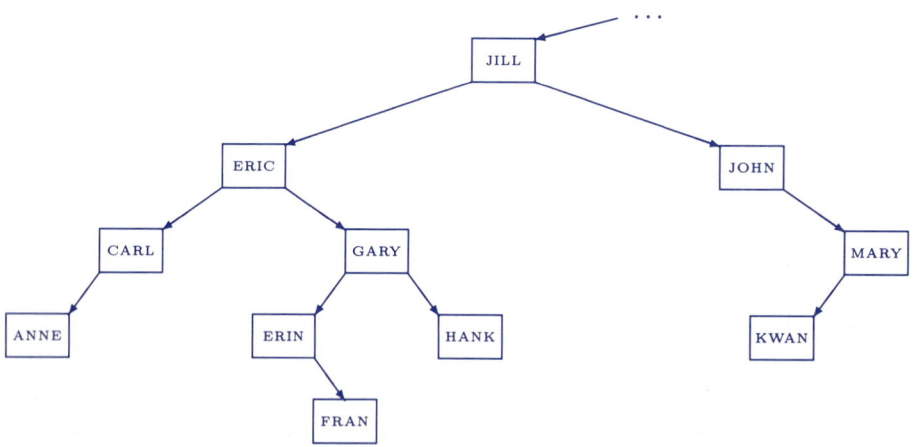

Figure 7.4 After Inserting `FRAN`

The point of all this is that you cannot tell where to insert a new name into the tree until you encounter a `nil` pointer, and it is *always* possible to insert the new node as a new leaf of the tree at that location.

If you follow pointers—following the left pointer if the name to be inserted comes before the name in the current node and following the right pointer if the new name is larger than the name in the current node—you will always be able to insert the new node at the point where you encounter a `nil` pointer. Thus, to insert a new name in the tree, you:

> *Start at the root and follow pointers to the left or the right depending on whether the name to be inserted is smaller or larger than the name in the current node until you find a nil pointer. When you get to a nil pointer, insert the new name at that point.*

A low-level recursive algorithm for this procedure would be:

```
START OF Insert(Root, Name)
Passed by value: Name
Passed by reference: Root

If Root = nil
    then
        insert Name at this point
    else
        if Name < Root^.Data
            then
                call Insert(Root^.Left, Name)
            else
                call Insert(Root^.Right, Name)

END OF Insert
```

Every time *Insert* is called, it is sent the root of the subtree where the name is to be inserted. These calls continue until *Insert* is called with a `nil` pointer. The *Name* is inserted at that point. The only thing that's left is to actually insert the new name into the tree and make the changes to the pointers. Since *Root is* the pointer that needs to be changed (it's passed by reference), all we have to do is call *Allocate* to get a new node, put the name in the new node, and set the two pointers in this node to `nil`. The completed algorithm is:

```
START OF Insert(Root, Name)
Passed by value: Name
Passed by reference: Root
Precondition: Name is not present in the tree

If Root = nil
    then
        call Allocate(Root)
        store Name in Root^.Data
        store nil in Root^.Left
        store nil in Root^.Right
    else
        if Name < Root^.Data
            then
                call Insert(Root^.Left, Name)
            else
                call Insert(Root^.Right, Name)

END OF Insert
```

We have called the parameter *Root*. Don't let the name confuse you. The original tree's root pointer is sent in the original call, but in subsequent calls, *Root* will be a pointer in a node. Since the parameter is passed by reference, when *Root* is eventually changed, the actual pointer that needs to be changed is the one that's changed.

Precondition for *Insert* Algorithm

You should note that this algorithm assumes, as a precondition, that the name being inserted is not already in the tree. The calling routine has, presumably, checked to make sure that this precondition is satisfied. You might not feel that this is a good way to do it since the calling routine will then have to first call *InTree* to determine whether or not the name is already in the tree. That means the tree will get searched twice: once in *InTree* and once in *Insert*. The algorithm could be modified to return a flag, "*Successful*," and have the flag set to true if the insertion took place and set to false if the name is already on the tree. The last *if ... then ... else* would have to be modified to include a check for equality. That's how we wrote the linked list *Insert* routine in chapter 4. We'll leave the details for an exercise.

7.7   Tree Traversal

Now that we can search the tree for a name and insert a new name into a tree, it would seem natural to look at deleting a node from a tree. Since deletion is considerably harder than insertion, let's wait a bit before we tackle it. Instead, let's look at the questions of traversing a tree and saving the tree in a file.

Since we want to be able to write the tree to a file and read it back from the file, we see that we need to be able to "look" or "visit" all the nodes in the tree. This is known as *tree traversal*.

Inorder Traversal

Our first goal was to maintain a list of names in alphabetical order; so let's start by seeing how to display the list of names in alphabetical order. This is known as *inorder traversal*.

To traverse a tree in inorder, you first traverse the left subtree, visit the root node and then traverse the right subtree. How do you traverse the left subtree? Recursively, of course. The algorithm is deceptively simple. Let's agree that "visiting" the root node just means displaying the name stored there. Here's the algorithm:

START OF InOrder(Root)
Passed by value: Root, a binary search tree

if Root ≠ nil
    then
        call InOrder(Root^.Left)
        display Root^.Data
        call InOrder(Root^.Right)

END OF InOrder

The above routine is obviously recursive and therefore must have a non-recursive case. Where is the non-recursive case? It occurs when a `nil` pointer is reached. What do you want to do when you get to a nil pointer? Nothing. What does the above algorithm do when a `nil` pointer is reached? Nothing! The non-recursive case is hidden in the *if ... then* by not having an *else* part.

Let's trace the algorithm on a very simple tree. Consider the tree in figure 7.5.

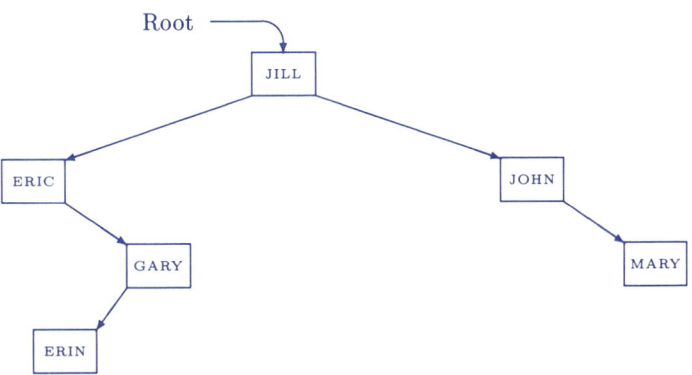

Figure 7.5 A Simple Tree

We start by passing *InOrder* a pointer to the tree itself. Since this pointer is non-`nil`, the routine calls itself, passing a pointer to the node containing **ERIC**. Since this pointer is non-`nil`, it calls itself, passing the left pointer of the node containing **ERIC**. But since this pointer is `nil`, the routine does nothing. Then the contents of the node containing **ERIC** are displayed. (That is, **ERIC** is displayed.) *InOrder* is called and passed the right pointer of the node containing **ERIC**. This pointer is non-`nil` and so before **GARY** can be displayed, a call is made to *InOrder* passing the left pointer of the node containing **GARY**. This pointer is non-`nil` so the routine recurses once more, passing the (nil) left pointer of the node containing **ERIN**, which causes nothing to happen. Then **ERIN** is displayed. Then the (nil) right pointer of **ERIN** is passed to *InOrder* which does nothing. Now `GARY` is displayed. Next, the right pointer of `GARY` is passed. Since this pointer is `nil`, nothing happens. Now the name stored in the original node, `JILL`, is displayed.

The original call to *InOrder* is not yet done; the right pointer of the node containing `JILL` is now passed to *InOrder*. Since this pointer is non-`nil`, the left pointer in the node at which it's pointing (which is `nil`) is passed, and nothing happens. The name stored there, `JOHN`, is displayed and then the right pointer of the node containing `JOHN` is passed. Since both of the pointers in the node containing `MARY` are `nil`, only the `MARY` gets displayed. Finally all of the calls are completed and the original call to *InOrder* is finished.

If you look back at what was displayed in the above paragraph, you'll see that the names were displayed in the order:

```
ERIC  ERIN  GARY  JILL  JOHN  MARY
```

as desired. An inorder traversal of a tree which satisfies the fundamental property causes the elements of the tree to be visited in ascending order of the key fields.

Writing the Tree to a File

Now, suppose we replace the "*display Root^.Data*" in the above algorithm with "*write Root^.Data to the file.*" If the calling routine took care of the details of the file for writing, and we included the file as a parameter, then we would have a routine which would write the entire tree to a file. Another routine would then be needed to read the names from the file and insert them into the tree but that routine would be trivial to write.

Are we done then with this part of the solution? Can we go on to the problem of deleting a node? *No!* What we have is not acceptable!

Consider what the tree would look like after reading a file created by the routine just discussed. That is, suppose we wrote the above routine, created a textfile and wrote the names into the file. If we read the file and insert the names back into a tree, the tree will look like figure 7.6.

This is a tree all right, but a terrible tree. Even if we start off with a nicely balanced tree like that in figure 7.1, the resulting tree will be nothing more than a linked list with some `nil` left pointers. A traversal of this tree would take even longer than a traversal of a linked list since we would have to compare the left pointers to `nil` over and over. Clearly this is not acceptable. We cannot use a routine which turns nicely balanced trees into linked lists.

Preorder Traversal

The solution to this problem is a different way of traversing a tree, known as *preorder traversal*. Rather than traversing the left subtree before visiting the

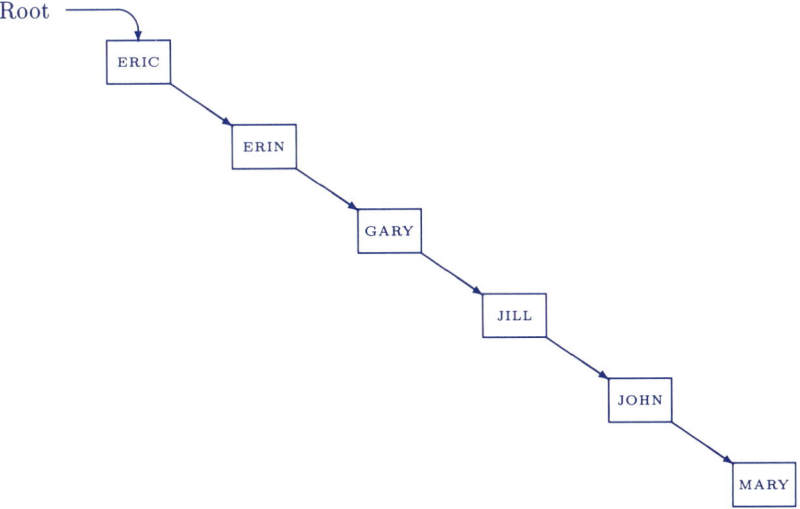

Figure 7.6 A Terrible Tree

root node, we simply visit the root node and then traverse the left and right subtrees, in that order. As an algorithm, we would have:

START OF PreOrder(Root)
Passed by value: Root, a pointer to a node of a tree.

if Root ≠ nil
    then
        display Root^.Data
        call PreOrder(Root^.Left)
        call PreOrder(Root^.Right)

END OF PreOrder

If you trace this algorithm, using the tree in figure 7.5, you'll see that the nodes are visited in the order:

```
JILL   ERIC   GARY   ERIN   JOHN   MARY
```

And, as you should verify, if the nodes are read from a file in that order and inserted into a tree, the same tree as that in figure 7.5 will be created.

To summarize, if you intend to save the tree in a file, do *not* use an inorder traversal to write the file. Instead, use a preorder traversal. Then, when you read the file and recreate a tree by inserting the nodes one by one from the file, the tree created will be the same as the tree you had when the file was written.

Postorder Traversal

There is a third way of traversing a tree that has probably occurred to you: *postorder traversal*. First, traverse the left subtree, then the right subtree and then visit the root. We'll leave the algorithm for postorder traversal for the exercises.

You might guess from the names that inorder, preorder and postorder traversals are somehow related to the infix, prefix and postfix methods of writing arithmetic expressions. They are indeed related, and we'll discuss this in the next chapter.

7.8   Deleting a Node from a Tree

Let's turn now to the reverse problem of inserting a new name: deleting a node from a binary tree. While it's always possible to insert a new name as a leaf, deletion is not nearly as easy. The node being deleted might be a leaf, in which case the deletion is easy, or the node might be somewhere in the middle of the tree, in which case the deletion has to be done with care. In general, we have three cases, which we'll consider separately:

- deleting a leaf,

- deleting a node with one `nil` pointer,

- deleting a node with two non-`nil` pointers.

Deleting a Leaf

Consider the tree in figure 7.7. Suppose we want to delete the node containing `FRED`. Since `FRED` is a leaf, all we have to do to delete it is to change the pointer in the node pointing to `FRED` (the left pointer in `GARY`) to `nil` and `FRED` will disappear. We will also want to return the memory used by `FRED` to the operating system so a call to *Deallocate* will have to be made.

Deleting a Node with One `nil` Pointer

Consider figure 7.7 again. This time, suppose we want to delete the node containing `JOHN`. `JOHN` is not a leaf, but because its left pointer is `nil`, deleting `JOHN` is simple. Change the right pointer of `JOHN`'s parent to point at the node currently pointed at by `JOHN`'s right pointer. That is, change `JILL`'s right pointer to point at `MARY`.

These two cases (deleting a leaf and deleting a node with one `nil` pointer) can be combined. If the node to be deleted has at least one nil pointer, modify the pointer pointing to this node by making it equal to the node's *other* pointer. This will be easier to say in an algorithm. Suppose that *Root* is the pointer that points at the node to be deleted. Also suppose that we know one of the pointers in the node pointed at by *Root* is `nil`. We can delete the node pointed

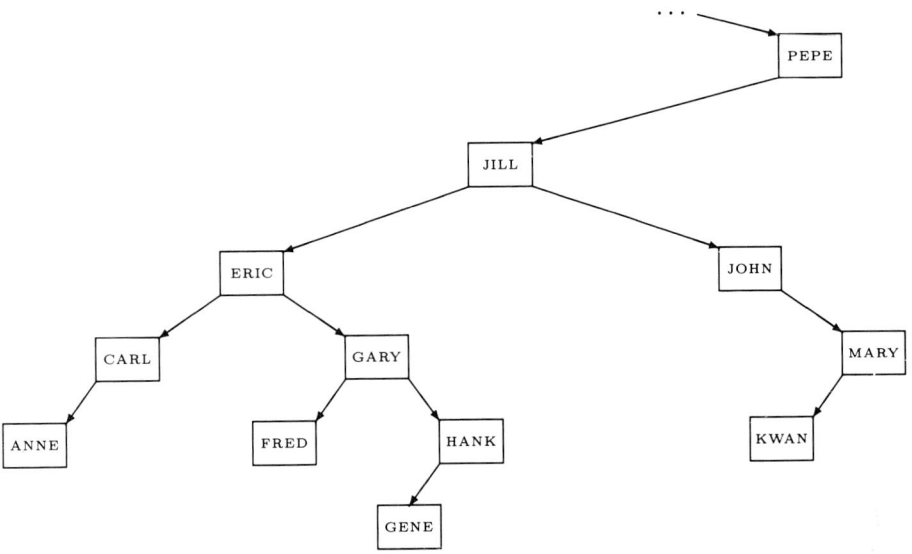

Figure 7.7 Before Deleting FRED or JOHN

at by *Root* by simply changing the pointer to point at the appropriate child. That is, by:

if Root^.Left = nil
    then
        store Root^.Right in Root
    else
        if Root^.Right = nil
            then
                store Root^.Left in Root
call Deallocate(Root)

There is a problem with this. We cannot deallocate *Root* after reassigning it to one of its pointers, and we cannot deallocate it before we reassign it since we need to have access to the pointers. The solution is to use a temporary pointer, say *OldRoot*, and store the pointer to the node to be deallocated in this variable. The case where the node being deleted has one **nil** pointer becomes:

store Root in OldRoot
if Root^.Left = nil
    then
        store Root^.Right in Root
    else
        if Root^.Right = nil
            then
                store Root^.Left in Root
call Deallocate(OldRoot)

That takes care of the easy cases. Be sure you understand this part before you go on.

Deleting a Node with Two Non-nil Pointers

We turn now to the hard case: deleting a node that has two non-**nil** pointers. Before we can write an algorithm, we must figure out how to accomplish what we need to accomplish. Let's look at the tree from figure 7.7 again.

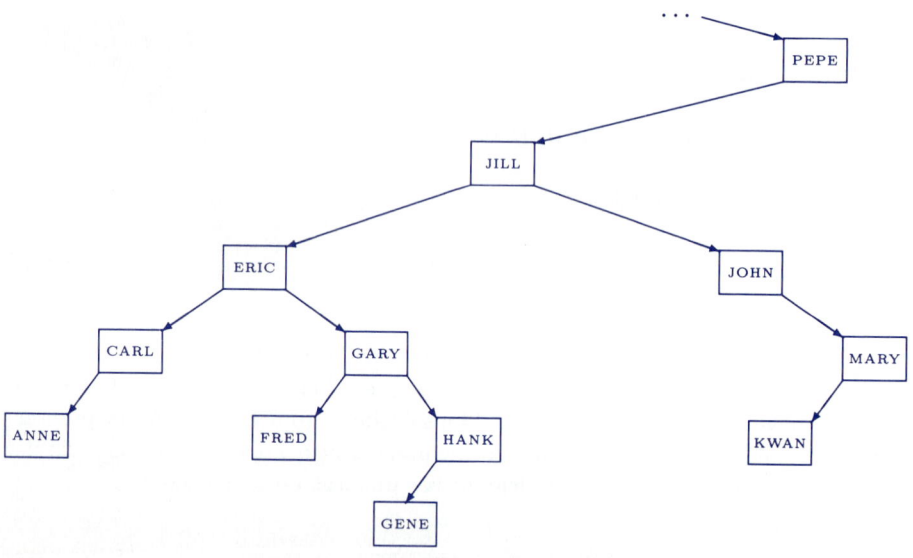

Figure 7.8 Before Deleting JILL

Suppose we want to delete the node containing JILL. Both of the pointers in this node are non-**nil**. We want to avoid moving data in the nodes, if possible, and would like to accomplish it by just changing pointers.

Perhaps the easiest solution is to find another node that can replace the node being deleted. In figure 7.8, which name comes just before JILL? In other words, which name is the inorder predecessor of JILL? The inorder predecessor of JILL is HANK. Since HANK doesn't have a right child, if we can somehow put HANK in the place of JILL, the tree will still satisfy the fundamental property. We could move HANK to the node containing JILL but can accomplish the same thing by just changing pointers. Consider what happens if we:

1. make HANK's right pointer point to JOHN,

2. make GARY's right pointer point to GENE,

3. make HANK's left pointer point to ERIC, and

4. make PEPE's left pointer point to HANK.

And then we deallocate the node containing JILL. In figure 7.9, we show the tree with the nodes in the same place as before, but the old pointers are eliminated and the new pointers are darker.

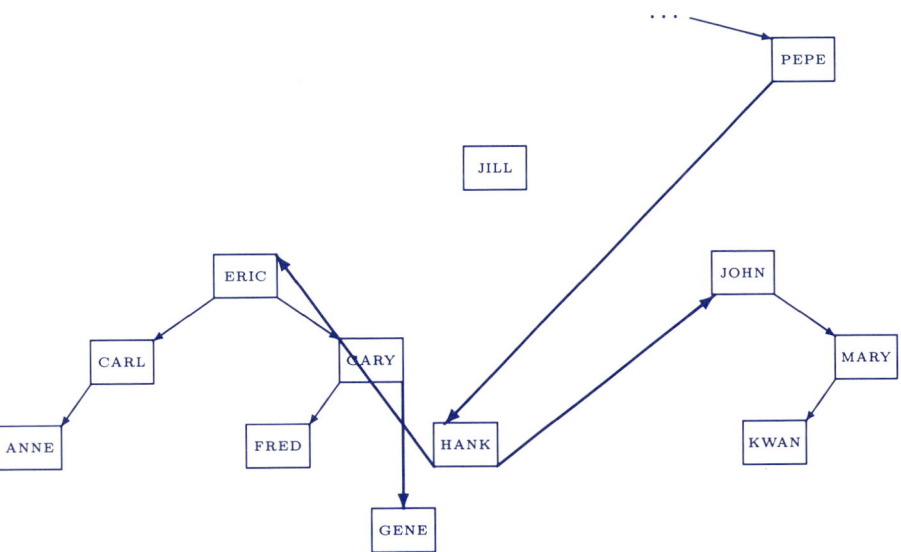

Figure 7.9 After Deleting JILL

In figure 7.10, we show the same tree but with the nodes and pointers drawn normally. Notice that we could have used the inorder successor rather than the inorder predecessor; the choice is arbitrary since both of the pointers in JILL are non-nil.

Now that we have an idea of how to accomplish what we want, we have to turn our solution into an algorithm. Assume that we have been able to find the inorder predecessor of the node we want to delete, and suppose that we have a

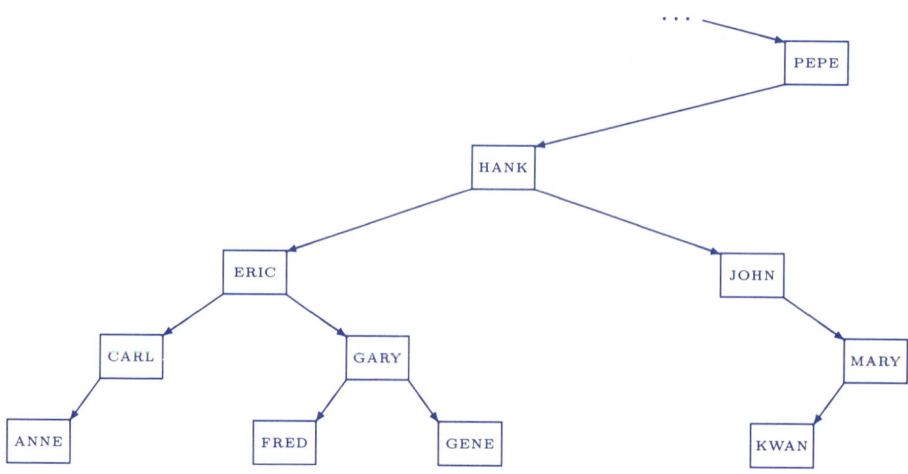

Figure 7.10 After Deleting JILL

pointer pointing at this node, say *Temp*. We need to change the right pointer in the parent node of this node; so assume we have a pointer, *Parent*, pointing at the parent of *Temp*. We also have to change the pointer pointing to the node being deleted, *Root*. With these pointers available, what we did above was:

1. store $Root^\wedge.Right$ in $Temp^\wedge.Right$,

2. store $Temp^\wedge.Left$ in $Parent^\wedge.Right$,

3. store $Root^\wedge.Left$ in $Temp^\wedge.Left$, and

4. store *Temp* in *Root*.

There is still a situation to consider. In figure 7.8 we show the inorder predecessor, HANK, to be several nodes to the right of the left child of the node being deleted, ERIC. That doesn't have to be the case. It could turn out that the right pointer of the left child of the node being deleted is nil. In this case, the left child itself is the inorder predecessor of the node being deleted, and we don't have to go "down to the right" to find it. To be able to tell if this is the case, we start *Parent* off at nil and use a *loop while* to follow right pointers until we get to a nil right pointer. If we don't have to go anywhere to find one, *Parent* will still be nil and we can use that fact to tell us that we didn't go anywhere. In this case, steps 2 and 3 in the above list are not needed. (If you don't see the importance of this, start all over and assume you want to delete the node containing ERIC instead of the node containing JILL.)

Here is the complete algorithm:

```
START OF Delete(Root, Name)
Passed by value: Name.
Passed by reference: Root.
Precondition: The Name is in the tree.

if Name < Root^.Data
    then
        call Delete(Root^.Left, Name)
    else
        if Name > Root^.Data
            then
                call Delete(Root^.Right, Name)
            else
                store Root in OldRoot
                if Root^.Left = nil
                    then
                        store Root^.Right in Root
                    else
                        if Root^.Right = nil
                            then
                                store Root^.Left in Root
                            else
                                store nil in Parent
                                store Root^.Left in Temp
                                loop while Temp^.Right ≠ nil
                                    store Temp in Parent
                                    store Temp^.Right in Temp
                                store Root^.Right in Temp^.Right
                                if Parent ≠ nil
                                    then
                                        store Temp^.Left in Parent^.Right
                                        store Root^.Left in Temp^.Left
                                store Temp in Root
                call Deallocate(OldRoot)

END OF Delete
```

Be careful to notice that the order of steps is very important. We use *Root^.Left* and *Root^.Right* and must be sure we don't change *Root* until we have moved these two pointers.

It should be pointed out again that the algorithm works because we are passing *the* pointer to the node being deleted, not just a pointer to the node; *Root* is passed by reference. Recursion makes the algorithm straightforward; an iterative version is not as easy to follow.

Precondition for *Delete* Algorithm

As we saw when we worked on *Insert*, the precondition can be a problem. We have to first call *InTree* to make sure the name is in the tree and call this routine only after we're sure the name is there. This would mean the tree gets searched twice. A better way would be to modify *Delete* by adding a Boolean variable parameter, *Successful*, and use it to determine whether or not the name was actually deleted. If this change is made, there are some other changes that will have to be made in the algorithm. We'll leave the details for the exercises.

7.9   Balancing a Tree

A harder problem is taking a tree that is misshapen and turning it into a balanced tree. It should be clear that a balanced search tree is much more efficient than one that is way out of balance, as is the tree in figure 7.6. After inserting and deleting nodes over a period of time, it is possible for a tree to get very unbalanced. There is no "easy" way to balance an unbalanced tree. By "easy," we mean with an order of magnitude that is similar to that of the other algorithms.

AVL Trees

One way to handle the problem is to modify the *Insert* algorithm so that the tree is balanced before and after the insertion. This is not nearly as easy to accomplish as the insertion routine we wrote. Furthermore, the delete algorithm would also have to be modified to keep the tree balanced. That algorithm would also be considerably more complicated. In the real world, when search trees are maintained and when it is important that the search of the tree be as efficient as possible, the extra work required to develop the more complicated algorithms might be worth the effort.

A class of trees that use algorithms for *Insert* and *Delete* that keep the tree nearly balanced at all times are known as *AVL trees* (named for the inventors Adel'son-Vel'skiĭ and Landis). These trees add an extra field to each node that keeps track of how nearly balanced the tree is. Typically, this field, called the *balance* of the tree, would contain the difference between the heights of the left subtree and the right subtree. If the tree is balanced, the balance of each node would be one of the three values -1, 0 or 1; e.g., if the balance is -1, then the left subtree of this tree has a height 1 smaller than the balance of the right subtree. As nodes are inserted and deleted from the tree, the balance field is examined and nodes are "rotated" from one subtree to another to keep the balances equal to -1, 0 or 1. These algorithms are non-trivial and, especially in the case of *Delete*, more complicated than we wish to deal with in this text.

2-3 Trees and B-trees

Another solution to the problem of non-balanced trees is the notion of a *2-3 tree*, which leads to a more complicated sort of tree, a *B-tree*. 2-3 trees and B-trees are discussed in chapter 9.

7.10   Count-balanced Trees

It is also possible to write a "balance" routine, a routine that takes a binary tree and balances it. Let's examine how such a routine might be written.

To begin with, we need to examine the notion of balance more carefully. We said earlier that a tree is balanced if it has minimum height. Since the minimum height for a tree with N nodes is

$$\lceil \log_2(N+1) \rceil,$$

a balanced tree was defined as a tree whose height is $\lceil \log_2(N+1) \rceil$.

An alternate definition of "balanced" might be: A tree is balanced if the number of nodes in every left subtree differs by at most one from the number of nodes in the corresponding right subtree. We'll call this notion *count-balanced*.

If the number of nodes in the left and right subtrees of a tree differs at most by one, then the tree seems "balanced." If a tree cannot be made shorter, i.e., it has minimum height, then it also seems "balanced." Our intuition tells us that these two definitions are similar, but are they equivalent? We'll delay a comparison of the two definitions until after we've discussed the second definition in more detail.

The second definition leads us to an elegant algorithm to balance a tree. Suppose that a tree's left subtree contains seven nodes and the right subtree contains three; the tree is out of balance according to our definition. To bring it into balance, we would like both subtrees to contain five nodes. We could accomplish this by moving two nodes from the left subtree to the right. But, of course, we cannot just move any two nodes from one subtree to another without destroying the nature of the tree. That is, we must be careful to preserve the fundamental property of a binary search tree.

Rather than trying to move two nodes from one subtree to another, let's see how we might move just one node. Suppose we can locate the "largest" element in the left subtree. If we can move the root of the tree into the right subtree—making it the smallest element in the right subtree—and take the largest element of the left subtree and make it the new root of the original tree, then the left subtree will have one fewer node, the right subtree will have one more node, and the fundamental property of the entire tree will be preserved. We'll call this a "right-shift."

In other words, a right-shift on a binary search tree will:

- locate the largest element in the left subtree,

- move the root of the tree into the right subtree, making it the smallest element of the right subtree, and

- move the largest element of the left subtree to the root.

The "largest" node in the left subtree is the inorder predecessor of the root node. After one right-shift, the old root node will be in the right subtree, and the inorder predecessor will be the new root. Surely a picture will help. Consider figure 7.11.

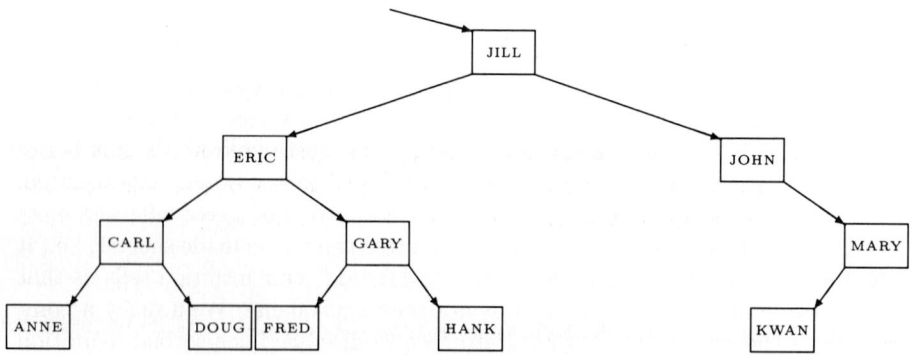

Figure 7.11 Before First Right-shift

The root node contains `Jill` and the largest element in the left subtree is the node containing `Hank`. After one right-shift, the tree will look like the tree in figure 7.12.

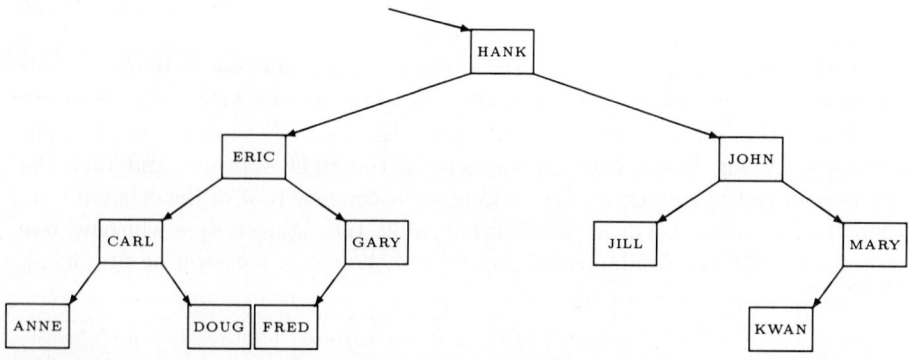

Figure 7.12 After First Right-shift

We wanted to move two elements from the left subtree to the right subtree. After another right-shift, the tree will look like the tree in figure 7.13.

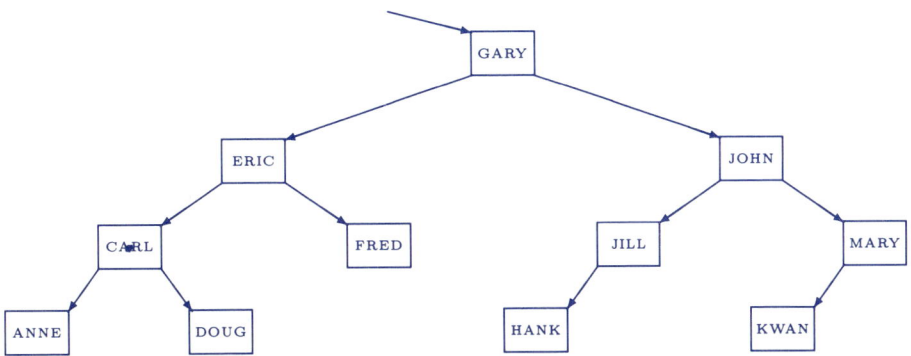

Figure 7.13 After Second Right-shift

Now the two subtrees have the same number of nodes: five. Is the tree balanced? No, not according to definition of count-balanced. The left subtree of `Eric` contains three nodes while the right subtree contains only one. We need to apply our routine to the subtree at `Eric`.

It's crucial you understand that in order for this process to work, it must be applied to the two subtrees, (and all their children) too; the procedure is recursive. Once we have finished with the root, we have to apply the same process to the left and right subtrees, continuing until we get to the leaves of the tree. After applying the balance routine to all the non-leaf nodes, the tree will look like the tree in figure 7.14.

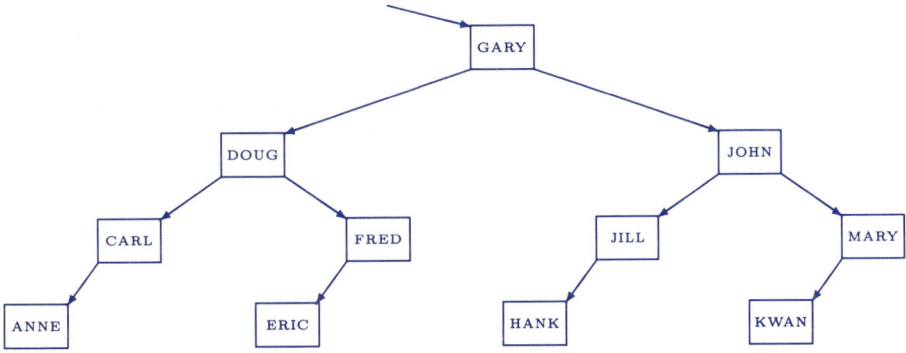

Figure 7.14 After Count-balancing the Entire Tree

Here's the algorithm for what we have developed:

```
START OF Balance(Root)
Passed by reference: A tree, Root

if Root ≠ nil
    then
        store the number of nodes in Root^.Left in LeftNum
        store the number of nodes in Root^.Right in RightNum
        if LeftNum ≥ RightNum
            then
                loop for i going from 1 to (LeftNum - RightNum) ÷ 2
                    Right-Shift(Root)
            else
                loop for i going from 1 to (RightNum - LeftNum) ÷ 2
                    Left-Shift(Root)
        call Balance(Root^.Left)
        call Balance(Root^.Right)

END OF Balance
```

We still have to write the routines *Right-Shift* and *Left-Shift*. These two routines will rearrange several pointers, *à la Delete*, and it will not be neccessary to move any data around. The general case requires changing seven pointers, but some cases require less. Remember that we are not moving any data in the nodes, we only reassign some pointers. Look back at figures 7.11 and 7.12. The seven pointers that changed were:

- The root, which originally pointed to JILL, now points at Hank.

- JILL's left pointer, which used to point at ERIC, now is nil.

- JILL's right pointer, which used to point at JOHN, now is nil.

- HANK's left pointer, which was nil—but didn't have to be—now points at ERIC.

- HANK's right pointer, which had to be nil, now points at JOHN.

- GARY's right pointer, which used to point at HANK, now points where HANK's left pointer used to point (it didn't have to be nil).

- JOHN's left pointer, which used to be nil, now points at JILL.

We'll leave the completion of *Right-Shift* and *Left-Shift* for the exercises.

A function that counts the number of nodes in a tree will prove necessary, too. If you think about this problem recursively, it will be easy to solve. We'll leave it for the exercises as well.

Equivalence of Definitions

Before we conclude this section, we should return to the question concerning the equivalence of the two definitions of "balanced." Are the two definitions equivalent? If a tree has minimum height, is it count-balanced? Clearly not. The tree in figure 7.11 has height 4 which is the minimum height for a tree with eleven nodes, but it's not count-balanced. On the other hand, if a tree is count-balanced, is it height-balanced? Does it have minimum height? This is straightforward to prove if you are familiar with the method of mathematical induction. We'll leave the proof for the exercises.

Notice that the result of applying our algorithm to a tree produces more than just a tree with minimum height. Is that good? Is a count-balanced tree preferable to a tree with minimum height? Look again at figures 7.11 and 7.13. Which of these two trees would result in a quicker search time? The actual difference in practice is insignificant.

7.11   Orders of Magnitude

Before we code these routines in Pascal, let's take the time to examine their efficiencies. Reviewing first, recall that we obtained the following results in earlier chapters:

Task	Unordered Array	Ordered Array	Linked List
Search	N	$\log N$	N
Insertion	1	N	N
Deletion	N	N	N

If the tree is badly out of balance, it looks and behaves much like a linked list. Let's assume the tree we are working with is balanced; otherwise it's of no real use. What is the order of magnitude of a search in a balanced binary search tree? The search proceeds much like that of a binary search in an ordered array; that is, about half of the remaining collection of nodes are eliminated at each look, so the search is $O(\log N)$.

How about an insertion? Since the insertion first finds a leaf at which the insertion actually takes place, the insertion is at least $O(\log N)$. After finding the point to do the insertion, one call to *Allocate* and three assignments are required to complete the process. Therefore, we can conclude that an insertion in a balanced binary tree is $O(\log N)$.

A deletion requires a search to find the node. If the node is an internal node, the search continues until a leaf is reached. This constitutes the same search as the insertion routine. The deletion then requires at most a handful of assignments and a call to *Deallocate*. Thus, a deletion from a balanced binary search tree is also $O(\log N)$.

All three of our routines are $O(\log N)$, which is a considerable improvement over all the earlier data structures considered. For storing large amounts of data in a manner that allows it to be searched and modified quickly, a binary search tree is an appropriate choice in many situations.

Let's add our results to the table presented above:

Task	Unordered Array	Ordered Array	Linked List	Binary Tree
Search	N	$\log N$	N	$\log N$
Insertion	1	N	N	$\log N$
Deletion	N	N	N	$\log N$

You might wonder if there are even better choices. The answer is yes. If the amount of data is huge—rather than just large—it might not all fit into memory at one time, and we have to again wrestle with the tradeoffs between saving time and saving space. In chapter 9 we will discuss "2-3 trees" and "B-trees" as well as "hashing." These concepts can be called upon to handle even larger amounts of data than can be handled with binary trees, and can perform some of the above mentioned tasks more efficiently.

7.12   Pascal Implementation of Tree Program

As we have seen many times, once algorithms have been written as carefully as they have been in this chapter, it's relatively straightforward to complete the code. The following discussion should illustrate that fact again.

First, the data types need to be defined. Let's agree on the following:

```
const
  MAXLENGTH = 10;
type
  NameType = packed array [1 .. MAXLENGTH] of char;
  Tree     = ^TreeNode;
  TreeNode = record
        Data        : NameType;
        Left, Right : Tree
     end;
```

These definitions are very similar to those used earlier for a linked list. The chief difference is that nodes now have two pointers rather than just one.

The various routines can be developed quickly. Here's `InTree`:

```
function InTree(Root : Tree; Name : NameType) : Boolean;

{  This function searches the tree pointed at by Root to  }
{  determine whether or not Name is present in the tree.  }

begin
  if Root = nil
    then
      InTree := false
    else
      if Name = Root^.Data
        then
          InTree := true
        else
          if Name < Root^.Data
            then
              InTree := InTree(Root^.Left, Name)
            else
              InTree := InTree(Root^.Right, Name)
end;
```

We'll leave `Insert` and `Delete` as exercises. The routines that traverse the tree are easy; all you have to do is translate the algorithm into Pascal. Here's `InOrder`:

```
procedure InOrder(Root : Tree);

{  This procedure lists the names stored in the tree in inorder.  }

begin
  if Root <> nil
    then
      begin
        InOrder(Root^.Left);
        write(Root^.Data, ' ');
        InOrder(Root^.Right)
      end
end;
```

If you sent this procedure the tree in figure 7.8, it would display:

ANNE CARL ERIC FRED GARY GENE HANK JILL JOHN KWAN MARY PEPE

Which, as you can see, is in alphabetical order.

Displaying the Tree as a Tree

The structure of the tree is not apparent, however. There is a cute trick that you can use to allow you to see the tree, if you wish. Include another parameter, `Tab`, modify the procedure `InOrder` as follows, and call this routine with `Tab` set to 0.

```
procedure InOrder(Root : Tree; Tab : integer);

{  This procedure lists the names stored in the tree in inorder.  }

begin
  if Root <> nil
    then
      begin
        InOrder(Root^.Left, Tab + 5);
        writeln(' ' : Tab, Root^.Data);
        InOrder(Root^.Right, Tab + 5)
      end
end;
```

Now each name will be printed on a separate line, but before printing the name, it will first print **Tab** spaces. **Tab** increases by five on each recursive call. The result is a listing that looks like:

```
                        ANNE
                  CARL
            ERIC
                  FRED
            GARY
                        GENE
                  HANK
      JILL
            JOHN
                  KWAN
            MARY
      PEPE
```

The structure of the tree is now apparent. (Compare this listing with the tree in figure 7.8.) The same trick can be applied to your `PreOrder` and `PostOrder` procedures, if desired.

The completion of the program will be left for the exercises. You'll probably want to write the program so that it allows the user to choose between searching the tree, inserting a name into the tree, deleting a name from the tree, traversing the tree (choosing which method of traversal to use), quitting the program without saving the new tree, and exiting and saving the new tree. The menu displayed could be very similar to that used in chapter 4 for the dictionary program.

7.13 Summary and Review

- In this chapter we started with the problem of maintaining a database of names. We introduced the notion of a binary tree, along with some terminology and definitions.

- We discussed binary search trees and introduced the fundamental property of binary search trees.

- We developed algorithms for searching a tree, inserting a node, traversing a tree and deleting a node.

- We discussed the implementation of these algorithms in Pascal.

7.14   Exercises

1. Write an iterative version of *InTree*.

2. On page 168 we indicated that the algorithm for *Insert* assumed, as a precondition, that the name being inserted was not already in the tree. As indicated, this would require that the tree be searched twice, once to see if the name is there, and once to insert it. Modify the algorithm by adding an additional parameter, say *Successful,* that will require only one search, and will return either true or false in *Successful* indicating whether the insertion took place.

3. On page 178 we indicated that the algorithm for *Delete* assumed, as a precondition, that the name being deleted was in the tree. This would require two searches of the tree, one to see if the name is there, and one to delete the name. Modify the algorithm by adding another parameter to remove the need for the extra search. See the previous exercise.

4. Write an iterative version of *Insert*.

5. Write an iterative version of *Delete*.

6. Write the algorithm for *PostOrder*.

7. Would you want to write iterative versions of *PreOrder, PostOrder* or *InOrder*. Why?

8. Write an algorithm and the code for a function that will determine the number of nodes in a binary tree.

9. Write an algorithm and the code for a function that will determine the height of a binary tree.

10. Prove that a binary search tree that is count-balanced (page 180) is also balanced according to the first definition, i.e., has minimum height.

11. Write the algorithms for *Right-Shift* and *Left-Shift* to complete the count-balance routine.

12. Complete the Pascal implementation of the tree program. Write the program so that it allows the user to choose between searching the tree, inserting a name into the tree, deleting a name from the tree, traversing the tree (choosing which method of traversal to use), quitting the program without saving the new tree, and exiting and saving the new tree. The menu displayed could be very similar to that used in chapter 4 for the dictionary program. If you worked exercises 8, 9 and/or 11, then include these in your program and in the menu of choices.

13. On page 183 we said that trees that are out of balance behave more like linked lists, and thus are not as efficient to search as balanced trees. If one were to do a search of a tree in general, the efficiency of the search is directly related to the average path length of the nodes in the tree. By "path length" we mean the level of a node, where the root node is on level 1. Consider the tree in figure 7.5. There are six nodes and the levels of the six nodes are: 1, 2, 2, 3, 3, 4. The sum of these levels is known as the "*internal path length*" of the tree. The internal path length of the tree in figure 7.5 is 15. A *successful* search of this tree would end up at one of the six nodes, and thus would require 1, 2, 2, 3, 3, or 4 comparisons. That is, the average number of comparisons required by a successful search would be the internal path length of a tree divided by the number of nodes in the tree; for the tree in figure 7.5, the average number of comparisons required by a successful search would be 15/6 or 2.5. By comparison, notice that the tree in figure 7.6 has an internal path length of 21, and the average number of comparisons required by a successful search would be 21/6 or 3.5.

    Write a routine that accepts a tree as a parameter and returns its internal path length. Use this routine to determine the average number of comparisons required by a successful search.

14. In the previous exercise we discussed the average number of comparisons required by a successful search. We can also discuss *unsuccessful* searches. When a search is not successful, it continues until it encounters a nil pointer. Thus the average number of comparisons required by an unsuccessful search is the average length of the levels of the nil pointers in the tree. Using the tree in figure 7.5 as an example again, the tree contains seven nil pointers, and they are on levels: 3, 3, 4, 4, 4, 5, and 5. (The level of a nil pointer is one more than the level of the node containing it.) We define the "*external path length*" of a tree to be the sum of the levels of the nil pointers contained in the tree. The average number of comparisons required by an unsuccessful search is the external path length divided by the number of nil pointers. For the tree in figure 7.5, it's 28/7. For the tree in figure 7.6, it's 34/7.

    Write a routine that accepts a tree as a parameter and returns its external path length. Use this routine to determine the average number of comparisons required by an unsuccessful search. You will also need to determine the number of nil pointers in the tree.

Chapter 8

Other Binary Trees

Sometimes I think we're alone.
Sometimes I think we're not.
In either case, the thought is staggering.
—Buckminster Fuller

8.1   Overview of the Chapter

This previous chapter introduced the concept of a binary tree. We saw how a binary search tree can be used to provide an efficient way of storing data that is easy to add to, delete from, and search.

We now want to discuss binary trees that do not satisfy the fundamental property of a binary search tree. We'll see how a binary tree can be searched even when it does not satisfy the fundamental property, and we'll discuss "threaded binary trees." We'll also see how a binary tree can be used to hold an arithmetic expression.

8.2   Introduction

When a binary tree does not satisfy the fundamental property of a binary search tree, it cannot be searched with the algorithms developed in the last chapter. The fundamental property allowed us to use a strategy very similar to a binary search of a sorted array; i.e., about half of the remaining data is discarded at each "look" into the tree. Non-search trees can still be searched, of course. In this chapter we'll look at two well known strategies: a depth-first search and a breadth-first search.

A threaded binary tree (actually "threaded binary search tree") replaces the `nil` pointers in the leaves of the tree with pointers that point at the inorder predecessor and successor of the current node (when present). The inclusion of these pointers makes it possible to traverse a tree with non-recursive routines rather than the recursive routines we wrote in the previous chapter. We'll take

191

a brief look at some of the iterative routines that manipulate threaded binary trees, and leave other routines for the exercises.

The familiar operations of elementary arithmetic: addition, subtraction, multiplication and division, are *binary* operations. This means that each operator has two operands. A binary tree is ideal to hold the two operands of a binary operation. We'll develop the algorithms for a program that manipulates a binary expression tree. This will also require some new Pascal for the notion of a "variant record," which will also be developed.

8.3   Searching Non-Search Binary Trees

Any tree that has two (or fewer) pointers in each node is a binary tree. As a simple example, you could construct a binary tree that consists of you, your parents, your grandparents, etc., for as far back as you could find ancestors. The left pointer in each node could point at the father of the occupant of the node, and the right parent could point at the mother. (You will have to be careful about the notation; we are also using 'child' to refer to these pointers.) Such a binary tree would be a simpler tree than a normal family tree since siblings, step-parents, etc. are being left off.

It is often necessary to search a binary tree that is not a binary search tree. Using the simple family tree mentioned above as an example, suppose you need to know if a given name is somewhere in the tree. Since the tree does not satisfy the fundamental search property, you cannot split the tree in two at each look. You will have to exhaustively look at every node in the tree to see if the name you are looking for is there. There are two strategies for conducting such a search, a breadth-first strategy and a depth-first strategy. As the names imply, you either follow pointers until you get to the end of a branch—depth-first—or you examine all the nodes on a given level before looking at the nodes on the next level.

Depth-first search

Let's make this more explicit. Here's a high-level algorithm for a depth-first search of a binary tree:

START OF Depth-First(Root, Key, Found)
Passed by value: Root, Key.
Passed by reference: Found

store False in Found
if Root is non-nil
    then
        Push Root onto a stack
        loop
            Pop a pointer, Ptr, from the stack
            if the node pointed at by Ptr equals the Key
                then
                    store true in Found
                else
                    Push all non-nil pointers in the node pointed at by
                    Ptr onto the stack
        until Found or the stack is empty

END OF Depth-First

Using the tree in figure 8.1 as an example, suppose we are searching for the name *Chris*. (We've picked a name that could be either a man's name or a woman's name because we don't want to consider gender.)

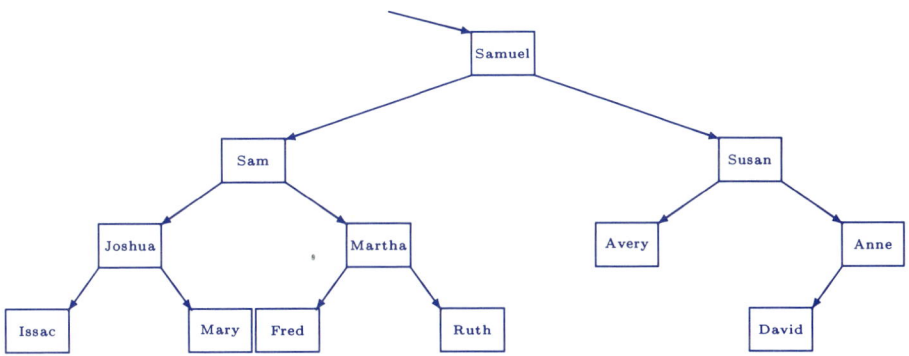

Figure 8.1 A Binary Non-Search Tree

The depth-first search would look at the name in the root node, (*Samuel*), then the name in one of the two children nodes, (*Sam* or *Susan*), then the name in one of the children's children's nodes. When the end of a branch is reached, no new pointers are pushed onto the stack, and the strategy essentially moves up one level and follows another branch, continuing until either the searched for name is found, or the tree is exhausted. We are not concerned—in this top-level algorithm—with which pointer is pushed onto the stack first, but for the sake of seeing the order of the search, let's assume that the left pointer is always pushed first, then the right. The tree in figure 8.2 has numbers above the nodes indicating which order they would be considered.

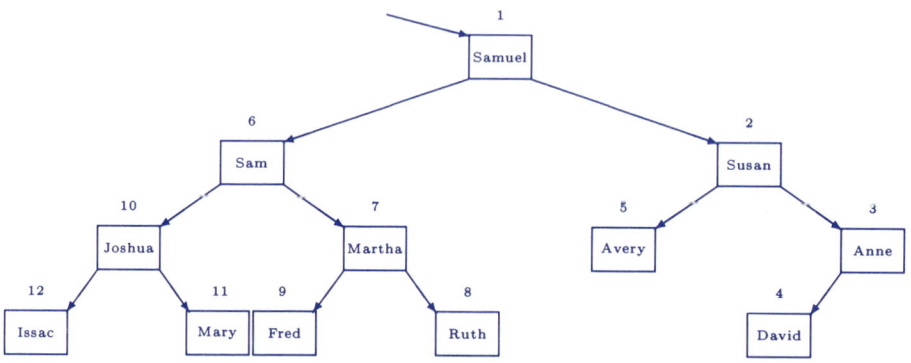

Figure 8.2 Order of a Depth-First Search

Be sure you see that the search is indeed "depth-first."

Breadth-first search

Now, let's consider a breadth-first search of a binary non-search tree. How can we modify the strategy used above so that we search all the nodes on the top level, then all the nodes on the second level, then all the nodes on the third level, etc. until we either find the name we are looking for or exhaust the tree? Hopefully you have already seen the answer. It's an elegant modification: all we have to do is change from using a stack to using a queue. Rather than push and pop the names from a stack, we enqueue and dequeue them from a queue. This simple change is all that is needed to change the strategy from depth-first to breadth-first. Here's another top-level algorithm:

```
START OF Breadth-First(Root, Key, Found)
Passed by value: Root, Key.
Passed by reference: Found

store False in Found
if Root is non-nil
    then
        Enqueue Root onto a queue
        loop
            Dequeue a pointer, Ptr, from the queue
            if the node pointed at by Ptr equals the Key
                then
                    store True in Found
                else
                    Enqueue all non-nil pointers in the node pointed at by
                    Ptr onto the queue
            until Found or the queue is empty

END OF Depth-First
```

Using the same tree from figure 8.1, suppose we are again searching for the name *Chris*, and suppose we are enqueueing the left pointer and then the right. Figure 8.3 shows the order of the nodes searched using the breadth-first strategy.

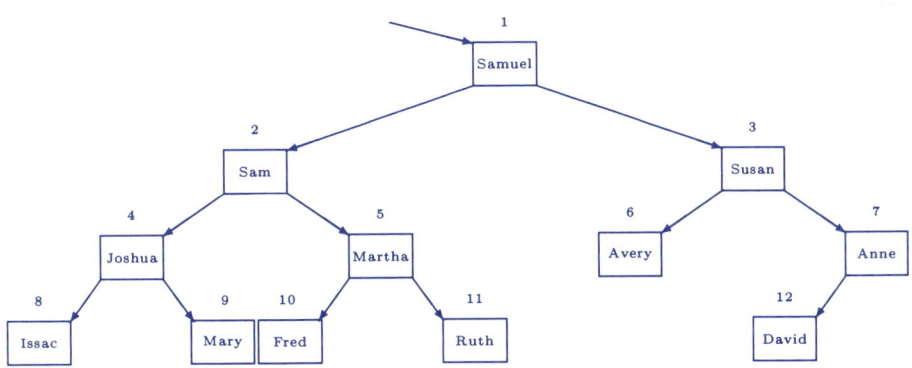

Figure 8.3 Order of a Breadth-First Search

In general, without knowing more about the data stored in a binary tree, there's no reason to prefer a depth-first strategy over a breadth-first strategy. Both get every node looked at exactly once (unless the search terminates successfully before examining every node), and both use about the same amount of memory, if the tree in question is balanced—or nearly balanced. Both strategies have the same order of magnitude.

We'll leave the refinement and implementation of these algorithms, as well as the determination of their orders of magnitude, for the exercises.

8.4   Threaded Binary Trees

If you consider the structure of the pointers in a binary tree for a moment, you'll agree that most of the pointers in the tree are not being used very efficiently. Indeed, about half of them contain the `nil` pointer. Over the years several people have made use of these pointers, and one of the most useful modifications results in a kind of tree known as a "threaded binary tree," or, more simply, just "threaded tree." While there are variations on the theme, we'll only mention one kind of threaded tree.

Rather than put `nil` pointers in the leaf nodes, consider what would happen if we use these pointers to point at the inorder predecessor and successor. (We'll call such a pointer a *thread*.) With a normal binary search tree, when you do an inorder traversal of the tree, you depend on a stack to hold the pointers to the ancestors of a current node. Once you reach a `nil` pointer as you follow right pointers, you need to unwind the recursion (i.e., pop elements off the stack) to get to the next element in inorder.

However, if you store a pointer to the inorder successor in the right child rather than the `nil` pointer, you can go directly to that node rather than have to unwind the recursion. Indeed, you can then write the inorder traversal routine iteratively rather than recursively. Simlarly, in the left child you can store a pointer to the inorder predecessor instead of the `nil` pointer. This won't be very useful when doing a normal traversal, but it does make it possible to traverse the tree in reverse order very easily.

Iteration vs. Recursion

If you decided to follow this suggestion, it would likely be due to a problem with using recursion. Perhaps you were using a language that didn't support recursion, or perhaps your recursive routines were causing the computer to run out of memory. In either case, if you did plan to construct a program that manipulated a threaded binary tree, you would likely intend to write all of the routines iteratively. For this reason, the algorithms we write for the remainder of this section will not use recursion.

Two kinds of pointers

Continuing with the solution, there are two problems that have to be resolved. First, since the pointers in the nodes are sometimes pointers to children and sometimes pointers to successors (or predecessors), we will have to be able to tell the difference. An easy solution to this problem is to just use another field in the node, a Boolean field, say *Thread*, that will tell us whether the pointer is a thread or a normal pointer. Second, what do we do when we come to the extreme left and right ends of the tree? These nodes don't have predecessors or successors (respectively). An easy solution to this is to just let them contain the `nil` pointer to indicate the left and right ends of the tree.

Figure 8.4 shows a threaded tree where the threads are shown as darker lines than the other pointers. Notice also that the threads always point upwards. For the sake of simplicity in the figure, we'll not show the Boolean field. If the pointer is a dark line and points upward, *Thread* will be true, and false otherwise. Notice that whenever a thread is followed, it leads you to either the predecessor (left pointer), or the successor (right pointer) of the current node. When a pointer is not a thread, it could be `nil`, in which case it indicates the end (left or right) of the tree.

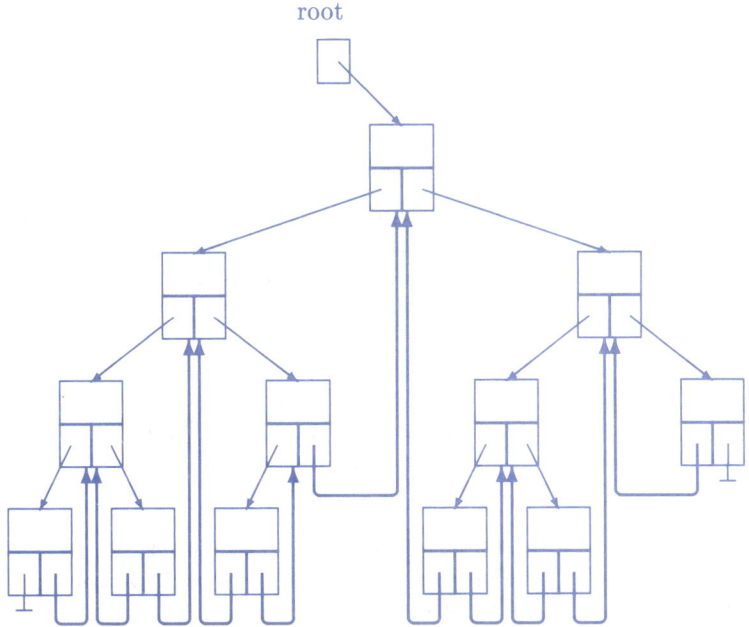

Figure 8.4 A Threaded Binary Tree

Successors and Predecessors

It is easy to find the successor of any node: if the right child of a node is a thread, it points at the successor. If it isn't a thread, we go right one time, and then follow left pointers until we come to a thread. A similar statement can be made about finding the predecessor of a node.

Let's examine a function that has a pointer as a parameter, and returns a pointer to the successor of the node pointed at by the parameter. It's possible that the node in question doesn't have a successor; we'll simply have the function return `nil` to indicate this. As a precondition, we'll assume that the pointer being sent is non-`nil`.

> START OF Successor(P)
> Precondition: P is not nil.
>
> if P^.Right.Thread { the right pointer is a thread }
>   then
>   return P^.Right.Ptr
>   else
>   store P^.Right.Ptr in P
>   if P is not nil
>   then
>   loop while not P^.Left.Thread
>   store P^.Left.Ptr in P
>   return P
>
> END OF Successor

You should notice that we're assuming something about the data structure. We're assuming that what used to be the pointer fields of the node are now two fields: a pointer and a flag indicating what type of pointer it is. *Right.Ptr* is the right pointer, and *Right.Thread* is *true* if the right pointer is a thread, and *false* otherwise.

Inorder Traversal of a Threaded Binary Search Tree

With this function, it's very easy to do an inorder traversal of a threaded binary search tree. Here is an algorithm for such a routine:

```
START OF InOrderTraversal(Root)
Passed by value: Root
Passed by reference: none
Precondition: Root points to a threaded binary search tree.

if Root ≠ nil
    then
        loop while Root^.Left is not nil
            store Root^.Left in Root
        display Root^.Data
        store Successor(Root) in Root
        loop while Root is not nil
            display Root^.Data
            store Successor(Root) in Root

END OF InOrderTraversal
```

We made no use of the left thread in either of the above routines. If it were necessary to do an inorder traversal of a threaded binary tree, but in reverse order rather than the normal forward order, the left threads would be used. We'll leave these algorithms for the exercises.

Maintaining a Threaded Binary Search Tree

Now let's think about maintaining the tree in the first place. It would be necessary to allow for new nodes to be inserted into the tree, and it would be necessary to allow for the deletions of nodes. It might also be necessary to be able to balance the tree. We'll not take the time to discuss all of the possible routines, but we'll look at doing an insertion.

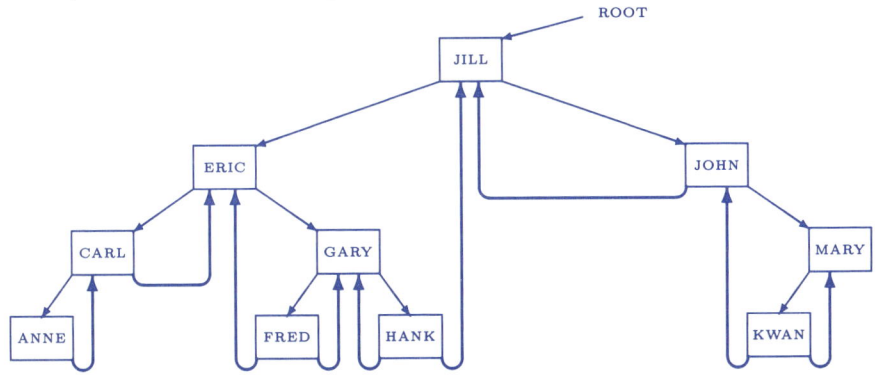

Figure 8.5 Before Inserting **FRAN**

Consider the tree in figure 8.5. Suppose we need to insert the name **FRAN** into the tree. Where should it go and what should be done to put it there? As with non-threaded trees, new nodes always get inserted as leaves. You know you're at a leaf (or semi-leaf) if the pointer there is either `nil` or is a thread. As before, memory is allocated for the new node, the data to be inserted are put in the new node, and the various pointers get adjusted. After inserting `FRAN`, the tree would look like figure 8.6.

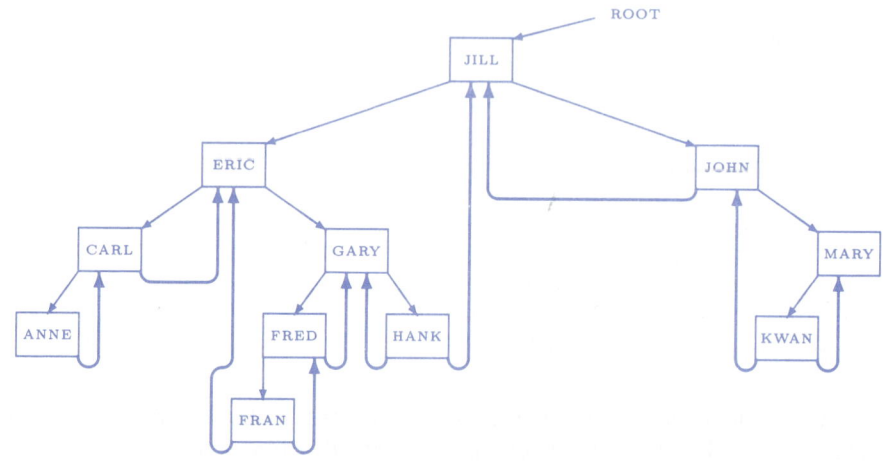

Figure 8.6 After Inserting `FRAN`

Recall that we intend to write the routine without relying on recursion. Here's an algorithm for the task:

START OF Insert(Root, Key, Successful)
Passed by value: Key
Passed by reference: Root, Successful
Postcondition: Key is inserted into the threaded tree and
Successful is set to true, unless it's already there, in which
case, Successful is set to false.

store true in Successful
if Root is nil
   then
      call Allocate(Root)
      store Key in Root^.Data
      store nil in Root^.Left.Ptr
      store nil in Root^.Right.Ptr
      store false in Root^.Left.Thread
      store false in Root^.Right.Thread
   else
      store Root in P
      store false in Done
      loop while not Done
        if Key = P^.Data
          then
            store true in Done
          else
           if Key < P^.Data
             then
               if P^.Left.Thread or P^.Left.Ptr = nil
                 then
                   store true in Done
                 else
                   store P^.Left.Ptr in P
             else
               if P^.Right.Thread or P^.Right.Ptr = nil
                 then
                   store true in Done
                 else
                   store P^.Right.Ptr in P
          { end of loop while not Done }

```
{ if Root is nil, else part continued }
if Key = P^.Data
    then
        store false in Successful
    else
        if Key < P^.Data
            then
                store P^.Left.Ptr in Q
                store P^.Left.Thread in Temp
                call Allocate(P^.Left.Ptr)
                store P^.Left.Ptr in R
                store Key in R^.Data
                store P in R^.Right.Ptr
                store true in R^.Right.Thread
                store Q in R^.Left.Ptr
                store Temp in R^.Left.Thread
            else
                store P^.Right.Ptr in Q
                store P^.Right.Thread in Temp
                call Allocate(P^.Right.Ptr)
                store P^.Right.Ptr in R
                store Key in R^.Data
                store P in R^.Left.Ptr
                store true in R^.Left.Thread
                store Q in R^.Right.Ptr
                store Temp in R^.Right.Thread

END OF Insert
```

We'll leave the other routines that manipulate threaded trees for the exercises.

8.5   Binary Expression Trees

The "binary" property of binary trees makes them useful in many different applications other than as binary search trees. The word 'binary' might remind you of the "binary operators" of arithmetic, i.e., addition, subtraction, multiplication and division. A binary tree can be used to hold an arithmetic expression, and the resulting tree makes it very easy to see the expression. Consider figure 8.7.

As usual, we are using '+' for addition, '–' for subtraction, '*' for multiplication and '/' for division. It is quite easy to determine the value of this expression; it's 56 (normally written as $(3 + 8 \div 2) \times (13 - 5))$. In fact, a re-

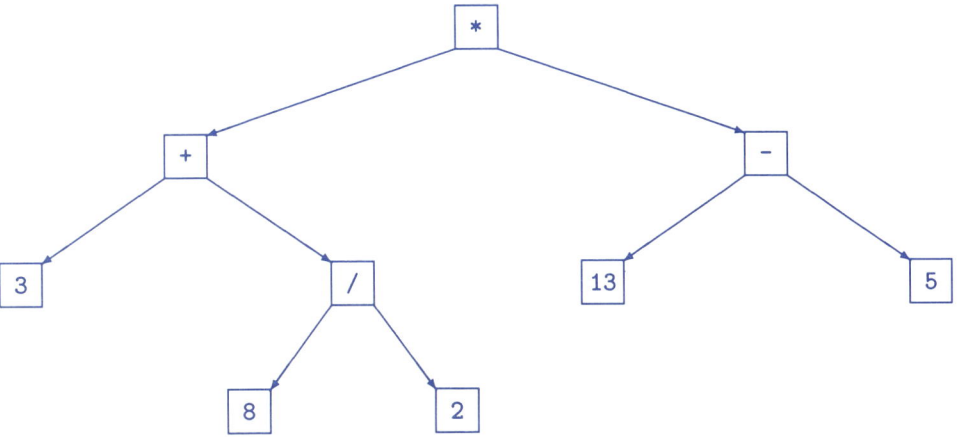

Figure 8.7 A Binary Expression Tree

cursive description of the value of the expression seems to jump out at us: the value of the expression is just the indicated operation applied to the values of the two subtrees. It should be that easy to write a routine that evaluates an arithmetic expression stored in a binary expression tree.

Define the Problem

However, before we start to write such a routine, we should be in agreement on just what the routine is to do. Let's agree that the problem we want to solve is:

> Write a program that will maintain a binary expression tree. The program should allow the user to build the expression, view the expression as an infix, prefix or postfix expression and evaluate the expression.

We have included the ability to view the expression tree and you probably won't be surprised to learn that the expression can be viewed as a prefix expression simply by doing a preorder traversal of the expression tree.

Before we go any further with the problem, we should decide what a binary expression tree really consists of. Take another look at figure 8.7 and notice that all the nodes of the tree contain either one of the four operators: '+', '-', '*' or '/' or a number. Notice that the numbers are always leaves of the tree and notice that there are no nodes which have only one child.

A recursive definition of a binary expression tree is:

A binary expression tree is a pointer which is either:

1. the nil pointer,

2. a pointer to a node containing a number, or

3. a pointer to a node containing an operator and two non-nil binary expression trees.

A node contains a data field and two pointer fields.

For our purposes, we'll only consider **real** numbers and the four operators: '+', '-', '*' and '/'. An exponentiation operation and/or the integer division operations (**div** and **mod**) could be added, if desired. We'll leave these extensions as exercises.

According to our definition, if a node contains a number, it doesn't matter what the pointers are; we'll assume the two pointers are nil when the node contains a number. Further, when a node contains an operator, neither pointer contained in that node is nil. However, notice that when the node contains an operator, either of the two pointers in the node could point at a node containing a number or at a node containing another operator.

Solve the Problem

The solution to the problem consists in writing a program that will contain most of the standard features of other programs developed in this book. It should display an introduction for the user and allow the user to build an expression. The program should put the expression into a binary expression tree (and the user does not have to know that the expression is being held in a tree). The program should then allow the user to see the expression (in either prefix, infix or postfix) and should allow the user to see the value of the expression. It would be nice to repeat this step until the user is ready to proceed. Perhaps we could decide to allow the user to enter another expression if he wishes. Finally, a concluding message should be displayed.

Here's an algorithm for the main program:

```
START OF Binary Expression Tree

call Introduce
loop
    display "Enter a binary expression tree (in prefix, of course)."
    call EnterExpression(Expr)
    loop
        display "Do you want to:"
        display "(D)isplay the expression,"
        display "(E)valuate the expression,"
        display "(Q)uit."
        accept Choice
        when Choice is
            'D', call DisplayExpression(Expr)
            'E', display "The value is", Evaluate(Expr)
        until Choice is 'Q'
    display "Do you want to enter another expression?"
    accept Choice
    until Choice is No
call Conclude

END OF Binary Expression Tree
```

The Data Structure of a Node

Unlike what we have done previously, the data field does not always contain the same type of data. For some nodes, the data is an operator; for others, a number. In Pascal, the data type of the operator fields will be **char**, and the type of the number fields will be **real**. We have not yet discussed how to do this. We will, after some more discussion of the problem.

Introduction and Conclusion

The routines that display the introduction and conclusion should be nearly trivial by now, but they still need to be written. We'll leave them for you.

Entering the Expression

The routine that allows the user to enter the expression is interesting. We'll agree to let the user choose to enter either an operator or a number. If the user chooses to enter a number, the routine will accept that number and exit. If the user chooses to enter an operator, the routine will accept the operator and then let the user enter the two expressions the operator will operate on. The last step will be done by calling the routine recursively. In both cases, the data entered by the user will be put into a new node, and the pointer passed to the routine will be changed to point at the new node. Here's an algorithm:

```
START OF EnterExpression(Expr)
Passed by reference: Expr, a pointer to the node containing the expression

call New(Expr)
display "Do you want to enter an operator or a number?"
accept Choice
if Choice is number
     then
          display "Enter a number: "
          accept Number
          store Number in Expr^.Data
          store nil in Expr^.Left
          store nil in Expr^.Right
     else
          display "Enter an operator: "
          accept Operator
          store Operator in Expr^.Data
          call EnterExpression(Expr^.Left)
          call EnterExpression(Expr^.Right)


END OF EnterExpression
```

Notice that this routine does not allow the user to create an empty expression. The only time an empty expression is allowed is at the very beginning of the program. Once the user enters an expression, it will no longer remain empty. This is in keeping with our definition of a binary expression tree.

Displaying the Expression

The routines that display the expression will be very much like the tree traversal routines written earlier in the previous chapter. We will have to make some decisions about parentheses in the infix display. Since we've already developed algorithms for traversals of binary trees, we'll leave the completion of these routines for later when we write the code.

Evaluating the Expression

Finally, the routine that evaluates the expression—the routine that got us started on this problem in the first place—will look at the contents of a node. If it is a number, the routine will just return the number. If the node contains an operator, the routine should return the value of the indicated operation applied to the values of the two subtrees. An algorithm for this routine is straightforward:

START OF Evaluate(Expr)
Precondition: Expr is a non-nil binary expression tree

if the node contains an operator
    then
        when the Operator is a
            '+', return Evaluate(Expr^.Left) + Evaluate(Expr^.Right)
            '−', return Evaluate(Expr^.Left) − Evaluate(Expr^.Right)
            '*', return Evaluate(Expr^.Left) × Evaluate(Expr^.Right)
            '/', return Evaluate(Expr^.Left) ÷ Evaluate(Expr^.Right)
    else
        return the number in the node

END OF Evaluate

The routine calls itself whenever a node contains an operator. This requires that all the numbers in the tree are leaves of the tree, but that's just what we have agreed.

Pascal for Binary Expression Trees

The single biggest problem facing us with the implementation of this program in Pascal is how to handle the fact that the nodes don't always contain the same type of data; some nodes contain operators (**chars**) while others contain **real** constants. To handle this, we need *variant records*. A variant record is a record that contains a field having variant types of data. Let's look at the syntax diagram for a *record* and for a *field list*. Consider figure 8.8.

Looking carefully at the syntax diagram for *field list*, you'll notice that there is an optional part that must come at the end of a field list and it cannot occur more than once. This extra part is the *variant part*. The "tag-field" is the name of the field that varies and must be of an ordinal type. The ordinal type is almost always a user-defined type that is defined in the same type definition part and is merely a list of constants that can be in the variant part. These constants are the "case constants." We can make this more clear by using our current problem as the example.

We need to define a node in such a way that it contains either a number or an operator and, of course, left and right pointers. Our earlier definitions put the pointers after the data field, but, since the variant part must come last, we now have to put the pointers first. Here are the type definitions:

record type:

field list:

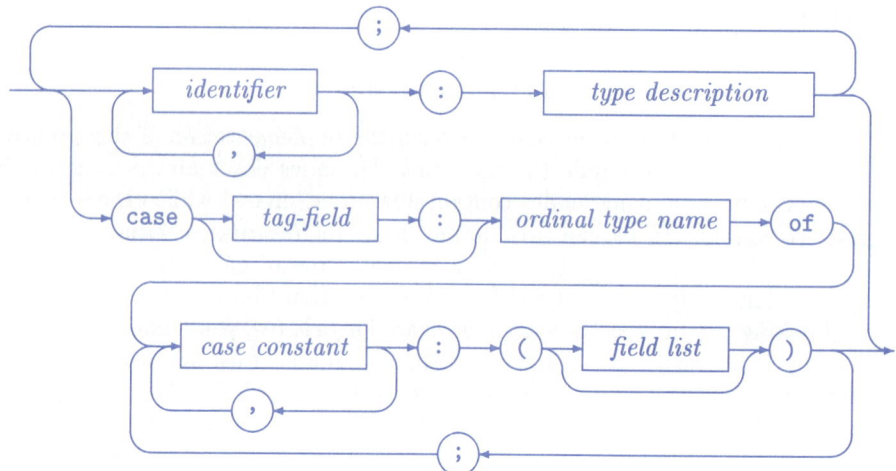

Figure 8.8

```
type
  OpType = (Operand, Operator);
  Tree = ^TreeNode;
  TreeNode = record
        Left,
        Right : Tree;
        case KindTag : OpType of
            Operand  : (Value : real);
            Operator : (Op    : char)
      end;
```

The tag-field (`KindTag`) allows us to examine the variant part to determine which kind of field is being used. That is, we can store either `Operand` or `Operator` in `KindTag` when the data are stored in the node and later examine `KindTag` to see what we put there. This too will make better sense when we look at an example. The code that we can use to actually enter a value into one of these nodes is on the next page.

```
procedure EnterExpression(var Expr : Tree);
var
   Number : real;
   Oper, Choice : char;
begin
   New(Expr);
   write('Do you want to enter an operator or a number? (O/N): ');
   readln(Choice);
   while not (Choice in ['O', 'o', 'N', 'n']) do
      begin
         write('Please enter ''O'' or ''N'': ');
         readln(Choice)
      end;
   if Choice in ['N', 'n']
      then
         begin
            write('Enter a number:  ');
            readln(Number);
            Expr^.KindTag := Operand;
            Expr^.Value := Number;
            Expr^.Left := nil;
            Expr^.Right := nil
         end
      else
         begin
            write('Enter an operator: ');
            readln(Oper);
            while not (Oper in ['+', '-', '*', '/']) do
               begin
                  write('Please enter a valid operator: ');
                  readln(Oper)
               end;
            Expr^.KindTag := Operator;
            Expr^.Op := Oper;
            EnterExpression(Expr^.Left);
            EnterExpression(Expr^.Right)
         end
end;
```

Style Considerations

Before we conclude this chapter, let's say a few more things about the syntax
used for variant records. First, you will have noticed that it is awkward to
find names for things. That's just the nature of it. You will often find yourself

struggling to devise good names for the tag-field, the ordinal type and the names of the fields. There's no simple cure for this problem; you just have to figure out some names. We sometimes add the word `Type` to an identifier if we're defining a type; similarly, we have added the word `Tag` in naming our tag field `KindTag`.

Second, the variant part is somewhat similar to a Pascal ⟨*case statement*⟩. The word `case` is there, as is the word `of`. Don't let yourself get fooled into thinking it is a ⟨*case statement*⟩, though. The construction is similar, but what we are doing here is quite different from what happens when we use a ⟨*case statement*⟩. The main reason for the similarity of the construction is due to the fact that you will often use a ⟨*case statement*⟩ to look at the tag-field. Then the constants in the ⟨*case statement*⟩ will match the case constants, one statement for each constant. You'll see this when you write the code for `Evaluate`.

Finally, notice that the word `end` does not appear at the end of the variant part. Since the variant part comes at the end of a field list, the `end` that ends the record definition suffices to end the variant part as well.

Displaying the Expression

We mentioned earlier that the routines we wrote earlier to traverse a binary tree would suffice for displaying a binary expression tree. To display the expression in prefix, we need merely to do a preorder traversal of the tree. And to display it in postfix, we need merely to do a postorder traversal.

The problem of displaying the expression in infix is almost as easy but there is the problem of what to do about precedence. When you see the infix expression 4 + 5 * 6, you know that the multiplication is to be performed first and the addition second. Similarly, when you see 4 * 5 + 6, you know again that the multiplication needs to be performed first. The prefix and postfix notation requires no parentheses and does not depend on any precedence understanding. One solution to this problem is to simply put in all the parentheses, whether they are needed or not. Then the above two examples would be displayed as (4 + (5 * 6)) and ((4 * 5) + 6).

Here's a Pascal procedure that will display a binary expression tree in infix putting in all the parentheses:

```
procedure InFix(Ptr : Tree);

{  This procedure displays the expression in infix,    }
{  fully parenthesized.  It is recursive.              }

begin
   case Ptr^.KindTag of
      Operator :  begin
                     write('(');
                     InFix(Ptr^.Left);
                     write(Ptr^.Op : 2, ' ');
                     InFix(Ptr^.Right);
                     write(')')
                  end;
      Operand : write(Ptr^.Value : 1 : 2)
   end
end;
```

The remaining routines are even easier. Another procedure could let the
user decide which of the three notations is used.

We'll leave the completion of the program for the exercises.

8.6   Summary and Review

- We introduced the notion of searching binary trees that do not satisfy the
  fundamental property of a binary search tree. We looked at algorithms
  for a depth-first search and a breadth-first search.

- We discussed the concept of a threaded binary tree, and saw how non-
  recursive algorithms could be developed to search, traverse and maintain
  threaded binary trees.

- We introduced binary expression trees and discussed the data structure
  we need to implement such a tree.

- We developed algorithms for a program to enter an expression into a
  binary expression tree and allow it to be evaluated and displayed in various
  ways.

- We discussed the Pascal implementation of these algorithms, and in particular, we discussed variant records.

8.7   Exercises

1. Write a low-level version of the depth-first search algorithm; see page 193. Implement the algorithm in Pascal. You will have to create the binary tree in some manner. A program that allows the user to enter the names into a binary tree would suffice.

2. Write a low-level version of the breadth-first search algorithm, see page 195. Implement the algorithm in Pascal. As with the previous exercise, you will have to create the binary tree in some manner.

3. What are the orders of magnitude of a depth-first and breadth-first search? The claim in the text is that these orders are the same. Do you agree?

4. Given a balanced binary tree containing N nodes, what is the average number of elements on the stack while doing a depth-first search? What is the average number of items on the queue while doing a breadth-first search? What are the maximum and minimum values for these numbers? If the tree is badly out of balance, is one strategy more memory efficient than the other?

5. On page 199 ff we developed algorithms for a function that returns the successor of a node, and a procedure that did an inorder traversal of a threaded binary search tree. Write similar algorithms for *Predecessor* and for a procedure that does a reverse inorder traversal.

6. We developed a routine that inserted a new node into a threaded binary search tree (see page 201). The problem of how to delete a node from such a tree does not have as simple a solution. Indeed, there is no obvious strategy to follow. Design a strategy that deletes a node from a threaded binary search tree, and turn your solution into an algorithm. You might want to use the same strategy we used in chapter 7.

7. Turn the algorithms for successor, predecessor, traverse, insert and delete into a complete Pascal program that maintains a threaded binary search tree.

8. Complete the code for a complete program that maintains a binary expression tree. Your program should allow the user to build a binary expression tree (i.e., enter a binary expression), view the expression as an infix expression, postfix expression or prefix expression, and evaluate the expression.

9. Extend the problem definition for the binary expression tree problem and your solution to allow for an exponentiation operator. You will have to decide how to handle the situationsof a base and an exponent that lead to undefined values. That is, your program should handle $(-3)^{0.5}$ in some reasonable manner.

10. Extend the problem definition for the binary expression tree problem and your solution to allow for integer division operators (i.e., `div` and `mod`). You might want to use single characters for these operators. You could, for example, use \ for integer division and % for the remainder. You will have to decide how to handle the situation wherein the operands are not integers while the operator is one of these integer operators.

Chapter 9

Non-Binary Trees and Hashing

His filing system was such that no one but he had the
slightest idea where any paper or information could be found,
but he himself could put his finger on things unerringly.
His method was always to put everything where
he would first think of looking for it.
— Dick Francis

9.1 Introduction

In this chapter we will discuss multiway trees, 2-3 trees and B-trees. These notions rely on direct access files, so even though Pascal does not support them, we'll discuss direct access files as an option. We'll also discuss hashing.

9.2 Multiway Trees

As the name implies, a multiway tree is a tree that is not limited to only two children per node, as is a binary tree. As with the binary trees of the previous chapter, we will discuss multiway *search* trees, that is, our multiway trees will satisfy a fundamental search property that makes them useful in storing and retrieving data. We begin by defining a *multiway search tree of order m*. A multiway search tree of order m is a pointer to a new kind of node. Rather than having one item of data and two pointers per node, each node will contain at least two, and at most $m + 1$, pointers to other nodes and at most m items of data. The number of items of data will always be one less than the number of pointers. For example, a node in a multiway search tree of order 4 could contain from two through five pointers to other nodes. If the node contains five pointers, then it will contain four items of data. If it contains three pointers, it will contain two items of data. The items of data in each node should be thought of as a record containing—in general—several fields, one of which is

215

the key field. The data items in each node must be arranged in order according
to these key fields.

Moreover, a multiway search tree will satisfy a fundamental search property
like that of a binary search tree. All the data items in the nodes pointed at by
the pointers in a node must be in order as well. If a non-nil pointer is between
two keys, then all the keys in the node pointed at by that pointer, as well as all
the keys in the data items of descendant nodes, must be between the two keys
in the first node. If a non-nil pointer is at the left end of the node, then all the
keys in the node pointed at by that pointer, and the keys of the descendants,
must be less than the first key in the node. Similarly, if a pointer is at the right
end of a node, then all the keys in that tree must be greater than the rightmost
key in the node.

To make this clearer, let's look at an example. To keep it simple, let's
assume the key field is the only field in the data record, and let's assume the
key field contains an integer. Figure 9.1 contains a multiway search tree of order
4. Notice that some nodes contain as few as two pointers, but no node contains
more than five pointers. The numbers in the nodes represent the data. The
numbers in each node are in ascending order and the numbers in all descendant
nodes are "between" the values in the parent nodes. As before, we will call this
the fundamental search property of the tree.

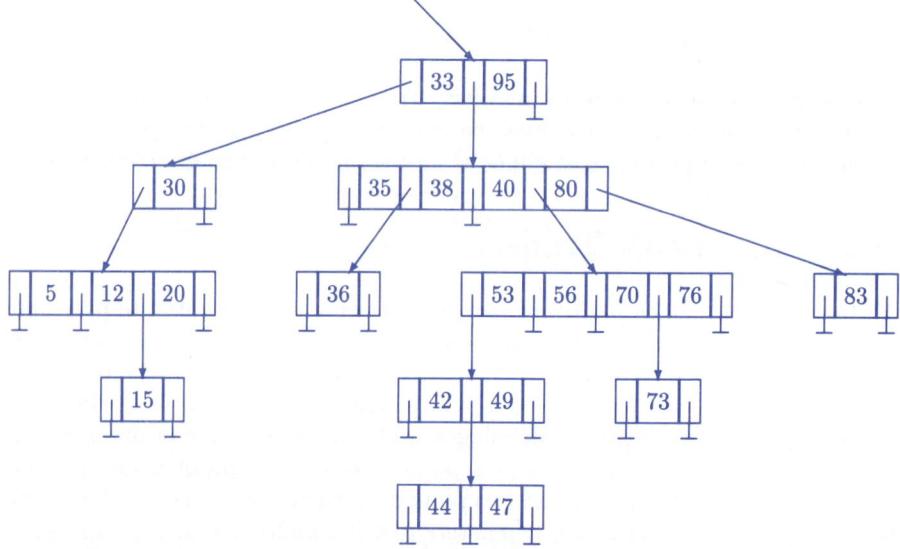

Figure 9.1 A Multiway Tree

While it's probably an implementation detail, we can also assume that each
node contains another integer indicating the number of items in that node.
There must be some way of ascertaining and modifying this number; we might
as well add the number as another field, say *NumItems*. Adding this field to

the tree changes its appearance to that of the tree in figure 9.2. Be careful not to confuse this number with the numbers in the key fields.

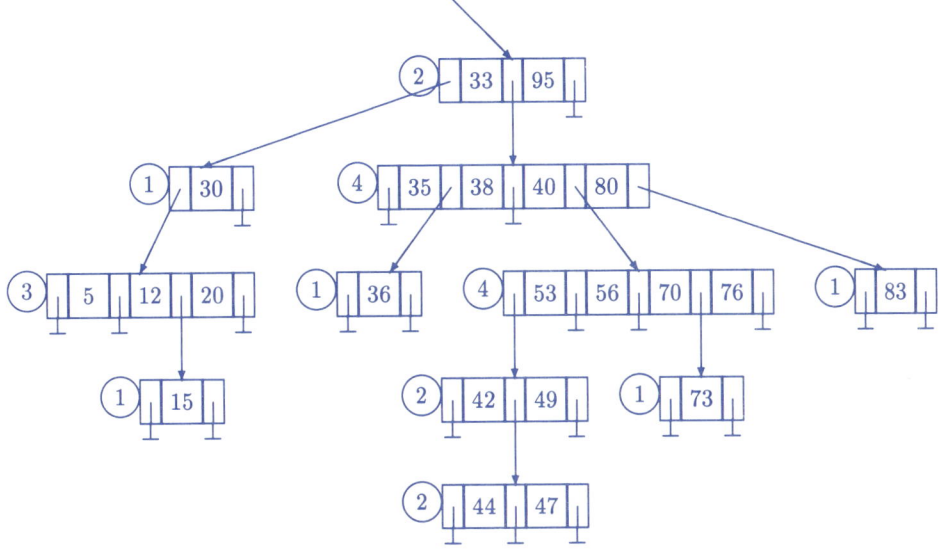

Figure 9.2 A Multiway Tree with a *NumItems* Field

Formally, a multiway search tree of order m is either a nil pointer or a pointer to such a node.

(By the way, some authors let m refer to the number of children rather than to the number of data items; it doesn't matter which notation is used as long as you don't forget. For us, the number m will refer to the maximum number of data items in each node.)

The notation we used for binary trees can be adopted for multiway trees. A *leaf* is a node such that all the pointers in the node are nil pointers. Some authors define a *semi-leaf* as a node that contains at least one nil pointer and at least one non-nil pointer. Each of the pointers in a node is a *subtree*. A multiway tree is *balanced* if all of its semi-leaves are on the same level. A node is a *full node* if it has all m data items.

If P is a non-nil multiway tree, then let $P^\wedge$ be the node to which P is pointing. We need to be able to refer to the data items in that node as well as the pointers. Let N be the node; we'll use $N.NumItems$ to refer to the number of items in the node. Then $N.Data_i$ will refer to the ith data item, and $N.K_i$ will refer to the ith key, for i between 1 and $N.NumItems$, and $N.P_i$ will refer to the ith subtree in the node, for i between 0 and $N.NumItems$. Notice that we are starting the pointer array at 0 instead of 1.

Searching a Multiway Tree

With this notation it is fairly easy to write a search routine. We'll present a recursive version and leave an iterative version for the exercises.

Our routine will have two parameters: a multiway tree (a pointer) and a search key. If the search is successful, the routine will return true, and false otherwise. The search will be unsuccessful if the pointer is a nil pointer. If the pointer is not nil, we'll look at the keys of the data items in the node, returning true if any of these match the search key. If we encounter a key in a data item that is larger than the search key, we'll follow the pointer just prior to that item and search down that path. If we get past the last item in the node without finding a match, we'll follow the last pointer in the node. Since we're going to make it a Boolean-valued function, we'll give it a functionlike name, *InTree*. Here's the algorithm:

```
START OF InTree(P, Key)
Passed by value: P, a multiway tree, and Key

if P = nil
    then
        return false
    else
        store Index(P, Key) in i
        if P^.Ki = Key
            then
                return true
            else
                return InTree(P^.Pi, Key)

END OF InTree
```

This function calls another function, *Index*, to determine the index of the array where the last data item is found that is either less than or equal to the *Key*. If the first data item is bigger than the *Key*, then *Index* should return 0. Here's a high-level description of *Index*.

```
START OF Index(Ptr, Item)

return the last subscript of Data such that Data_i ≤ Item

END OF Index
```

The items in a node are ordered, so it would be possible to write *Index* so that it does a binary search of the items in a node. If the maximum number of items in a node is large, such a binary search would speed things up considerably.

If the number is small, a linear search would probably work just as well. We'll leave the refinement of this algorithm for the exercises.

Traversing a Multiway Tree

A traversal of a multiway tree is also quite similar to what we have already discussed in chapter 7 for binary search trees. The fundamental property makes a recursive algorithm easy to write:

```
START OF Traverse(P)
Passed by value: P, a multiway tree

if P ≠ nil
    then
        call Traverse(P^.P₀)
        loop for i going from 1 to P^.NumItems
            visit P^.Dataᵢ
            call Traverse(P^.Pᵢ)


END OF Traverse
```

We are not specifying what a "visit" of a data item consists of. It may involve just printing the data in the item or it may involve some sort of processing of that data. The structure of the algorithm does not depend on what needs to be accomplished at each visit.

Notice also that this constitutes an "inorder" traversal of the tree. If you needed to save a multiway tree in a file, you would want to traverse it in preorder while it's being written to the file, just as with a binary tree. We won't write algorithms for either preorder or postorder traversals of a multiway tree; they are very similar to the above algorithm.

Rather than discuss general multiway trees further, we'll discuss two particular kinds of multiway trees: 2-3 trees and, later, B-trees. These particular types of multiway trees are more commonly used than general multiway trees.

9.3   2-3 Trees

In this section we will discuss 2-3 search trees. Since we're not going to discuss 2-3 trees in general, just 2-3 *search* trees, from this point on when we say "2-3 tree," we will mean "2-3 search tree."

A 2-3 tree is much the same as a multiway search tree of order 2. Every node contains either two or three pointers and one or two data items. However, a 2-3 tree must satisfy one additional requirement: all the nodes containing nil pointers must contain only nil pointers, and they must all be on the same level. This means, in other words, that there are no semi-leaves, just leaves. This requirement, as we will see, causes the tree to behave in a manner analogous to height-balanced binary search trees. Indeed, if all the nodes in the 2-3 tree have exactly two subtrees—rather than the three that they would be allowed— then the 2-3 tree would be a height-balanced binary search tree. By allowing the nodes to have either two or three subtrees, we can insert and delete nodes without the complicated algorithm required by, for example, AVL trees.

As in our earlier examples, we'll let the data field of each node contain just the key field. Remember, this is a simplification that really makes the tree useless. The techniques we learn, however, will apply to real 2-3 trees with real data in each node. Figure 9.3 contains a 2-3 tree that we will use in several of our later examples. Notice that each data field contains just an integer, and notice that the integers in the subtrees are always between those in the parent nodes.

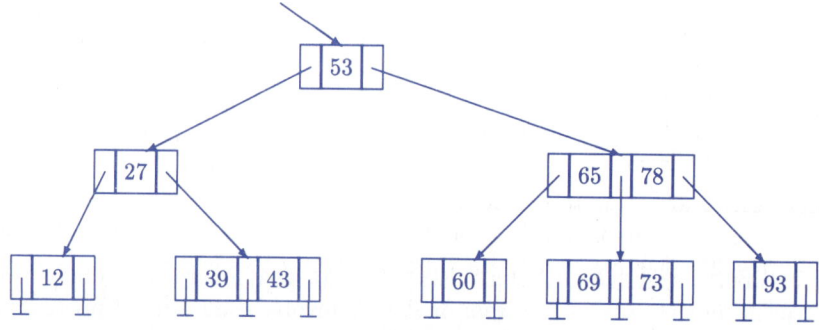

Figure 9.3 A 2-3 Tree

Notice also that all the leaves are on the same level. That's an important property that we must preserve at all times—along with the fundamental search property.

In the previous sections, we developed algorithms for searching and travers- ing multiway search trees. Since a 2-3 tree is a multiway search tree and neither searching nor traversing changes the structure of a tree, these same algorithms will suffice for the jobs of searching or traversing a 2-3 tree. Consequently, we'll not discuss searching or traversing 2-3 trees, and will move right on to inserting and deleting nodes.

Inserting a New Node in a 2-3 Tree

Consider again the 2-3 tree in figure 9.3. Suppose that you need to insert the number 15 into the tree. As always, the new node will be a leaf of the tree. Where would it belong? 15 follows 12 in numerical order and precedes 27 so it belongs in the same node as 12. That node currently has only one data item and two pointers, so it's easy just to add another number to the node. The tree will now look like the tree in figure 9.4.

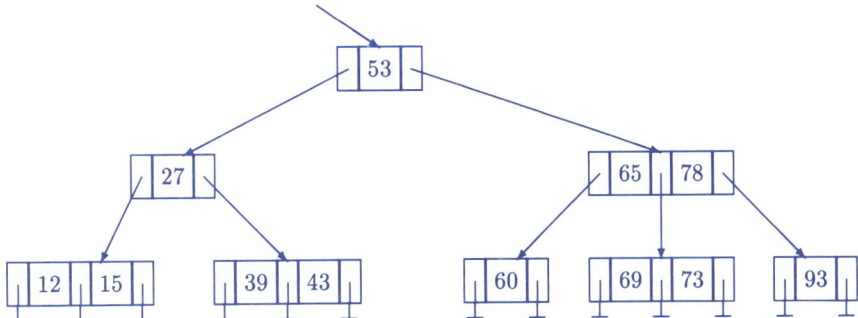

Figure 9.4 The 2-3 Tree, after Inserting 15

Suppose that we now want to insert **22**. Since 22 is smaller than 27, we get to the same node as before, i.e., the one that now contains 12 and 15. But since this node already has two data items, we cannot add 22 to this node. You might be tempted to think that a new leaf will be added at this point, but that's not what happens! A 2-3 tree always has all its leaves on the same level and we cannot add a new leaf without destroying this property. Instead, we temporarily add the 22 to the node and then split it into two leaves by moving the middle value up one level to the parent. In this case, the parent—the node containing 27—has only one data item and thus there is room for the middle value: the **15**. This value is added to the node containing 27, the pointers are adjusted, and the tree in figure 9.5 results.

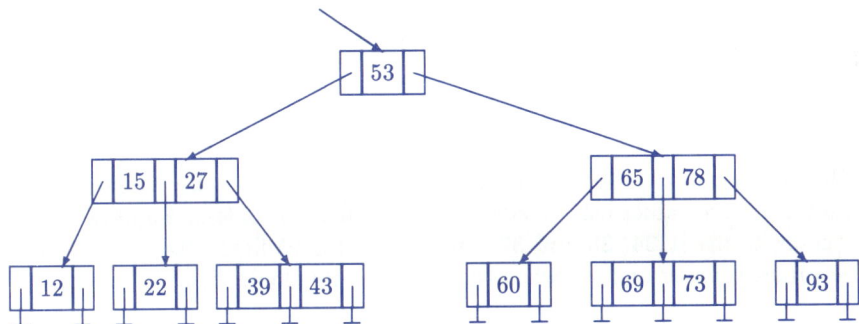

Figure 9.5 The 2-3 Tree, after Inserting 15 and 22

Now suppose we want to insert **32** in the tree in figure 9.5. As always, we follow pointers until we come to a nil pointer, indicating we are at a leaf. In this case, we come to the leaf node containing 39 and 43. Since this node already has two data items, we must split the node and pass the middle value—**39**—up one level to the parent. This would yield the tree in figure 9.6.

There's an obvious problem, however. There are now three data items and four subtrees in the node that received the 39, and no node is allowed to have more than two data items.

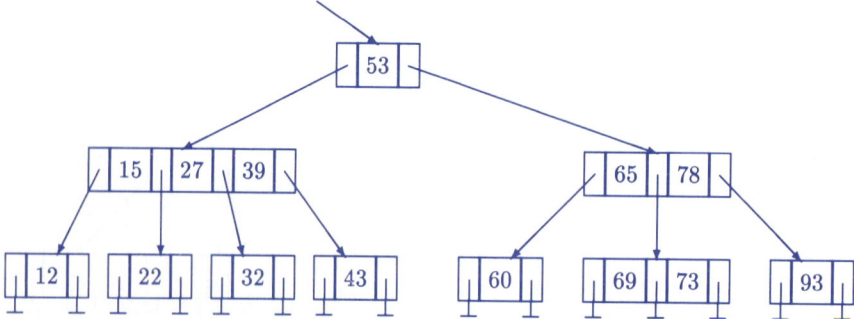

Figure 9.6 The 2-3 Tree, Trying to Insert **32**

The next step is to again split the node and pass the middle value—this time the **27**—up one level to the next node. After passing the **27** up one level, the tree in figure 9.7 results.

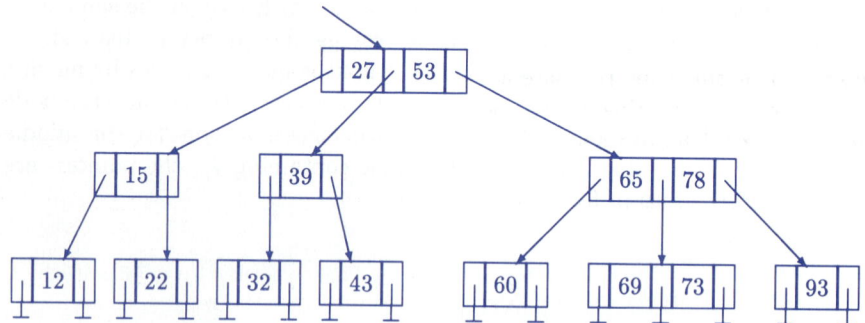

Figure 9.7 The 2-3 Tree, after Inserting **32**

Now most of the nodes in the left side of the tree have only one data item and several more values can be added without much problem. Suppose we are now going to insert **34**, **35** and **37**. Before looking at figure 9.8, try inserting these values yourself and see what the resulting tree looks like.

After inserting **34**, **35** and **37** into the tree in figure 9.7, the tree in figure 9.8 results.

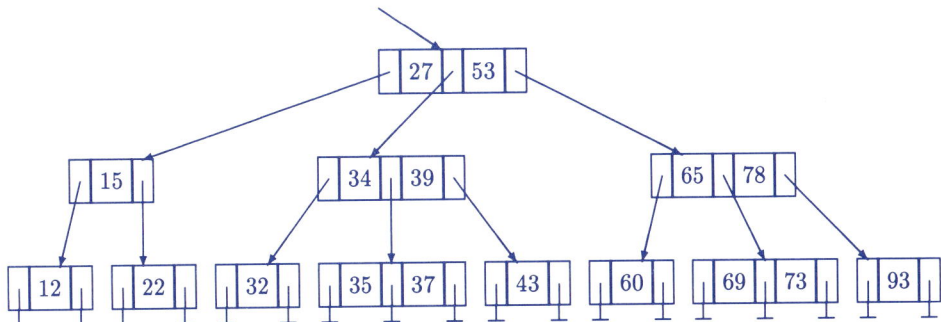

Figure 9.8 The 2-3 Tree, after Inserting 34, 35 and 37

Now suppose we want to insert **36**. Since the node where **36** belongs—the node containing **35** and **37**—already has two data items, it must be split into two nodes and the middle value—the **36**—passed up one level. The **36** won't fit in the node above since it already has two data items: **34** and **39**. That node also has to be split into two nodes and the middle value again passed up to the parent node. This node also already has two values, **27** and **53**, and it needs to be split. But this time the parent node is the root node. When the root node is split, the middle value cannot be "passed" up to the next higher node since there is no next higher node. In this case, the value that would otherwise be passed up becomes the new root of the entire tree. The tree in figure 9.9 results. Notice that the figure shows only that part of the tree that was changed by the insertion routine.

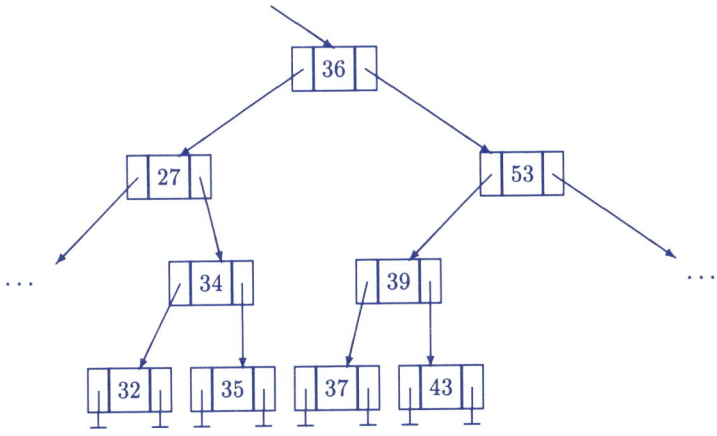

Figure 9.9 The 2-3 Tree, after Splitting the Root

A 2-3 tree grows wider as nodes are inserted, and, when necessary, grows taller *at the root!* As nodes are inserted into a 2-3 tree, it becomes very broad, and tends to stay short. As we saw in chapter 7, short squat trees are preferable to tall skinny trees; they yield faster search times.

Let's summarize what we do when we insert a new node. We can pretend, for the sake of understanding what happens, that a node can temporarily hold three data items:

- The new item is always inserted in a leaf node.

- If the node now has three items, the node is split and the middle value is passed up to the parent.

- If a node being split is the root node, the middle value is put into a new node, which becomes the new root of the tree.

It is, of course, necessary to correctly assign the various pointers at each of these steps. It's time to turn our solution into an algorithm.

The Parent of a Node

Since the algorithm often makes it necessary to pass a data item up to a node's parent, it is necessary to somehow keep track of the parents of the nodes. As we search down the tree looking for the correct leaf into which the new item should be inserted, we have to keep track of each node's parent in case it becomes necessary to pass an item up to a parent node when a node is split. That presents a problem that we must resolve before going much further with the development of the algorithm.

Two ways of keeping track of the parents come to mind. One way would be to add another field, a parent pointer, to each node. As the tree is constructed, the parent of each node would be stored in this field; later, when necessary, we can follow that pointer back up the path to the parent of the node being split. This is a workable solution but does involve quite a bit of overhead. It will be necessary to make sure that whenever pointers are adjusted, the parent pointers are adjusted too. In particular, when a node is split, one of the data items is put in the new node. This item is surrounded by two trees which also need to be placed in the new node. But then, since the children have a different parent, their parent pointers have to be changed.

Using a Stack for the Parent Pointers

There's another solution. Since the path that has to be followed back was already followed in the forward direction when the node where the insertion is to be done is located, all we need to do is retain that path somehow and then, when necessary, follow it backward. An appropriate data structure for such a task would be a stack. As we move down the tree, we can push the old pointer onto a stack. As we need to move back up the tree, we can pop a pointer off the stack.

It's an implementation question which could be handled later, but let's examine how we might write the stack. Two choices come to mind, based on our experiences from earlier chapters. We could use an array or we could use a linked list. One of the lessons of chapters 3 and 4 is that arrays are often difficult to deal with since the size of the array has to be determined in advance. If we were working with binary search trees rather than 2-3 trees, we would have a hard time determining how big to make the array. As nodes are added to the tree, it would be impossible to determine how big the array would have to be. If the tree is a binary tree, it would always be possible that a series of insertions could take place that would create, essentially, a linked list of nodes.

However, we're dealing with 2-3 trees, not binary trees. A 2-3 tree is always very balanced. Repeated insertions never cause a 2-3 tree to get out of balance. Indeed, it can be shown that a 2-3 tree containing m items will always have a height less than or equal to $\lceil \log_2(m + 1) \rceil$, the same as the minimum height of a binary tree. Therefore, if we use an array that will hold, say 40 pointers, the number of items the tree will hold will be about 2^{40}, or around one trillion. Thus, we can reasonably pick a size for the array that will work in all possible cases, and that will not require a great deal of storage. In summary, using a stack to hold the parent pointers, and implementing that stack with an array, will be reasonable choices for appropriate data structures.

The Structure of a Node

We have already agreed to use two arrays in each node: one for the data items and one for the subtrees. To make it possible to temporarily have three data items in a node before splitting it, let's agree that these arrays will hold a maximum of three and four elements, respectively. We'll also assume there is a field that contains the number of items in the node—this field will normally equal one or two. In summary, the fields of each node will consist of:

- *NumItems*, the number of data items in the node, between one and three. It will only equal three when the node needs to be split.

- *Data*, an array of data items. This array would likely be an array of records in a real example. It will always contain *NumItems* actual data items.

- *P*, an array of subtrees. There can be up to four elements in this array. It will always contain *NumItems* + 1 actual subtrees. If the node is a leaf, all of the subtrees will be nil pointers.

To insert the new item, we must first examine the *Root*; if it's nil then the tree is empty, and a new node has to be created. In this case various pointers have to be assigned. The more interesting case, of course, occurs when the *Root* is not nil. Then we have to follow pointers until we come to a nil pointer. Since there are either two or three pointers in each node, we'll use *Index* again to determine which pointer to follow. Look back at our description of *Index* and the version you wrote to make sure it works for *InTree* as well as for *Insert*.

The loop will end when we encounter a nil pointer, but in that case we will have gone one level too far. Since we're pushing the pointers onto a stack, it will be easy to simply pop one pointer off the stack. We'll call the pointer to the leaf node where the insertion should be done *Ptr*.

After finding the correct node, we just add the item to those already there, moving those that are bigger to the right. This is accomplished by another subroutine, *AddToNode*.

After adding the item, it may be that there are now three items in that node and the node needs to be split. This can happen again and again so we use a *loop while* that works its way back up the tree, using the stack of pointers to take us back to each node's parent. This loop continues as long as the node we're at has four subtrees. Another routine, *Split*, actually does the job of calling *Allocate* to get a new node and splitting the old node apart. When a node is split, the new node will adopt the rightmost data item from the old node as well as the two rightmost subtrees. These routines need to be written carefully, and you should think about how you would write them before reading further.

The complete algorithm is on the next page.

```
START OF Insert(Root, Item)
Passed by value: Item
Passed by reference: Root, a 2-3 tree
Precondition: Item is not in the tree
Postcondition: Item is in the tree

if Root = nil
    then
        call Allocate(Root)
        store Item in Root^.Data₁
        store nil in Root^.P₀
        store nil in Root^.P₁
        store 1 in Root^.NumItems
    else
        call InitStack(Stack)
        store Root in Ptr
        loop
            call Push(Stack, Ptr)
            store Index(Ptr, Item) in i
            store Ptr^.Pᵢ in Ptr
            until Ptr = nil
        call Pop(Stack, Ptr)
        call AddToNode(Ptr, i+1, Item, nil)
        loop while Ptr^.NumItems = 3
            call Split(Ptr, Temp)
            store Ptr^.Data₂ in Item
            if Ptr = Root
                then
                    call Allocate(Root)
                    store Ptr in Root^.P₀
                    store Temp in Root^.P₁
                    store Item in Root^.Data₁
                    store 1 in Root^.NumItems
                    store Root in Ptr
                else
                    call Pop(Stack, Ptr)
                    store Index(Ptr, Item) in i
                    call AddToNode(Ptr, i+1, Item, Temp)

END OF Insert
```

START OF Split(Ptr, Temp)
Passed by value: Ptr, a 2-3 tree
Passed by reference: Temp, a 2-3 tree
Precondition: Ptr is a 2-3 tree with three data items, and needs to be split

call Allocate(Temp)
store $Ptr^\wedge.Data_3$ in $Temp^\wedge.Data_1$
store $Ptr^\wedge.P_2$ in $Temp^\wedge.P_0$
store $Ptr^\wedge.P_3$ in $Temp^\wedge.P_1$
store 1 in $Temp^\wedge.NumItems$
store 1 in $Ptr^\wedge.NumItems$

END OF Split

START OF AddToNode(Ptr, Place, Item, Temp)
Passed by value: Ptr, Temp (2-3 trees), Place, Item

add 1 to $Ptr^\wedge.NumItems$
loop for i going from $Ptr^\wedge.NumItems$ down to Place + 1
    store $Ptr^\wedge.Data_{i-1}$ in $Ptr^\wedge.Data_i$
    store $Ptr^\wedge.P_{i-1}$ in $Ptr^\wedge.P_i$
store Item in $Ptr^\wedge.Data_{Place}$
store Temp in $Ptr^\wedge.P_{Place}$

END OF AddToNode

Deleting a Node from a 2-3 Tree

We turn now to the complementary problem of deletion. We want to be able to
delete a node from a 2-3 tree, and we must be sure to retain the two properties
of a 2-3 tree: the fundamental search property and the property of having all
the leaves of the tree on the same level. In chapter 7 we saw that deletion is
more difficult than insertion in a binary tree. The same is true for a 2-3 tree.
Even the previously simplest case of deletion—that of deleting a leaf node—is
harder with a 2-3 tree since we cannot just remove a leaf if it contains only one
data item. In that case, the node above it would become a leaf or a semi-leaf,
and that cannot happen. Let's take another look at the tree in figure 9.3 to see
how some deletions might be accomplished. Figure 9.10 contains the same tree
for easy reference.

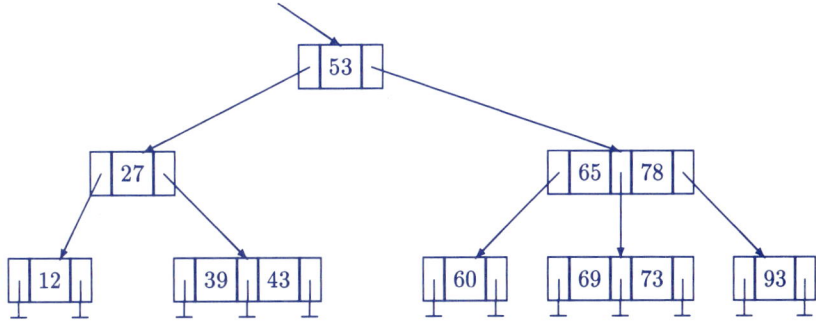

Figure 9.10 A 2-3 Tree

It would be a simple matter to delete **39**. Since the node containing **39** has two items, just removing **39** from the tree would not alter either fundamental property. The same could be said for deleting **43**, **69** and **73**. We'll not delete these nodes; just remember this situation for later.

How would you delete **12**? Think about it before you read on.

Since deleting **12** would leave that node empty, some sort of remedial action must be taken. In this case, the easiest action would be to adopt a data item from a sibling that has an extra item of data. In particular, since the sibling to the right has two items (**39** and **43**), it can spare the **39**. Of course, this item would have to be moved to the parent node, not just moved over. This action would result in the tree in figure 9.11.

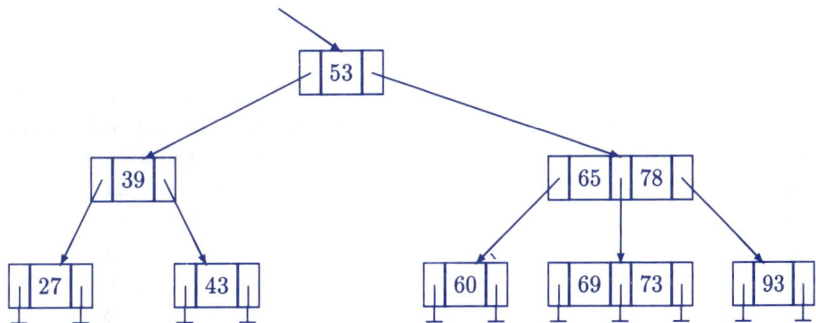

Figure 9.11 A 2-3 Tree, after Deleting 12

Be sure to notice how the **39** was moved up to the parent, and the parent data—**27**—was moved down to the node where the **12** was. The strategy here is that when you delete an item that would leave a node empty, adopt an item from a sibling, if possible.

Before we discuss what to do if it isn't possible to borrow an item from a sibling, let's look at the problem of deleting an item from a non-leaf node. All of the examples we have considered so far illustrated deleting an item from a leaf.

Deleting an Internal Item

Look at figure 9.11 again and consider how we might delete the 65. The 65 is in an internal node (as opposed to a leaf node). There is an elegant solution to this problem. Since the 65 is in an internal node, there must be a leaf node that contains its "inorder successor." By "inorder successor," we simply mean the next item in inorder. The inorder successor of 65 is 69 and that item is in a leaf node. To delete the 65, we simply replace the 65 with the 69 and delete the 69 from the leaf. That process destroys the order property of the tree, temporarily, but since were going to delete the extra 69, the property will be restored quickly. After replacing the 65 with 69, and deleting the 69 in the leaf node, the tree will look like that in figure 9.12.

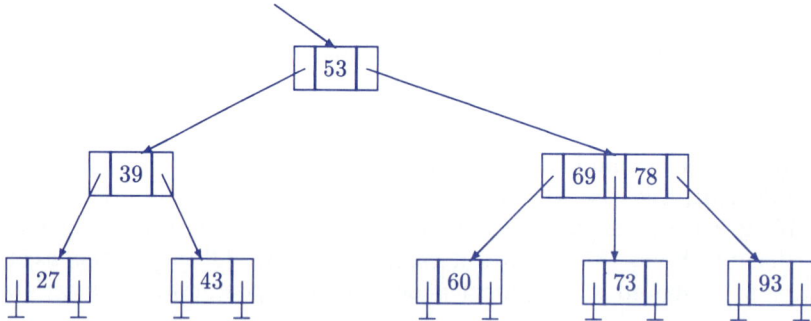

Figure 9.12 A 2-3 Tree, after Deleting 12 and 65

This strategy will always work: any time the item to be deleted is in an internal node, simply find the inorder successor—which must be in a leaf node—replace the data in the internal node with its inorder successor, and delete the item from the leaf node. Notice that this requires an actual assignment of the data in the nodes. We avoided moving data earlier because that has a potentially high cost. Now, however, we cannot accomplish the deletion by simply rearranging pointers. The data item is in a node, which means it is in an array in the node, and we cannot simply rearrange some pointers to remove it.

Since we see now that we can always delete an item from an internal node by replacing it with an item in a leaf node, from this point on we'll only consider deleting nodes from leaf nodes, assuming the replacement can be taken care of, when necessary.

Deleting from a Leaf Node

Look back again at figure 9.11. Suppose this time we want to delete 60. The 60 is in a leaf node, and deleting this item would leave that node empty, so we have to try to adopt an item from a sibling. Again, this is possible; the sibling node to the right contains two items, 69 and 73. We can adopt the 69. As before, the 69 is not just moved over to this node but rather is moved up to the parent and the corresponding item in the parent, the 65, is moved down. This results in the tree in figure 9.13.

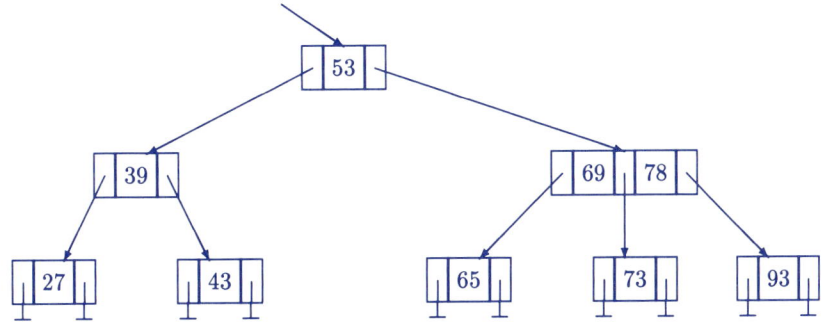

Figure 9.13 A 2-3 Tree, after Deleting 60 instead of 65

It's important to understand that we'll only adopt an item from an adjacent sibling that has one to spare. In both of the examples we've looked at, the sibling that we adopted from was an adjacent sibling. It might be the case that the adjacent sibling does not have an item to spare but the other sibling does. For example, if we were deleting from a far left node, and the "middle" sibling had only one item while the far right sibling had two items, we could adopt one from that node. This would require moving an item from the far right node to the parent, moving one of the parent's items down to the middle child node, moving the original item in the middle node up to the parent, and moving the far left item in the parent node down to the node that is being left vacant by the deletion. This makes the process more complicated than necessary. If the adjacent siblings each have only one item, we'll just combine two nodes and pull down an item from the parent, which is the next case we consider.

Deleting an Item When the Siblings Can't Spare an Item

Let's consider that case: deleting an item from a leaf node when the siblings can't spare any. The process in this case is the reverse of what happens when we insert an item, and the node has to be split. When we split an node, we pass one item up to the parent node. Now we have to combine two nodes (one of which is empty) and pull an item down from the parent.

Look at figure 9.13. To delete the 73, we just combine this node with a sibling node, say the node containing 65, and pull down the 69 from the parent, producing the tree in figure 9.14.

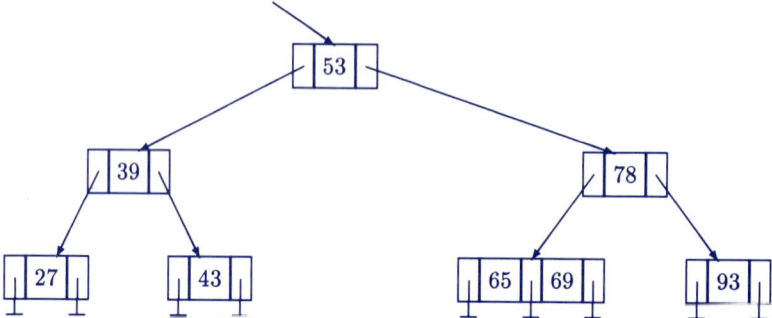

Figure 9.14 The Tree from Figure 9.13, after Deleting **73**

Deleting an Item When the Siblings Can't Spare an Item, and the Parent Has Only One Item

The next case to consider is the case where we want to delete an item from a node that only contains one item, where the adjacent sibling node(s) have no items to spare, and where the parent node only has one item. Consider, once again, the tree in figure 9.13. Suppose we want to delete the **43**. The node containing **43** has only the one item. The sibling node has only the **27**. If we combine these nodes, pulling down an item from the parent, we obtain the tree in figure 9.15.

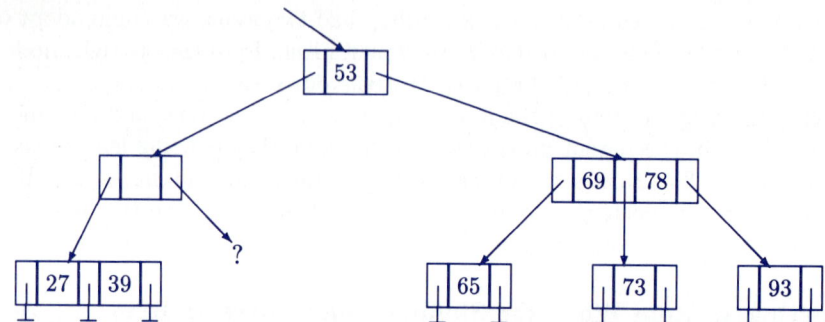

Figure 9.15 A 2-3 Tree, Trying to Delete **43**

But, as you can see, when we pulled down the **39** from the parent, it left the parent node empty. The remedy is similar to the one we used earlier: we look at an adjacent sibling to see if it can spare an item. In this case, the parent's sibling has two items, **69** and **78**, so we can move one item over. As before, the item is moved to the parent, and the item in the parent is moved down. Notice, however, that when this adjusting is done, the children of the node being adopted have to be moved over too. The pointer to the node containing **65** is moved from the right node to the left node. This produces the tree in figure 9.16.

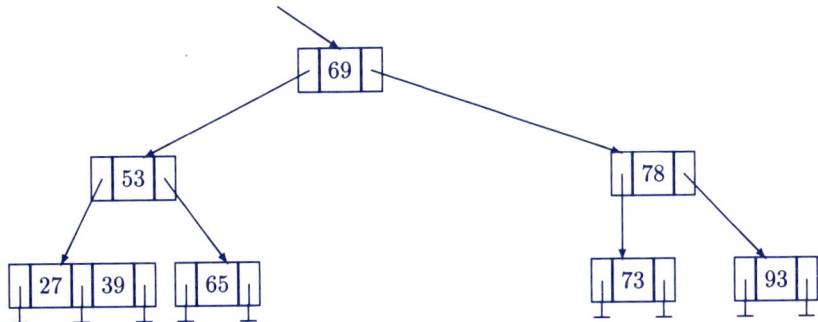

Figure 9.16 A 2-3 Tree, after Deleting 43

It's important to see that we cannot pass the 27 up to the node containing 39 in this case. If we were to do so, the leaves of the tree would not all be on the same level, and it would not satisfy the fundamental property of a 2-3 tree.

Deleting an Item When the Siblings Can't Spare an Item, the Parent Has Only One Item, and the Parent's Siblings Can't Spare an Item

Now, suppose that the item being deleted is the only item in the node, the siblings of the node don't have any items to spare and the siblings of the parent don't have any items to spare. The solution should be obvious: pull down an item from the parent and combine two nodes. That leaves the parent empty and the parent's siblings can't spare any items, so pull down an item from the parent's parent and combine the parent node with one of the parent's siblings. This process would be repeated until one of the following three things happens: (1) a node with two items is encountered, (2) a node with an adjacent sibling that has an item to spare is encountered, or (3) the root node is reached. In the last case—that of reaching the root node—two children of the root will be combined, the root node deallocated, and the combined node will become the new root—the tree will be one level shorter.

This has turned into a complicated process. It's time to write an algorithm for the solution.

Algorithm for Deletion from a 2-3 Tree

Let's start by reducing our solution to a "high-level" algorithm. One problem in writing the algorithm is deciding which steps need to be repeated. When an item is removed from a node, the process will end if that node still contains another item; i.e., if that node is non-empty. If the node is empty, then there is more work to be done. The essential steps we need to accomplish are:

find the node containing the item to be deleted
point Ptr to that node
if it's an internal node
    find the inorder successor of the item being deleted
    replace the item with its inorder successor
    retool the data for deleting the successor instead
remove the item from the node pointed at by Ptr
loop while the node pointed at by Ptr is empty
    if Ptr is the root node
        then
            point Root at its successor
            deallocate the root
        else
            adjust the tree

The work that needs to be done is to either reassign the root pointer—if that's the node that is empty—or adjust the tree adopting a child from a sibling or by pulling down an item from the parent. We've left this step as just *adjust the tree*, and we must think about that process in more detail.

We adjust the tree by either adopting an element from a sibling or by pulling an item from the node's parent. In the latter case, the parent node might now be empty. As long as we point at the correct node, we can use a *loop while* to tell us when more work needs to be done; i.e., we can loop while the node pointed at is empty.

We can identify some useful subroutines. Earlier we used a routine, *Add-ToNode*, that moved items over to make room for a new item. The complement of this, say *RemoveFromNode*, can be used to slide items to the left to remove the item that is either being deleted or has been sent down to a child.

In the process of adjusting the tree, sometimes we find a spare item in the node to the right; sometimes we find a spare item in the node to the left. We'll use two routines, *AdoptFromRight* and *AdoptFromLeft*, to accomplish these tasks.

There are different cases in which nodes need to be combined. One case is when the leftmost child is empty and is being combined with the second child. Another is when the second child is empty and is being combined with the leftmost node. A third case is where an empty third child is being combined with the second node. Notice that the case of an empty second node being combined with the third child can be avoided; in this case the first child has only one data item and it can be used instead of the third. We'll call these three cases *Combine1With2*, *Combine2With1*, and *Combine3With2*. In each of these cases an item will be pulled down from the parent.

Here's *Delete* using these ideas:

```
START OF Delete(Root, Item)
Passed by value: Item
Passed by reference: Root, a 2-3 tree
Precondition: Item is in the tree
Postcondition: Item is not in the tree


call InitStack(Stack)
store Root in Ptr
store Index(Ptr, Item) in i
loop while Ptr^.K_i ≠ Item
    call Push(Stack, Ptr)
    store Ptr^.P_i in Ptr
    store Index(Ptr, Item) in i
if Ptr^.P_0 ≠ nil { it's in an internal node }
   then
        call Push(Stack, Ptr)
        store Ptr^.P_i in Temp
        loop while Temp^.P_0 ≠ nil
            call Push(Stack, Temp)
            store Temp^.P_0 in Temp
        store Temp^.Data_1 in Ptr^.Data_i
        store Temp^.Data_1 in Item
        store 1 in i
        store Temp in Ptr
call RemoveFromNode(Ptr, i)
loop while Ptr^.NumItems = 0
    if Ptr = Root
       then
            store Ptr^.P_0 in Root
            call DeAllocate(Ptr)
            store Root in Ptr { to get the loop to end }
       else
            call Pop(Stack, Parent)
            call AdjustTheTree(Ptr, Parent, Item)
            store Parent in Ptr


END OF Delete
```

We are using a procedure *AdjustTheTree* to handle the situation that occurs when we have to either adopt an item from an adjacent sibling or pull an item down from the parent. Here's an algorithm for *AdjustTheTree*:

START OF AdjustTheTree(Ptr, Parent, Item)
Passed by value: Ptr, Parent (2-3 trees) and Item

if Item is the leftmost child of Parent
    then
        store Parent^.P$_1$ in Temp
        if Temp^.NumItems = 2
            then { right sibling can spare an item }
                call AdoptFromRight(Ptr, Parent, 0)
            else{ have to pull one down from Parent }
                call Combine1With2(Ptr, Temp, Parent)
    else
        if Item is the middle child of Parent
            then
                store Parent^.P$_0$ in Temp
                if Temp^.NumItems = 2
                    then { left sibling can spare an item }
                        call AdoptFromLeft(Ptr, Parent, 1)
                    else
                        if Parent^.NumItems = 2 and Parent^.P$_2$^.NumItems = 2
                            then { right sibling can spare an item }
                                call AdoptFromRight(Ptr, Parent, 1)
                            else { have to pull one down from Parent }
                                call Combine2With1(Ptr, Temp, Parent)
            else { Item is the rightmost child of Parent }
                store Parent^.P$_1$ in Temp
                if Temp^.NumItems = 2
                    then { left sibling can spare an item }
                        call AdoptFromLeft(Ptr, Parent, 2)
                    else{ have to pull one down from Parent }
                        call Combine3With2(Ptr, Temp, Parent)

END OF AdjustTheTree

The routines AdoptFromRight and AdoptFromLeft are called if it is determined that either the right or left sibling, respectively, has an item it can spare. AdoptFromRight will move over the leftmost item from the right sibling of Ptr. AdoptFromLeft moves over the rightmost item from the left sibling of Ptr. The extra parameter helps determine which child Ptr is of Parent.

If none of the siblings can spare an item, one of the three versions of Combine is called to combine the nodes Ptr and Temp.

Here's AdoptFromRight:

START OF AdoptFromRight(Ptr, Parent, Num)
Passed by value: Ptr, Parent (2-3 trees) and Num
Precondition: Node pointed at by the (Num+1)st pointer in Parent
            has an item to spare

store $Parent^\wedge.Data_{Num+1}$ in $Ptr^\wedge.Data_1$
store $Parent^\wedge.P_{Num+1}$ in Temp
store $Temp^\wedge.P_0$ in $Ptr^\wedge.P_1$
store $Temp^\wedge.Data_1$ in $Parent^\wedge.Data_{Num+1}$
store 1 in $Ptr^\wedge.NumItems$
call RemoveFromNode(Temp, 1)

END OF AdoptFromRight

We'll leave *AdoptFromLeft* and the three *Combines* for the exercises.

Notice that the function *Index* returns the index of the array item if it's found in the array. This is, of course, what we want it to return if the item is in the array and we're doing a search. A more subtle situation arises in the case of *Delete*. When *Index* is used by *Delete* it will be necessary to have it give us the index of a pointer even when the item it's searching for is in the node being searched. Remember that the *Delete* algorithm we wrote replaced an internal item with its inorder successor. As we move up the tree, combining nodes and pulling items from their parents, it becomes necessary to use *Index* to find the correct subtree to examine. Since we have replaced the item being deleted by its inorder successor, and have replaced *Item* by this same data item, we have to be sure that when we use *Index* on the parent node, it will direct us to the correct node. *Item* does not have the same value as it did when we searched down the tree for its inorder successor; we changed it to the value in the leaf node. Now when we use *Index*, it will actually find a data item equal to *Item* in an internal node, and we must be sure the correct path will be followed. When an algorithm for *Index* is written, it must work as described.

Pascal Implementation of the 2-3 Tree Routines

After completing the algorithms, their implementations in Pascal will be straightforward. There's no new Pascal required. Let's look at a couple of the Pascal routines and leave the remainder for the exercises. Here are some Pascal definitions and declarations that are consistent with the decisions made in the chapter:

```
const
  MAX = 3;
type
  Tree = ^Node;
  Node = record
    Data : array [1 .. MAX] of integer;
    P : array [0 .. MAX] of Tree;
    NumItems : integer
  end;
```

Refer to the earlier discussion regarding *Index* (page 237). Recall that *Index* is used by *Delete* and *InTree*—as well as by *Insert*—and that it has to be carefully written to make sure it gives us the correct subscript. A careful examination of Index below will reveal that we follow the pointer to the right of Item when a data item equal to Item is encountered. This is primarily due to the fact that we indexed the array of pointers from 0 rather than from 1.

Here's a version of Index that will work for 2-3 trees as well as multiway trees:

```
function Index(Ptr : Tree; Item : integer) : integer;
var
  i : integer;
begin
  i := 1;
  while (i <= Ptr^.NumItems) and (Ptr^.Data[i] < Item) do
    i := i + 1;
  if (i <= Ptr^.NumItems) and (Ptr^.Data[i] <= Item)
    then
      Index := i
    else
      Index := i - 1
end;
```

There is a problem with this function, however. As mentioned earlier, it would be possible to do a binary search through the keys in a node rather than a linear search since the keys are in order. If the tree is a 2-3 tree, or if it is a multiway tree of a small order, then this linear search will be satisfactory. For multiway trees of larger orders, the linear search should be replaced with a binary search.

Here's our version of Delete; notice how similar it is to the algorithm.

```
procedure Delete(var Root : Tree; Item : integer);

{  This procedure deletes the node containing Item from  }
{  the 2-3 tree Root.                                    }

var
  i, j : integer;
  Ptr, Temp, Parent : Tree;
  S : Stack;

begin
  InitStack(S);
  Ptr := Root;
  i := Index(Ptr, Item);
  while Ptr^.Data[i] <> Item do
    begin
      Push(S, Ptr);
      Ptr := Ptr^.P[i];
      i := Index(Ptr, Item)
    end;
  if Ptr^.P[0] <> nil  { not a leaf }
    then
      begin
        Push(S, Ptr);
        Temp := Ptr^.P[i];
        while Temp^.P[0] <> nil do
          begin
            Push(S, Temp);
            Temp := Temp^.P[0]
          end;
        Ptr^.Data[i] := Temp^.Data[1];  { move successor up }
        Item := Temp^.Data[1];          { replace item }
        i := 1;
        Ptr := Temp
      end;
  RemoveFromNode(Ptr, i);
```

```
while Ptr^.NumItems = 0 do
  begin
    if Ptr = Root
      then
        begin
          Root := Ptr^.P[0];
          dispose(Ptr);
          Ptr := Root
        end
      else
        begin
          if not EmptyStack(S)
            then
              Pop(S, Parent)
            else
              writeln('Error, stack empty.');
          AdjustTree(Ptr, Parent, Item);
          Ptr := Parent
        end
  end
end;
```

We'll leave the coding of the remaining subroutines for the exercises.

9.4   Direct Access Files

In all of the preceding discussion in this text, we have assumed that the data structures we deal with are held entirely in memory. We have, for example, worked with binary trees that we read from and wrote to a file, but we assumed that when we read the tree from the file, the entire tree could be in memory at once. That assumption enabled us to learn about these data structures and, hopefully, you have learned a great deal about them. However, in the real world it is often necessary to deal with much larger amounts of data that would not fit in the memory of even the largest of today's computers. This section and the remaining sections of this chapter deal with this situation.

This immediately presents us with a problem. The sort of files that are needed to deal with huge amounts of data are "direct access files." A direct access file is a file that allows us to directly obtain any record in the file. Standard Pascal does not support direct access files, only sequential access files.

Pascal was originally designed as a teaching language, not as a production language, and it was deemed unnecessary to include direct access files in a teaching language. Pascal has, as we all are aware, become an enormously popular language despite the original intentions for the language. As a result it became necessary to add to the language the ability to support direct access files. Virtually all of the Pascal compilers were extended to support direct access files. Unfortunately, the different compiler writers had no standard to refer to when adding this extension and they didn't all do it the same way. This destroys the transportability of programs that use direct access files written in Pascal, and a programmer who needs to move such a program from one compiler to another is usually forced to rewrite part of the code.

We have committed ourselves to using Standard Pascal in this text, but obviously we cannot stay within the standard regarding direct access files when there is no mention of them in the Pascal Standard. To make the following programs as transportable as possible,we have decided to adopt a very simple picture of a direct access file and assume that anyone who wishes to turn the following programs into "real" programs on a particular compiler will be able to add whatever statements are needed to make them run.

Sequential Access Files

A sequential access file in Pascal is treated like you might imagine a long tape file. You can start reading or writing the file from the beginning and can move only in the forward direction. In the case of reading a file, you can simply start at the beginning of the file and read one record after another until reaching the end of the file. In the case of writing, you can only start writing at the beginning of the file and can simply add new records to the file one after another at the end. Every time you start writing to a file, you create a new file; any other file with the same name is overwritten and lost. When reading from a file, you cannot back up except to back up all the way to the beginning. When writing, you cannot back up at all.

Direct Access Files

We will assume that we can deal with files that can be both read from and written to. We will assume that we can directly access any record in the file and can either read that record or write that record. We will assume that all our files are files of records of some type. A record could be as simple as a single character or a single integer, or could be as complicated as a Pascal `record`. We will assume that when we read the file, we always read an entire record. Similarly, when we write to the file we always write an entire record.

We will assume the following primitive operations:

- *NumRecords(FileName)* A function that will return the number of records currently in the file.

- *ReadRecord(FileName, i, Record)* A procedure that will read the *i*th record from the file. Parameters will be the file *FileName*, the record number *i*, and a record *Record* to be read into. We assume as a precondition that all record numbers used are between 1 and *NumRecords(FileName)*.

- WriteRecord(FileName, i, Record) A procedure that writes a record to the file onto the ith position. Parameters will be the file FileName, the record number i, and the record Record to be written. We assume that it is possible to write a record to the $n + 1$st position in the file when there are only n records currently in the file. This essentially allows us to add a new record at the end of the file. We assume as a precondition that all record numbers used are between 1 and NumRecords(FileName) $+ 1$.

We'll see how these routines are used in the following sections.

It should be noted that real direct access files probably don't work this way. When a real direct access file is read from or written to, it is likely done in *blocks*. A block can be thought of as a collection of records, the largest number that the hardware can read or write at once. This allows for fewer actual disk accesses and makes for less wear and tear on the hardware. It doesn't affect our routines to imagine that records are read and written one at a time even though it might happen in practice in blocks. This does become a matter of consideration when we choose the size of a multiway tree. It's a good idea to choose this size so that a tree node is about the same size as a block. Then, each time a block is read, one tree node is read. We'll return to this question in a few pages.

9.5   B-trees

A B-tree is similar to a 2-3 tree. It's a multiway tree that has all its leaves on the same level. The number of children per node is not two or three; however, the number is much larger. There is an integer m such that every node—except possibly the root node—has between $m/2$ and m items. The root node can have as few as zero items—when the tree is entirely empty—and as many as m items. This is the only node that can have fewer than $m/2$ items. When a node other than the root node has fewer than $m/2$ items, either an item will be adopted from an adjacent sibling or they will be combined with a sibling. This adoption and combining happens as items are deleted from the tree, as with 2-3 trees. It's convenient to let m be an even integer. Remember that the number of subtrees in a multiway tree is always one greater than the number of items, so a B-tree of order m has between $m/2 + 1$ and $m + 1$ subtrees (except possibly for the root).

It should be mentioned again that different authors use different terminology. Some authors refer to the number of subtrees, some refer to the number of items. Thus, to some authors a B-tree of order m is a multiway tree that can have between $m/2$ and m *subtrees* rather than between $m/2$ and m *data items*. It is of little difference which terminology is chosen. To us it seems easier to think in terms of the number of items rather than the number of children. A 2-3 tree can have one or two items per node, so a 2-3 tree is a B-tree of order 2, according to our definition. The name "2-3 tree" refers to the maximum number of items (2) and the maximum number of children (3).

While we could spend several pages discussing B-trees in general terms, the actual real world use of a B-tree occurs in conjunction with direct access files. One would only use a B-tree when there was a great deal of data being maintained, more data than could be held in memory at one time. Thus, in the following pages when we discuss B-trees, we'll discuss them in the context of direct access files. Indeed, we'll assume that each node is a record, and that each record is being stored in a direct access file. To follow pointers, then, means to read records from such a file. Rather than being pointers in the sense we've used in the past, a pointer now will be the record number of a record in the file. The B-tree itself will be the file rather than a pointer to a node.

The number m is chosen, in practice, in accordance with the hardware and software being used. Since the B-tree will be used with direct access files, and since with each access of a direct access file there is a maximum amount of data that can be read or written, m is chosen so that one access of the file grabs as large a chunk as possible. For example, if one access of a direct access file on a particular machine retrieved at most 2k bytes of data, the number m would be chosen so that a record in the B-tree consisted of just 2k bytes or less. It would not be unusual for m to be 100 or more. If m does equal 100, then there will be at least 50 data items in every node (except possibly the root node). Assuming the nodes have about 75 data items each, the number of items on the first level would be 75, the number on the second level about 75×75, or about 5,625. The third level would contain around $75 \times 75 \times 75$ items, or about 421,875. You can easily see that B-trees of high orders containing millions of items will be very short. We'll return in the exercises to the relationship between the height of a B-tree and the number of items it contains.

When we discussed 2-3 trees, we made the simplifying assumption that the key field was the only field in the record, and in fact we assumed that the key field was an integer. B-trees will be different. A data item in the B-tree itself will consist of two fields: the key field and a record number. The record number will be the number of a record in another file, called the data file. When, for example, a successful search is performed, the value returned by the search will be the record number of a record in the other file, and an access of that record in that file will produce the rest of the actual data.

When a new record is inserted into the tree, the new record will be placed in the data file and the record number of that record along with the key field will be inserted into the B-tree. Figure 9.17 contains a picture of these two files and the records in them.

Notice that every record (node) in the B-tree contains three fields; the first field, Num, is an indication of the actual number of items in the record. The second field is an array of pointers. This array actually contains record numbers, P_i, of other records in the file. To indicate what we considered the nil pointer before, we'll use the number 0. The last field will be another array, an array of pairs, each pair containing a key field, K_i, and a record number, R_i, for the corresponding record in the data file. We drew these arrays as if they were separated, with the pointers and the keys interspersed with one another. In actuality they won't be, of course.

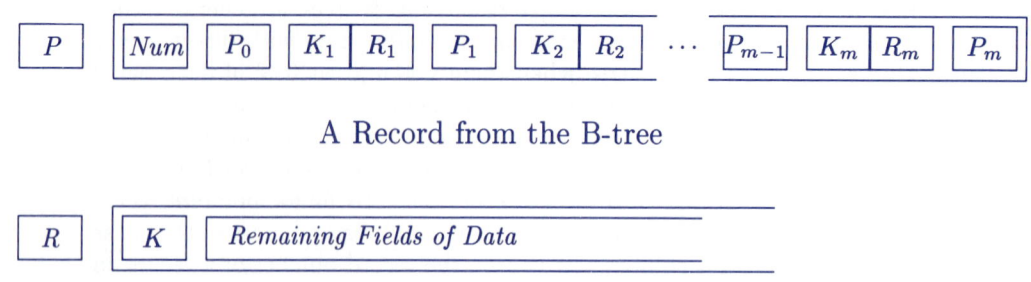

A Record from the B-tree

A Record from the Data File

Figure 9.17 The Structure of a B-tree

Notice that in the figure we also show a box to the left of the record, this box contains the record number of the record. The record number is not a part of the record but is associated with each record.

It is also necessary to keep track of where the root is. As new nodes are added to the tree (that is, to the file), these new nodes, on occasion, will become the root of the tree—remember the tree grows at the root, not at the leaves. When a new node is added and that new node becomes the root, it will be necessary to change the designation of the root. It is not necessary for our purposes to worry about how the designation of the root is retained, but in a real program, it has to be retained somewhere and it has to be able to be changed.

Searching a B-tree

The search procedure is a good place to start since it's an easy routine to understand and since its goal does not require adding or removing records.

To search a B-tree, we will start with the root record and look for the key field. As before, we'll use a function that will return the index of the last position in the key array that is less than or equal to the key being searched for. The search function will have to return an indication as to whether or not the key was found, and, if found, where it is in the data file. Let's write it as a function and have it return the record number of the record in the data file if the key field is found. If the key is not found, we'll have it return 0. In the past, we have written this function as a Boolean-valued function and named it *InTree*. Since it now returns a record number, let's name it *DataIndex*.

Here's an algorithm:

```
START OF DataIndex(B-tree, Root, Key)
if Root is 0
    then
        return 0
    else
        ReadRecord(B-tree, Root, Record)
        store Index(Record, Item) in i
        if Record.Data.Key_i = Key
            then
                return Record.Data.R_i
            else
                return DataIndex(B-tree, Record.P_i, Key)

END OF DataIndex
```

This function is nearly identical to those written earlier. The two differences are the fact that it reads records from a file and that it returns an integer rather than a Boolean value. The calling routine can now access the correct record in the data file, if the function returns a non-zero value. Notice that we still are calling a function, $Index$, that tells us which path to follow. The coded version of $Index$ presented earlier—in the section on 2-3 trees—used a linear search. But now, since the order of the tree is likely to be large, an order of 100 or more would not be unusual. The linear search should definitely be replaced by a binary search.

Traversal

Traversal of a B-tree is identical to traversal of a multiway tree except that rather than following pointers, we follow record numbers. The same algorithm used earlier will suffice except that the references to pointers need to be replaced with file accesses.

Here's a version:

```
START OF Traverse(B-tree, Ptr)
Passed by value: Ptr
Passed by reference: B-tree

if Ptr ≠ 0
   then
        call ReadRecord(B-tree, Ptr, Node)
        call Traverse(B-tree, Node.P₀)
        loop for i going from 1 to Node.NumItems
            visit Node.Dataᵢ
            call Traverse(B-tree, Node.Pᵢ)


END OF Traverse
```

As in our earlier versions, this one is also recursive. Since the height of the tree should be very small, the recursion will not get very deep, and a shortage of memory should not become a problem.

Insertion into a B-tree

Now let's tackle the more interesting question of doing an insertion into a B-tree. There are some simple cases that can be dealt with easily. If the tree is empty, we simply write a single record into the file. The three fields in this record will indicate that the record has one item, i.e., Num will be set to 1, the two pointers P_0 and P_1 will be set to 0, and the data item will get a value assigned. Before this can be done, we'll have to access the data file and add a new record to that file. Then that record number and the key will become data item number 1 in the tree file.

In the past we have referred to "nodes" of a tree. In a B-tree, each node becomes a record. In the future, we'll often use "record" in addition to "node" when referring to the nodes of a B-tree.

Suppose the root node is the only record in the tree and it has fewer than m items. Then the root node can hold another and the new item is just added. Indeed this is just what's done whenever the record reached can hold another item. As always, insertions are done in a leaf. We follow "pointers" until we come to a leaf. We add the new item to that leaf. If that causes the item to have more than m items, we split the record, placing the rightmost $m/2$ items in a new record, leaving the first $m/2$ items in the current record and passing the middle item to the parent. That tells us that we have to be able to move back up the tree to a node's parent. We'll keep track of the parent pointers with a stack, as before. If the record being split is the root, a new record is added and that record becomes the new root. This makes it necessary, as before, to pass the root by reference.

The steps are similar to those of the 2-3 tree insertion routine. The major differences are the need to watch for a node having more than m items, rather than more than two, and the need to add records to files rather than allocating more memory. As items are added, a data item record is added at the end of the data file. When it is necessary for the tree to grow (at the root), a new record is added to the B-tree file. Since the root of the tree changes, it will be necessary to store the root somewhere so that the program can find it each time the program begins. This detail has to be handled by the main program.

Here's our algorithm. You might want to compare it with the 2-3 insert algorithm.

```
START OF Insert(B-tree, Data, Root, Item)
Passed by value: Item
Passed by reference: B-tree, Data (direct access files) and Root (the record
                     number of the root record)
Precondition: Item is not in the B-tree
Postcondition: Item is in the B-tree

if Root = 0
    then
        call WriteRecord(Data, 1, Item)
        store 1 in Node.NumItems
        store Item.Key in Node.Data₁.Key
        store 1 in Node.Data₁.R
        store 0 in Node.P₀
        store 0 in Node.P₁
        call WriteRecord(B-tree, 1, Node)
        store 1 in Root
```

```
else
    call InitStack(Stack)
    store Root in Ptr
    call ReadRecord(B-tree, Ptr, Node)
    loop while Node.P_0 ≠ 0
        call Push(Stack, Ptr)
        store Index(Node, Item.Key) in i
        store Node.P_i in Ptr
        call ReadRecord(B-tree, Ptr, Node)
    store NumRecords(Data) + 1 in Num
    call WriteRecord(Data, Num, Item)
    store Num in Item.R
    call AddToNode(Node, i+1, Item, 0)
    call WriteRecord(B-tree, Ptr, Node)
    loop while Node.Num = m + 1
        call Split(B-tree, Ptr, Temp)
        store Node.Data_{m/2+1} in Item
        if Ptr = Root
            then
                store NumRecords(B-tree) + 1 in Root
                store Ptr in Node.P_0
                store Temp in Node.P_1
                store Item in Node.Data_1
                store 1 in Node.NumItems
                call WriteRecord(B-tree, Root, Node)
            else
                call Pop(Stack, Ptr)
                call ReadRecord(B-tree, Ptr, Node)
                store Index(Node, Item.Key) in i
                call AddToNode(Node, i+1, Item, Temp)
                call WriteRecord(B-tree, Ptr, Node)

END OF Insert
```

```
START OF Split(B-tree, Ptr, Temp)
Passed by value: Ptr
Passed by reference: B-tree (a direct access file), Temp
Precondition: Ptr is the number of a record that has m + 1 data items,
              and needs to be split

call ReadRecord(B-tree, Ptr, Node)
store m/2 in Node.Num
call WriteRecord(B-tree, Ptr, Node)
store NumRecords(B-tree) + 1 in Temp
loop for i going from 1 to m/2
    store Node.Data_{m/2+1+i} in Node.Data_i
loop for i going from 0 to m/2
    store Node.P_{m/2+1+i} in Node.P_i
call WriteRecord(B-tree, Temp, Node)

END OF Split


START OF AddToNode(Node, Place, Item, Temp)
Passed by value: Place, Item, Temp
Passed by reference: Node

add 1 to Node.NumItems
loop for i going from Node.NumItems down to Place + 1
    store Node.Data_{i-1} in Node.Data_i
    store Node.P_{i-1} in Node.P_i
store Item in Node.Data_Place
store Temp in Node.P_Place

END OF AddToNode
```

Deletion from a B-tree

As you would expect, the algorithm for deletion is considerably more complicated. We will not present the algorithm here, but will discuss some of the subtle points for your consideration. The completion of the algorithm and the completion of a program that maintains a B-tree is a major undertaking, an undertaking that is unlikely to be assigned in a course such as this.

First we need to comment on what happens when an item is deleted from a B-tree. The record in the data file will, presumably, not be wanted any more. If several deletions are performed and the records in the data file are just left there, several "holes" in the data file will develop. After many such deletions, the number of holes could be a major problem. It would not be reasonable to "slide" other items up to fill the holes because the number of items could conceivably be in the millions. A better solution would be to maintain a list of these holes, and when a new item is to be inserted, check this list to see if there are holes in the data file. If the list is non-empty, then put the new item there and remove that record number from the list. If the list is empty, append the new data item onto the end of the data file. This, of course, results in a change in the insertion algorithm presented above as well.

Also, since a deletion could cause the tree to shrink in height, there could be similar holes left in the B-tree file as well. Another list of holes in the B-tree should also be maintained. When an item is deleted, and that deletion causes the old root to be discarded, the number of that record should be added to the list of available places in the B-tree file. As items are inserted, if it becomes necessary to add a level to the tree, this list would be checked; if it is not empty, a record number would be removed from it and the new root put there. If the list is empty, the new root would be appended at the end of the B-tree as we did above.

Both of these lists would have to be stored somewhere in permanent memory, i.e., on the disk, along with the files representing the B-tree, the root of the B-tree, and the data.

Next, the case of deletion from an internal node must be handled. As before, we can replace such an item with its inorder successor and the successor deleted instead. That process is almost exactly the same as before, the chief difference again being dealing with records in files rather than with pointers and the nodes to which they point.

Finally, the deletion algorithm will have to handle—as in the case of the 2-3 tree—the situation where a node other than the root node contains fewer than $m/2$ items. As before, when this happens an item will be borrowed from an adjacent sibling that can spare one—i.e., has more than $m/2$ items—or, if neither adjacent sibling can spare an item, will have to be combined with an adjacent sibling and an item pulled down from the parent. This could leave the parent record too short, so the process has to move up the tree until either a parent that has enough items is located, one of the adjacent siblings is able to spare an item, or the root is reached. The root record can have fewer than $m/2$ items, but must have at least one, unless the entire tree becomes empty.

There are several additional details that must be taken care of carefully. For instance, if the record being considered is the first child of its parent, then it cannot have a left sibling and only the right sibling needs to be examined when trying to see if a sibling has an item to spare or needs to be combined. Similarly, the rightmost child does not have a right sibling to consider when looking for a spare item. And, when combining records, there are at least two cases to consider: combining a record with fewer than $m/2$ items with a sibling on its right that contains exactly $m/2$ items, and combining a child with fewer than $m/2$ items with a sibling on its left that contains exactly $m/2$ items.

9.6 Orders of Magnitude

We saw, in chapter 7, that a balanced binary tree has much more efficient search, insert and delete routines than those for unsorted arrays, sorted arrays, and linked lists. Let's examine these same routines for 2-3 trees and B-trees.

The efficiencies of all the algorithms depend on the maximum heights of the trees involved. That is, the maximum number of "looks" into a 2-3 tree required to determine whether or not a particular item is there will depend on the height of the tree; one never has to do more looks than the number equal to the height of the tree. A 2-3 tree with N elements will have a height of at most $\lfloor \log_2(N+1) \rfloor$ (see the exercises). Therefore, the search algorithm is $O(\log N)$.

How about a B-tree? The most costly operation involved with a B-tree is the disk access. To measure the efficiency of an algorithm, count the maximum number of disk accesses required. Once again, this is directly related to the height of the tree; one never has to make more disk access than the number equal to the height of the tree. What is the maximum height of a B-tree of order m containing N data items? We leave this question for the exercises. After determining this number, you should be able to show that the order of magnitude of a search of a B-tree is $O(\log N)$.

How about insertions? To insert a new item into either a 2-3 tree or a B-tree, you have to follow pointers until you get to a leaf. Then you insert the new item and, maybe, split nodes moving back up the tree. You never have to split more nodes than there are levels in the tree, so we again see that the efficiency is related to the height of the tree. At worst you would have to walk all the way down the tree and then all the way back up. Thus, the worst case is the number equal to twice the height of the tree. Since the height is at worst $\lfloor \log_2(N+1) \rfloor$, and since the constant 2 is discarded, an insertion is $O(\log N)$.

There might be more work to do at each level when doing a deletion, but again the most that can happen is to walk all the way down the tree and then all the way back up, combining nodes as necessary. This again results in an order of magnitude of $O(\log N)$.

These results are not really unexpected. We saw earlier that a balanced binary search tree behaved very nicely. Both 2-3 trees and B-trees are data structures that stay balanced. Since $\log_2 N$ and $\log_m N$ differ by only a constant—albeit a large constant—the efficiencies of 2-3 tree algorithms and B-tree algorithms are the same as for balanced binary search trees.

9.7 Hashing

We see that balanced binary search trees and their relatives, 2-3 trees and B-trees, provide us with $O(\log N)$ efficiencies for searching, inserting and deleting items. That's very good in comparison to arrays and linked lists. We might, however, ask if it's possible to do even better.

The answer to the query is a limited yes. Under certain conditions we could improve on even these results. We've mentioned the trade-offs that are often

made between saving time and saving space. If we had all the space in the
world, we could always search, insert and delete using routines that are of order
of magnitude 1, having a unique place for each possible item. To search for an
item, look in its place to see if it's there. To insert an item, just put it in its
unique place, and to delete an item, just remove it from its place. If that looks
too easy, remember we said "each possible item." This means that, for example,
if a company were going to use this method for their employee database, they
could set aside one place for each person in the world. Assign each person in the
world a unique ID, say from 1 to 10 billion. If the person with ID n is employed
by the company, mark his or her spot as occupied and place the necessary data
in that spot. It would never be necessary to move items around when doing an
insertion since each item would always have its own place to occupy. Of course,
this would require enough memory to hold all the data necessary on each person
10 billion times. If each person's individual record required, say, 1,000 bytes
of data, the computer would have to be capable of holding 10 trillion bytes of
data. While such memories are coming available, it's obvious that this is still
a poor solution to the problem. It simply wastes far too much space. If the
company employed 100 people, 99.999999% of the memory would be empty.

This is a silly solution, but it does suggest another that might work. Suppose
we assign each person a unique ID as before—for example, a social security
number. Suppose we could put aside 100 places to hold the data for the 100
employees in the company, and suppose we could devise a way of assigning
each person one of the places in the array. (Naturally this could be done by
assigning each person a number between 1 and 100, but we're looking for a
scheme that doesn't require assignment of different IDs.) If we could look at a
person's social security number and easily determine his or her unique place in
the array, then we could search, insert and delete records in order of magnitude
$O(1)$. Suppose, for example, we just look at the last two digits of the social
security number. This number is a number between 0 and 99. We could simply
allow each person a unique cell in the array determined by the last two digits
of his or her social security number. The obvious problem with this method is
that two people might have different social security numbers but their last two
digits could be the same; indeed, there must be hundreds of people with the
same last two digits.

If we can resolve the problem of what to do when two people have the same
last two digits, and if we can assume that the use of the last two digits gives
us a fairly uniform distribution of the population, we have reduced our original
problem to about $1/100,000,000$ of its original size.

This attack is a simplified description of a method known as *hashing*. In the
remainder of this section, we'll discuss hashing, but will not go into as great an
amount of detail as we have for the other methods discussed. Our goal will be
to leave the reader with an overall understanding of the method.

The essential idea of hashing is to take any item to be handled and quickly
assign it a number. This number can be thought of as either an index in an
array or as a record number in a direct access file. We'll use arrays for the
discussion but in the real world the amount of data that is being held is usually

too large to be held in memory all at once, and so direct access files are usually used instead.

Let P be the data item to be stored. We send P to a function, called a *hashing* function, which returns its index. Then we simply go to that location in the array and either store the item there or retrieve it. Since we must have a place for every possible value returned by the hashing function, let's assume that the hashing function returns numbers in the range 0 to $m - 1$, and that the array is dimensioned from 0 to $m - 1$. It's usually easier to have the array dimensioned from 0 to $m - 1$ since we often use hashing functions that use integer division and remainders. Dividing by m always leaves a remainder between 0 and $m - 1$.

In our earlier example, m equals 100, the hashing function—i.e., taking the last two digits—yields a number between 0 and 99. This is the same as dividing the social security number by 100 and looking at the remainder.

This doesn't solve the problem of what to do when two items yield the same value from the hashing function. This problem will always exist since the number of cells in the array is fixed and the number of potential items is always much larger. If that weren't the case, we would be back in the situation of having a unique cell for each possible item, a situation which we saw was not realistic.

When two items yield the same value from the hashing function, this is called a *collision*. A major portion of the hashing methodology has to do with the resolution of collisions, and there are a number of schemes used to resolve collisions.

If a perfect hashing function existed, i.e., we were in a situation where each item had a unique cell and where no collisions ever occurred, then the number of cells could be exactly equal to the number of items that needed to be stored. This is extremely unlikely, so the normal case is to have a few extra cells in the array. We can likely afford to waste a few cells, especially if that will result in fewer collisions.

Returning to our example of employees in a company, if we could assume that we would never employ more than 100 people at a time, we might choose m to be 120, wasting 20 cells or so hoping to avoid collisions. Then rather than dividing by 100 and looking at the remainder, we would divide by 120 and look at the remainder.

This still leaves the problem of resolving collisions. Regardless of what we do, it will always be possible that our hashing function will return the same value for two different items. What should happen then?

The resolving of a collision is called a *rehash*. There are several ways to rehash.

One way of resolving collisions is to simply start looking through the array for an empty cell. That is, suppose we have already stored an item in the array with a hashing value of h. If another item is encountered that yields a hashing value of h, we look there in the array and see that the cell is occupied. We could just look at position $h + 1$, $h + 2$, ..., until we find an empty cell, and put the item there. Later if we search for the same item, we would start at h, see that that cell is occupied, but the item is not the one we want. We would search the next few cells until we either find the item or come to an empty cell. If the hashing function did a good job of distributing items uniformly, rather than doing a linear search on the entire array, this would be essentially the same as doing a linear search on $1/m$th of the array. This has the same order of magnitude, but a much smaller constant. In this case we have to be careful about deletions. We could not simply mark a cell as empty when we do a deletion. If we did, then a subsequent search for a different item could encounter the empty cell and return the erroneous result that the searched for item was not present when it might, indeed, be the next item in the array. A solution to this problem would be to mark a cell as either empty or deleted, as appropriate. All cells would be marked as empty at the beginning.

Another solution to the collision problem is more elegant. Rather than just storing one item in each cell, we could store a data structure there—for example, a linked list. Each time we do an insertion, we send the item to the hashing function to determine the hash number, h. We go directly to that cell and insert the item at the head of the list at that position. An insert is of $O(1)$. To do a search, we find the hash number and start a search of a linked list at that location. If the hashing function is a good one, then the list should be very short and the search should be very efficient. A deletion would be similar. If the hashing function is a good one, the deletion will be essentially a deletion from a very short linked list.

Yet another solution would be to store an even more efficient structure in each cell. For example, you might store a binary search tree in each cell rather than a linked list. Then searches, insertions, and deletions would be as good as $O(1)$ and never worse than $O(\log N)$.

You will have noticed that we said "if the hashing function is a good one" several times above. The whole concept of hashing depends very heavily on finding good hashing functions. Over the years there has been a huge amount of research done on the subject of hashing and hashing functions. Much has been learned about the selection of a good hashing function. We do not intend to discuss these results, but will mention that, for example, if you plan to use a function that divides something by m and uses the remainder, make m a prime number. It can be shown that if m is not prime, the hashing numbers "cluster" around certain values.

Before we leave the subject of hashing, let's think a bit about traversals. Since a good hashing function assigns each item a number that is uniformly distributed in the range 0 to $m - 1$, it is not at all easy to traverse the items of data in an orderly manner. A traversal of the data in order of the key items is a very inefficient routine, in general. As a result, if you need to store data in a structure that provides you with a means of traversing the data in a particular order, you probably shouldn't choose to use hashing.

9.8   Summary and Review

- We discussed multiway trees, a tree structure that allows more than two children in each node as with binary trees. We wrote routines that would permit us to search and traverse a multiway tree.

- We discussed 2-3 trees in considerable detail. Every node of a 2-3 tree contains either two or three pointers to children nodes and one or two data items. The primary advantage of 2-3 trees is the fact that they are very balanced at all times. A 2-3 tree is a multiway tree that appears very similar to a height balanced binary tree. As a 2-3 tree grows, it grows at the root of the tree rather than at the leaves. All the leaves of a 2-3 tree are on the same level. We wrote routines for inserting and deleting new items in a 2-3 tree. These routines were also implemented in Pascal.

- We discussed direct access files. The Pascal Standard only supports sequential access files, but there are many real world needs for files that allow access to any record stored in the file.

- We discussed B-trees. Our discussion described B-trees stored in direct access files. A B-tree of order m is a multiway tree of order m with all the leaves on the same level. We described a situation where each node of the B-tree contained up to as many as m data items where m is an even integer. In actual applications m would be quite large, perhaps around 100 or even larger. We saw that a B-tree of order 100 would be very squat, allowing access to millions of records with only a small number of disk accesses. Each node of the B-tree contained a collection of key fields and record numbers. The record number associated with each key is the location in another file, the data file, where the rest of the data pertaining to that key can be found. The B-tree thus becomes an index into the data file.

- We briefly introduced the concept of hashing, a technique that can, in the right circumstances, result in storage and retrieval performance even greater than that afforded by binary and multiway trees.

9.9   Exercises

1. Write an iterative version of *InTree*, a routine that will search a multiway tree.

2. Write a lower-level algorithm for *Index*. Assume the number of children per node is large so that a linear search would not be efficient, and therefore a binary search should be used instead.

3. Write algorithms for pre-order and post-order traversals of a multiway tree.

4. Demonstrate that a 2-3 tree with height k can hold between $2^k - 1$ and $3^k - 1$ items.

5. Determine the maximum height of a 2-3 tree with m items.

6. In the text, we wrote a routine that inserted an item in a 2-3 tree. The routine we wrote relied on a precondition that the item being inserted was known not to be in the tree already. This requires two searches of the tree: one to determine whether or not the item is in the tree and one to find the leaf node in which to do the insertion. The second search follows exactly the same path as the first, and the routine is therefore not as efficient as it could be. Add a flag, *Successful*, to the parameter list of *Insert* and do away with the precondition. If the item is located during the process of attempting to find the place where the insertion should be done, the flag should be assigned the value "false" and the procedure terminated. If the insertion is successful, the flag should be assigned the value "true." This is the same strategy followed in earlier chapters.

7. In the text, we wrote a routine that deleted an item from a 2-3 tree. The routine we wrote relied on a precondition that the item being deleted was known to be in the tree already. This requires two searches of the tree: one to determine whether or not the item is in the tree and one to find the node where the item is located (and the node containing the inorder successor, when necessary). The second search follows exactly the same path as the first, and the routine is therefore not as efficient as it could be. Add a flag, *Successful*, to the parameter list of *Delete* and do away with the precondition. If the item is not located during the process of attempting to find the node containing the item, the flag should be assigned the value "false" and the procedure terminated. If the deletion is successful, the flag should be assigned the value "true."

8. Write the algorithms for *AdoptFromLeft* and the three versions of *Combine* discussed on page 234.

9. Write a complete program that manipulates a 2-3 tree. Your program should allow you to search, traverse, insert a node into, and delete a node from a 2-3 tree.

10. Determine the minimum and maximum number of items that can be stored in a B-tree of order m.

11. Determine the maximum height of a B-tree of order m with n items.

12. Write a complete program that manipulates a B-tree and a corresponding data file. This is a major program that will require a good deal of effort.

13. Suppose that you need to develop a hashing function for a group of people who do not have social security numbers. You could use their names instead. Discuss the problems with using names and suggest some possible hashing functions that use names. Try to determine whether your suggested functions are "good hashing functions."

Chapter 10

Advanced Sorting

> To iterate is human, to recurse divine
> — Anonymous

10.1 Introduction

In this chapter we will see more examples of recursive routines and will see again how the order of magnitude of a recursive routine can be determined. We'll study some more sorting algorithms—in particular, the quicksort, merge sort, and radix sort algorithms. We'll also discuss external sorting, i.e., sorting of data stored in files.

We'll introduce the notion of a loop invariant and begin to see how this notion can lead to a formal method of proof of correctness of a program.

10.2 Loop Invariants and Quicksort

A *loop invariant* is a condition that does not vary during the execution of a loop. More precisely, it's a statement of the status of things that can be shown to be true before the loop is executed, after each iteration of the loop, and after termination of the loop. To see a particular example of a loop invariant, let's look at another sorting algorithm, the *Quicksort*. The quicksort algorithm was invented by C. A. R. Hoare, a giant in the history of computer science. His algorithm is one of the fastest algorithms known for sorting a randomly arranged collection of numbers, and is relatively easy to understand and implement.

The Quicksort Algorithm

As before, let's assume we have an array that we want to sort into ascending order. Also, to keep our focus on the essentials, let's assume that the array is simply an array of numbers; more complicated arrays can be handled in similar ways later. The quicksort algorithm accomplishes the task by "partitioning" the array into sections and then sorting these sections. The sections are sorted by the same method, so the algorithm is recursive.

Fundamental to the algorithm is the notion of partitioning the array—actually, partitioning a portion of the array—so let's first look at what is meant by partitioning the array. To partition the array from, say, *Left* to *Right*, where *Left* and *Right* are subscripts indicating the left and right ends of that portion of the array to be partitioned, we choose one element in the array, called the *pivot*, and rearrange the elements in the array so that all the elements smaller than the pivot are to the left of it, and all the elements that are greater than it are to the right. If there happen to be elements that are equal to the pivot, they are to end up adjacent to it. Let's look at an example.

Pivot

Left   *Right*

646	203	385	509	706	819	390	385	205	310	706	895	390	209	389	295
31	32	33	34	35	36	37	38	39	40	41	42	43	44	45	46

Figure 10.1 The Array before Partitioning

In the array in figure 10.1, we only want to consider the portion of the array from *Left* (31) through *Right* (46). For reasons to be explained later, let's choose the element midway from *Left* to *Right* as the pivot, i.e., the element in position 38, namely 385.

Pivot

385

Left   *Right*

295	203	209	310	205	385	385	390	819	706	895	390	706	389	509	646
31	32	33	34	35	36	37	38	39	40	41	42	43	44	45	46

Figure 10.2 The Array after Partitioning

Consider figure 10.2, which shows the array after partitioning. Notice that the elements in positions 36 and 37 equal the pivot element, 385. Also, notice that all the elements between 31 and 35, inclusive, are smaller than 385, while all the elements between 38 and 46 are larger. Had there been other elements equal to 385, we would want them next to positions 36 and 37. It wouldn't matter whether they are to the left or right of positions 36 and 37, just that they are adjacent.

The regions to the left and right are not sorted, but we have made progress towards that goal. We can now partition the region between 31 and 35 and partition the region between 38 and 46. If we continue doing this until all the regions contain at most one element, the entire array will be sorted. That's the quicksort algorithm.

Partitioning the Array

There are many ways that the partitioning can be done. Let's look at an example where it's relatively easy to use a loop invariant. What we will do is to break up the array from *Left* to *Right* into four regions. One region will contain numbers smaller than the pivot, another will contain numbers equal to the pivot, a third will contain numbers that are greater than the pivot and the fourth region will contain numbers that have not yet been partitioned, the "not-done" region. When the partition routine begins, the not-done region will contain all the numbers and the other three will be empty. When the routine is finished, the not-done region will be empty and the other three regions will contain all the numbers. Of course we'll arrange the regions so that the first is to the left of the second, and the second is to the left of the third. Let's look at a picture. Consider figure 10.3.

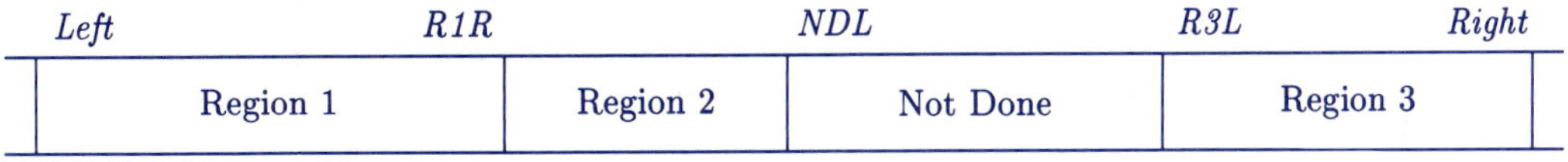

Left		*R1R*		*NDL*		*R3L*		*Right*
	Region 1		Region 2		Not Done		Region 3	

Figure 10.3 The Four Regions

We are using *R1R* for the right end of region 1, *NDL* for the left end of the not-done region, and *R3L* for the left end of region 3. As you will see, these three indices, along with *Left* and *Right* will be sufficient to delimit all four regions. We could, of course, use indices like *R2L*, *R2R* and *R3*, but they aren't needed—*R2R* is just one smaller than *NDL*, and *R3R* is just *Right*.

With this in mind, the loop invariant becomes:

> All the elements in region 1 (in positions *Left* to *R1R*) are smaller than the pivot; all the elements in region 2 (in positions $R1R + 1$ to $NDL - 1$) are equal to the pivot; all the elements in region 3 (from *R3L* to *Right*) are greater than the pivot; and all the elements in the not-done region (from *NDL* to $R3L - 1$) have not yet been partitioned.

If we initialize *R1R* to $Left - 1$, *NDL* to *Left*, and *R3L* to $Right + 1$, we can guarantee that the invariant is true at the outset of the algorithm. Then if we can guarantee that whatever we do to the elements of the array keeps the invariant true, and that the not-done region eventually becomes empty, we will be able to guarantee that the partitioning algorithm works correctly.

The not-done region will shrink to zero width by looking at the elements in the region one at a time, moving one element out of the not-done region into its proper region, and continuing until there are none left. The actual movement is simple, but somewhat tricky. We must be careful to preserve the invariant and we want to keep the movement of array elements to a minimum. We start by looking at the element in position NDL. There are three possibilities: this element will be smaller than the pivot, equal to it or greater than it.

Since region 2—those elements equal to the pivot—is just to the left of the element in position NDL, the second case is very easy to handle. If the element in position NDL equals the pivot, all we need to do is increment NDL by one and the invariant is preserved.

The case that the element in position NDL is greater than the pivot is not much harder. We can swap this element with the element in position $R3L - 1$, decrement $R3L$, and the invariant will be preserved. Notice that NDL does not get incremented in this case since we will have placed an element in position NDL that has not yet been partitioned.

The remaining case is only slightly more complicated. When the element in position NDL is smaller than the pivot, it needs to be moved into region 1. That can be accomplished by swapping the leftmost element in region 2 with this element and incrementing both $R1R$ and NDL. The leftmost element in region 2 is in position $R1R + 1$, so if we increment $R1R$ first, it will point at the leftmost element in region 2. This element gets swapped with the element in position NDL and then NDL gets incremented.

Here are these three cases as well as the necessary initializations written in our algorithmic language:

```
START OF Partition(A, Left, Right, R1R, R3L)
Passed by value: Left, Right
Passed by reference: A, R1R, R3L

store Left − 1 in R1R
store Left in NDL
store Right + 1 in R3L
store A_(Left+Right)/2 in Pivot
loop while NDL < R3L
    if A_NDL = Pivot
        then
            add 1 to NDL
        else
            if A_NDL > Pivot
                then
                    subtract 1 from R3L
                    call Swap(A_NDL, A_R3L)
                else
                    add 1 to R1R
                    call Swap(A_NDL, A_R1R)
                    add 1 to NDL

END OF Partition
```

Let's trace this on the example presented earlier. Consider figure 10.4. Notice that the first three numbers, i.e., those in positions 31, 32 and 33, cause all three cases to occur. The element in position 31 is greater than the pivot, the element in position 32 is smaller than the pivot and the element in position 33 equals the pivot.

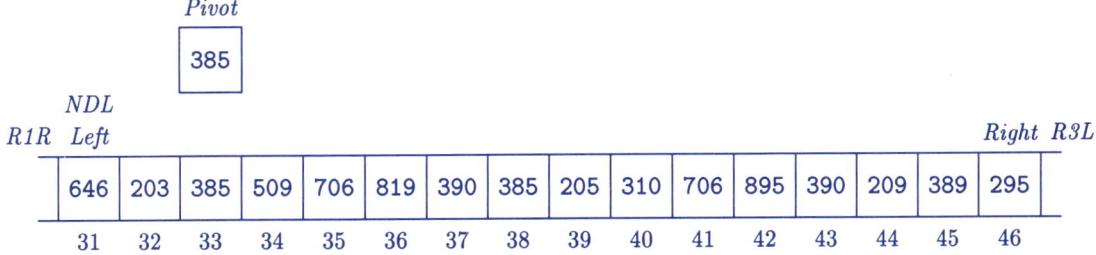

Figure 10.4 The Array before Partitioning

When the 646 in position 31 is exchanged with the 295 in position 46, *R3L* is decremented, but *NDL* doesn't change. See figure 10.5.

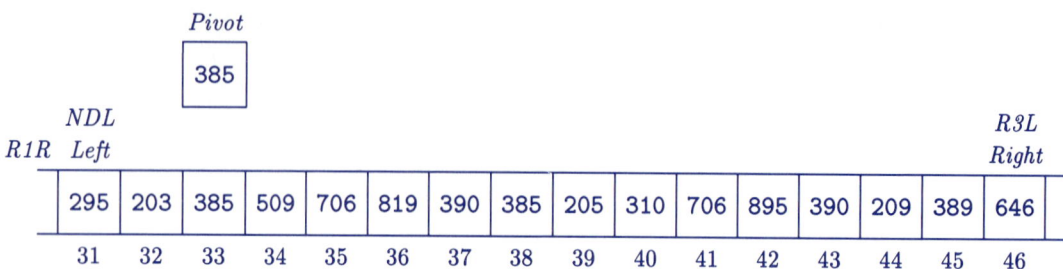

Figure 10.5 The Array after Swapping the 646 and 295

The next two elements are smaller than 385 and hence belong in region 1. *R1R* is incremented and the element at *NDL* is exchanged with the element at *R1R*, and then *NDL* is incremented. This actually amounts to swapping the elements with themselves, but *NDL* does get moved over each time. After these two steps, the array will look like figure 10.6.

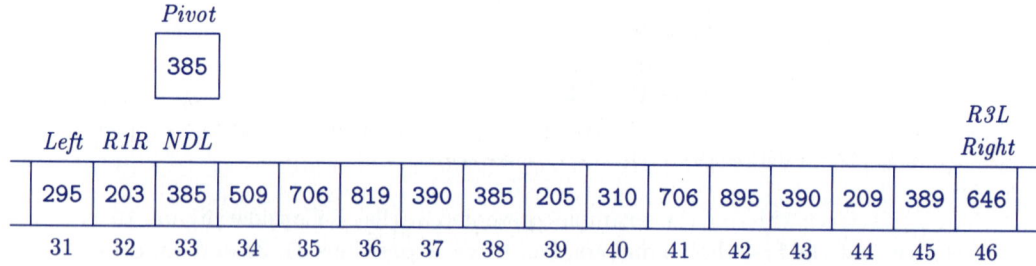

Figure 10.6 The Array after moving *NDL* past 203

The element in position *NDL* this time equals 385 and *NDL* is simply incremented by one. The array looks like figure 10.7.

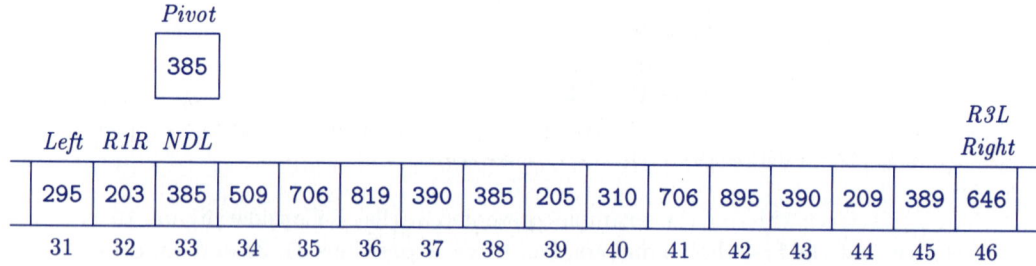

Figure 10.7 The Array after moving *NDL* past 385

Trace the algorithm for a few more elements and see what happens.

Figure 10.8 shows the array after five more iterations of the loop.

Pivot

385

Left | | | *R1R* | *NDL* | | | | | | | *R3L* | | | *Right*

295	203	209	310	385	819	390	385	205	706	895	390	706	389	509	646
31	32	33	34	35	36	37	38	39	40	41	42	43	44	45	46

Figure 10.8 The Array after Several More Moves

Be sure that you see that the invariant is true after each iteration. Before the loop is entered, regions 1, 2 and 3 are empty, preserving the invariant. After each iteration of the loop, exactly one action has taken place. Each of the actions preserves the invariant. Since either *NDL* is incremented or *R3L* is decremented during each iteration, the loop will terminate after exactly *Right* − *Left* + 1 iterations. At this point, the not-done region will be empty and the array from *Left* to *Right* will be partitioned.

Loop Invariants vs. Earlier Algorithmic Development

The difference between what we have done in the past and what we have done here may not be clear. In the past we have examined algorithms carefully and have learned to "see" when they work correctly. This method works on short straightforward algorithms, but won't work in more complicated situations simply because of the complexity. What we have done here is to state a loop invariant that we can guarantee will lead to successful completion of the process. Then we can examine the algorithm and prove that the invariant is preserved.

Quicksort completed

We have finished *Partition* and now can turn to the completion of the quicksort algorithm itself. Recall that after the array is partitioned, regions 1 and 3 are not sorted. All the elements in region 1 will stay in that part of the array, but they are not necessarily in order. We call the routine recursively to accomplish the task on the entire array. So as to keep the original call to *Quicksort* parallel to the other sorting algorithms, we'll rewrite it so that it calls a subroutine, *Sort*, and this routine calls itself.

```
START OF Quicksort(A, N)
Passed by value: N
Passed by reference: A, an array of N numbers

call Sort(A, 1, N)

END OF Quicksort

START OF Sort(A, Left, Right)
Passed by value: Left, Right
Passed by reference: A, an array of N numbers

if Left < Right
    then
        call Partition(A, Left, Right, R1R, R3L)
        call Sort(A, Left, R1R)
        call Sort(A, R3L, Right)

END OF Sort
```

10.3   Pascal for Quicksort

There's absolutely no new Pascal involved with the implementation of this algorithm. It is a routine process to turn the steps into code. Rather than spend any time discussing the process, let's just include the code for your inspection. It begins on the next page.

```
procedure Quicksort(var A : List; N : integer);

{ This procedure sorts the array A with the Quicksort algorithm }

   procedure Partition(var A : List;
                   Left, Right : integer;
                   var R1R, R3L : integer);

   { This procedure partitions the array A from Left to Right,    }
   { leaving the element initially in position (Left + Right) / 2 }
   { in its final place.                                          }

   var
      NDL : integer;
      Pivot : real;

   begin
      R1R := Left - 1;
      NDL := Left;
      R3L := Right + 1;
      Pivot := A[(Left + Right) div 2];
      while NDL < R3L do
         begin
            if A[NDL] = Pivot
               then
                  NDL := NDL + 1
               else
                  if A[NDL] > Pivot
                     then
                        begin
                           R3L := R3L - 1;
                           Swap(A[NDL], A[R3L])
                        end
                     else
                        begin
                           R1R := R1R + 1;
                           Swap(A[NDL], A[R1R]);
                           NDL := NDL + 1
                        end
         end
   end;
```

```
procedure Sort(var A : List; Left, Right : integer);

{  This procedure sorts the region from Left to Right by }
{  partitioning it and then sorting the two regions.     }

var
  R1R, R3L : integer;

begin
   if Left < Right
      then
         begin
            Partition(A, Left, Right, R1R, R3L);
            Sort(A, Left, R1R);
            Sort(A, R3L, Right)
         end
end;

begin  { Main Statement Part of Quicksort }
   Sort(A, 1, N)
end;
```

10.4   Order of Magnitude of Quicksort

In order to determine the order of magnitude of the quicksort, we need to estimate how much work is done during each call to *Sort*, and how many calls are made. Looking first at how much work is done during each call, notice that other than the recursive calls to *Sort*, all the work is done in *Partition*. The partitioning step requires that we scan through the array from *Left* to *Right*, looking at each element once. (The element in position *NDL* changes when we exchange it with the element in position *R3L* so, even though *NDL* doesn't change, we don't look at the same element twice.) This means that *Partition* is of order N when we consider comparisons. If the elements occur randomly in the array, then the number of times that we'll have to move an element will also be of order N since if we double the size of the array, the number of times elements will move will double. Thus, we conclude that the *Partition* module is of order N with respect to both the number of comparisons and the number of assignments.

Next we need to determine how many times the *Partition* module will be called. If we are lucky and choose a pivot element that ends up near the middle of the portion of the array being partitioned, i.e., about halfway between *Left* and *Right*, then each time we split it, we'll be splitting it about in half. An array of size 100 will get split into two arrays of about 50. Each of these will get split into two arrays of about 25. Each of these into two of about 12, then two of about six, then about three and finally about 1. The number of different sizes is 7, the first integer bigger than $\log_2 100$. Thus, the number of different array sizes is $\log_2 N$. On the other hand, if we're unlucky and the pivot element ends up near one end or the other of the array, i.e., near either *Left* or *Right*, then we will only reduce the size of the array being partitioned by a value near one. In this case, we'll end up calling the routine about N times. In conclusion, we can say that the quicksort has an order of magnitude in the best case of $N \log_2 N$ and worst case of N^2.

The worst case could happen if the array happened to be sorted already, and we selected as a pivot element either A_{Left} or A_{Right}. That's why we decided to use the element in position $(Left + Right)/2$ as pivot.

It could happen that the array is in some random order, but whenever a pivot is selected, it happens to belong near one end or the other of the portion being partitioned. In this case, the performance of the quicksort can be as bad as that of an insertion sort or even a bubble sort. The demonstration is beyond us at this point, but rest assured that it can be shown that this is very unlikely. It can be shown that for randomly arranged arrays of numbers, the quicksort algorithm almost always performs at an order of magnitude of $N \log_2 N$. Indeed, the quicksort is one of the fastest known routines for sorting large arrays of randomly arranged numbers.

10.5   Merge Sort Algorithm

We now turn to a discussion of another well-known recursive algorithm for sorting, the *merge sort*. If two arrays are already arranged in ascending order, a single pass through the two arrays can "merge" them together into one sorted array. This requires another array and three indices. Suppose that the first array is A, the second is B and the third is C. Suppose we know that A contains *NumA* elements and B contains *NumB* elements. If i, j and k all start off at 1, the following scheme works quite nicely:

```
loop while i ≤ NumA and j ≤ NumB
    if A_i < B_j
        then
            store A_i in C_k
            add 1 to i
        else
            store B_j in C_k
            add 1 to j
    add 1 to k
```

Of course we'll come to the end of one array before we come to the end of the other, and will then have to move the remaining elements from the other array into C. That can be accomplished with a pair of *loop whiles*:

```
if i > NumA
    then
        loop while j ≤ NumB
            store B_j in C_k
            add 1 to j
            add 1 to k
    else
        loop while i ≤ NumA
            store A_i in C_k
            add 1 to i
            add 1 to k
```

And, as a matter of fact, since the body of a *loop while* is only executed when the test is true, we can eliminate the *if...then...else*:

```
loop while j ≤ NumB
    store B_j in C_k
    add 1 to j
    add 1 to k
loop while i ≤ NumA
    store A_i in C_k
    add 1 to i
    add 1 to k
```

Putting these three loops together yields an algorithm that nicely merges two sorted arrays into a third. That, however, is not a job that needs doing very often. One seldom encounters two sorted arrays that need to be merged into a third. What happens much more frequently is to have a completely unsorted array that needs to be sorted. Suppose for the moment that we can somehow split the array in the middle and sort each half. We could then make some small changes to the above algorithm and merge the two halves into one sorted whole:

```
store N div 2 in Mid
store 1 in i
store Mid + 1 in j
store 1 in k
loop while i ≤ Mid and j ≤ N
    if A_i < A_j
        then
            store A_i in C_k
            add 1 to i
        else
            store A_j in C_k
            add 1 to j
    add 1 to k
loop while j ≤ N
    store A_j in C_k
    add 1 to j
    add 1 to k
loop while i ≤ Mid
    store A_i in C_k
    add 1 to i
    add 1 to k
loop for i going from 1 to N
    store C_i in A_i
```

Notice that we replaced *NumA* with *N div 2*, and *NumB* with *N*; we replaced references to array B with references to A, and we initialized j to *N div 2 + 1*. Since we wanted to get the array A sorted, we added a *loop for* that moves the elements from C back into A.

Let's consider this process in light of our earlier discussion of loop invariants. Before the first loop begins, we can be certain that the elements in array C are in order since the array is empty. After each iteration of the first loop, exactly one element has been placed into C, and that element is the smaller of the two current elements in A and B, thus keeping C in order. Since A and B are finite and one element gets moved each iteration of the loop, we are certain that the loop will terminate with C still in order. Finally, the same invariant can be applied to each of the following loops, and we can be confident that each element in A and B will have been placed into C, and that C is arranged in ascending order. The *loop for* simply puts the elements back into array A.

This process surely gets A sorted, but there's still the question of how to get the two halves of A sorted in the first place. If you're thinking recursively, you've already seen the answer; just use the same procedure on the two halves, continuing to recurse until you get down to sub-arrays that have only one element. To make this change we have to be careful not to initialize the indices to 1, but instead to the left end of the array being sorted. Let's assume that the merge routine accepts four parameters: the array, the left and right ends of the portion to be sorted, as well as the position mid-way between *Left* and *Right*. The following algorithm will take care of the merge part:

```
START OF Merge(A, Left, Middle, Right)
Passed by value: Left, Middle, Right
Passed by reference: A, an array of N elements

store Left in i
store Middle + 1 in j
store Left in k
loop while i ≤ Middle and j ≤ Right
    if Aᵢ < Aⱼ
        then
            store Aᵢ in Cₖ
            add 1 to i
        else
            store Aⱼ in Cₖ
            add 1 to j
    add 1 to k
loop while j ≤ Right
    store Aⱼ in Cₖ
    add 1 to j
    add 1 to k
loop while i ≤ Middle
    store Aᵢ in Cₖ
    add 1 to i
    add 1 to k
loop for i going from Left to Right
    store Cᵢ in Aᵢ


END OF Merge
```

The array C is a local variable used to store the array while the merge is taking place. (And, of course, we don't have to call it C; that's just left over from our earlier thinking.)

After completing *Merge*, the *MergeSort* routine is almost trivial if you think recursively. Once again, to keep this algorithm parallel to the other sorting algorithms in the book, we'll call it initially with just two parameters and have it call a module, *Sort*, that calls itself:

```
START OF MergeSort(A, N)
Passed by value: N
Passed by reference: A, an array of N elements

call Sort(A, 1, N)

END OF MergeSort


START OF Sort(A, Left, Right)
Passed by value: Left, Right
Passed by reference: A, an array of N elements

if Left < Right
    then
        store (Left + Right) div 2 in Middle
        call Sort(A, Left, Middle)
        call Sort(A, Middle + 1, Right)
        call Merge(A, Left, Middle, Right)

END OF Sort
```

Pascal for MergeSort

As with the quicksort, this sorting technique requires no new Pascal. This time, however, we'll leave the completion of the code for the exercises.

10.6   Order of Magnitude for MergeSort

The order of magnitude of the merge sort is easy to determine. Sort calls itself until the piece being sorted has fewer than two elements left. Consequently, all the work is really done in Merge. The merging process requires that we make a pass all the way through the array, looking at each element exactly once. If the portion being merged doubles, the number of assignments and comparisons also doubles. Merge is of order N. Since we exactly halve the array on each recursive call, we are going to need $\log_2 N$ calls. Therefore, the merge sort algorithm is $O(N \log N)$.

It's interesting to note that the merge sort is of order $N \log N$ in the best case as well as the worst case. If the quicksort is unlucky, it can take a lot longer than the merge sort. However, if the quicksort is lucky, it will run faster than the merge sort. The primary reason is the extra overhead that the merge sort requires to move the elements back into A from C. While it's beyond us to show it, it can be shown that the quicksort is more likely to be lucky than it is to be unlucky. On random data, the quicksort will almost always perform faster than a merge sort.

10.7 External Sorting

All of the sorting algorithms discussed so far in this book have been *internal sorts*. An internal sort is a sorting algorithm that will work when the data being sorted will fit into memory all at once. These techniques we've discussed work fine on arrays when the entire array can be held in the computer's main memory. There are many times in the real world, however, when the data being sorted simply won't fit in memory all at once; consider trying to sort a database containing all the records being manipulated by the Infernal Revenue Service, for example.

A sorting algorithm that handles this situation is called an *external sort*. We'll assume that the data to be sorted exists in a large file and that it is not possible to hold the entire file in memory. While there are a number of techniques that will work, we'll just consider one. Indeed, we have already seen the core of this technique, the merge sort.

Merge Sort on Two Files

Consider the first version we wrote for *Merge*:

```
loop while i ≤ NumA and j ≤ NumB
    if Aᵢ < Bⱼ
        then
            store Aᵢ in Cₖ
            add 1 to i
        else
            store Bⱼ in Cₖ
            add 1 to j
    add 1 to k
loop while j ≤ NumB
    store Bⱼ in Cₖ
    add 1 to j
    add 1 to k
loop while i ≤ NumA
    store Aᵢ in Cₖ
    add 1 to i
    add 1 to k
```

If we think about this algorithm and assume that we're talking about files instead of arrays, and assume that A and B are files containing data that have already been sorted, and that we want to write these data into a third file *C* in ascending order, we see that it's easy to modify:

```
loop while not at the end of file A and not at the end of B
    if the current element in A < the current element in B
        then
            write the current element in A into C
            advance to the next element in A
        else
            write the current element in B into C
            advance to the next element in B
loop while not at the end of B
    write the current element in B into C
    advance to the next element in B
loop while not at the end of A
    write the current element in A into C
    advance to the next element in A
```

Of course this assumes we can take care of the details of preparing the three files to be read from and written to, and that we can read and write from the files as indicated. These are details that every programming language supports and we'll worry about these details in Pascal later.

There are other problems remaining, however. We indicated above that it's not all that often that you run into two arrays that need to be merged. In fact, what we did was to recursively apply the merge routine to smaller and smaller pieces of one array to get it sorted. It's not that easy with files. The recursive nature of the algorithm requires that we are able to pass the index of a particular location in the array. To be able to accomplish the same thing with files would amount to requiring that we be able to directly access each record in a file. Such files exist, and they're known as *direct access files*, but we're not going to deal with direct access files here for two reasons.

First, even though it would be possible to write a merge sort algorithm that would work with direct access files, it would not be practical. The resulting routine would require many many file accesses. These repeated file accesses would be time consuming and hard on the hardware. While direct access files are designed in such a manner that any record can be accessed directly, the hardware and software (operating system) usually work together in such a manner that large chunks of data (buffers) are read from the file all at once, and the operating system gives just a piece of that chunk to the requesting program. A recursive program that did many many accesses to a file, requesting one record at a time, would result in the hardware being asked to jump around in the file over and over. This can result in a lot of extra wear and tear on the hardware and is simply not a good idea.

The second reason is even simpler: Standard Pascal only supports sequential access files and does not support direct access files at all. Many Pascal compilers have added the ability to work with direct access files as an extension to the language, but these extensions are not standard. Even if they were, we would not write a recursive routine to sort a direct access file.

Sequential Files

To read a file sequentially, you read the first record into memory, then the second, then the third, and so on until you reach the end of the file. A sequential file is created in a similar manner, the records are written into the file one at a time starting with the first one and continuing, in order, until all the records have been written.

Let's see if we can write a sorting algorithm that will sort a sequential access file. Notice that the merge routine works just fine on sequential files. One sequential pass through each file is made.

In the real world, the data stored in the file would consist of records containing multiple-type fields. One of these fields would be the key field and our goal is to rearrange the records in the file so that they are in (ascending) order according to this key field. Such a file can easily be envisioned by considering the database of students at some school. Each record would contain a student's name, address, grade point average, list of courses completed, etc. Imagine that one field is the student's identification number and that you want to sort the file according to this field.

While this is easy to imagine, it's not necessary, and it might get cumbersome worrying about the records and the remaining fields. Since the principles are the same, let's simplify things by assuming the file in question is just a file of integers and that we want to sort the file into ascending order.

Merge Sort on One File

If a file contains a collection of integers arranged randomly, there will be portions of the file that are in ascending order, we'll call these *runs*. A run can be very short—as short as one number—but in general there will be long runs and short runs. (If all the runs are only one number long, the file is actually in descending order.) Suppose, for example, that the file A contains the following numbers:

```
A =    16   23   37   28   12   58   36   43   95   83   18   20   73   62   50   82
```

This file contains eight runs. The algorithm we're going to develop involves writing these runs into two temporary files and then merging these files together. The result will not necessarily be a sorted file, but it will be a file that has longer runs than the one we started with. Let's look at the above numbers to see what we mean. Suppose we distribute the runs into two files, say B and C as follows:

```
B =    16   23   37   12   58   83   62

C =    28   36   43   95   18   20   73   50   82
```

and then we merge these two files back into A:

A =   16   23   28   36   37   12   43   58   83   62   95   18   20   73   50   82

Notice that this is the same collection of numbers, but there are only five runs now. Distributing them again results in:

B =   16   23   28   36   37   62   95   50   82

C =   12   43   58   83   18   20   73

After merging these two files, A will look like:

A =   12   16   23   28   36   37   43   58   62   83   18   20   73   95   50   82

And now there are only three runs. If we continue this process until there is only one run, the file will be sorted.

Before we forget what the goal is, let's look at the processes we're using to make sure they satisfy our requirement of working with sequential files. We've already confirmed that the merge routine is sequential, how about the distribute routine? It will require a single pass through the first file, reading each number from that file and writing it to either file B or C depending on whether a new run is encountered or not. So distribute is a sequential process as well. It's time to write an algorithm for *Distribute*.

```
START OF Distribute(A, B, C)
Passed by reference: A, B and C, three files

prepare A to be read from
prepare B and C to be written to
start with B as the output file
store −∞ in Previous
loop while not at end of file A
     read the Current value from A
     if Current < Previous
          then
               change output files
     write Current to the output file
     store Current in Previous

END OF Distribute
```

We're treating −∞ as a large negative number, and we're storing −∞ in *Previous* so that when the first number is read from the file, it will not be considered the beginning of a new run. It isn't actually important, however. As long as *Previous* has some value, the first number read from file A will either be considered as belonging to the first run or the start of another run. In either case, the routine works; the only thing that changes is which of the two temporary files is written to first. It's not clear how we'll change output files, but that's an implementation problem that we'll leave for the coding step. We'll probably use `-maxint` for $-\infty$ but that's an implementation detail as well.

Let's write *Merge* as an algorithm:

```
START OF Merge(A, B, C)
Passed by reference: A, B and C, three files

prepare A and B to be read from
prepare C to be written to
loop while not at the end of file A and not at the end of B
    if the current element of A < the current element of B
        then
            write the current element of A into C
            advance to the next element of A
        else
            write the current element of B into C
            advance to the next element of B
loop while not at the end of B
    write the current element of B into C
    advance to the next element of B
loop while not at the end of A
    write the current element of A into C
    advance to the next element of A


END OF Merge
```

All that's left is the routine that calls these two routines. We are not going to call them recursively, but we are going to have to call them repeatedly. How do we know when to stop? When the file created by *Merge* contains only one run, it is sorted. Unfortunately, there's no easy way to distinguish between runs during the merge process. It is, however, easy to tell when a new run starts during *Distribute* and we can count runs there. We'll add another parameter to a Distribute that returns the number of runs encountered and continue distributing and merging until the number of runs encountered is one. Here's the algorithm:

```
START OF FileMergeSort(A)
Passed by reference: A, a sequential file

loop
    store 1 in Runs
    call Distribute(A, B, C, Runs)
    if Runs > 1
        then
            call Merge(B, C, A)
    until Runs = 1

END OF FileMergeSort
```

We're treating *B* and *C* as local variables. They're the temporary files that the routine uses. *Runs* is also a local variable, and it's passed by reference to *Distribute*. We have to remember to modify *Distribute* to accept the additional parameter; we'll take care of this in the next section when we write the code.

10.8 Pascal for FileMergeSort

There are some interesting aspects of this program that are revealed when we get around to coding it so let's work on the code.

To begin, let's assume that the file is a file of integers—remember this is a simplification that doesn't make much sense in the real world. You'll probably never have occasion to sort a file of integers. However, you may very well have occasion to sort files of records where the sort key is one field of the record. The algorithms and code developed here can easily be modified later to handle this. Let's assume the following type definition:

```
type
    IntFile = file of integer;
```

Distribute

The **Distribute** procedure follows directly from the algorithm:

```
procedure Distribute(var A, B, C : IntFile; var Runs : integer);
var
  Current, Previous : integer;
  UsingB : Boolean;

begin
  reset(A);
  rewrite(B);
  rewrite(C);
  UsingB := true;
  Previous := -maxint;
  while not eof(A) do
    begin
      read(A, Current);
      if Current < Previous
        then
          begin
            Runs := Runs + 1;
            UsingB := not UsingB
          end;
      if UsingB
        then
          write(B, Current)
        else
          write(C, Current);
      Previous := Current
    end
end;
```

You should notice how we use **eof** to determine whether or not the end of file A has been encountered. You should also notice how we used a Boolean variable, UsingB, to decide which file to write the current integer to. Finally, notice that Runs gets incremented only when an integer smaller than the previously read integer is encountered; i.e., when we come to the start of a new run.

Merge

The procedure **Merge** is not as easy. The algorithm requires that we look at the first elements of both A and B and write the smaller one into C. How do we do that? The first thing that comes to mind is probably something like:

```
while not eof(A) and not eof(B) do
  begin
    read(A, M);
    read(B, N);
    if M < N
      then
        ...
```

But that won't work. This reads a new element into both M and N every time. We only want to read a new element into the one that was written to C. Consider this modification:

```
while not eof(A) and not eof(B) do
  begin
    if M < N
      then
        begin
          write(C, M);
          read(A, M)
        end
      else
        begin
          write(C, N);
          read(B, N)
        end
  end;
  ...
```

But now we have to make sure M and N have values before the loop begins. Thus, we might want to add:

```
read(A, M);
read(B, N);
while not eof(A) and not eof(B) do
  begin
    if M < N
      then
        begin
          write(C, M);
          read(A, M)
        end
      else
        begin
          write(C, N);
          read(B, N)
        end
  end;
  ...
```

The problem now is that one of these two files might very well be empty when
Merge is called. Then you might want to modify the first two statements to
say:

```
if not eof(A)
  then
    read(A, M);
if not eof(B)
  then
    read(B, N);
while not eof(A) and not eof(B) do
  begin
    if M < N
      then
        begin
          write(C, M);
          read(A, M)
        end
      else
        begin
          write(C, N);
          read(B, N)
        end
  end;
  ...
```

But now eof might be false when we try to read the file the first time, but might be true before the loop starts—that is, the file might contain exactly one integer. In this case, either M or N (or both) will contain an integer that has not yet been written to the third file. In fact, due to the way eof works in Pascal, there will always be an integer stored in either M or N that has not yet been written when the loops exits. The problem is with eof. eof always "looks ahead" to see if the file is empty. If we try to use eof to stop the loop and if we have read the current integer into M or N and not yet processed it, we'll have a very hard time getting the loop to stop at the right time. This could lead to a lot of extra code testing to see whether or not a particular integer has been written, etc.

The solution to the dilemma—and if you don't think it's a dilemma, then you need to try to solve it yourself before reading further—is to not use eof to terminate the loop. Rather, use a pair of flags, say AEnd and BEnd. If we are at the end of file A, we'll set AEnd to true, similarly, if we're at the end of file B, we'll set BEnd to true. They'll be false otherwise. Now consider this code:

```
reset(A);
AEnd := false;
if not eof(A)
  then
    read(A, M)
  else
    AEnd := true;
reset(B);
BEnd := false;
if not eof(B)
  then
    read(B, N)
  else
    BEnd := true;
```

```
rewrite(C);
while not AEnd and not BEnd do
  if M < N
    then
      begin
        write(C, M);
        if not eof(A)
          then
            read(A, M)
          else
            AEnd := true
      end
    else
      begin
        write(C, N);
        if not eof(B)
          then
            read(B, N)
          else
            BEnd := true
      end;
  ...
```

At first glance, this doesn't seem to be any different than just using eof. To see the difference, say to yourself, "eof(A) tells me about the status of the file *after* reading a number into M, that is, just before attempting to read the next number; AEnd tells me about the *current* status of the file."

This is a subtle point that you'll have to think about carefully to see. Try to write the procedure yourself using eof and not using any flags. Then trace the code below and decide whether or not it accomplishes the task.

Our code for Merge begins on the next page.

```
procedure Merge(var A, B, C : IntFile);

{  This procedure merges the two files A and B into one file, C    }
{  Precondition: The data stored in A and B are stored in ascending }
{  order.                                                           }
{  Postcondition:  The data from A and B are in file C and in       }
{  ascending order.                                                 }

var
  M, N : integer;
  AEnd, BEnd : Boolean;

begin
  reset(A);
  AEnd := false;
  if not eof(A)
    then
      read(A, M)
    else
      AEnd := true;
  reset(B);
  BEnd := false;
  if not eof(B)
    then
      read(B, N)
    else
      BEnd := true;
  rewrite(C);
  while not AEnd and not BEnd do
    if M < N
      then
        begin
          write(C, M);
          if not eof(A)
            then
              read(A, M)
            else
              AEnd := true
        end
      else
        begin
          write(C, N);
          if not eof(B)
            then
              read(B, N)
            else
              BEnd := true
        end;
```

```
      while not BEnd do
        begin
          write(C, N);
          if not eof(B)
            then read(B, N)
            else BEnd := true
        end;
      while not AEnd do
        begin
          write(C, M);
          if not eof(A)
            then read(A, M)
            else AEnd := true
        end
    end;  { end of Merge }
```

FileMergeSort

Finally the Pascal procedure that calls these two procedures until the file is in
order also follows the algorithm directly:

```
procedure SortFile(var A : IntFile);
var
  B, C : IntFile;
  Runs : integer;

    . . .

begin { Statement Part of SortFile }
  repeat
    Runs := 1;
    Distribute(A, B, C, Runs);
    if Runs > 1
      then
        Merge(B, C, A)
    until Runs = 1
end;
```

We'll leave it as an exercise to write a program that tests **FileMergeSort**.
Your routine should create a file of integers and should provide for a way to see
the three files as they are being written and read.

10.9   K-way Merge

The merge sort just completed works well, but it can be improved in a fairly direct manner. We used just three files, the main file and two supplemental files into which the main file was distributed and then merged back together. It took several passes over the main file to sort it. There's no reason we have to only use two supplemental files. It would be possible to reduce the number of passes over the main file by using several files instead. Let's suppose we use $k + 1$ files. The idea is: take the main file, distribute the runs as before, but cycle through k files, distributing each run to the next file in the cycle—after using the kth file, start over with the first file. When all the runs have been distributed, merge the k files together back into the main file.

This solution requires rewriting both *Distribute* and *Merge*. Rather than distributing A to two files, distribute it to k files. Then, rather than merging two files, *Merge* would have to merge k files. The basic idea is just the same, but the two algorithms are more complicated. The decision as to which file to use for output becomes more complicated since there has to be a way to decide which file is currently being used and a way to decide how to use the next file when a new run begins. *Merge* has to merge the k files and when the end of each of the k files is reached, the remaining numbers in the other files still have to be written (in order) to the main file. While these ideas are easy to conceptualize, their implementation is non-trivial.

For example, here's the code we wrote for `Distribute5`; it will illustrate the modifications that need to be made:

```
procedure Distribute5(var A, F1, F2, F3, F4, F5 : IntFile;
      var Runs : integer);

{  This procedure distributes the data in file A into five  }
{  files: F1 through F5.                                     }

var
  Current, Previous : integer;
  Using : integer;

begin
  reset(A);
  rewrite(F1);
  rewrite(F2);
  rewrite(F3);
  rewrite(F4);
  rewrite(F5);
  Using := 0;
  Previous := -maxint;
  while not eof(A) do
    begin
      read(A, Current);
      if Current < Previous
        then
          begin
            Runs := Runs + 1;
            Using := (Using + 1) mod 5
          end;
      case Using of
        0 : write(F1, Current);
        1 : write(F2, Current);
        2 : write(F3, Current);
        3 : write(F4, Current);
        4 : write(F5, Current)
        end;
      Previous := Current
    end
end;
```

This solution only works for a fixed value for k (5). If you want to write a general procedure that allows k to be a parameter, you'll have to be a lot more clever. The procedure MergeK is more complicated than this, but straightforward once you see the need for k flags. We'll leave the rest of the implementation for the exercises.

10.10 Additional Comments on External Sorting

Before leaving this topic, we need to say a few more words about external sorting. First, while the routines we just wrote work, they do require a lot of disk accesses, even for relatively small files. If you have a real world problem where a file is being maintained and the data in that file needs to be accessed in a particular order, the best solution probably will not involve continually adding records to the end of the file and then sorting the file. This simply takes too much time and causes too much wear and tear on the hardware. There are several better solutions available. You could maintain the file as a binary tree—as long as it will all fit in memory—and insert and/or delete records as we did in chapter 7.

If the file will not fit entirely in memory—which is the normal situation— you'll likely want to resort to direct access files. Given the ability to access the records stored in a file directly, there are several nice solutions to the problem.

One solution involves simply writing each new record to the very end of a file and never moving it. We'll call this file the "data file." The records in the data file are accessed according to another file, the "index file." The index file contains the key fields from each record and the record number. If the index file can be held entirely in memory, then it can be read in when the program begins and treated as a binary search tree. When a new record is added to the database, it's appended to the end of the data file, and the node containing the record number and the key field is inserted in the tree. Whenever a search is conducted, the tree is searched for the key; when it's found, the record number is used to read the appropriate record from the data file.

If the database gets even bigger and the index file also cannot be held in memory, you could create a B-tree to hold the index file (B-trees were discussed in chapter 9).

Since direct access files are not supported in Standard Pascal, we'll not discuss these ideas any further in this chapter. Chapter 9 treats direct access files in more detail, but remember that the extensions needed to support them differ from compiler to compiler.

10.11 The Radix Sort

In this chapter we have looked at ways of sorting arrays (the Quicksort and the Merge Sort) and files (the File Merge Sort). As a final example of advanced sorting techniques we'll consider sorting another data structure: the linear linked list.

The method we'll use to sort the linked list is based on a time-honored method called the *radix sort*. This method was used to sort punched cards, a data storage medium from the early days of tabulating machines. To illustrate this sorting technique, consider the task of sorting a deck of cards so that the suits are in order (ie., ♣ < ◊ < ♡ < ♠), and within each suit, the cards themselves are in order (A < 2 < ... < Q < K).

We might think of the cards as representing two-digit numbers such as ♡6, where the least significant digit (the 6) can take on one of 13 values, and the most significant digit (the ♡) can take on one of four values. Using the radix sort, you would first sort the deck on the least significant digit, forming 13 piles of four cards each. Then you pick up these piles in order and sort them again, this time on the most significant digit (the suit). When you gather up the four piles this time, the entire deck will be sorted. You should try this yourself to see how it works.

In general, in the type of radix sort we're discussing, we sort the data into piles on each pass, based on the least significant digit first, then the next most significant, and so on. The number of piles on each pass equals the number of values the corresponding digit can take on, and the number of passes equals the maximum number of digits the data can have. To make our explanation simpler, let's say the data in our linked list consists of integers with at most 3 digits. We can sort the list with 3 passes, making 10 piles on each pass.

Let's see how this works with a small sample of such integers, before we begin designing the data structure and the algorithm we'll need. Consider this sequence of integers:

833   354   205   224   992   719   800   38   530   228

After the first pass these numbers would be in order by the ones digit:

800   530   992   833   354   224   205   38   228   719

After the second pass, they would be in order by the tens digit. Notice that numbers sharing the same tens digit are also in order by their ones digits:

800   205   719   224   228   530   833   38   354   992

Finally, sorting this list by the hundreds digit results in an ordered list:

38   205   224   228   354   530   719   800   833   992

Now consider a linked list containing three-digit integers in a data field. We wish to sort this list by the radix method, so we will need ten "piles" into which to put the data on each pass. For each pile, all we need is a pointer to the top of the pile and a pointer to the bottom. The piles themselves will be linked lists, subsets of the original list. After each pass, the piles can be linked together in order, to reform a list with the same length as the original, but now partially sorted. The data itself need not be moved, only the pointers will be rearranged.

Since we need ten piles, we'll use an array of ten pointers to point to the top of each pile, and another such array to point the the bottom of each pile. Here's a high-level algorithm for the radix sort:

```
START OF RadixSort(Head)
passed by value: none
passed by reference: Head

loop for i going from 1 to the number of digits in the data
    initialize the pile pointers to nil
    store Head in P
    loop while P is not nil
        let k be the iᵗʰ digit of P^.Data
        add P^ to the top of the kᵗʰ pile
        point P at the next node in the list
    point the top of each nonempty pile
                at the bottom of the next nonempty pile
    store the bottom of the first nonempty pile in Head
    store nil in the pointer field of the node at the top
                of the last pile

END OF RadixSort
```

We'll leave the completion of this algorithm and the corresponding code for the exercises.

Order of Magnitude for the Radix Sort

How fast is the radix sort? Remember that the number of piles into which we divide the list is equal to the number of digits in the data; it doesn't depend on N. Let's call the number of digits d. We make d passes through the list, no matter how long the list is. Initializing the pile pointers, linking the piles together and cleaning up the ends of the list are also processes that don't depend on N. We may be tempted to conclude that we make dN comparisons in sorting the list, so the sort is $O(N)$ since d is constant.

The catch in the above argument is that d isn't really independent of N in practice. The number of different integers with d decimal digits is 10^d, and as N increases beyond 10^d the list just includes more and more duplicates. It's reasonable to require that as N increases, d should increase so that $d \approx \log_{10} N$; i.e., d is $O(\log N)$. This means that the number of comparisons, dN, is $O(N \log N)$.

10.12   Summary and Review

- We discussed two more sorting algorithms, the quicksort and the merge sort. Both of these algorithms were written recursively.

- We used the notion of a "loop invariant" to begin to see how one could go about proving the correctness of an algorithm.

- We saw that the quicksort algorithm is $O(N \log N)$ in the best case and $O(N^2)$ in the worst case. It is very unlikely that the worst case will happen so the quicksort is an extremely useful method of sorting numbers; one of the fastest algorithms known.

- We saw that the merge sort algorithm is only slightly slower than the quicksort. The merge sort is $O(N \log N)$ in both the best and worst case.

- We saw that the ideas involved in the merge sort can be used to sort an external collection of data, i.e., a file. We wrote a program that used the merge sort algorithm on a file.

- We saw that eof and the way that files are read in Pascal call for special care when implementing routines that read files.

- We examined the notion of doing a k-way merge sort on a file.

- We discussed sorting a linear linked list using the radix sort.

10.13   Exercises

1. The partitioning method we used in the quicksort algorithm can also be used to determine the kth smallest element in an array of numbers. (After partitioning the array, if the number of numbers in region 1 is less than or equal to k, then the kth smallest number in region 1 is also the kth smallest number in the original array. On the other hand, if the number of numbers in region 1 and 2 combined is smaller than k, then the kth smallest number in the original array is the k minus this number smallest number in region 3. Finally, if the number of numbers in region 1 is smaller than k, but the number of numbers in regions 1 and 2 combined is greater than or equal to k, then any of the numbers in region 2 equals the kth smallest number in the original array.) Using the *Partition* procedure, write the algorithm and the code for a function that will return the kth smallest element in an array of real numbers. What is the order of magnitude of the function?

2. Is the quicksort stable?

3. Complete the coding for a procedure that implements the *MergeSort*.

4. Add the quicksort and merge sort procedures to the program developed in chapter 2. Your enlarged program should compare the speeds of these two algorithms in addition to those already included in the program. See exercise 3, page 44.

5. Is the merge sort stable?

6. Complete the program that sorts the data stored in a file. As indicated on page 286, you should create a file of integers, and use that file to test your program. Your program should also allow for some sort of "debug" printing, a way to see the contents of the files as the sort is happening.

7. Complete the program that does a "k-way merge sort." Your program should probably assume a constant value for k. You will want to write an algorithm for `MergeK` before you write the code.

8. Write a Pascal function `Kth` that extracts the kth digit from the right (i.e., the kth least significant digit) of a given integer. The integer itself and k are passed as parameters.

9. Complete a lower-level algorithm for the radix sort of a linked list. Code the algorithm in Pascal, and write a short test program that creates a linked list, displays it, sorts it using the radix sort, and displays the list again.

Chapter 11

Graphs

> The Second Law of Thermodynamics:
> Probable events happen more frequently
> than improbable events.
> — Mark Schindler

11.1 Introduction

In this chapter we will discuss a few of the elements of *Graph Theory*. We will see once again how computer programming involves the use of appropriate data structures as well as the development of algorithms that manipulate these data structures. We will begin to see how some of the data structures we have already discussed can be viewed as variations of graphs.

11.2 The Beginnings of Graph Theory

In 1736, the Swiss mathematician Leonhard Euler published an elegant solution to a problem that is now known as "The Seven Bridges of Königsberg." This solution and the methodology it introduced are considered to be the origin of subject known as "graph theory." Here's a statement of the problem:

> The city of Königsberg, located on the banks of the river Pregel, had seven bridges that connected the city with various islands in the river. The people of Königsberg enjoyed strolling through the city and across the bridges. Someone once wondered if it was possible to stroll across the bridges in such a manner as to cross each bridge exactly once and return to the point where the stroll had begun. Either find such a stroll or demonstrate that it is not possible.

A picture of the river Pregel and the seven bridges connecting parts of the city of Königsberg is contained in figure 11.1. Euler solved the problem; he

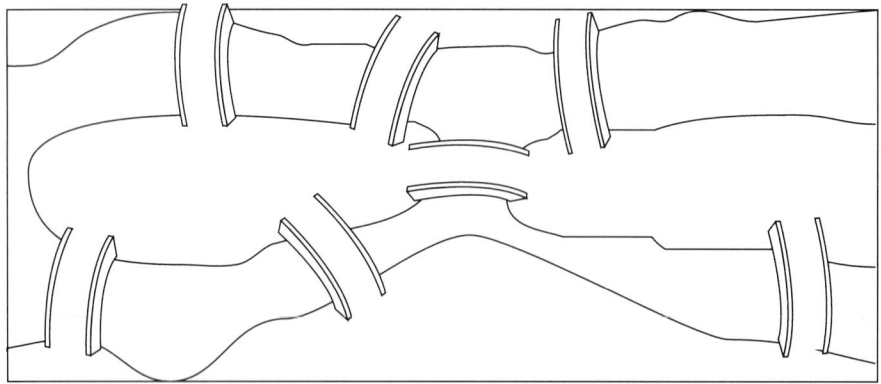

Figure 11.1 The Seven Bridges of Königsberg

answered the question as to whether or not such a stroll could be found. You
might want to try to find a stroll yourself before reading on.

Before we can understand Euler's solution, we need to introduce some terminology.

Definitions and Terminology

A *graph* consists of two sets, a set V of *vertices*, and a set E of *edges*. Each
edge must connect exactly two distinct vertices. We will say that the edge is
"incident with" (i.e., "on") the two vertices. When two vertices are connected
by an edge, we will say that the vertices are "adjacent." We will often say
that two vertices are "on" an edge, as well as saying the edge connects the two
vertices. No two vertices may be on more than one edge. No edge connects a
vertex to itself.

When we draw pictures of graphs, we draw the vertices as dots and the
edges as line segments connecting the dots. A picture of a graph can be drawn
in several ways, and we will try to draw it so that the edges only intersect at the
vertices, but it's not always possible. Regardless of how we draw the picture,
the graph is not the picture. The graph is the collection of vertices and edges.
Figure 11.2 shows a simple graph with five vertices and six edges. Vertices A
and B are connected by one edge, vertices B and C are adjacent as well. Vertex
B is on three different edges.

There are various ways that graphs can be represented; just listing the two
sets is one way. We'll examine ways to represent a graph in the computer in a
few pages.

While many things can be done with graphs, the Seven Bridges of Königsberg
problem requires a generalization of the notion, called a "multigraph." A *multigraph* also consists of two sets of vertices and edges, but an edge in a multigraph
may have the same vertex on both ends (such edges are called "loops"), and

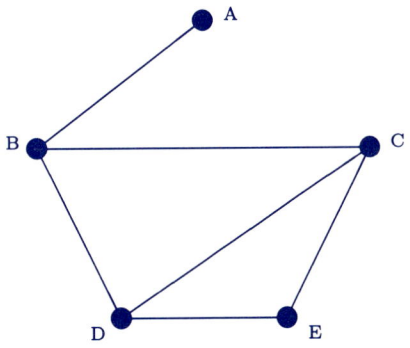

Figure 11.2 A Simple Graph

there may be more than one edge connecting the same two vertices. Figure 11.3 contains a picture of a multigraph.

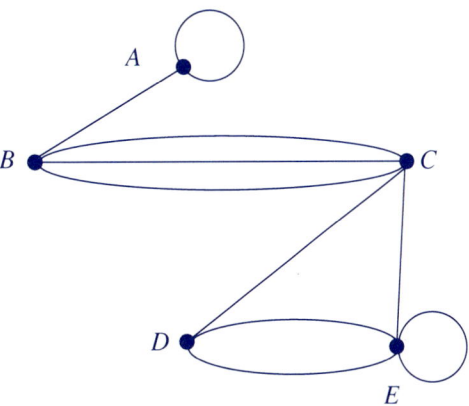

Figure 11.3 A Multigraph

This multigraph has five vertices and ten edges. There are, for example, three distinct edges connecting vertices B and C.

A *path from U to V* in a multigraph is an alternating series of vertices and edges,

$$V_0 \ e_1 \ V_1 \ e_2 \ V_2 \ \ldots \ e_n \ V_n$$

where $U = V_0$ and $V = V_n$, and with the property that edge e_i has vertices V_{i-1} and V_i as its endpoints. A *simple* path is one in which the vertices are not repeated.

Two vertices, U and V, in a multigraph are *connected* if there exists a path from U to V. By definition, we agree that every vertex is connected to itself. Notice that we say that an edge connects two vertices, and we say that two vertices are connected if there is a path from one to the other. When this leads to confusion, we'll say that two vertices are 'adjacent' rather than 'connected' if they are on the same edge.

A multigraph is *connected* if every pair of vertices in the multigraph are connected.

In figure 11.4, we show two multigraphs. In 11.4 (a), vertices A and B are not connected by any path, and thus the multigraph is not connected. In 11.4 (b), every pair of vertices is connected by a path, and therefore, the multigraph is connected.

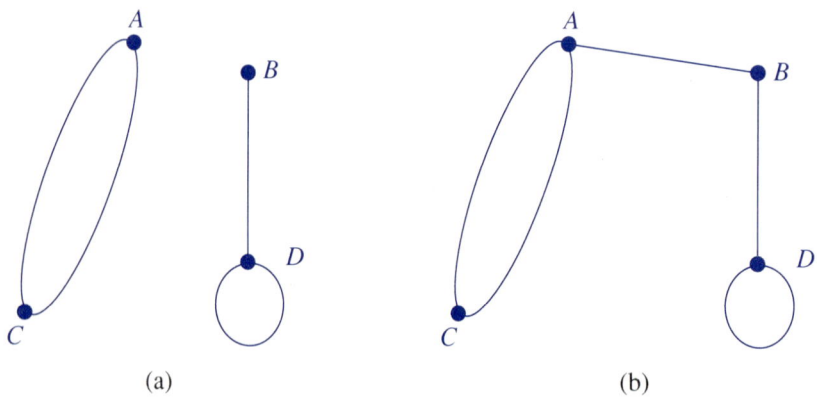

(a)   (b)

Figure 11.4 Two Multigraphs

A *circuit* is a path

$$V_0 \; e_1 \; V_1 \; e_2 \; V_2 \; \ldots \; e_n \; V_n$$

such that $V_0 = V_n$ and for $i = 1 \ldots n, j = 1 \ldots n$, whenever $i \neq j$, then $e_i \neq e_j$. In other words, the starting and ending vertices are the same and the edges are distinct.

In honor of Euler, an *Euler path* is a path that has different starting and ending vertices and includes every edge in the multigraph exactly once.

An *Euler circuit* is a circuit that contains all the edges of the multigraph.

We need one more definition before we can return to the solution of the Seven Bridges of Königsberg problem. We define the *degree* of a vertex to be the number of edges incident on it. If the vertex is on both ends of an edge, that is, if the edge is a loop, we count the edge twice in determining the degree of the vertex. In figure 11.5, vertex A has degree 3, and vertex B has degree 5. Vertices C and D both have degree 4. We denote the degree of a vertex V by $\deg(V)$.

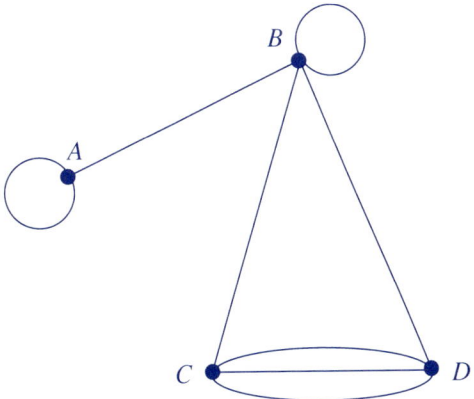

Figure 11.5 A Connected Multigraph

You can see that these definitions are leading us towards a solution to the Seven Bridges of Königsberg problem. Before we can continue, we need to redraw our picture of the city. The shores and the islands become vertices and the bridges become edges. Figure 11.6 contains a representation of the city as a multigraph. Notice that this is a multigraph, not a graph.

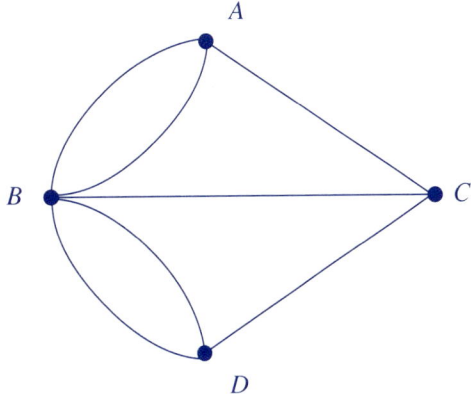

Figure 11.6 The Seven Bridges as a Multigraph

Theorems Concerning Multigraphs

We are ready to state the theorem that solves the Seven Bridges of Königsberg problem:

Theorem 11.1 *If a connected multigraph G has an Euler circuit, then every vertex has even degree.*

Proof: Since every vertex on the Euler circuit, including the starting vertex, has to be entered exactly once every time it is exited, and since every edge has to be used exactly once, the degree of every vertex must be even.

If we consider an Euler path instead of an Euler circuit, we get a similar theorem:

Theorem 11.2 *If a connected multigraph G has an Euler path, then exactly two vertices have odd degree and every other vertex has even degree.*

Proof: The starting vertex of the Euler path is exited one more time than it is entered; the ending vertex is entered one more time that it is exited, so these two vertices have odd degree. The other vertices are exited exactly once every time they are entered so they all have even degree.

Now, using these two theorems, we can examine the multigraph in figure 11.5 and see if it has either an Euler circuit or an Euler path. If there was an Euler circuit, every vertex would have an even degree. Since *every* vertex has an odd degree, it's clear that no Euler circuit exists. The same can be said about Euler paths since it is not the case that exactly two vertices have odd degree. This solves the original Seven Bridges problem. There is, of course, a great deal more that can be said about graphs and multigraphs, and these notions lead to several other fascinating topics. We'll examine a few of these topics in the remainder of this chapter.

An Additional Theorem Concerning Multigraphs

Our first theorem has a converse that Euler also proved:

Theorem 11.3 *If every vertex of a connected multigraph G has even degree, then the multigraph has an Euler circuit.*

Proof: Suppose G is a connected multigraph and suppose every vertex of G has even degree. Select a vertex, call it V_0. Select an edge on V_0, say e_1. Let V_1 be the other endpoint of e_1. If possible, choose a different edge, say e_2, on V_1. Since $\deg(V_i)$ is even, this is always possible, unless $V_1 = V_0$ and all the edges on V_0 have been used up. Continue adding edges and vertices to this path until it is not possible to add any more. This results in a circuit:

$$V_0 \ e_1 \ V_1 \ e_2 \ V_2 \ \ldots \ e_n \ V_n$$

where $V_n = V_0$. Since every vertex has even degree, it is always possible to leave a vertex unless that vertex equals V_0, so we must get back to V_0. This, however, may not be an Euler circuit because we may not have used all the edges of G. To complete the construction, continue the next steps until all the edges of G have been used:

1. Find the first vertex, say V_j of the circuit that has an unused edge, e.

2. Construct a circuit

$$V_j \ e \ \dots \ V_j$$

that starts with the unused edge and continues until no more edges can be added. Again, this circuit will end up at V_j since all vertices have even degree.

3. Enlarge the original circuit by "splicing" these two circuits together:

$$V_0 \ e_1 \ V_1 \ \dots \ e_j \ V_j \ e \ \dots \ V_j \ e_{j+1} \ \dots \ e_n \ V_n$$

Since G is connected, every edge will eventually be used, and this process constructs an Euler circuit of G. This completes the proof.

The proof also constitutes an algorithm for constructing an Euler circuit when one exists. We'll use that algorithm below in a computer program.

11.3   Graphs on a Computer

Now that we know what graphs and multigraphs are, let's use the computer to do some elementary graph theory. As always, we need a problem to solve. Using the above descriptions of graphs, multigraphs, path and circuits, we can state a problem that involves these concepts:

> Write a computer program that will allow a user to enter a multigraph, and determine whether or not it's connected. If it is connected, determine whether or not an Euler circuit exists. If an Euler circuit exists, find one and display it. If the graph is not connected or does not have an Euler circuit, then display an appropriate message.

Solve the problem

Think back to our FIVE + STEPS from chapter 3. The first step is to define the problem; that we've done. The second step is to find a solution to the problem, choosing appropriate data structures for the representation of the data involved. How would you represent a multigraph in a computer?

Once you've answered that question, ask yourself how you could represent a circuit.

Neither of these questions has a trivial answer, and they surely require some thought. A multigraph consists of two sets, a set of vertices and a set of edges.

Should we represent a graph as two sets? If so, how would we represent the set of edges? We could make an edge an ordered pair, say (A, B) where A and B are vertices, but that isn't quite satisfactory. Since a multigraph can have more than one edge joining two vertices, we will need to be able to have two edges, say (A, B) and (A, B), joining the same pair of vertices. If we put both these pairs into a set, then they will not be counted as distinct elements.

Another representation that is possible is a matrix. If we imagine a matrix where the rows and columns are numbered by the vertices, we can indicate the number of edges connecting vertex A to vertex B by the number in row A column B (as well as in row B column A). For example, if you look back at the multigraph in figure 11.3, you will see that it could be represented by the matrix:

$$
G = \begin{pmatrix}
2 & 1 & 0 & 0 & 0 \\
1 & 0 & 3 & 0 & 0 \\
0 & 3 & 0 & 1 & 1 \\
0 & 0 & 1 & 0 & 2 \\
0 & 0 & 1 & 2 & 2
\end{pmatrix}
$$

Remember loops are counted twice; i.e., the loop connecting A to itself is represented by the 2 in the first row and first column. Notice also that the matrix is symmetrical along the main diagonal, that is, the number in row R column C equals the number in row C column R. That is because there are the same number of edges connecting U to V as there are connecting V to U.

The matrix alone might not be sufficient. Since a matrix is a two-dimensional array, and since arrays have to have their sizes determined in advance, we should also assume there is a "size" number associated with each multigraph representing the number of vertices in the multigraph. We can assume that a multigraph is a record consisting of a two-dimensional array of integers and an integer field representing the number of vertices in the multigraph.

Entering a Multigraph

Given this structure for representing a multigraph, it is easy to develop an algorithm that allows a user to enter a multigraph. Here's a simple version:

```
START OF EnterGraph(G)
Passed by reference: G, a multigraph

display "How many vertices in the multigraph?"
accept G.NumVertices
loop for V going from 1 to G.NumVertices
    display "How many loops from vertex", V, "to itself?"
    accept Num
    store 2*Num in G.Matrix[V, V]
    loop for U going from V + 1 to G.NumVertices
        display "How many edges connecting", V, "to", U, "are there?"
        accept Num
        store Num in G.Matrix[V, U]
        store Num in G.Matrix[U, V]

END OF EnterGraph
```

Main Algorithm

An algorithm like this gets us started on the solution, and we can sketch an outline of the main program very readily. It would likely go something like this:

```
START OF Euler

call EnterGraph(G)
if G is connected
    then
        if G has an Euler circuit
            then
                construct an Euler circuit and display it
            else
                display "The multigraph does not have an Euler circuit."
    else
        display "That multigraph is not connected."

END OF Euler
```

This clearly leaves some modules to be written. We will have to be able to tell whether or not a multigraph is connected. We will have to be able to determine whether or not an Euler circuit exists in a connected multigraph. If an Euler circuit exists, we will have to be able to construct and display one.

Existence of an Euler Circuit

The second task is easy so let's tackle it first. We can take the matrix and determine the degree of each vertex by just summing the numbers in the row corresponding to that vertex. Here's a Boolean valued function, *HasEulerCircuit* that will do that job.

```
START OF HasEulerCircuit(G)

store true in HasCircuit
store 1 in V
loop while V ≤ G.NumVertices and HasCircuit
    store 0 in Sum
    loop for U going from 1 to G.NumVertices
        add G.Matrix[V, U] to Sum
    add 1 to V
    if Sum is odd
        then
            store false in HasCircuit
return HasCircuit

END OF HasEulerCircuit
```

Two major modules remain. We have to be able to tell whether a multigraph is connected, and we have to be able to construct an Euler circuit if one exists.

Connected

Let's tackle "connected" first. How can we determine whether or not a multigraph is connected? If a multigraph is connected, it must be possible to start with any vertex and find a path to every other vertex. If we start with, say, the first vertex and keep track of all the vertices that are adjacent to this one, and keep track of all those that are adjacent to these, and all the vertices that are adjacent to these, until no more vertices can be added, then this collection will contain all the vertices in the multigraph if it is connected. If it isn't connected, the set of vertices that can be reached from the starting vertex will be a proper subset of the set of all vertices.

We're talking about sets. Can we work with sets in Pascal? The answer is yes, but we shouldn't really care. We can write the algorithm using sets and then find a way to implement that algorithm even if the language doesn't support sets. So, let's continue with the algorithm.

Let's call the first vertex A. We want to add all the vertices adjacent to A to a set and then add all the vertices adjacent to each of these vertices, continuing until no more vertices can be added. How can we keep track of those vertices that we are putting in the set? Easy—put them onto another data structure and work with them later. It doesn't matter whether we use a FIFO structure or a LIFO structure; i.e., it doesn't matter whether we use a stack or a queue. Let's use a stack. Our algorithm will look something like this:

```
START OF Connected(G)
Passed by value: G, a multigraph

pick any vertex, say A
store A in a set C
push A onto a stack
loop
    pop a vertex, say V, from the stack
    loop for U going from 1 to G.NumVertices
        if G.Matrix[V, U] is non-zero and U is not in C
            then
                add U to C
                push U onto the stack
    until the stack is empty
if C contains all the vertices of G
    then
        return true
    else
        return false


END OF Connected
```

We could refine this algorithm, rewriting it in our lower-level algorithmic language, but we'll leave that and the coding of the algorithm for the exercises.

Sets in Pascal

The *Connected* algorithm is interesting in that it uses several different data structures: a record consisting of a two-dimensional array and an integer, a set, and a stack. The stack is an abstract data type that has to be implemented in some manner similar to that used in the earlier chapters of the book, and we'll leave that implementation for you. We should, however, say a bit about sets in Pascal, as they have scarcely been mentioned before.

First, it is possible to define a "set type." For example, if we need to have a set that can hold vertices, we can define a new type, say `SetType` as follows:

```
type
  SetType = set of Vertex;
```

Of course, this requires that we first define `Vertex`. To do that, we have to decide what a vertex is. The simplest way to handle it would be to just allow a vertex to be a character from `'A'` to `'Z'`. This will limit us to 26 vertices, but that should not prove to be a real limitation. It's hard to imagine wanting to enter a multigraph with more than 26 vertices. If it happens that we need to, we can redefine things so that a vertex is an integer instead. Thus, we could include:

```
type
  Vertex = 'A' .. 'Z';
  SetType = set of Vertex;
```

We would then need to declare vertices V and U as variables of type Vertex and a variable C to be of type SetType. This is done in the usual manner:

```
type
  Vertex = 'A' .. 'Z';
  SetType = set of Vertex;
var
  U, V : Vertex;
  C : SetType;
```

Then we can make C the set containing vertex 'A' by just writing:

```
C := ['A']
```

To see if U is in set C, we can code:

```
if U in C
  then
    ...
```

And then, if we need to add vertex U to the set, we can use "set union," represented in Pascal by the + symbol, as follows:

```
C := C + [U]
```

We wouldn't want to spoil your fun in writing this code, but perhaps it will be beneficial to show just the *loop for* in Pascal. Using the above declarations, the code from the middle of **Connected** will look something like:

```
    ...
    for U := 'A' to chr(G.NumVertices - 1 + ord('A')) do
      if (G.Matrix[V, U] <> 0) and not (U in C)
        then
          begin
            C := C + [U];
            Push(S, U)
          end
    ...
```

Notice that we have defined G.Matrix to be a two-dimensional array using characters as subscripts. Notice also that a **for** statement can loop from character to character as well as from integer to integer. The construction chr(G.NumVertices - 1 + ord('A')) is likely to reoccur several times, and we might want to make it a variable, e.g., LastVertex. We'll leave Connected for you to complete, and go on to the task of constructing an Euler circuit.

Constructing an Euler Circuit

Our solution to the problem of constructing an Euler circuit and our algorithm use the same process that was outlined in the proof of theorem 3: we start with a vertex, say A, and follow edges until we come back to A. Since the degree of every vertex is even, we'll have to get back to A eventually. We will then have a circuit that connects A to A but we would not necessarily have an Euler circuit; there will likely be some unused edges in the multigraph. To complete the Euler circuit, we start over at A and follow the edges in the circuit we have constructed until we come to a vertex, say V, that has an unused edge. We start at V and construct another circuit that comes back to V. This circuit can be spliced into the original circuit which is then still a circuit from A to A. This process continues until all the edges are used. Let's look at a picture to see how this works. Consider figure 11.7.

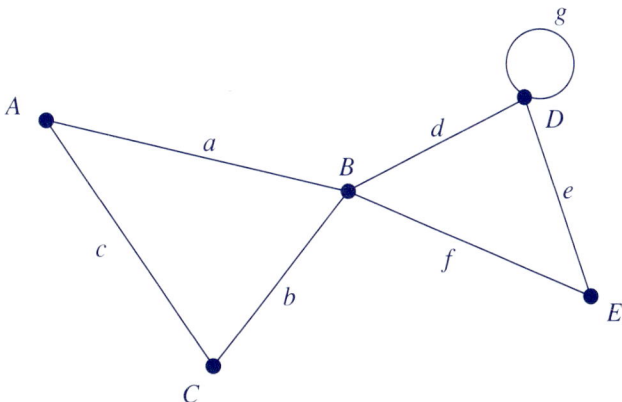

Figure 11.7 A Multigraph that has an Euler Circuit

There is an Euler circuit of this multigraph since every vertex has even degree. If we start at A and follow the edges a, b and c, we come back to A. The circuit $A\,a\,B\,b\,C\,c\,A$ does not contain all the edges of the multigraph so we come to the second stage. We follow edges of this circuit until we come to a vertex with an unused edge. That takes us to B. We find a circuit starting at B using the unused edge, say $B\,d\,D\,e\,E\,f\,B$. This circuit is spliced into the original circuit, producing $A\,a\,B\,d\,D\,e\,E\,f\,B\,b\,C\,c\,A$. This is still not an Euler circuit since there are still unused edges; the second step is repeated until all the edges are used. The circuit $D\,g\,D$ is spliced into the original circuit, producing $A\,a\,B\,d\,D\,g\,D\,e\,E\,f\,B\,b\,C\,c\,A$, and the Euler circuit is complete.

That solves the problem; let's turn the solution into an algorithm. How are we going to represent the circuits? A reasonable data structure would be a linked list since it's easy to splice linked lists together. We won't have to keep track of the names of the edges, but we will have to keep track of when an edge has been used. We can use a copy of the matrix for this. We can simply subtract 1 from the number of edges connecting two vertices whenever we use one in constructing a circuit—and we have to also subtract 1 from the symmetric place in the matrix, since an edge connecting A to B also connects B to A.

A first cut at the algorithm might look like this:

```
START OF FindEulerCircuit(C, G)
Passed by value: G a connected multigraph
Passed by reference: C, an Euler circuit
Precondition: G is connected and every vertex has even degree
Postcondition: C is an Euler circuit of G


choose a vertex, say A
build a circuit from A to A
loop while there are unused edges
    follow edges on C until you come to a vertex, say V, with an unused edge
    build a circuit from V to V
    splice that circuit into C

END OF FindEulerCircuit
```

We will refine this algorithm, but before we do, let's look at a routine that builds a circuit. We will have to send it a vertex so it can start building the circuit at that point. We will also pass the circuit that's being built to the routine (by reference, of course). And we will have to send the multigraph since as edges are added to the circuit, they will have to be removed from the matrix. Here's a first cut at the algorithm:

START OF BuildCircuit(A, C, G)
Passed by value: A, a vertex
Passed by reference: C, a circuit, and G a multigraph
Precondition: A has an unused edge incident with it.
Postcondition: C is a circuit from A to A.

initialize C to contain A alone
store A in U
loop
    find an unused edge on U, say e
    store the other end of e in V
    add the vertex V to the circuit
    subtract 1 from G.Matrix[U, V]
    subtract 1 from G.Matrix[V, U]
    store V in U
    until U equals A

END OF BuildCircuit

We *loop until U equals A* since we want the circuit to come back to A eventually. The step:

    find an unused edge on U

will be accomplished by just looking down row U in the matrix until we come to a non-zero value. That needs to be a *loop while* since it's possible the vertex in the first row and first column has an unused edge: a loop. We will also have to pass the number of edges—by reference—so that each time an edge is added to the circuit, we can subtract 1 from the number remaining to be added; that will enable us to tell when all the edges have been added. Here's an improved version of the algorithm:

START OF *BuildCircuit(A, C, G, NumEdges)*
Passed by value: A, a vertex
Passed by reference: C, a circuit; G, a multigraph; NumEdges
Precondition: A has an unused edge incident with it.
Postcondition: C is a circuit from A to A

initialize C to contain A alone
store A in U
loop
    store the first vertex in V
    loop while G.Matrix[U, V] = 0
        store the next vertex in V
    add the vertex V to the circuit
    subtract 1 from G.Matrix[U, V]
    subtract 1 from G.Matrix[V, U]
    subtract 1 from NumEdges
    store V in U
    until U equals A

END OF *BuildCircuit*

Notice that we are not putting edges in the circuit, just the vertices. Since the edges don't exist in our matrix representation, there's no way we can actually put them in a circuit. When we display the circuit later, we'll just display the vertices.

If we assume we can determine the total number of edges in the multigraph—which will be easy to do using the matrix—we can refine the earlier algorithm and write it:

START OF *FindEulerCircuit(C, G)*
Passed by value: G a connected multigraph
Passed by reference: C, an Euler circuit
Precondition: G is connected and every vertex has even degree
Postcondition: C is an Euler circuit of G

choose a vertex, say A
store the number of edges of G in NumEdges
call BuildCircuit(A, C, G, NumEdges)
loop while NumEdges > 0
    follow edges on C until you come to a vertex, say V, with an unused edge
    call BuildCircuit(V, C_1, G, NumEdges)
    call Splice(C, C_1)

END OF *FindEulerCircuit*

The remaining step:

> *follow edges on C until you come to a vertex, say V, with an unused edge*

can be accomplished with a *loop while* just like the one used in *BuildCircuit*:

> $\vdots$
>
> *store the first vertex in V*
> *loop while G.Matrix[A, V] = 0*
>   *store the next vertex in V*
>
> $\vdots$

This leaves the problems of adding a vertex to a circuit, and of splicing the circuits C and C_1 together. Since we're imagining the circuits as linked lists, the splicing is straightforward. We'll leave the completion of the algorithm for the exercises.

11.4 Directed Graphs and Multigraphs

The notion of a "directed" graph is similar to that of a graph, the difference is simply that each edge has an assumed direction involved with it. A *directed edge* is an edge *from* one vertex to another. Think of the directed edges as one-way streets—or perhaps, thinking of the Seven Bridges of Königsberg, as one-way bridges. Then there might be an edge from vertex U to V while there might *not* be an edge from V to U. This same notion can be extended to *directed multigraphs*. In this case, each ordered pair of vertices, (U, V), may have any number of directed edges from U to V. If you think about the adjacency matrix, what this implies is that the matrix is no longer symmetric along the main diagonal.

The vertices of a directed graph or multigraph no longer have degrees; rather, each vertex will have an *indegree* and an *outdegree*. The *indegree* of vertex V is the number of edges *from* V to another vertex, and the *outdegree* of V is the number of edges from another vertex *to* V. A familiar looking theorem results:

Theorem 11.4 *In a directed graph or multigraph, the number of directed edges equals the sum of the indegrees of the vertices, which is also equal to the sum of the outdegrees of the vertices.*

A directed multigraph can have *directed loops* as well as *parallel directed edges*. For directed multigraphs we can define *directed paths* and *directed circuits* in a manner similar to our earlier definitions. Likewise, we can define a notion similar to the notion of "connected," called "strongly connected." A directed multigraph is *strongly connected* if for every pair of vertices (U, V), there is a directed path from U to V. Everything would remain much the same as before except that we would have to follow directed edges rather than just following edges.

Finally, if we imagine the Seven Bridges of Königsberg problem as involving one-way bridges, we can imagine having to find a *directed Euler circuit* of the seven bridges, or a *directed Euler path* from some vertex to another.

A theorem (which we will not prove) similar to our major result for simple multigraphs then follows:

Theorem 11.5 *Suppose G is a directed multigraph that is strongly connected. Then there is a directed Euler circuit of G if and only if the indegree of every vertex equals its outdegree.*

Notice how similar this is to requiring that the degree of each vertex in a simple multigraph is even.

There is a similar theorem concerning the existence of a directed Euler path, which we'll leave as an exercise.

Directed Multigraphs on a Computer

We have introduced the notion of directed graphs in order to pose the following problem:

> Write a computer program that will allow a user to enter a directed multigraph, and determine whether or not it's strongly connected. If it is strongly connected, determine whether or not a directed Euler circuit exists. If a directed Euler circuit exists, find one and display it. If the graph is not strongly connected or does not have a directed Euler circuit, then display an appropriate message.

The solution to this problem will be similar to the earlier solution, and we leave the completion of the solution as well as the coding of the program as an exercise.

11.5   Coloring Maps

Another famous problem involving graphs is the map-coloring problem. For centuries people have drawn maps and have used different colors to indicate different regions on the maps. Two adjacent regions on the map must be colored with different colors so they can be told apart. By "adjacent," we mean they share a common border; two regions that only meet in a point can use the same color. Two questions arise: "How can a map be colored so that two adjacent regions have different colors?" and "What is the minimum number of colors needed to color a map?"

It was observed in 1850 by a student, Francis Guthrie, that all the maps he tried could be colored with no more than four colors, and he wondered if all two-dimensional maps could be colored with no more than four colors. He mentioned this to others, and the problem finally reached some prominent mathematicians of the day. They attacked it, but could neither prove that four colors were always sufficient nor find an example of a map that required five colors. For decades mathematicians worked on this problem. No matter how hard they tried, they could not find an example of a map that required more than four colors, but they could not prove that every map could be colored with four colors or fewer.

Finally, in 1976, the Four Color Map Problem was solved. Two mathematicians from the University of Illinois, K. Appel and W. Haken, proved that any two-dimensional map could be colored using four or fewer colors.

The announcement of this result excited the world mathematics community. It was the conclusion of a quest that thousands of mathematicians had struggled with for over a hundred years. What makes this result even more interesting to us is the fact that the proof used a computer. The proof consisted of exhaustively checking thousands of cases, requiring over 1200 hours of computer time on a very large computer. This is the first example of a major mathematical theorem that was proved with the help of a computer. The method used is simply not available to human mathematicians; 1200 hours of computer processing time translates into hundreds of human lifetimes. No human working alone could ever have done it that way. Indeed, to some mathematicians this is not considered a valid proof, and they are still looking for a "better" way of proving the result.

Obviously, we are not going to try to reproduce the proof used by Appel and Haken. What we can do, however, is use an well-known algorithm to solve the first of the two problems posed above; i.e., to color a map. Let's make this our problem:

> Write a program that will allow a user to enter a two-dimensional map, and will assign to each region of the map a color in such a manner that two adjacent regions have different colors.

Solve the Problem

Thanks to the Four Color Map Theorem, we know we should be able to get the job done using four or fewer colors. Since this is an extremely hard task, if we want it to be efficient, we'll not make it a requirement that our coloring results in a minimal number of colors. It would be nice, of course, to use a "small" number of colors, that is, it would be nice to use an algorithm that is relatively straightforward while not requiring too many colors. How would you color the map in figure 11.8 using as few colors as possible?

While you can use "trial and error" to get that map colored using four colors, a more systematic process will be useful. A well-known algorithm for coloring a map—the Welsh and Powell algorithm—exists, and we'll use that algorithm below in our program.

Figure 11.8 A Map to be Colored

Choose the Data Structures

But first, we realize that we need to choose some way of representing the map
in the computer. A graph will do the job. If we let each region of the map be
represented by a vertex and use edges to indicate that one region (vertex) is
adjacent to another, we can represent the map quite nicely as a graph. Notice
that this results in a graph, not a multigraph, since two vertices can either be
adjacent or not; they cannot have more than one edge connecting them. (And,
no region is adjacent to itself, so there won't be any loops.) Figure 11.9 shows
the map from figure 11.8 as a graph. Notice that we have assigned each region
(i.e., each vertex) a letter.

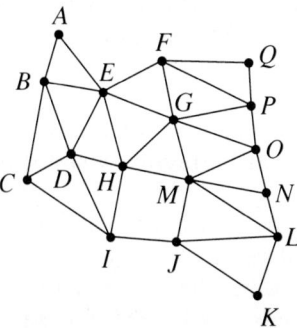

Figure 11.9 A Graph Representing the Map

We will also have to decide how to represent the colors assigned to each
region. Since we have to have a maximum number of regions (because we're

using a two-dimensional array for the graph), we might as well use an array to represent the colors too. Let's make it an array of pairs, each pair will contain the vertex letter and the assigned color. We'll initialize each pair to zero to indicate that no color has been assigned.

A Map Coloring Algorithm

Now that we can represent a map and its colors, we need to find an algorithm that will color the map. Perhaps a method has occurred to you already. Perhaps you had the thought: "Color the regions that have the largest number of adjacent regions first." This turns out to be a good start, and is essentially the Welsh and Powell algorithm mentioned earlier. Here's how it goes.

START OF ColorGraph (Welsh and Powell Algorithm)

Arrange the vertices in order according to degree, largest degree first.
(if there are several vertices with the same degree, put them
in any order.)
store 0 in N
loop while there are uncolored vertices
    add 1 to N
    Color the first vertex in the list that is uncolored with color N.
    Go down the list and assign color N to any uncolored vertex that
    is not adjacent to a vertex colored with color N.
N represents the number of colors used.

END OF ColorGraph

Now we see that we have to keep track of each vertex's degree as well as its color. Let's make the list an array of triples rather than pairs. Each triple will contain the vertex letter, the color, and the degree. Let's call the triples vertices; i.e., each vertex will be a triple that contains a letter, a color and a degree.

Using our map from figure 11.8 as an example, after rearranging the vertices by degree, the list of vertices and degrees would look like that in figure 11.10.

Vertex:	E	G	M	D	H	B	F	I	J	L	O	P	C	N	A	K	Q
Degree:	6	6	6	5	5	4	4	4	4	4	4	4	3	3	2	2	2

Figure 11.10 The Vertices in order by Degree

Following the Welsh and Powell algorithm—and using numbers for the colors—the resulting list would look like figure 11.11.

Refine the Algorithm

We need to solve some sub-problems. It's not hard to

Vertex:	E	G	M	D	H	B	F	I	J	L	O	P	C	N	A	K	Q
Degree:	6	6	6	5	5	4	4	4	4	4	4	4	3	3	2	2	2
Color:	1	2	1	2	3	3	3	1	2	3	3	1	4	2	2	1	2

Figure 11.11 The Vertices after Colors have been Assigned

> *Color the first vertex in the list that is uncolored with color N.*

To accomplish this; we simply go down the list, starting at the top, look at the color field of each triple and see if it's zero or not. If it is not zero (meaning it's already been colored), we keep looking. That is, we can just

```
store 1 in i
loop while Vertexᵢ.Color ≠ 0
    add 1 to i
store N in Vertexᵢ.Color
```

This assumes we will reach an uncolored vertex before we run out of vertices, which we will since the outer loop will get exited if all the vertices have been colored.

It's a little harder to

> *Go down the list and assign color N to any uncolored vertex that is not adjacent to a vertex colored with color N.*

but we can use the adjacency matrix for this. We can start at i, and look further down the list for uncolored vertices. When we find one, say V, we look to see if V is adjacent to a vertex with color N. If none of the vertices adjacent to V have color N, we assign V the color N. Here are the steps that will do the job:

```
loop for j going from i + 1 to G.NumVertices
    if Vertexⱼ.Color = 0
        then
            store true in Ok
            loop for k going from 1 to j − 1
                if G.Matrix[j, k] ≠ 0 and Vertexₖ.Color = N
                    then
                        store false in Ok
            if Ok
                then
                    store N in Vertexⱼ.Color
```

With these refinements added, the algorithm looks like:

START OF ColorGraph (Welsh and Powell Algorithm)

Arrange the vertices in order according to degree, largest degree first.
(If there are several vertices with the same degree, put them
in any order.)
store 0 in N
loop while there are uncolored vertices
    add 1 to N
    store 1 in i
    loop while $Vertex_i$.Color ≠ 0
        add 1 to i
    store N in $Vertex_i$.Color
    loop for j going from i + 1 to G.NumVertices
        if $Vertex_j$.Color = 0
            then
                store true in Ok
                loop for k going from 1 to j − 1
                    if G.Matrix[j, k] ≠ 0 and $Vertex_k$.Color = N
                        then
                            store false in Ok
              if Ok
                then
                    store N in $Vertex_j$.Color
N represents the number of colors used.

END OF ColorGraph

While this will get the map colored, the question remains open as to whether a minimum number of colors is used. We'll leave that question open for the time being.

Entering the Map and Designing the Output

The input to the program will be just a graph, which we can hold in a matrix. We can allow the user to enter the regions one at a time and indicate which regions are adjacent to which regions. The input routine could look much like the one we wrote earlier for multigraphs, but it becomes tedious to enter it this way. Since the regions have to be adjacent in a stronger sense than with graphs in general, it will be easier to enter a list of regions that are adjacent to a given region. In other words, we could use a loop for that went through each of the vertices and asked for a list of regions adjacent to that one. The entire matrix could be initialized to zero first and then particular locations changed to ones.

We also need to decide what the output of the program should be. Let's just have the program print a list of regions (vertices) and assign each one a color. Then let's have the program display the number of colors it required.

With our program, we set it up so that a run of the program looked like the following:

```
This program allows a user to enter a map and color it.  If the map
is not connected, you will be so advised, otherwise a coloring is
found.  You will need to enter the number of regions (vertices) and
you will need to indicate which regions are adjacent to each other.

How many regions does the map have?  (1 to 26): 17

Which regions are adjacent to region A?   B E
Which regions are adjacent to region B?   AEDC
Which regions are adjacent to region C?   BID
Which regions are adjacent to region D?   B D I H E
Which regions are adjacent to region E?   ABDHGF
    ...


The map is colored as follows:
Region E has degree 6 and is assigned color 1
Region G has degree 6 and is as·igned color 2
Region M has degree 6 and is assigned color 1
    ...


It required 4 colors to color this map.
```

Notice that we wrote it so that the adjacent regions can be entered in any order, and so that the user could enter spaces or not as he wished.

The completion of this program, while not trivial, should be fairly routine, using techniques we've already discussed elsewhere in this book. We'll leave the completion for the exercises.

Minimal Number of Colors

Before we go on to our next topic, let's return to the question concerning minimal number of colors. Does the Welsh and Powell algorithm produce a minimal number of colors? While our intuition might tell us it does, as a matter of fact, it does not. This algorithm produces a "reasonable" number of colors (whatever that means), but not a minimal number of colors. When a map is sufficiently complicated, the program will often produce a coloring that uses more colors than are needed. It is a very hard problem to develop an efficient algorithm that produces a minimal coloring. Indeed, if by 'efficient,' we mean with order of magnitude N^2, or even N^m where m is some integer, then no such algorithm has yet been found. This is a problem that is well beyond what we intend to accomplish here, so we'll content ourselves with what we have.

11.6 Weighted Graphs and Shortest Paths

As a final example of how computer programs can manipulate graphs, let's take a look at "weighted graphs" and a famous algorithm that finds the shortest path through a weighted graph.

A *weighted graph* is a graph where each edge has been given a weight. We'll assume that the weights are positive values. Each edge has been assigned a positive number representing, in some sense, the "cost" of following that edge. For example, the vertices could represent cities and the weights could represent the distance between the cities. Or, the vertices could represent different energy states and the weights on the edges could be the change in energy from one state to another. Figure 11.12 contains a weighted graph that we'll use for our discussion.

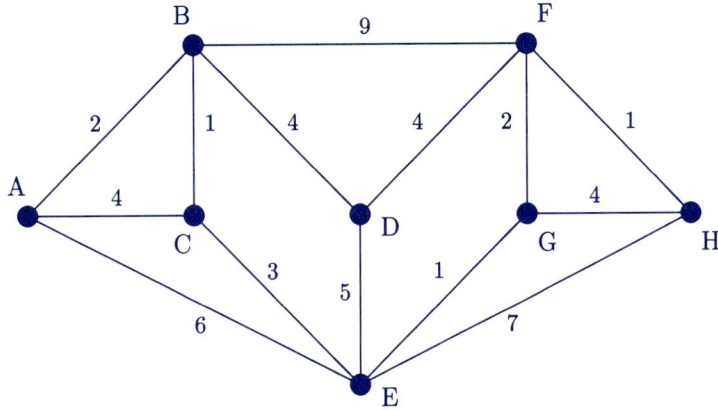

Figure 11.12 A Weighted Graph

The notion of a weighted graph leads us the the notion of "shortest path" from one vertex to another. The definition of a path is unchanged from our earlier discussion; it's still a series of vertices and edges that start at one vertex and end at another. However, we now want to add the notions of "distance" and "length of a path."

Given a weighted graph, the *distance* between two adjacent vertices is the weight of the connecting edge. The *length of a path* is the sum of the weights of the edges in the path.

In figure 11.12 there are many paths from vertex A to vertex H. We want to find a path with the smallest length; i.e., a "shortest path."

Once again, by trial and error one could find a shortest path, but there are rigorous ways to find one without resorting to trial and error. A famous algorithm that finds the shortest paths from a given vertex to every other vertex in the graph is due to Edsger Dijkstra, and we'll use his algorithm in the following.

The algorithm depends on the notion of a "predecessor" to a given vertex and on the ability to assign a label to a vertex. The predecessor of a vertex is another vertex. The label assigned to a vertex is a positive number. The algorithm also depends on a collection of values $W(U, V)$ defined for all pairs of vertices, U, V, in the graph. When two vertices are connected by an edge, $W(U, V)$ equals the weight of that edge. If two vertices are not connected by an edge, $W(U, V)$ equals ∞. In the algorithm, S represents the set of vertices with permanent labels, and P is an array of predecessors. When the main loop in the algorithm is completed, the labels assigned to each vertex represent that vertex's distance from the given vertex, and to find a shortest path from the given vertex to any other vertex, you start with the ending vertex and follow predecessors back to the start.

Here's Dijkstra's algorithm:

START OF ShortestPaths(A, G, L, P) — Dijkstra's Algorithm
Passed by value: A, a given vertex; G, a weighted graph
Passed by reference: L, an array of lengths; P, an array of predecessors
Precondition: All the weights in G are positive.
Postcondition: $L[V]$ is the length of the shortest path from A to V,
* $P[V]$ is the predecessor of V on a shortest path from A to V.*

initialize $L[V]$ to $W(A, V)$, for $V \neq A$
store 0 in $L[A]$
initialize $P[V]$ to A, for $V \neq A$
store $\emptyset$ in $P[A]$
initialize S to $\{A\}$
loop
*   let V be a vertex such that $V \notin S$ and $L[V]$ is minimal*
*   add V to S*
*   for every U that is adjacent to V and $U \notin S$*
*   if $L[V] + W(V, U) < L[U]$*
*   then*
*   store $L[V] + W(V, U)$ in $L[U]$*
*   store V in $P[U]$*
*   until every vertex in G is in S*

END OF ShortestPaths

We store 0 in $L[A]$ because the length of the shortest path from A to A is 0. We store $\emptyset$ in $P[A]$ because A has no predecessor. When the algorithm is implemented, something else—depending on data types used—will have to be stored in $P[A]$.

This algorithm will require some effort to refine. The step:

let V be a vertex such that $V \notin S$ and $L[V]$ is minimal will require the ability to find a vertex that is not in S, whose current length from A is minimal. It's not obvious how we can efficiently keep track of the lengths in such a way as to be able to find a vertex with minimal length, and at the same time quickly access $L[V]$ for a particular vertex V. A single pass through the array looking for the smallest value will do the job, but if there are a lot of vertices, this single pass will get expensive.

Similarly, the step:

for every U that is adjacent to V and U ∉ S

is some sort of a loop that only considers vertices that are adjacent to V and are not in S. This can be a loop *for* that looks at every vertex but only works on those that are adjacent to V and not included in S. However, this too can be quite inefficient. Again, if there are a lot of vertices, this can take a long time. A better way of storing the set of edges might be needed. For example, we could store the edges in "adjacency lists." Each vertex would head a list of vertices that are adjacent to it. Such a list would make it easier to look just at those vertices that are adjacent to a particular vertex, but the need for the weights remains. In the interest of getting the program finished, and at the expense of not writing the most efficient program, let's just do with a loop *for*.

Let's trace the algorithm on the weighted graph in figure 11.12. Assuming that the given vertex is A. After initializing L and P, they will equal:

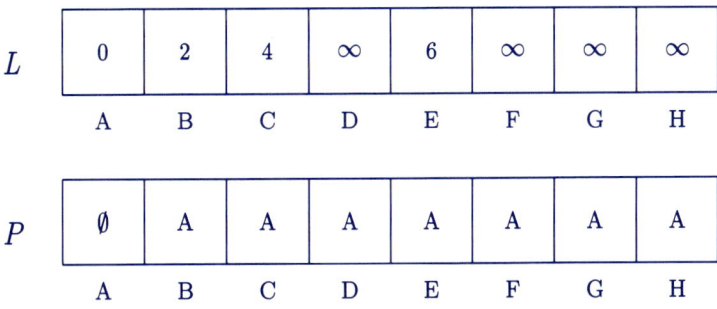

Figure 11.13 The Initial Arrays L and P

The vertex that is not in S and has the smallest label is vertex B. We add B to S and we examine those vertices that are adjacent to B and not in S, namely C, D and F. $L[C]$ is currently 4, $L[B] + W(B, C)$ is 3, so $L[C]$ is changed to 3 and B is made the predecessor of C. Similarly, $L[D]$ and $L[F]$ are changed and B becomes the predecessor of both D and F. Arrays L and P will look like those in figure 11.14.

Now the vertex that is not in S that has the smallest label is C. We add C to S and we examine those vertices that are adjacent to C and not in S. That

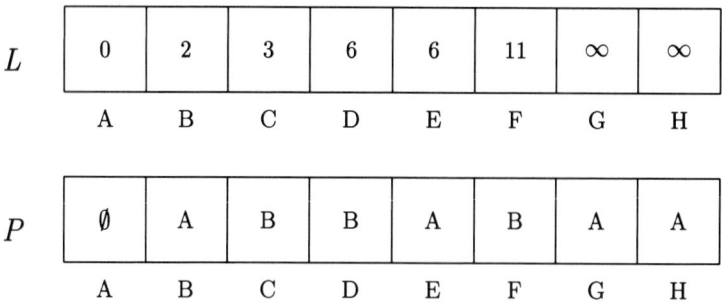

Figure 11.14 The Arrays L and P after B has been added to S

includes only E. Since $L[E] = 6$ and $L[C] + W(C,E) = 6$, we don't change either the label or E's predecessor. The only thing that gets changed is S.

When we now look at the labels to find the next vertex to add to S, we see that there are two vertices with label 6. It doesn't matter which one we work with, so let's take them in alphabetical order. D is added to S, and those vertices adjacent to D are examined. That includes E and F. The label on E is smaller already than the sum of $L[D]$ and $W(D,E)$ so nothing changes for E. The label on F, however, changes to 10 since $L[D] + W(D,F) < L[F]$. Also, the predecessor of F changes from B to D. Now things look like figure 11.15:

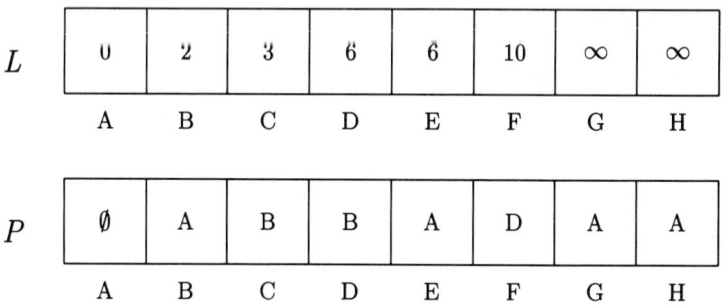

Figure 11.15 The Arrays L and P after D has been added to S

Stop reading and finish the trace of the algorithm yourself.

Your final arrays should look like those in figure 11.16.

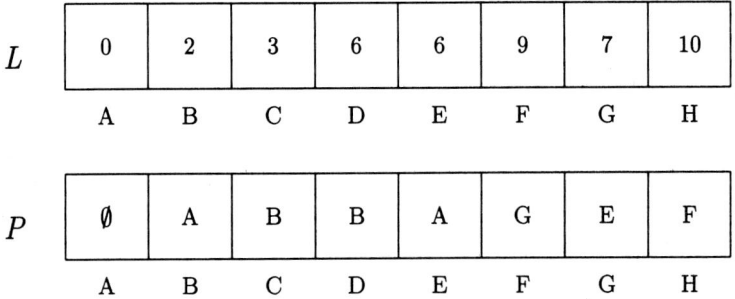

Figure 11.16 The Final Arrays L and P

Did you notice how at first it looked like the shortest path to F was through vertex B, then it changed to be through D, and finally it turned out to be through G? If you didn't, then you should go back and actually trace it.

Now, to find the shortest path from A to H, for example, we "backtrack" from H to F, from F to G, from G to E and then from E to A.

Notice also that this is *a* shortest path, not *the* shortest path. The path $A\,B\,C\,E\,G\,F\,H$ has the same length as the one found by the algorithm.

Pascal Implementation

The data structures for the Pascal implementation are straightforward; we'll use a two-dimensional array of integers for the matrix. This is exactly the same as the structure we used for our first program in this chapter. Here are the definitions and declarations from our program:

```
const
  MAX = 26;

type
  Vertex = 'A' .. 'Z';
  Graph = record
      Matrix : array [Vertex, Vertex] of integer;
      NumVertices : integer
    end;
  Labels = array [Vertex] of integer;
  Pred = array [Vertex] of Vertex;

var
  G : Graph;
  L : Labels;
  P : Pred;
  A, V, LastVertex : Vertex;
  Again : char;
```

We're using `P : Pred` as the array of predecessors, and we're using `L : Labels` as the list of labels for the vertices. These follow the algorithm exactly.

We can use an input routine very similar to the routine from our first program in this chapter with some minor changes: we'll ask for the weights rather than ask for the number of edges; we won't ask about loops, and we'll initialize the places in the matrix where no edges exist to `maxint` rather than 0.

Our main program allows the user to enter the weighted graph and then asks the user to enter a particular vertex. It then calls Dijkstra's algorithm to find the shortest path from that vertex to every other vertex in the graph. The user is then allowed to enter another vertex or quit.

Here's our main program, for reference:

```
begin  { WeightedGraphs }
  writeln('This program allows a user to enter a weighted graph and');
  writeln('a particular vertex.  It then finds the shortest path from');
  writeln('that vertex to every other.');
  Initialize(G);
  LastVertex := chr(G.NumVertices - 1 + ord('A'));
  repeat
    write('Which vertex do you want to start with?  ');
    readln(A);
    while (A < 'A') or (A > LastVertex) do
      begin
        write('Invalid vertex, try again:  ');
        readln(A)
      end;
    Dijkstra(G, A, L, P);
    writeln('The length of a shortest path from ', A, ' to the others is:');
    for V := 'A' to LastVertex do
      if V <> A
        then
          write(V : 5);
    writeln;
    for V := 'A' to LastVertex do
      if V <> A
        then
          write(L[V] : 5);
    writeln;
    writeln('with predecessors:');
    for V := 'A' to LastVertex do
      if V <> A
        then
          write(P[V] : 5);
    writeln;
    write('Enter another vertex?  ');
    readln(Again)
  until Again in ['n', 'N'];
  writeln('That concludes the program.')
end.
```

These remaining routines are very similar to the algorithms, and we'll leave their completion for the exercises.

11.7   Trees and Graphs

This chapter has been treated as somewhat separate from the earlier chapters on trees. It should be made clear that trees and graphs are actually closely related. Indeed, a tree is a graph. We defined a graph as a collection of vertices and a collection of edges. Surely a tree can be viewed as a collection of vertices plus a collection of edges. Each node is a vertex, and the non-nil pointers are the edges.

It is not the case that a graph is a tree; a tree is a special kind of graph. The definition used by most authors is:

> Any graph which is connected and has no cycles is a tree.

A *cycle* is a path with at least three vertices that begins and ends with the same vertex. It's clear that the trees we've worked with in earlier chapters don't have cycles. It's also clear that the trees we've worked with have been connected. Thus it's not surprising that trees are connected graphs that contain no cycles. It's not quite as obvious that every connected graph containing no cycles is a tree. There are several other statements about graphs that are equivalent to the above definition.

This is not a mathematics text, and we don't want to get too far afield, but we will state (without proof) a theorem concerning graphs and trees that should help you gain some insight about trees and graphs.

Theorem 11.6 *Given a graph G, the following are equivalent:*

1. *G is a tree.*

2. *G is connected and the number of edges in G is one less than the number of vertices.*

3. *G has no cycles and the number of edges in G is one less than the number of vertices.*

4. *There is exactly one simple path between every two vertices in G.*

5. *G is connected, and the removal of any one edge will cause G to not be connected.*

6. *G has no cycles, and the addition of any edge will cause G to have a cycle.*

By "equivalent," we mean that if any one of the above statements is true, they are all true.

Rooted Trees

The trees we have been dealing with satisfy another property that makes them special kinds of trees: they have each had a root. A *rooted tree* is a directed graph that satisfies two conditions: (1) when the directions on the edges are ignored, the graph is a tree, and (2) there is exactly one vertex that has indegree 0, and all other edges have indegree 1.

With this definition, and with the understanding that `nil` pointers are ignored, all the trees other than threaded trees we discussed in chapters 7–9 are rooted trees. Threaded trees are rooted trees as long as the threads are ignored. To insure that a graph is a binary tree, we would only have to add a provision that the outdegree of each vertex is less than three.

A great deal more can be said about graphs and trees. It can be shown, for example, that every connected graph contains (as a subset) a special kind of tree, a *spanning tree*, that contains all the vertices of the graph. Conversely, if a graph has a spanning tree, it must be connected. These results are fully covered in a course in Discrete Mathematics, and we'll leave further discussion of these topics for such a course.

11.8   Summary and Review

This chapter was concerned with several topics from elementary graph theory.

- We discussed the famous Seven Bridges of Königsberg problem that was solved by Leonhard Euler in the eighteen century.

- We introduced the concepts of graphs and multigraphs. Both graphs and multigraphs are collections of vertices and edges. Multigraphs differ from graphs in that multigraphs can have more than one edge connecting a pair of vertices, and they can have edges which connect a vertex to itself. Neither of these things can happen in a graph.

- We defined the notions of connectedness, paths, circuits, the degrees of the vertices, Euler paths, and Euler circuits. We used these notions to state and prove several theorems concerning graphs and multigraphs. These theorems led to a demonstration of the solution to the Seven Bridges problem.

- We stated a problem relating to multigraphs and the Seven Bridges problem that could be solved on a computer. This problem was to allow a user to enter a multigraph and find an Euler circuit if one existed. The solution of the problem involved a number of different data structures, including sets. We used this to introduce some of Pascal's ability to work with sets.

- We defined several notions similar to those for graphs and multigraphs but for *directed* graphs and multigraphs instead. These notions lead to similar results as those for regular multigraphs, which we left for the exercises.

- We discussed another famous problem from mathematics that involves graphs, the Four Color Map Problem. We showed how graphs can be used to find a coloring of a map, but we did not attempt to show how to find a minimal coloring of a map.

- We introduced the concept of a weighted graph, where each edge has a particular weight, and the notion of a shortest path through a weighted graph. We used Dijkstra's algorithm to find the shortest path from a given vertex in a weighted graph to every other vertex. We worked on a computer program that allows a user to enter a weighted graph, and find the shortest path from a given vertex to every other vertex in the graph, continuing until the user wants to exit the program.

- We briefly discussed the relationship between graphs and trees. We indicated that every tree is a graph, but graphs are not necessarily trees. We stated without proof a theorem that gives several characterizations of a tree. We mentioned the notion of a rooted tree.

The programs in this chapter served to illustrate how a knowledge of different data structures can be used to solve a variety of problems involving graphs. There are many other interesting problems in graph theory that were not mentioned.

11.9   Exercises

1. If the citizens were to tear down one of the Seven Bridges of Königsberg, could they choose one that would allow an Euler circuit of the city? If so, which bridge should they tear down?

2. If the citizens were to tear down one of the Seven Bridges of Königsberg, could they choose one that would allow an Euler path of the city? If so, which bridge should they tear down?

3. Could the citizens of Königsberg build one more bridge that would allow either an Euler circuit or an Euler path?

4. Refine the algorithm for *Connected* from page 305, and code it. You will have to use some of Pascal's ability to manipulate sets.

5. Complete the algorithm for *FindEulerCircuit* on page 310. You will need to decide how to add a vertex to a circuit and how to splice two circuits together. In the text we imagined this as involving linked lists, but you could use other data structures as you saw best.

6. The problem on page 301 was concerned with finding an Euler circuit, if one exists. It might be possible that an Euler circuit does not exist but an Euler path does. Modify the statement of the problem to say that if either an Euler circuit or an Euler path exists, the program should find it and display it. Then modify the algorithms and code appropriately to solve this problem.

7. State the theorem similar to the theorem on page 312 for the existence of a directed Euler path in a directed multigraph.

8. Using the concept of a directed multigraph and the related concepts of indegrees, outdegrees, directed edges, strong connectedness, and directed Euler paths and circuits, solve the problem presented on page 312. You will need to find a solution to the problem, turn your solution into an algorithm, choosing appropriate data structures for the solution, and code the program.

9. Could you assign directions to the Seven Bridges of Königsberg in a manner that would allow either a directed Euler circuit of the seven bridges or a directed Euler path?

10. Complete the solution to the map coloring problem. Your program should allow a user to enter a map, and then color it according to the Welsh and Powell algorithm. Write the input routine so that the user only has to enter the regions adjacent to a given region (see the example on page 318).

11. If the people of the state of California decided to split the state into two states: Northern California and Southern California, the map in figure 11.8 could be colored with three colors. Find such a coloring. Does the program you wrote in exercise 10 color the map with just three colors?

Figure 11.17 A Map with a Border

12. Suppose the map in figure 11.8 has a border added to it, producing the map in figure 11.17. Suppose also that the border region needs to be colored as well. At first you might think that, since the original map requires four colors, and since each of these four colors could be on regions that are adjacent to the new border, the new map must require five colors. However, the Four Color Map Theorem says that every map can be colored using no more than four colors. Find a coloring of the map in figure 11.17 using only four colors. Does the program you wrote in exercise 10 color the map with just four colors?

13. Complete the program for a weighted graph. Your program should allow a user to enter a weighted graph, and then allow the user to enter a particular vertex and find a shortest path from that vertex to every other vertex. The user should be able to continue entering vertices or quit.

Chapter 12

Random Numbers (Optional)

> Anyone who considers arithmetical methods
> of producing random digits
> is, of course, in a state of sin.
> — John von Neumann

12.1 Overview of the Chapter

This chapter will open with a brief discussion of the meaning of the term "random" in connection with sequences of numbers generated by a computer program. We will analyze the random number generator presented earlier in the book, and generalize on this example. We will present ways to generate numbers in a variety of distributions, and give examples of how each can be used. Finally, we will discuss tests to which we can subject our generators, to check for various aspects of what are generally accepted to be properties of a properly "random" sequence.

12.2 What Does *Random* Mean?

Let's say we're playing some sort of game where we ask a person to pick a number between 1 and 10. What we expect is that our friend will choose some number in that range in such a way that we can't predict which number it is. We would expect that if we were to try to guess the chosen number, we would have a one in ten chance of being correct.

Imagine our friend chooses the number four. Now we ask her to choose another number between 1 and 10. This time she again chooses four. Do we start to get suspicious? Why? If a four was random the first time, why shouldn't it be random the second time, or the third, for that matter? The point is that although we may want random numbers generated one at a time, the notion of "randomness" doesn't really come into play until we see a *sequence* of them.

Now consider these sequences of numbers from 1 to 10: (4, 4, 4), (1, 2, 3) and (1, 9, 6). Which of these sequences is the most "random?" Of course we would be tempted to say that the last sequence is, because the first two seem to have such obvious patterns. In fact, though, the chances of randomly choosing the sequence (4, 4, 4) are exactly the same (namely one in a thousand) as those of choosing (1, 9, 6). The reason we might object to the first or second sequence is that we seem to have more information about the *fourth* number in the sequence than we should have (although that may not be the case at all). What we're after, then, is a sequence of numbers such that each number is independent of the other numbers in the sequence, and each number is equally likely to occur.

There may be situations where we want the numbers in the sequence to have we would be tempted to say that the last sequence is, because the first two unequal probabilities. For example, when we roll a pair of dice, the possible values are the numbers between 2 and 12. The game of craps is based on the fact that the likelihood of rolling a 2 or a 12 is much less than that of rolling a 7. There is a specific *distribution* of probabilities associated with rolling dice. Assuming that each die yields a value between 1 and 6, with equal probability, there are $6 \times 6 = 36$ possible outcomes in rolling two dice. Of those possible outcomes, there is only one way to get a two, so the chances of getting a two are one in 36. There are six ways to get a 7, however, so the chances of getting a seven are six in 36, or one in six. We would call this distribution a *non-uniform* distribution, as distinguished from a *uniform* distribution, for which each outcome is equally likely.

In general, when we ask for a random number we want the next number in a sequence of independent numbers with a particular (possibly uniform) distribution of probabilities.

12.3   Pseudo-random Numbers

When we ask a *computer* to generate a random sequence we are asking the impossible. The computer only follows the instructions in a program, and anyone who knows those instructions could predict the sequence. We can, however, instruct the computer to generate a sequence that *appears* to be random, even though it's not. Such a sequence is called a *pseudo-random* sequence, and from now on when we use the term "random" in reference to a computer-generated sequence we will really mean "pseudo-random."

In the examples we have discussed so far, we have been concerned only with random integers; there are cases where we might be interested in random real numbers. For example, an economic simulation game might generate a random number of births and deaths in a country every year (integers), and the annual rainfall (a real). The former kind of random number sequence is called *discrete* and the latter is called *continuous*. We will first concern ourselves with generating a continuous random sequence of reals between zero and one; as we will see, this will enable us to build continuous and discrete sequences with various probability distributions.

As an example, consider the problem of generating a random integer between 1 and 10. If we were given a random real number R such that $0 \leq R < 1$, then we could divide the interval from 0 to 1 into ten equal parts, and return 1 if R is in the first part, 2 if it's in the second, and so on. Another way would be to multiply R by 10 and truncate the result. This would give us an integer between 0 and 9, and we could add 1 to that. Either way, if we have a sequence of R's that is uniformly distributed between 0 and 1, then the corresponding sequence of integers will be uniformly distributed between 1 and 10.

Computers, however, cannot represent real numbers with complete accuracy. On a given computer, there is a finite number of reals between zero and one that can be represented. There are various means for generating a sequence of real values between zero and 1, and in the next section, we'll examine one of the most popular methods.

12.4   The Linear Congruential Method

What we actually do is choose an integer between zero and some maximum integer N. The real number we return is that integer divided by N. Every number in the sequence we generate depends on the previous number in the sequence. We start with one number, called the *seed*, and generate another number from it. That number becomes the seed for the next number, and so on.

A common method of generating a number from the seed involves multiplying the seed by some fixed number, adding a second fixed number, dividing by a third and setting the new seed to the remainder of that division. A sequence generated by this method is known as a *linear congruential* sequence. Let's consider the random number generator introduced in chapter 3:

```
function Random : real;

{  This function returns a pseudo-random real number   }
{  between 0 and 1.  Seed is a global integer variable. }

const
   MULTIPLIER = 40;
   INCREMENT  = 3641;
   MODULUS    = 729;

begin
   Seed := (Seed * MULTIPLIER + INCREMENT) mod MODULUS;
   Random := Seed / MODULUS
end;
```

This function starts with a seed less than 729. It generates another number between 0 and 728 by multiplying the seed by 40, adding 3641 and taking the remainder of the result divided by 729. That remainder becomes the seed for the next call, and the value returned is the new seed divided by 729.

At first glance it's not clear why the particular values of 40, 3641 and 729 were chosen. Let's see what we can determine about the sequences generated by this combination of numbers.

First of all, it's clear that the only real numbers that can be generated by this combination are

$$0, \frac{1}{729}, \frac{2}{729}, \frac{3}{729}, \dots, \frac{728}{729}.$$

That is, we are limited to at most 729 different real numbers, after which the sequence will start to repeat itself. In general, the *period* of a sequence is the number of numbers in the sequence before it starts to repeat. In a linear congruential sequence, the maximum period is equal to the modulus.

In any application that uses random numbers, the period of the sequence should be greater than the number of numbers needed by the application, so it makes sense to try to have as long a period as possible. It's clear, though, that in the Pascal function above, as MODULUS gets larger, MULTIPLIER must get smaller, so that their product doesn't exceed maxint.

There are other considerations involved in the choice of MODULUS, MULTIPLIER and INCREMENT; for a complete discussion see *The Art of Computer Programming, Volume 2* by Donald E. Knuth (1981, Addison-Wesley). We'll simply state here that MODULUS should be divisible by a high power of a prime number (note that $729 = 3^6$), MULTIPLIER $-$ 1 should be a multiple of every prime factor of MODULUS ($39 = 3 \times 13$), and INCREMENT and MODULUS should have no factors in common ($3641 = 11 \times 331$).

Avoiding the problem with maxint

It is possible, through the use of a clever coding trick presented by Brian Wichmann and David Hill in the March, 1987 issue of *Byte* magazine, to choose much larger values for MODULUS and MULTIPLIER without running into the problem of overflowing maxint. Consider, for example, the following choices:

```
const
  MULTIPLIER = 142;
  INCREMENT  = 3641;
  MODULUS    = 19683;
```

Note that $19683 = 3^9$ and $142 - 1 = 141 = 3 \times 47$. Clearly, the line

```
Seed := (Seed * MULTIPLIER + INCREMENT) mod MODULUS
```

can't be executed as written if `maxint` is 32767. However, we can always express
Seed as 138 * (Seed div 138) + (Seed mod 138), where, since 19683 div
142 is 138, `Seed div 138` will always be less than or equal to 142. In that case,

```
    Seed * MULTIPLIER + INCREMENT
```

becomes

```
    138 * (Seed div 138) * MULTIPLIER + (Seed mod 138) * MULTIPLIER +
    INCREMENT
```

which is

```
    19596 * (Seed div 138) + (Seed mod 138) * MULTIPLIER + INCREMENT
```

But $19596 = 19683 - 87$, so this is

```
    19683 * (Seed div 138) - 87 * (Seed div 138) +
            (Seed mod 138) * MULTIPLIER + INCREMENT
```

Now since we're taking this number mod 19683, the first term above can be
dropped, giving (with a little rearrangement)

```
    (Seed mod 138) * MULTIPLIER - 87 * (Seed div 138) + INCREMENT
```

which, in the worst case, will be comfortably less than `maxint`. We can then
take this number mod 19683 as the new Seed.

It should be noted that some compilers don't compute the mod of a negative
number properly, and it is possible that the number above could be negative.
For example, if Seed is 13800, then Seed mod 138 is 0, and Seed div 138
is 100, so the above number comes out to -5059. If your compiler doesn't
correctly take -5059 mod 19683 (it should equal 14624), you will have to add
a line to the function below that checks to see if Seed is negative, and if so,
adds `MODULUS` to Seed before determining the return value for the function.

Here's the new generating function:

```
function Random : real;

{  This function returns a pseudo-random real number     }
{  between 0 and 1.  Seed is a global integer variable.  }

const
  MULTIPLIER = 142;
  INCREMENT  = 3641;
  MODULUS    = 19683;
  DIVISOR    = 138;
  DIFFERENCE = 87;

begin
  Seed := ((Seed mod DIVISOR) * MULTIPLIER -
           DIFFERENCE * (Seed div DIVISOR) + INCREMENT) mod MODULUS;
  Random := Seed / MODULUS
end;
```

In cases where our first generator is inadequate, this one will prove to be significantly better. If you encounter an application where this one, too, becomes unworkable, you will probably then be in a position to do further research and come up with an even better version.

12.5   Discrete Distributions

We now assume that we have a generating function that will give us a sequence of real numbers uniformly distributed between zero and one. We turn to the task of generating sequences of integers with different distributions.

Uniform Distributions

When the likelihood of any number being chosen is the same as that of any other number, the distribution is uniform. When we roll a die, we expect that any number between one and six is equally likely. When we spin a roulette wheel, any outcome should be as probable as any other. As we mentioned earlier, it's easy to convert a uniform distribution of reals between zero and one into a uniform distribution of integers. Let's write a simple function, `RandInt`, that will return a uniformly distributed integer between `Min` and `Max`.

There are `Max - Min + 1` integers between `Min` and `Max`, inclusive. We multiply this number by the random number generated by our function and truncate the result. This gives us one of `Max - Min + 1` integers starting with zero. If we add `Min` to the result, we'll get an integer between `Min` and `Max`, inclusive. Here's a Pascal function:

```
function RandInt(Min, Max : integer) : integer;

{  This function returns a random integer between Min and Max,   }
{  inclusive.  It calls Random to obtain a real between 0 and 1. }
{  Precondition:  Min < Max                                      }

begin
   RandInt := trunc(Random * (Max - Min + 1)) + Min
end;
```

A similar function could be written to return a uniformly distributed real number in a particular range. We'll leave that one as an exercise.

Weighted Distributions

As we've seen, the outcomes when rolling a pair of dice is distributed over the values from 2 through 12, but not uniformly so. This is an example of a weighted distribution. Although it's easy to generate numbers with this distribution by simply calling `RandInt(1, 6)` twice and adding the results, it can also be done in a more general way, that can be applied with any weighted distribution.

The main idea behind a weighted distribution is that there is a discrete set of outcomes, each with its specific probability. Each probability is a fraction between 0 and 1, and all of the probabilities for the outcomes add up to 1. We could partition the number line between 0 and 1 by laying the probabilities "end to end" as it were, starting at 0. We can then generate a random number, see which partition it's in, and return the corresponding value.

More specifically, let's say there are N possible outcomes which for simplicity we'll label $1, 2, \ldots, N$, each with its corresponding probability $p_1, p_2, \ldots, p_N$. Our generator gives us a random real number R. A function that returns one of the N integers, weighted as above, would work like this:

if $R < p_1$
    then
        return 1
    else
        if $R < p_1 + p_2$
            then
                return 2
            else
                ...
                return N

This is a rather awkward and inefficient algorithm; it would make more sense to store the values $p_1, p_1 + p_2, \ldots$ in an array, and simply search the array for

R, returning the corresponding index. If N is small, a linear search of the array would be sufficient, otherwise you could use a binary search, since the array is in ascending order. We'll leave the coding of an example as an exercise.

As you can see, if N is large, it becomes very tedious to have to spell out each of the probabilities of the various outcomes. Fortunately, in most cases of interest, one can use other methods to generate random numbers with non-uniform distributions.

Binomial Distributions

Consider an event (say, rolling "doubles" with a pair of dice) that occurs with a certain probability p (in this case, there are 6 different ways to roll doubles out of 36 possible ways to roll the dice, so $p = 6/36 = 1/6$). We would expect that if we rolled the dice N times, we would roll doubles roughly $N/6$ times. We would say that the *expected value* of the number of doubles rolled out of N trials is $N/6$. In general, the expected value for N independent trials with probability p each time is Np.

We want a function that, given the probability p and number of trials N, returns one of a sequence of numbers with the expected value Np. That is, we want the function to generate a random number between zero and N that is non-uniformly distributed; it should be closer to zero if p is small, and closer to N if p is close to 1.

A function that does this would be generating numbers according to the *binomial* distribution. In general, the binomial distribution applies to situations where some number of independent events occur with a given probability. The outcome of each event can be characterized by one of two possibilities, usually called "success" and "failure."

It's easy to generate numbers with the binomial distribution, given the probability p and the number of events N. Simply generate N random numbers R, each time testing to see whether $R < p$, and return the number of times this happens. Here's an algorithm for the function:

```
START OF Binomial(N, p)

store 0 in Counter
loop for i going from 1 to N
    if Random < p
        then
            add 1 to Counter
return Counter

END OF Binomial
```

which is easy to turn into a Pascal function.

Geometric Distributions

A distribution related to the binomial distribution is the *geometric* distribution.
Imagine independent events occurring, each of which has one of two outcomes,
which we again call "success" and "failure." Imagine further that the probability of a success is p. The number of events that occur between successes is
distributed according to the geometric distribution.

Recall the `ServiceTime` function from the queue simulation in chapter 3:

```
function ServiceTime(AvgServTime : integer) : integer;

{  This function returns a random service time.  The times         }
{  returned over a long time interval will average to AvgServTime.  }

  var
    i    : integer;
    Temp : real;

  begin
    i := 0;
    Temp := 1/AvgServTime;
    repeat
      i := i + 1
      until Random < Temp;
    ServiceTime := i
  end;
```

The numbers returned by this function will be geometrically distributed.
The function counts "events," each of which has probability `1/AvgServTime`.
Notice that there is no limit to the size of the number returned; the function
keeps trying until a random number is generated whose value is less than this
probability.

Also notice the connection between this distribution and the binomial distribution. In the latter, we're counting the number of successes per N events.
In the former, we're counting the number of events per 1 success.

The routine above is a straightforward translation of the meaning of the
geometric distribution. One drawback of this method is that if the probability
p is small, the routine is proportionately slow; the `Random` function is called and
compared a number of times proportional to $1/p$. A faster, but less obvious,
method of generating a geometrically distributed random number is to use the
fact (which we will not prove) that if R is a uniformly distributed real number
between zero and one, then $\lceil \log_{1-p} R \rceil$ is geometrically distributed. We can use
the property of logs that

$$\log_b a = \frac{\ln a}{\ln b}$$

to write a simple generating function using the built-in Pascal `ln` function:

```
function Geometric(p : real) : integer;

{  This function returns a geometrically distributed random  }
{  integer.  p is the probability for each event.            }

var
   R : real;

begin
   repeat
      R := Random
      until R > 0;
   Geometric := trunc(ln(R) / ln(1 - p)) + 1
end;
```

Note that we have to guard against the rare case when **Random** returns a zero, since the logarithm of zero is undefined.

And, to be accurate, the above function doesn't always yield $\lceil \log_{1-p} R \rceil$. In the extremely rare event that `ln(R) / ln(1 - p)` is an integer, we would return the next integer. This will occur so seldom that it will not affect the distribution.

Poisson Distributions

The Poisson distribution describes a situation where a number of independent events occur over a specified time interval t. Let μ represent the average number of events that occur over the time t. μ must be proportional to t; i.e., we would expect twice as many events to occur over an interval twice as long. The probability associated with each number n of total events is

$$\frac{e^{-\mu}\mu^n}{n!}.$$

For example, assume that $\mu = 1$. That is, on the average, one event occurs during every time interval. The probability of a 0 (the event fails to occur within the time interval) is

$$\frac{e^{-1}1^0}{0!} \approx .368.$$

The probabilities of 1, 2 and 3 are, respectively,

$$\frac{e^{-1}1^1}{1!} \approx .368, \ \frac{e^{-1}1^2}{2!} \approx .184, \text{ and } \frac{e^{-1}1^3}{3!} \approx .061.$$

Even though there are an infinite number of probabilities, they add up to 1.

We can think of the number line between 0 and 1 as being partitioned similar to the way it was in the weighted distribution algorithm. To generate a

Poisson-distributed integer, then, we let our generator produce a real number R, uniformly distributed between 0 and 1, and we see which partition it's in, returning the corresponding integer. That's the strategy used in the following algorithm, where $Prob(\mu, n)$ is a function that returns the Poisson probability of n events with mean μ:

START OF Poisson(μ)

store 0 in Sum
store 0 in n
store a random number in R
loop
    add Prob(μ, n) to Sum
    add 1 to n
    until Sum > R
return n − 1

END OF Poisson

The straightforward way to write the function *Prob* is:

START OF Prob(μ, n)

return $\dfrac{e^{-\mu} * \mu^n}{n!}$

END OF Prob

In coding this function, you will need to do two things that are not supplied in Standard Pascal: raise a number to a power, and take the factorial of a number. You can avoid having to raise a number to a power by using the fact that

$$\mu^n = e^{n \ln \mu}$$

to simplify the Poisson probabilities:

$$\frac{e^{-\mu} \mu^n}{n!} = \frac{e^{-\mu} e^{n \ln \mu}}{n!} = \frac{e^{n \ln \mu - \mu}}{n!}$$

You can now use the **exp** and **ln** functions for the numerator. You'll still have to write a **Factorial** function, and you'll have to be careful to avoid **maxint** problems.

It's also possible to write the *Prob* function recursively. Note that if $n > 0$,

$$\frac{e^{-\mu} \mu^n}{n!} = \frac{e^{-\mu} \mu^{n-1}}{(n-1)!} \cdot \frac{\mu}{n}$$

so that $Prob(\mu, n) = Prob(\mu, n - 1) * \mu \,/\, n$. The basis case is when $n = 0$:

START OF Prob(μ, n)

if $n = 0$
   then
      return $e^{-\mu}$
   else
      return Prob(μ, $n - 1$) * μ / n

END OF Prob

This is as good a way as any to write *Prob*, and will avoid some of the problems with `Factorial` and `maxint`. We'll leave the coding of `Poisson` and `Prob` as exercises.

12.6   Continuous Distributions

So far we have discussed methods of generating integers in a given range with a given distribution. Now we look at ways of producing real numbers in a similar fashion. Once again we assume the existence of a random number generator that returns R, a real number uniformly distributed between zero and one. The simplest continuous distribution is, of course, the uniform distribution; in the exercises, you are asked to write a function similar to `RandInt` that returns a uniformly distributed real number between two given real numbers.

Before we discuss other continuous distributions, it's important to point out some subtle distinctions between them and discrete distributions. Discrete random numbers take on certain values (usually integers) within a given range, but there are values in the same range that they *don't* take on. We might want to simulate, for example, flipping a coin 10 times and counting the number of "heads." We would generate an integer using an algorithm like *Binomial* with $N = 10$ and $p = \frac{1}{2}$. It would make no sense to generate a number like 3.5, because you can't flip heads 3.5 times.

Theoretically, continuous random variables can take on any value within a given range. They would be used to represent, for example, the height or weight of people boarding a plane, or the amount of rainfall per day in a jungle location.

With discrete variables, there is a set of possible outcomes which can be enumerated, and there is a definite probability associated with each outcome. Furthermore, the sum of the probabilities for all the outcomes is 1. In rolling dice, for example, the probability of rolling a 2 is $\frac{1}{36}$, as is the probability of rolling a 12. The probability of rolling a 2 *or* a 12 is the sum of these two probabilities, or $\frac{1}{18}$. The probability of rolling *any* number between 2 and 12 is the sum of all the corresponding probabilities, which is 1. This makes sense because you are certain to roll *some* number between 2 and 12.

With continuous variables, the notion of probability is not as clear-cut, and the notion of the "sum" of probabilities is also a bit more complicated. The question "What is the probability of measuring 1 inch of rainfall on a given day?" is poorly stated. It's very rare that a rainfall of *exactly* 1.0000... inches is measured. It makes more sense to speak of the probability of measuring rainfall within a certain range centered on 1 inch; for example, 1 ± 0.1 inches. The narrower the range is, the lower the associated probability.

It is still true that the total probability over all possible values is 1, even with continuous variables. For this reason, we represent the probability associated with a continuous variable by a curve such that the total area underneath has the value 1. The area under the curve between two given points represents the probability that the continuous variable falls between those two values.

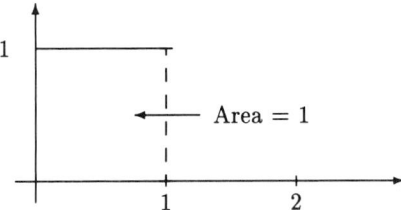

Figure 12.1 The Uniform Continuous Distribution

Let's look at a simple example: the uniform continuous distribution. In figure 12.1, we have drawn the distribution curve for this distribution, which is simply a horizontal line. Notice that the total area under the line is 1; the probability of generating *some* number between 0 and 1 is 1. To represent the probability of generating a number between 0.3 and 0.5, we draw dashed lines at 0.3 and 0.5, and consider the area under the curve between those dashed lines (see figure 12.2). This area is 0.2, the probability of generating a number between 0.3 and 0.5.

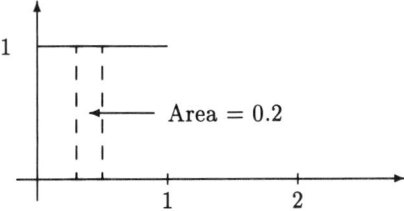

Figure 12.2 The Probability That $0.3 < R < 0.5$

We can generalize this notion by stating that *any* curve whose total area is 1 can represent a probability distribution. We usually specify the curve by its equation; for example, the equation for the uniform distribution is

$$f(x) = 1, \ 0 \le x \le 1.$$

There are many other functions that are used to represent continuous probability distributions; in what follows, we will consider two such functions associated with common continuous distributions, the *normal* and *exponential* distributions.

The Normal Distribution

A normal distribution is often referred to as a "bell-shaped" curve; the curve is symmetric, with a rounded peak in the middle and wedge-shaped tails at each end. This distribution can be used to describe many situations in the real world. For example, if we were to measure the heights of a large number of adult men, we would expect the values to be normally distributed. If we were to measure the heights of a large number of adult women, we would expect a normal distribution again, shifted a bit to the left.

Because the curve is symmetric, the average or *mean* value of the distribution occurs where the peak does. On either side of the peak, there is a point where the curve is momentarily a straight line; it changes from being concave downward to concave upward. The horizontal distance from these "points of inflection" to the center of the curve is called the *standard deviation* σ. Since the area under the curve is always 1, if σ is small (the curve is narrow), then the peak is high, and the numbers are mostly very close to the mean. If σ is large (the curve is broad), then the peak is low, and the numbers are more widely scattered. A normal curve can be completely characterized by its mean μ and standard deviation σ.

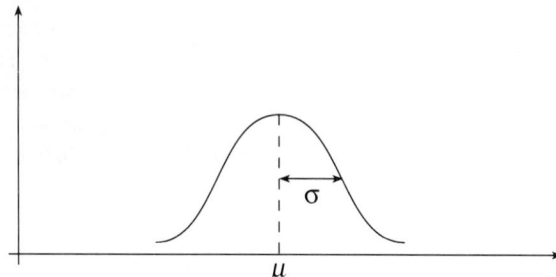

Figure 12.3 A Normal Distribution

The simplest normal curve is the one with mean 0 and standard deviation 1. As we will see, it is easy to generate numbers normally distributed with any mean and standard deviation based on numbers distributed with $\mu = 0$ and $\sigma = 1$. The distribution function for this curve is

$$f(x) = \frac{1}{\sqrt{2\pi}} e^{-\frac{x^2}{2}}, \quad -\infty < x < \infty.$$

Unfortunately, there is no obvious way to generate numbers with this distribution. One common method is known as the *polar* method, because its proof involves converting the Cartesian coordinates of a random point inside the unit circle to polar coordinates. The algorithm itself is easy to write, but

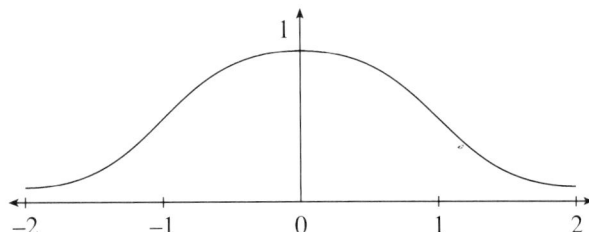

Figure 12.4 The Normal Distribution with $\mu = 0$ and $\sigma = 1$

understanding why the numbers it generates are normally distributed requires a little calculus. For a proof, see *The Art of Computer Programming, Volume 2* by Donald E. Knuth (1981, Addison-Wesley). The method is based on the following, which we will state without proof:

> If the point (x, y) is a random point in the unit circle a distance $r = \sqrt{x^2 + y^2}$ from the origin, then $\frac{-4x}{r} \ln r$ is normally distributed with mean 0 and standard deviation 1.

As a matter of fact, $\frac{-4y}{r} \ln r$ is also normally distributed, so with the following algorithm you get two for the price of one:

START OF Normal

loop
    call Random twice to generate X and Y.
    store $\sqrt{X^2 + Y^2}$ in R
    until $R < 1$
return either -4 * ln(R) * X / R or -4 * ln(R) * Y / R

END OF Normal

Generating numbers distributed with arbitrary means and standard deviations is easy once we have Normal. Simply multiply the result of Normal by σ and add μ, and the resulting numbers will be normally distributed with mean μ and standard deviation σ. In the exercises, you will be asked to write a function that returns real numbers normally distributed with a given mean and standard deviation.

The Exponential Distribution

We mentioned earlier the connection between the two discrete distributions: geometric and binomial. In generating numbers with the binomial distribution we count the number of successes per N events, whereas for the geometric distribution we count the number of events per success. A similar relationship exists between the Poisson distribution and a continuous distribution, called the *exponential* distribution.

Recall that for the Poisson distribution we are interested in the number of events that occur in a specific time. For the exponential distribution, we measure the elapsed time between successive events. For example, consider the single server queue simulation of chapter 3, which we implemented as a time-driven simulation. Essentially, only two types of events can occur in that simulation; either a new customer arrives at the bank, or the teller finishes serving a customer and starts serving another one. If we were to rewrite this simulation as an event-driven one, it would go something like this:

```
initialize necessary variables
loop
    generate an arrival time
    generate a service time
    whichever time is sooner,
        jump to that time and
        update appropriate variables
until the end of the day
```

We mentioned earlier that the `ServiceTime` function from chapter 3 returned numbers that were geometrically distributed. Strictly speaking, the `ServiceTime` function should return a continuously distributed number, since these times aren't really integers. We used the geometric distribution because we were taking "time slices" that were integers anyway, and the function was easy to write and produced reasonable results. It would be a better approximation to the real-world situation to generate real numbers distributed exponentially, then round them off to the nearest integer.

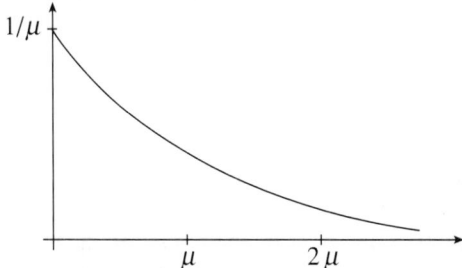

Figure 12.5 The Exponential Distribution

Figure 12.5 shows the exponential distribution function, whose equation is

$$f(x) = \frac{1}{\mu}e^{-\frac{x}{\mu}}, \; x \geq 0.$$

As you can see, it is more likely that the numbers generated will be less than the mean (that happens about 63% of the time), but the numbers greater than the mean could be very large, so they tend to balance out in the long run.

Fortunately, it's quite easy to use a uniformly distributed real number between 0 and 1 to generate an exponentially distributed real. If R is such a uniformly distributed real, then $-\mu \ln R$ is an exponentially distributed real with a mean value of μ. Note that R can't be zero, since the logarithm of zero is undefined. With this in mind, the algorithm is simple:

START OF *Exponential*(μ)

loop
    call Random *to generate* R
    until $R \neq 0$
return $-\mu \ln R$

END OF *Exponential*

We'll leave it as an exercise to rewrite the single server simulation as an event-driven simulation.

12.7   Testing Random

In the preceding pages we have made a great deal of use of a generating function that generates pseudo-random real values between zero and 1. We have seen that if we have such a function, we can use it to generate numbers according to many other distributions. The key to producing random numbers according to these distributions is the function that produces numbers between zero and 1, and we must test it to see that it does its job correctly. In this section, we will discuss a number of tests that can be used to test Random. (For the remainder of this chapter, we will assume that Random is a function that is supposed to return a sequence of numbers randomly distributed between zero and 1. Recall that zero is theoretically possible, while 1 is not.)

The Bucket Test

If Random is working correctly, every real number between zero and 1 must be equally likely. A simple test to see if this is happening is the "bucket test." Imagine that you have a bunch of golf balls and a bunch of empty buckets. If you start tossing balls into the buckets at random, after awhile all the buckets will have approximately the same number of balls in them. If some buckets were empty, or some had lots more balls than others, you would conclude that you weren't throwing the balls into the buckets at random. Also, if every bucket had exactly the same number of balls, you would also conclude that you were not throwing the balls randomly into the buckets.

This test is easy to do on the computer. What we would do is generate a series of integers (using Random of course) and check to see if each integer comes up about the same number of times. Let's use RandInt from page 337 to generate integers between 1 and 20 and count the number of times each number comes up. Here's a procedure that does just that:

```
procedure BucketTest;

{  This procedure tests the uniformity of the random  }
{  number generator.                                   }

const
  MAX = 20;

var
  Count : array [1 .. MAX] of integer;
  i, R, Times : integer;

begin
  for i := 1 to MAX do
    Count[i] := 0;
  write('How many numbers do you want to generate?  ');
  readln(Times);
  for i := 1 to Times do
    begin
      R := RandInt(1, MAX);
      Count[R] := Count[R] + 1
    end;
  writeln('The numbers from 1 to ', MAX : 1,
          ' occurred with the following frequencies:');
  for i := 1 to MAX do
    writeln(i : 5, Count[i] : 8)
end;
```

The numbers in each cell should be about the same, each about 1/20th the number of numbers generated. It would be possible to look at the frequencies, using some sort of statistical measurement, and determine whether the actual frequencies are about right; a *chi-square* test would be appropriate. Since this is not a statistics course, we'll not do the formal statistical testing but will resort to just eye-balling the results. If some of the frequencies are drastically different from others, we'll conclude that Random failed this test.

Here are the results of applying this test to the function Random on page 336.

```
Enter a seed: 456
How many numbers do you want to generate?  2000
The numbers from 1 to 20 occurred with the following frequencies:
         1       108
         2        91
         3       117
         4       117
         5       101
         6        91
         7        98
         8       111
         9       104
        10       100
        11        86
        12       100
        13        97
        14       103
        15        97
        16        94
        17        89
        18        93
        19        95
        20       108
```

The 2000 numbers should have been evenly spread out between 1 and 20, which means each of the numbers between 1 and 20 should have occurred about 100 times each. The numbers above seem about what we would expect if the numbers are random. Without fancier statistical methodology, we can only conclude that the generator didn't fail the test.

Note: We should remind you of the caution we made on page 335. Some compilers do not calculate the **mod** of a negative number according to the Standard. If yours doesn't, you will need to add an ⟨*if statement*⟩ to the function **Random**.

Now let's try it on the first example of a random number generating function presented in the chapter (see page 333). Here's the output:

```
Enter a seed: 456
How many numbers do you want to generate?  2000
The numbers from 1 to 20 occurred with the following frequencies:
     1       103
     2        99
     3       101
     4        98
     5       104
     6       101
     7        97
     8       101
     9        96
    10        94
    11        98
    12       104
    13        98
    14       104
    15        99
    16       106
    17       100
    18       102
    19        99
    20        96
```

At first glance, these results look even better, but we have to be careful. These numbers somehow seem too good. How would you feel if every value between 1 and 20 occurred *exactly* 100 times? You would suspect that things were too good, wouldn't you? If the numbers are truly random, there would have to be some variation. Indeed, we could generate "perfect" results by just generating the sequence 1, 2, 3, 4, 5, 6, 7, ..., 20 over and over again, a hundred times. No one would call that sequence "random." We conclude that the numbers have to be "close" to the predicted values, but not too close. Again, without resorting to statistical methodology, we can't say much more about the results here. Let's think about some more tests that could be run.

The Difference Test

Let's suppose we are generating random integers between 1 and 10. Consider the difference between two successive values. If the two numbers are uniformly distributed between 1 and 10, the differences should also be distributed according to some pattern. Could we get a difference of 10? No, that's not possible, but we could get a difference of 9 if the first number returned is 10 and the next number is 1. How likely is that? Not very; as we will see, it should happen about one one-hundredth of the time. Could we get a difference of 8? Yes, but only in two cases: when one number is 10 and the next is 2, and when one number is 9 and the next is 1. This is also not very likely but it is twice as likely as the first example. Continuing this argument, we see that the possible differences between successive numbers range from −9 to 9. A difference of 8 is twice as likely as a difference of 9, a difference of 7 is three times as likely as a difference of 9, and so on. There are ten ways that a difference of 0 can happen, so that result is 10 times as likely as a difference of 9. There are ten ways the first number can happen and ten ways the next number can happen, making a total of 100 different pairs that can occur. A difference of 9 can only occur in one way so that should happen about one one-hundredth of the time. A difference of 8 can occur in two ways so that should happen about two one-hundredths of the time. A histogram showing the distribution of differences between successive random numbers should look like a triangle.

We call this test the "difference test." Let's write a test program that conducts a difference test of a random number generator. This is also an easy program to write:

```
procedure DifferenceTest;

{  This procedure tests the variation in the difference between  }
{  pairs of numbers generated by the random number generator.    }

const
  MAXARRAY = 9;
  MAX = 10;

var
  Count : array [-MAXARRAY .. MAXARRAY] of integer;
  i, j, Diff, Times : integer;

begin
  for i := -MAXARRAY to MAXARRAY do
    Count[i] := 0;
  write('How many pairs of numbers do you want to generate?  ');
  readln(Times);
  New := RandInt(1, MAX);
  for i := 1 to Times do
    begin
      Diff := RandInt(1, MAX) - RandInt(1, MAX);
      Count[Diff] := Count[Diff] + 1
    end;
  writeln('The differences between pairs of numbers occurred with');
  writeln('the following frequencies:');
  for i := -MAXARRAY to MAXARRAY do
    writeln(i : 2, Count[i] : 5)
end;
```

It's important that the pairs of numbers be *independent* from each other, and that's why we pick two new integers each time rather than take the difference between successive random numbers.

We can make it a easier to see the results if we add the code to display a histogram showing the distribution. When we run the resulting program, using the generator on page 336, we get the following histogram:

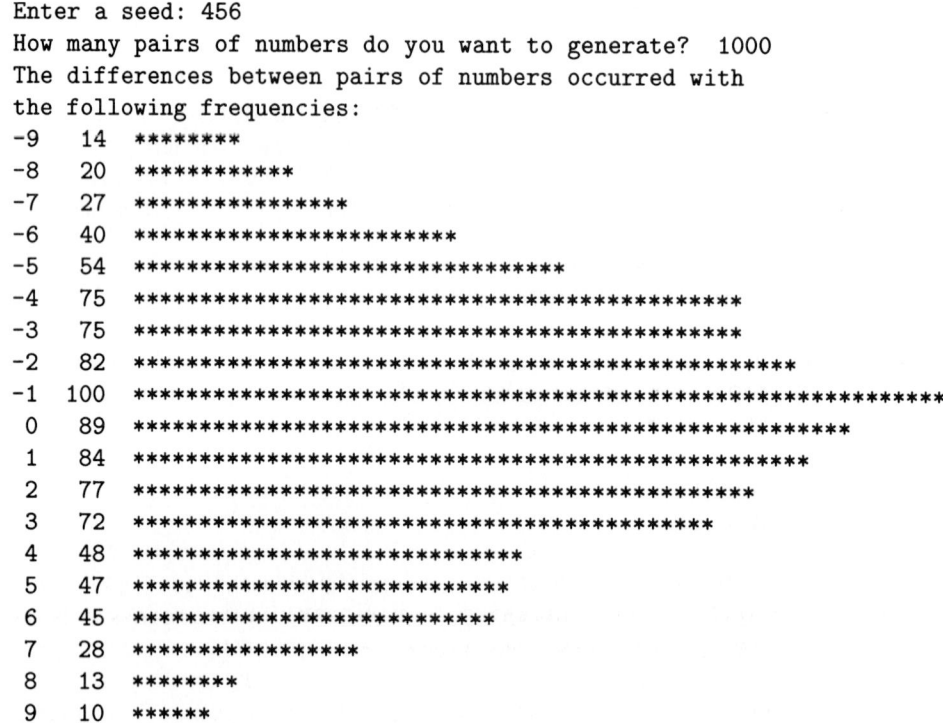

```
Enter a seed: 456
How many pairs of numbers do you want to generate?  1000
The differences between pairs of numbers occurred with
the following frequencies:
-9    14   ********
-8    20   ************
-7    27   ****************
-6    40   ************************
-5    54   ********************************
-4    75   *********************************************
-3    75   *********************************************
-2    82   **************************************************
-1   100   ************************************************************
 0    89   *****************************************************
 1    84   **************************************************
 2    77   *********************************************
 3    72   *******************************************
 4    48   ****************************
 5    47   ***************************
 6    45   **************************
 7    28   *****************
 8    13   ********
 9    10   ******
```

which looks pretty good. Again, we conclude that this function doesn't fail the test. Let's try it with the first function, the one on page 333:

```
Enter a seed:  123
How many numbers do you want to generate?  3000
The successive differences between the numbers occurred with
the following frequencies:
-9   33  *****
-8   63  **********
-7   88  **************
-6  120  *******************
-5  152  ************************
-4  180  *****************************
-3  212  **********************************
-2  241  ***************************************
-1  258  ******************************************
 0  295  ***********************************************
 1  270  *********************************************
 2  239  ***************************************
 3  214  **********************************
 4  182  *****************************
 5  149  ***********************
 6  124  ********************
 7   89  ***************
 8   58  *********
 9   33  *****
```

Once again these results look too good. Comparing this histogram with the first one, the first one seems to show the right amount of variability from the expected numbers. This one looks like it was rigged, somehow. There are statistical tests—such as the chi-square test mentioned earlier—which can tell us in more precise terms just how good is too good, and how bad is too bad. As mentioned, we'll just have to be satisfied with our intuition for this course.

As you can see, there are many ways in which a sequence can show its randomness. The bucket test provides one measure of how uniform the distribution is, but as we mentioned, it's easy to think of a sequence whose distribution is perfectly uniform, but is not random at all.

The sequence 1, 2, 3, … would fail the difference test dramatically. It's more difficult to think of a sequence that passes the difference test but fails the bucket test.

The Coupon Collector's Test

Another interesting test looks at a much more global aspect of a sequence. This test determines how long it takes for every possible number in the sequence to be generated at least once.

For example, let's say we're generating integers between 1 and 10. How many times do we have to call RandInt before it has generated each of these

numbers? We imagine that the numbers in the sequence are coupons, and we
have to collect every one in the set to get a prize. That's why it's called the
coupon collector's test.

Here's an algorithm for a routine to call `RandInt` and keep track of the
lengths of runs it takes to get a complete set of possible numbers:

> *accept Num*
> *initialize the Bucket$_i$'s to zero*
> *loop for i going from 1 to Num*
> > *store the null set in NumSet*
> > *store 0 in Counter*
> > *repeat*
> > > *call RandInt and include the number returned in NumSet*
> > > *add 1 to Counter*
> >
> > *until NumSet contains all possible numbers*
> > *add 1 to Bucket$_{Counter}$*
>
> *display statistics*

Based on this algorithm, here's a complete program (we don't show `Random`
or `RandInt`) that asks the user for a random number seed and the number of
times to generate a complete set, and displays the appropriate statistics:

```
program CouponTest(input, output);

{  This program runs the Coupon Collector's test.  }

const
   MAXRANGE = 10;
   MINRUNS  = 10;
   MAXRUNS  = 40;

type
   NumSetType = set of 1 .. MAXRANGE;

var
   Num, i, Seed, Counter, Overflow, Longest : integer;
   Bucket : array [1 .. MAXRUNS] of integer;
   NumSet, FullSet : NumSetType;

{  Random and RandInt go here...  }
```

```
begin { Main program }
   FullSet := [1 .. MAXRANGE];
   write('Please enter a seed: ');
   readln(Seed);
   write('Please enter the number of numbers: ');
   readln(Num);
   Overflow := 0;
   Longest := 0;
   for i := MINRUNS to MAXRUNS do
      Bucket[i] := 0;
   for i := 1 to Num do
      begin
         NumSet := [ ];
         Counter := 0;
         repeat
            NumSet := NumSet + [RandInt(1, MAXRANGE)];
            Counter := Counter + 1
            until NumSet = FullSet;
         if Counter > MAXRUNS
            then
               Overflow := Overflow + 1
            else
               Bucket[Counter] := Bucket[Counter] + 1;
         if Counter > Longest
            then
               Longest := Counter
      end;
   writeln('Coupon Collector''s Test Results:');
   writeln;
   for i := MINRUNS to MAXRUNS do
      writeln(i : 3, Bucket[i] : 5);
   writeln('>', MAXRUNS : 2, Overflow : 5);
   writeln('The longest run was ', Longest : 1, '.')
end.
```

When we run this program with our improved generator, generating 1000 runs, we get the following results:

Coupon Collector's Test Results:

10	0
11	2
12	4
13	7
14	13
15	20
16	26
17	44
18	27
19	44
20	47
21	31
22	44
23	44
24	49
25	43
26	32
27	40
28	53
29	36
30	31
31	36
32	32
33	31
34	25
35	33
36	16
37	13
38	13
39	8
40	8
>40	148

The longest run was 89.

As we would expect, runs of 15 or fewer should be possible, but rare. In fact, there are 10! ways of arranging the numbers 1 through 10 with no repetitions, and there are 10^{10} different ways of arranging the numbers 1 through 10 when repetitions are allowed, so the probability of getting all ten numbers in a run of ten is $10!/10^{10}$, or about 0.000363. If the numbers are being chosen randomly, in 1000 trials, we would expect to collect all ten numbers in a run of ten about 0.3 times. We'll leave the calculations of the remaining probabilities as an exercise.

Similarly, runs greater than 35 or so should be increasingly rare, but there should be some fairly long runs. The results above show 148 runs of more than 40; in fact, there was at least one run of length 89.

Once again, we will add the code to display a histogram showing the distribution. Here's what we get (using the same seed):

```
Coupon Collector's Test Results:

 10     0
 11     2   *
 12     4   **
 13     7   ****
 14    13   *******
 15    20   **********
 16    26   *************
 17    44   **********************
 18    27   **************
 19    44   **********************
 20    47   ***********************
 21    31   ***************
 22    44   **********************
 23    44   **********************
 24    49   ************************
 25    43   *********************
 26    32   ****************
 27    40   ********************
 28    53   **************************
 29    36   ******************
 30    31   ***************
 31    36   ******************
 32    32   ****************
 33    31   ***************
 34    25   ************
 35    33   ****************
 36    16   ********
 37    13   *******
 38    13   *******
 39     8   ****
 40     8   ****
>40   148
The longest run was 89.
```

Now we'll run the same program using the first generator, from page 333:

Coupon Collector's Test Results:

```
10     0
11     0
12     0
13     0
14     0
15     0
16    36    *****************
17     0
18    36    *****************
19   107    **********************************************************
20    70    ***********************************
21    35    *****************
22    71    ************************************
23    35    *****************
24    72    ************************************
25     0
26    36    *****************
27    36    *****************
28    71    ************************************
29   107    **********************************************************
30    72    ************************************
31     0
32    73    ************************************
33    36    *****************
34     0
35    35    *****************
36    36    *****************
37     0
38    36    *****************
39     0
40     0
>40    0
```
The longest run was 38.

As you can see, something quite non-random is happening here. There are run lengths that don't occur at all, and those that do occur seem to be multiples of about 36. It's easy to see without a detailed statistical analysis that our original generator fails the coupon collector's test miserably.

You might give a little thought to why this happens. A generator with a relatively short period is likely to do poorly in this test because it is called so many times; tens of thousands of times in the example above. Once it starts repeating itself it will continue to fill the same buckets in the same ratios.

From the results of the program above, it looks as if the generator repeats the following pattern: One each of 16, 18, 21, 23, 26, 27, 33, 35, 36 and 38; two each of 20, 22, 24, 28, 30 and 32; three each of 19 and 29. Calculate the total of all those runs. What do you get? Can you see why?

The Poker Test

One routine that tests several different things at once is known as the poker test. Essentially, the poker test uses the random number generator to generate poker hands and then compares the actual number of different kinds of hands generated with the expected number of each kind, to see how they are distributed. In some applications, this test only concerns itself with hands that contain pairs; i.e., are one of the following: one pair, two pair, three of a kind, full house, or four of a kind. Since it's also fun (and challenging) to work with straights and flushes, we'll consider them as well.

Before we go any farther, we had better say a little about the game of poker. A standard deck of playing cards has 52 cards of four different suits, spades (♠), hearts (♡), diamonds (♢) and clubs (♣). Each suit has thirteen cards with denominations ranging from an ace, king, queen, jack, ten, ..., deuce. A poker hand consists of five cards. A hand is said to contain one pair if two cards have the same denomination, and no other cards have the same denomination. For example, the hand containing ♠5, ♡5, ♢8, ♢3, and ♣Q contains one pair. A hand contains a flush if all five cards are from the same suit, but do not constitute a straight. A hand contains a straight if all five cards are in order; i.e., 4, 5, 6, 7 and 8, but do not constitute a flush. A hand contains a straight flush if all five cards are from the same suit and are in consecutive order. Normally an ace is considered either high or low in straights.

The following table lists the nine different kinds of poker hands that are possible, along with a couple of example hands from each kind:

Type of hand		
Straight flush	♠A, ♠K, ♠Q, ♠J, ♠10	♣5, ♣4, ♣3, ♣2, ♣A
Four of a kind	♠J, ♡J, ♢J, ♣J, ♠9	♠2, ♡2, ♢2, ♣2, ♠A
Full house	♠A, ♡A, ♢A, ♢K, ♣K	♡2, ♢2, ♣2, ♠A, ♡A
Flush	♡Q, ♡10, ♡8, ♡7, ♡2	♣6, ♣4, ♣3, ♣2, ♣A
Straight	♠8, ♡7, ♠6, ♠5, ♣4	♠A, ♠K, ♠Q, ♠J, ♡10
Three of a kind	♠2, ♢2, ♣2, ♡10, ♡5	♠A, ♡A, ♣A, ♢5, ♣Q
Two pairs	♠A, ♡A, ♢8, ♣8, ♠2	♢5, ♣5, ♠6, ♡6, ♡10
One pair	♠9, ♡9, ♡2, ♢A, ♣10	♡4, ♡3, ♠K, ♣4, ♢7
Flat hand	♠K, ♠9, ♡3, ♡A, ♢10	♠A, ♠K, ♠Q, ♠J, ♣4

Notice that the ace is treated as a high card—above a king—as well a low card—below a deuce—in straights and straight flushes. However, a hand containing ♠3, ♠2, ♡A, ♡K, ♢Q is a flat hand, not a straight.

We sometimes list the five cards in order in the above examples, but this is just for ease in examining the hand. It makes no difference what order the cards are in.

Now we can further discuss the poker test. Remember, we are not playing a card game here, we are testing a random number generator. The idea is to use the random number generator to shuffle the deck of cards, deal poker hands, and determine and count the kind of each hand. After dealing a large number of hands, compare the resulting frequencies with the expected frequencies. If the random number generator is doing its job well, the actual distribution of hands should be approximately the same as the expected distribution.

Expected Distribution of Poker Hands

If we are going to be able to interpret the results of this program, we are going to have to know the expected distribution of poker hands. There are $\binom{52}{5}$ different poker hands possible. That's a very large number: 2,598,960. Of these, there are exactly 40 hands that contain a straight flush. If we generated several thousand poker hands, we might not get any straight flushes at all. Only one out of every 72,193 poker hands is a straight flush (2,598,960 ÷ 40). Thus, the probability of getting a straight flush is 0.000014 (40/2598960).

Similarly, there are exactly 624 poker hands that contain four of a kind, so out of every 4,165 hands (2,598,960 ÷ 624) we would expect to get a hand containing four of a kind. The probability of getting a hand containing four of a kind is 0.000240 (624/2598960).

The table below lists the hands again, but this time we list the number of possible hands and the probability of getting a hand of this kind. Notice that the order is the same as before; that is, the most likely kind of hand is a flat hand, and the least likely is a straight flush.

Type of hand	Number	Probability
Straight flush	40	0.0000154
Four of a kind	624	0.0002401
Full house	3744	0.0014406
Flush	5108	0.0019654
Straight	10200	0.0039246
Three of a kind	54912	0.0211285
Two pairs	123552	0.0475390
One pair	1098240	0.4225690
Flat hand	1302540	0.5011774

Representing a Deck of Cards

There are 52 cards in a deck. How can we represent these 52 cards in the computer? Of course we could just use the numbers from 1 to 52. While that would work, it's better to use the numbers from 0 to 51. Do you see why? If we use the numbers from 0 to 51, then the first 13 numbers all have the quotient 0 when divided by 13. The numbers from 13 to 25 all have the quotient 1 when divided by 13. We can take any number from 0 to 51 and have that number div 13 represent the suit that the card is in. Similarly, we can use mod to determine the denomination. If we let an ace be low, then the number 12 could represent the King of clubs and the number 25 could represent the King of diamonds. Thus if M and N are two integers between 0 and 51, and M mod 13 equals N mod 13, then M and N represent cards of the same denomination. This will make it much easier to determine the kind of hand. Although it doesn't really matter, we'll consider the numbers from 0 to 12 to be the clubs, the numbers from 13 through 25 to be the diamonds, the numbers from 26 through 38 to be the hearts, and the numbers from 39 through 51 to be the spades.

Shuffling a Deck of Cards

Back to testing the random number generator. We can use Random to shuffle a deck of cards, deal several poker hands (from the 52 cards we can deal ten hands), examine each hand to see what kind of hand it is, add one to the appropriate counter, and repeat the process a large number of times. When we are finished, we can compare the percentage of actual hands dealt with the expected percentage (the probabilities in the above table) and see how well the random number generator is doing.

To begin with, we need to shuffle the deck of cards. How can this be done? There are several ways to solve this problem, and you should think about it yourself before looking at our solution. Maybe you'll come up with a better solution.

Here's one idea. We'll let the cards be represented by the numbers from 0 to 51, as mentioned above. We'll put these 52 numbers in an array indexed from 0 to 51, and each number will start off in a cell with its own index; i.e., number 0 will be in cell 0, number 1 will be in cell 1, etc. We'll pick a random number between 0 and 51 and swap the number in that cell with the number in cell 0. If the random number generator is producing a random sequence of numbers, this gives each number the same probability of being in position 0. Then we'll pick a random number between 1 and 51, and swap the number in that array position with the one in position 1. This process continues until we have swapped either the number in position 50 or the number in position 51 with the one in position 50. (Sometimes an array element will get swapped with itself, but that's as it should be.) If the random number generator does provide good pseudo-random values, the deck should be thoroughly shuffled. Did your method involve picking more than 51 random numbers?

Here's an algorithm for *Shuffle*, in case the above discussion is not clear.

```
START OF Shuffle(Deck)
Passed by reference: An array, Deck, that can hold 52 integers

loop for i going from 0 to 51
    store i in Deck_i
loop for i going from 0 to 50
    store RandInt(i, 51) in j
    call Swap(Deck_i, Deck_j)


END OF Shuffle
```

We are assuming the `RandInt` is, as before, a routine that calls `Random`, and returns a random integer between the two integer parameters (inclusive).

Determining the Kind of Hand Dealt

Since we can now shuffle the deck, it will be easy to write a routine that takes five cards off the deck and calls the five cards a hand. We'll leave writing that routine for the exercises.

How do we look at a poker hand and determine the kind of hand it is? There are a number of clever tricks that can be applied. For example, it's fairly easy to tell whether or not a hand is a flush. Suppose the five cards in a hand are represented by the five numbers 3, 5, 9, 10 and 11. Is that a flush? Sure, they are all in the first 13 numbers; i.e., they are all between 0 and 12, inclusive. How about 26, 30, 33, 35 and 38? Yes again, they are all between 26 and 38, inclusive. We can write a Boolean-valued function, *Flush*, that will return *true* if a hand is a flush and *false* otherwise:

```
START OF Flush(Hand)

store true in Flush
loop for i going from 2 to 5
    if Deck_i div 13 ≠ Deck_1 div 13
        then
            store false in Flush
return Flush

END OF Flush
```

Actually, this routine returns *true* when the hand is a straight flush as well as when it's a flush. A straight flush is not really a flush, according to our earlier definitions, but there's no reason we can't call the function *Flush* as long as we don't return the wrong number later. What we can do is write a similar function, say *Straight* that will return *true* if a hand has all five cards in sequence, and then consider the hand a straight flush if both these functions return *true*.

How can we determine whether a hand is a straight? If we know that there are no pairs, and if the values mod 13 of all five cards differ by at most 4, then the denominations of the five cards are in sequence. For example, consider the five numbers 46, 45, 21, 18 and 4. According to our earlier decisions regarding the suits and denominations, the 46 is the ♠8, the 45 is the ♠7, the 21 is the ♢9, the 18 is the ♢6, and the 4 is the ♣5. Thus, this hand is a straight. If we look just at the quotients of these five numbers divided by 13, we get 7, 6, 8, 5 and 4 respectively. The difference between the largest and the smallest of these five values is 4. However, we have to be careful. We have to know that the hand does not contain any pairs in order for this strategy to work. The five numbers 45, 31, 34, 19 and 4 also have the property that the maximum and the minimum of the five quotients differ by exactly 4, but that hand contains a pair, and is not a straight. Also, we must be careful to write this function so that it recognizes both ace-high straights and ace-low straights. It's a minor challenge to write the routine so that it will consider both kinds of straights, and to make it efficient as well.

It seems that it will be easier to determine whether or not a hand is a straight if we have already ruled out all the hands that contain pairs; i.e., four of a kind, full house, three of a kind, two pairs and one pair. Let's turn to that problem. How can we look at a hand and determine if it's one of these? Again we should let you find your own solution to this problem before looking at ours. How would you do it?

It turns out that there is a fast way of solving the problem, and it's quite elegant. For the time being, let's just consider the denominations—the remainders mod 13—of the cards. If we compare the cards to each other, starting on the left and counting the number of times two cards have the same denominations, we obtain a number which turns out to be a function of the kind of hand it is. That is, consider the hand: ♠A, ♡A, ♢A, ♡5, ♣5. If we start with the first ace and look to the right, we see that it matches two other cards. The second ace matches one other card, the third ace doesn't match any, the first 5 matches the second 5. This makes a total of four matches. It doesn't matter what order the cards are in; consider the hand: ♠K, ♠J, ♡K, ♢J, ♣K. Comparing each card to those on the right and adding up the number of matches again results in a total of four matches. Every hand containing a full house will result in four matches using this procedure.

If you examine the results of using this algorithm on all other kinds of hands, you'll see that a hand containing one pair will always have one match, a hand containing two pairs will have a total of two matches, etc. Flat hands, as well as flushes, straights and straight flushes will have no matches. In the exercises, you will be asked to write an algorithm for a function *Matches* that returns the

number of matches found in a given hand. You should think about the results
of a call to this function given the possible poker hands.

Matches gives us an easy-to-implement, fast way of deciding whether a hand
has one pair, two pairs, three of a kind, full house, four of a kind or something
else. The "something else" must be a straight, flush, straight flush, or flat hand.
The functions *Straight* and *Flush* can be used to discriminate between these
possibilities.

We'll interrupt our discussion of the solution at this point, leaving the completion of the algorithms and the coding of the various routines program for
the exercises.

The Poker Test Program

Here are our results of running the resulting Poker Test program, using the
function **Random** from page 336:

```
Enter a seed: 581
How many shuffles do you want?  1000
                    Occurred  Expected
   Straight flush:      1         0
   Four of a kind:      1         2
      Full house:      19        14
           Flush:      22        20
        Straight:      38        39
Three of a kind:      223       211
      Two pairs:      450       475
       One pair:     4190      4226
       Flat hand:    5056      5012
          Total:    10000
```

Here are our results of running the same program but using the **Random**
function from page 333.

```
Enter a seed: 581
How many shuffles do you want?  1000
                    Occurred  Expected
   Straight flush:      0         0
   Four of a kind:      8         2
       Full house:     18        14
            Flush:      4        20
         Straight:     63        39
  Three of a kind:    244       211
        Two pairs:    460       475
         One pair:   4211      4226
        Flat hand:   4992      5012
            Total:  10000
```

Comparing these two runs with the expected values in the table on page 360, we see that first set of results are fairly close to the expected values, but those from the second run are not as close. Notice that the number of flushes is far less than it should be, while the number of hands containing four of a kind is too large. If we wanted to write a poker playing game, we could probably get by with either version of **Random**, but the first version is better, as expected.

We also ran the program using Turbo Pascal's version of **Random** just for comparison; here are the results:

```
How many shuffles do you want?  1000
                    Occurred  Expected
   Straight flush:      0         0
   Four of a kind:      3         2
       Full house:      8        14
            Flush:     18        20
         Straight:     47        39
  Three of a kind:    214       211
        Two pairs:    482       475
         One pair:   4202      4226
        Flat hand:   5026      5012
            Total:  10000
```

These results demonstrate that the Turbo Pascal generator does a good job as well.

Then we ran the test one more time, using the first random number generator again, but this time we changed one number, the `MULTIPLIER`. Instead of using 142 for the `MULTIPLIER`, we made it 145. We got the following distribution:

```
Enter a seed: 123
How many shuffles do you want?  1000
                     Occurred  Expected
   Straight flush:       0         0
    Four of a kind:      0         2
       Full house:       0        14
            Flush:      49        20
         Straight:       0        39
 Three of a kind:      241       211
        Two pairs:     618       475
         One pair:    4188      4226
        Flat hand:    4904      5012
           Total: 10000
```

You should notice that there were no straights at all, nor were there any hands containing four of a kind or full houses. It's not unlikely that no hands containing four of a kind occurred, but there should have been around 14 full houses and around 39 straights. We can conclude that this generator failed the poker test.

12.8   Summary and Review

This chapter was concerned with the generation of pseudo-random sequences of integers and real numbers as well as the testing of such generators.

- We looked at the linear congruential method of generating random number sequences, and we examined ways of extending the period of the sequence.

- We discussed the difference between discrete and continuous distributions of random numbers.

- We described a number of different distributions, starting with what we called a uniform distribution. We saw that it is possible to use a uniformly distributed sequence of real values between zero and 1 to generate several other distributions. The foundation of all the distributions was a function that generates a uniform pseudo-random sequence of real values, R, such that $0 \leq R < 1$.

- We examined "weighted" distributions. We described a simple method of generating a weighted sequence, such as the distribution simulating the roll of a pair of dice.

- We discussed the "binomial" and "geometric" distributions. In both these distributions, we required the notion of a series of independent events where each event amounted to either a "success" or a "failure," and that a success had a given probability, p. The binomial distribution allows us to determine the probability of a certain number of successes in some number of events. The geometric distribution allows us to determine the number of events that occur between successes. We discussed writing functions that returned a sequence of numbers distributed according to either a binomial distribution or a geometric distribution.

- We discussed the Poisson distribution. The Poisson distribution is useful in determining the number of independent events that occur over a time interval, t. A Poisson distribution is completely characterized by the average number of events that occur in a unit of time. Once again, we we interested in developing a routine that would return a sequence of numbers according to a Poisson distribution.

- A discrete distribution is characterized by the fact that there are a discrete collection of values that are possible. These values are usually viewed as integers in some range. For example, in a discrete distribution, the events represented by the numbers 0, 1, 2, 3, etc. would be possible, and would each have a distinct probability, but there would be no event represented by the real number 1.5. A continuous distribution is a distribution where the possible events are represented by real values rather than integers. Theoretically, no single real value has a positive probability; instead, we discuss the probability that the number representing the event is between two real values. In other words, it makes no sense to ask, what is the probability that one inch of rain will fall tonight? Instead, we must ask questions like, what is the probability that there will be between $1/2$ inch and $1\frac{1}{2}$ inches of rain tonight? We discussed three continuous distributions, the uniform distribution, the normal distribution and the exponential distribution.

- The normal distribution is recognized by the familiar "bell-shaped curve." We developed a function that would return real values according to a normal distribution with a given mean and a given standard deviation.

- The exponential distribution is a counterpart to the Poisson distribution. Where the Poisson allows one to ask questions about the number of events in a given time period, the exponential allows one to inquire about the time interval between successive events. Notice that the Poisson is discrete—the number of events is an integer—and the exponential is continuous—the time period between events is a real number.

- We spent a good deal of time on the idea of testing a random number generator. Since all the generators used on computers rely on some sort of algorithmic process, and thus the sequence could be determined in advance, there will always be some test that a particular generator will fail. The goal is never to write a random number generator that can pass all tests of randomness, but rather, to write generators that pass more and more of the tests.

• We discussed the "bucket test." This test amounts to calling the function a large number of times, dividing the returned values into a number of buckets of equal sizes ('widths,' if you're thinking about the number line), and counting how many times each number comes up. Any random number generator that failed the bucket test would not be worthy of further consideration.

• We discussed the "difference test." This tests counts the number of times each possible difference between successive numbers happens. Essentially, it helps measure the "scatter" pattern of the random numbers.

• We discussed the "coupon collector's test." This test measures how many times the function being tested has to be called before a complete collection of integers in a given range has been returned. If the numbers are random, the resulting "runs" have a known distribution which can be compared with the actual counts.

• Finally, we discussed the "poker test." We had a program use the random number generator to shuffle a standard deck of playing cards, and we dealt poker hands, counting the number of hands of each type that were dealt. We could then compare the actual distribution of hands with the expected distribution. This test was more fun that the others as it allowed us to examine some other interesting problems; such as, how can a random number generator be used to shuffle a deck of cards?, and, how can you quickly look at a poker hand and determine what kind of a hand it is?

12.9 Exercises

1. Write a function called `RandReal` that will return a uniformly distributed real number in a particular range.

2. On page 337 we discussed a routine that returned numbers according to a weighted distribution. The routine we wrote could have been improved to use either a linear search or a binary search, as indicated on page 337. Write such a routine.

3. The text discusses the Poisson distribution and provides an algorithm for *Poisson* and *Prob* starting on page 341. Code the algorithms in Pascal. You will have to decide on a strategy to use to implement *Prob*. Your program should then call the `Poisson` function many times, keeping track of the values returned. Then have it draw a histogram of the distribution of returned values.

4. Write a Pascal function `Normal` that returns real numbers normally distributed with mean `Mu` and standard deviation `Sigma`. Write a program that calls the function and draws a histogram for a set of test data.

5. Write a Pascal function `Exponential` that returns real numbers normally distributed with mean `Mu`. Write a test program similar to the one in the previous exercise.

6. Rewrite the single-server queue program from chapter 3 as an event-driven simulation. Use the `Exponential` function from the previous exercise to generate arrival times and service times.

7. Add the code to the procedure `DifferenceTest` to display the histogram for the differences between the random numbers generated.

8. Calculate the probabilities associated with the Coupon Collector's Test as discussed on page 356. That is, assuming the numbers are truly random, what is the probability of collecting all ten numbers with only eleven calls of the random number generator? In general, what is the probability of collecting all ten numbers in a run of length $n, n \geq 10$?

9. Verify the values presented in the table on page 360. You might need to go to the library or otherwise find a book that discusses elementary counting methods in order to determine how to count the total number of hands containing four of a kind, a full house, etc.

10. Write the code for a Boolean function `Flush` based on the algorithm discussed on page 362.

11. Write the algorithm and the code for a Boolean function `Straight` based on the ideas presented on page 363, or on your own ideas. Be sure you consider both ace high straights and those with an ace as the lowest card.

12. Write the algorithm and the code for the function `Matches` to determine the number of matches found in a given hand.

13. Using the routines developed in the previous exercises, write a routine `KindOf` that returns the kind of hand passed to it. You may wish to use an `integer` code for each of the nine kinds of hand, or you could create an enumerated data type.

14. Finish the development of the Poker test program. You will have to decide how to take five cards at a time from a shuffled deck of cards and determine what kind of hand the five cards constitutes. Your program should allow the user to enter a number of shuffles, should aloow the deck to be shuffled that many times, should deal, identify and count ten hands from the deck after each shuffle, and then display the appropriate statistics.

15. Rewrite the two versions of `Random` discussed in the text, using various values for `MULTIPLIER`, `MODULUS`, etc. and test them with the tests developed in this chapter. If your computer system has a random number generator, test it as well with the various tests.

16. Try your own hand at developing a random number generator. Now that we have this collection of tests, we can run them on any pseudo-random number generating function we like. Think up a scheme that looks like it might generate a sequence of random numbers between zero and 1, and test it. For example, you might try this:

Start by storing an arbitrary real number in a global variable Seed

START OF Random

store $(Seed + 1.5)^2$ in Seed
replace Seed with its decimal part
return Seed

END OF Random

17. Do some research on statistics. Look up the chi-square test and see how it can be used to measure the results of our tests.

Appendix A

Syntax Diagrams

program:

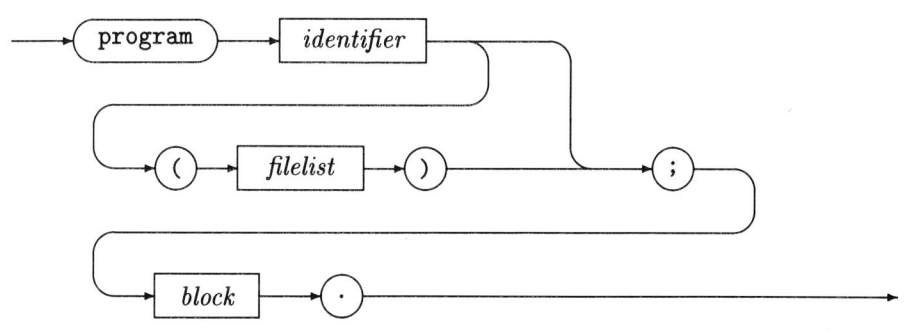

identifier:

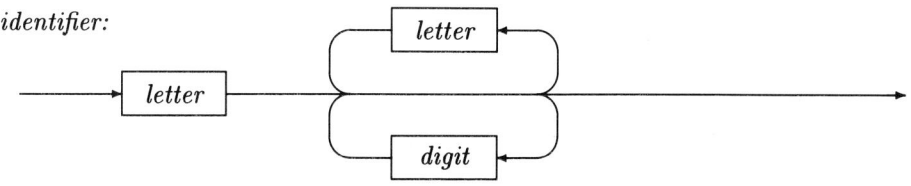

letter:

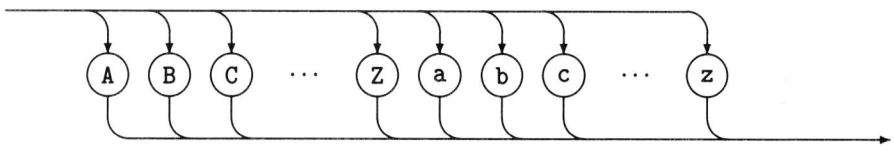

% digit

digit:

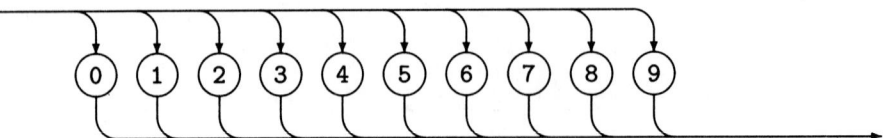

block:

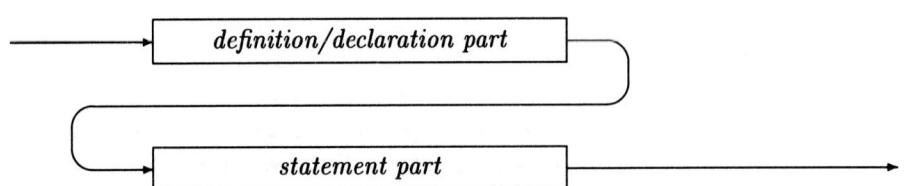

definition/declaration part:

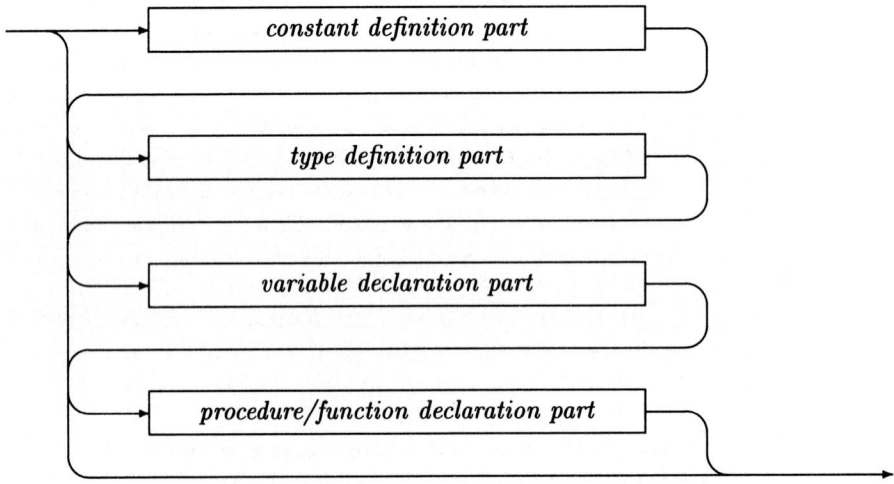

constant definition part:

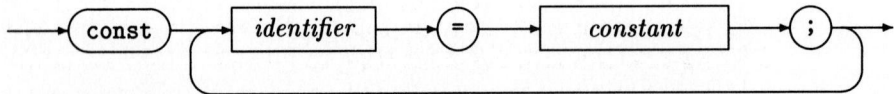

constant:

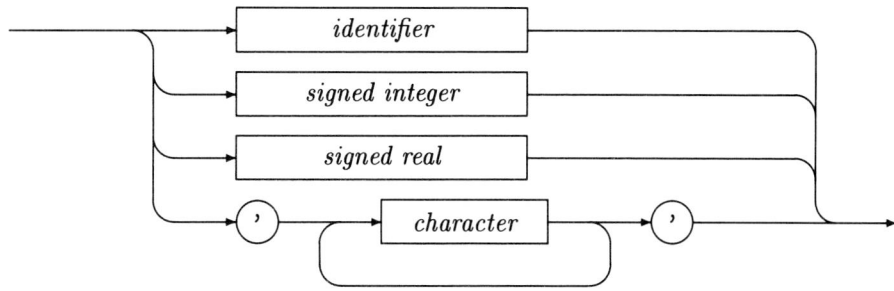

signed integer:

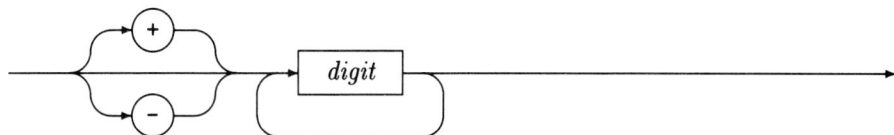

signed real:

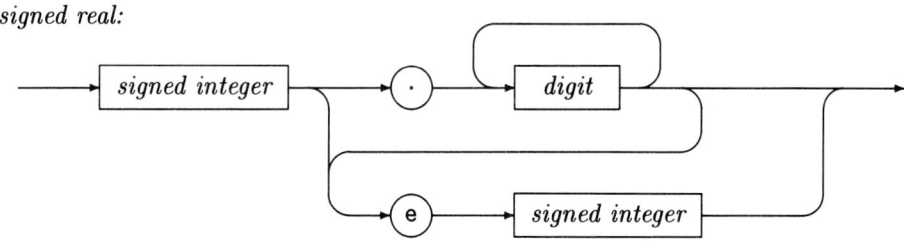

type definition part:

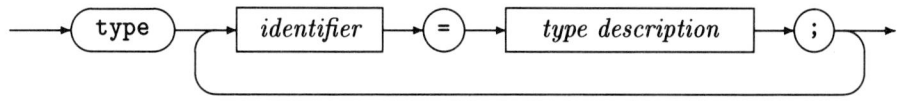

type description:

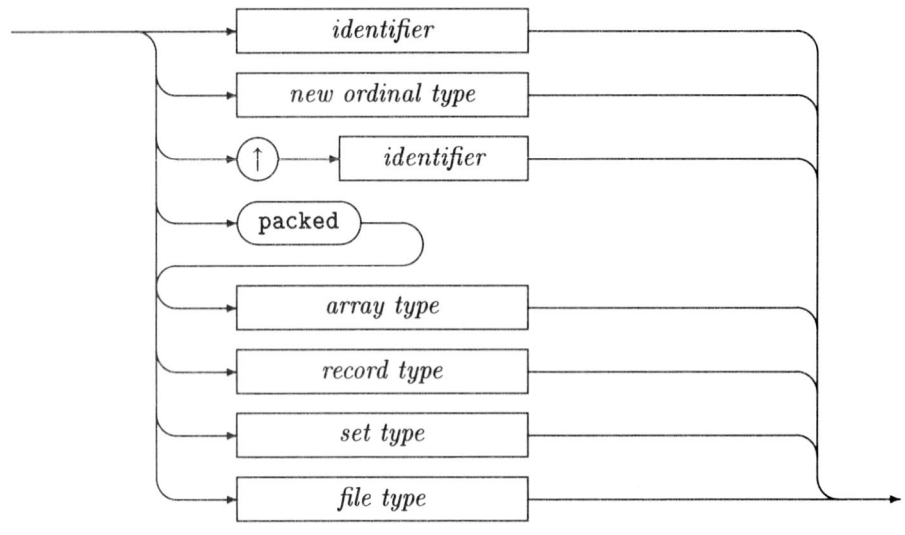

new ordinal type:

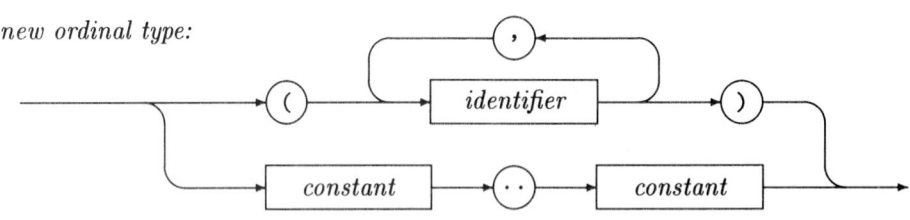

array type:

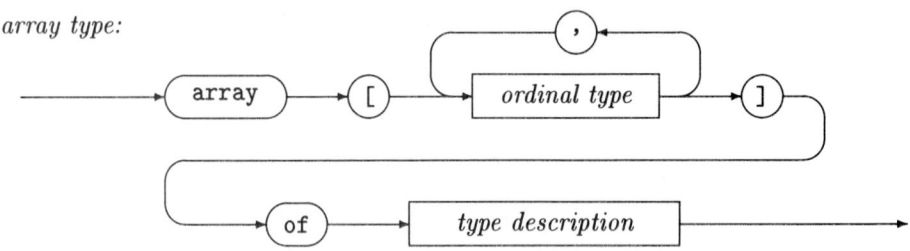

ordinal type:

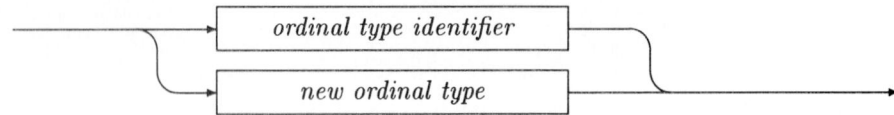

record type:

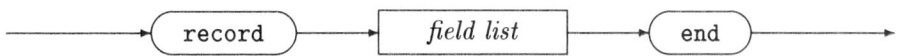

field list:

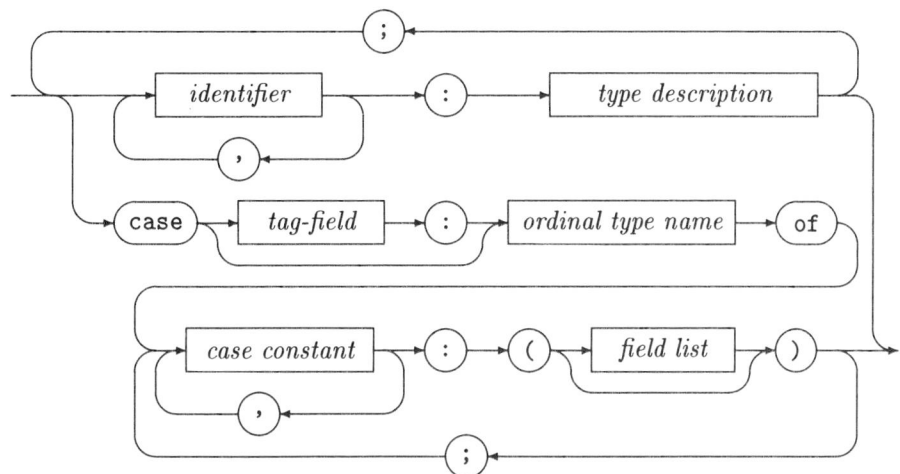

set type:

file type:

variable declaration part:

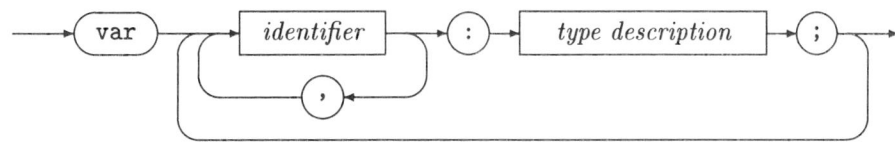

procedure/function declaration part:

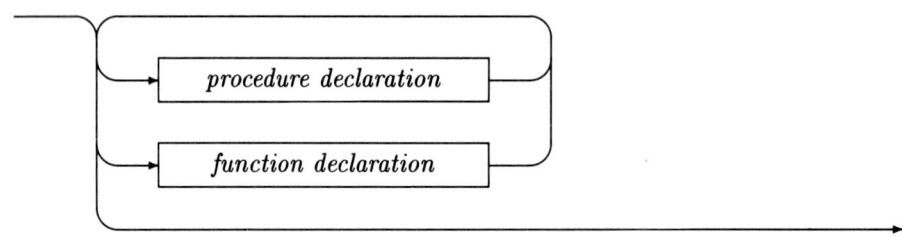

procedure declaration:

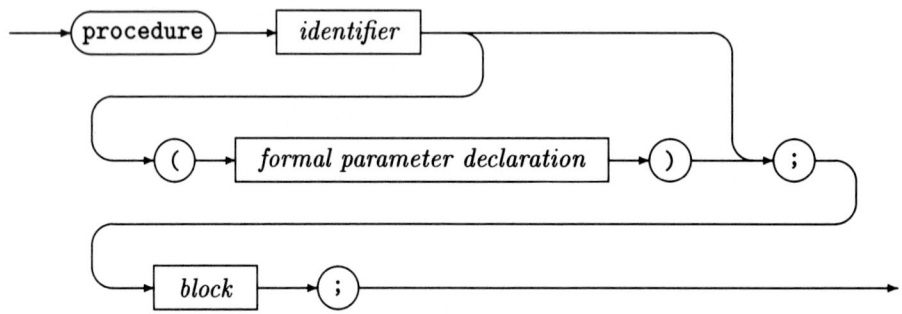

formal parameter declaration:

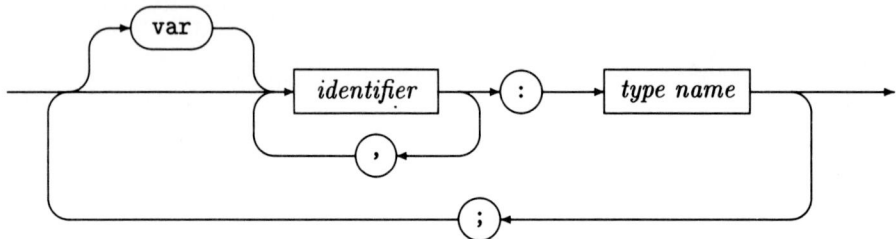

function declaration:

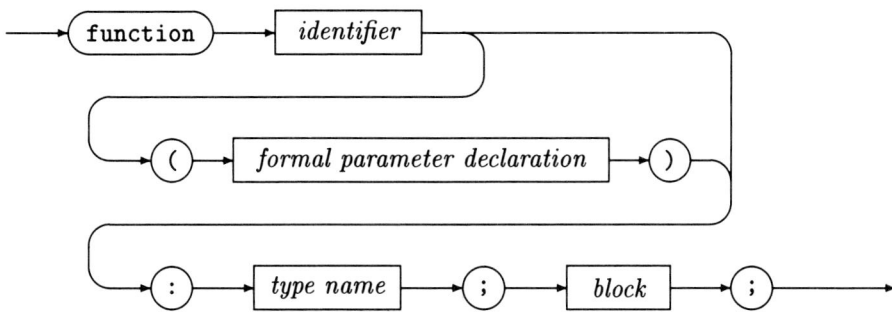

statement part:

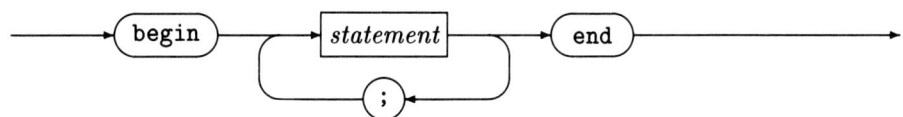

statement:

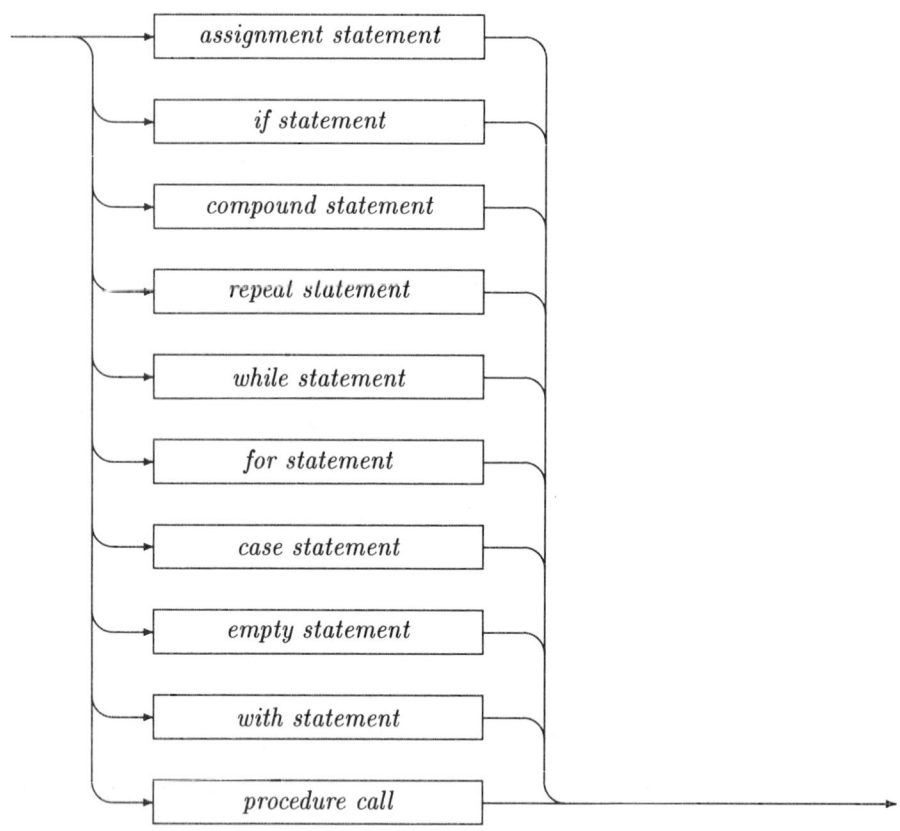

assignment statement:

expression:

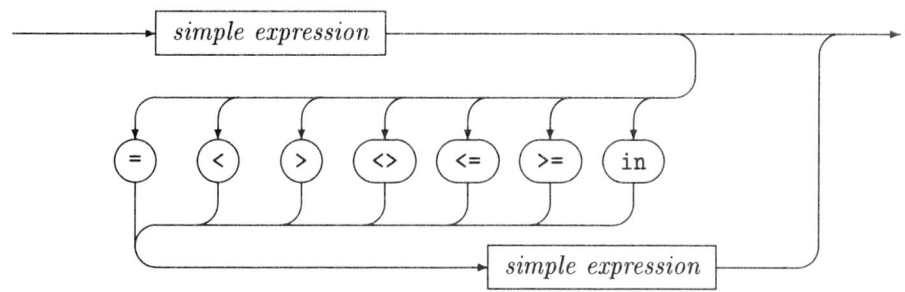

simple expression:

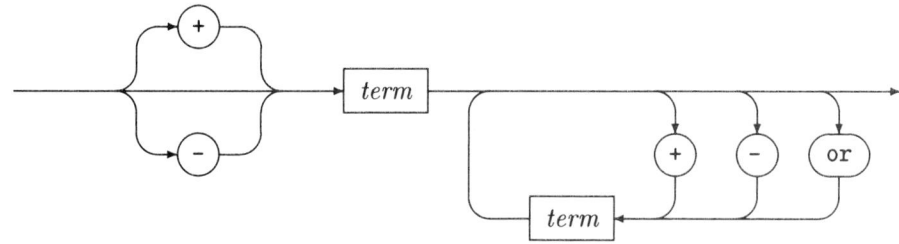

term:

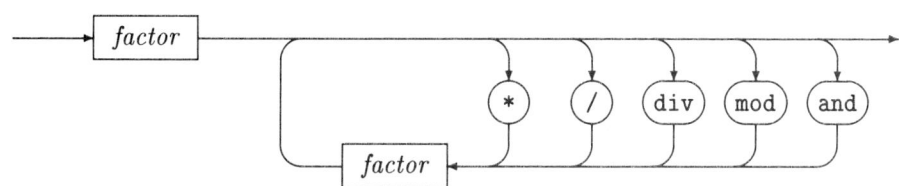

factor:

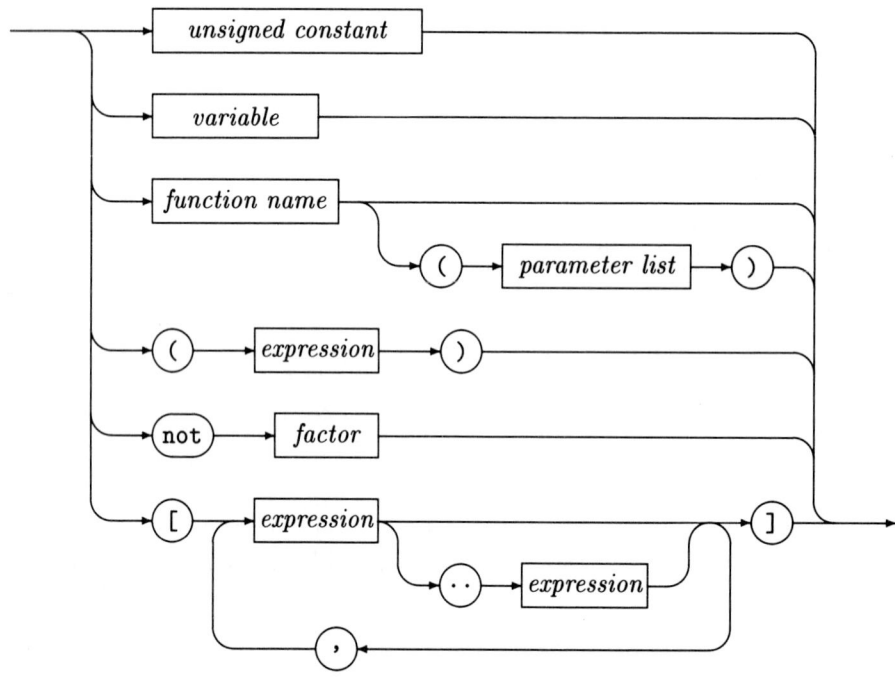

if statement:

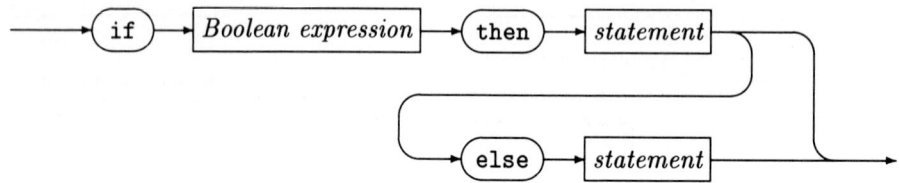

compound statement:

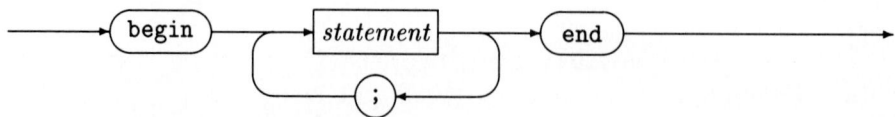

repeat statement:

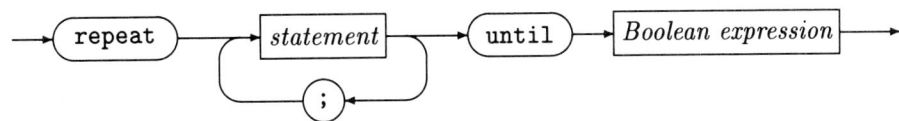

while statement:

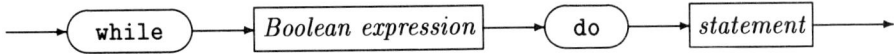

for statement:

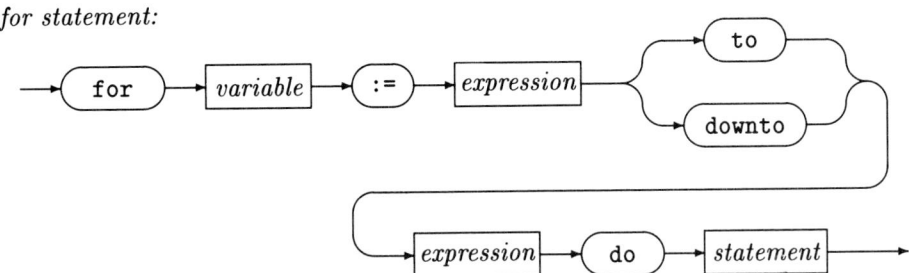

case statement:

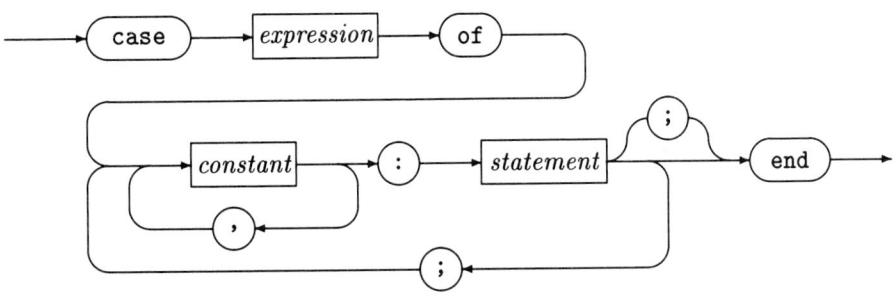

empty statement:

with statement:

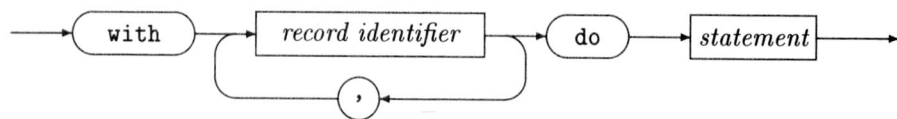

procedure call:

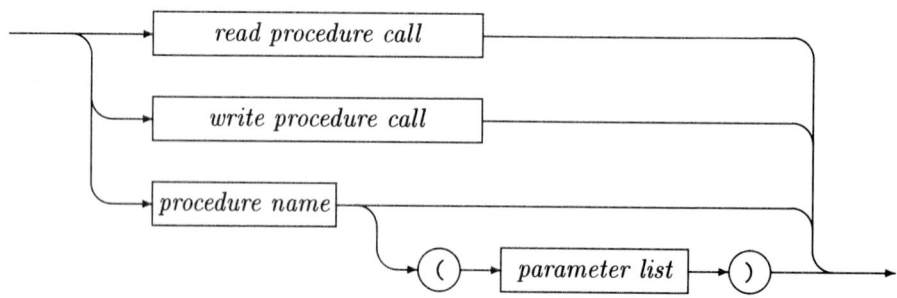

read procedure call:

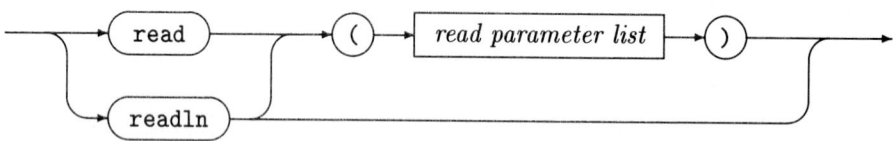

write procedure call:

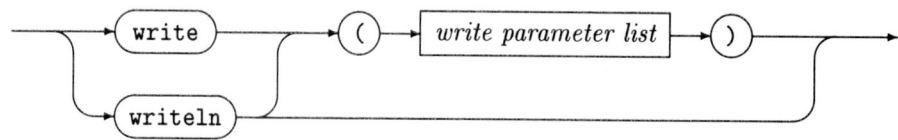

A.1 Index to Syntax Diagrams

Index